# The Indispensable
# University

# Part of the American Council on Education
## Series on Higher Education
## Susan Slesinger, Executive Editor

# The Indispensable University

## Higher Education, Economic Development, and the Knowledge Economy

Eugene P. Trani and Robert D. Holsworth

AMERICAN COUNCIL ON EDUCATION
® The Unifying Voice for Higher Education

ROWMAN & LITTLEFIELD PUBLISHERS, INC.
Lanham • Boulder • New York • Toronto • Plymouth, UK

Published in partnership with the American Council on Education

Published by Rowman & Littlefield Publishers, Inc.
A wholly owned subsidiary of The Rowman & Littlefield Publishing Group, Inc.
4501 Forbes Boulevard, Suite 200, Lanham, Maryland 20706
http://www.rowmanlittlefield.com

Estover Road, Plymouth PL6 7PY, United Kingdom

British Library Cataloguing in Publication Information Available

**Library of Congress Cataloging-in-Publication Data**

Trani, Eugene P.
 The indispensable university : higher education, economic development, and
the knowledge economy / Eugene P. Trani and Robert D. Holsworth.
     p. cm. — (American council on education series on higher education)
 Includes bibliographical references.
 ISBN 978-1-60709-079-3 (cloth : alk. paper)—ISBN 978-1-60709-081-6 (electronic)
 1. Education, Higher—Economic aspects—Cross-cultural studies. 2. Economic
development—Cross-cultural studies. I. Holsworth, Robert D. II. Title.
 LC67.6.T73 2010
 338.4′7378—dc22

                                                             2009042118

⊗™ The paper used in this publication meets the minimum requirements of
American National Standard for Information Sciences—Permanence of Paper for
Printed Library Materials, ANSI/NISO Z39.48-1992.

Printed in the United States of America

For our wives, Lois E. Trani and Susan W. Holsworth,
with deep appreciation for their support and understanding.

# Contents

# Foreword

*The Honorable Timothy M. Kaine*

During my time in public office I have learned that a collaborative creative process almost always strengthens the final product. That is why I am so glad that my friends Gene Trani and Bob Holsworth have compiled their collective wisdom, gained over decades in higher education, to produce a work that should be mandatory reading for any university or community leader seeking to fully realize the benefits of higher education. These are two men who lived the lessons they discuss. They have seen great victories and setbacks as they seek to advance their schools and communities.

I have known Gene Trani in many capacities—as a neighbor living near Virginia Commonwealth University, as a parent of three children born at the university hospital, as a city councilman and mayor working closely with him on the economic development of Richmond, and as governor of Virginia, where I wrote much of his budget and appointed his Board of Visitors. When I learned that Gene would be retiring after nineteen years as president of Virginia Commonwealth University, the governor in me was disappointed to lose one of the finest university presidents in the nation. But as a believer in the transformative power of education, I knew that Gene still had plenty to offer the world of higher education. I truly believe that this book is just part of a long list of contributions to the field. I have gotten to know Bob Holsworth over the years, both personally and professionally, and learned long ago that he is one of the sharpest minds in the Virginia political landscape and a true asset to our commonwealth's system of public higher education. Throughout my career in public service, I have found his analysis to be well researched and well supported, even when his conclusions weren't necessarily what I wanted to hear as a candidate. I have always admired his dedication to his teaching career, even when his considerable skills could have made him an in-demand consultant in the private sector.

The book these two gentlemen have produced, *The Indispensable University*, offers a thorough and thoughtful history of the development of the university system, but more importantly it offers a vision for where the system is going and what it can contribute to its broader community. Anyone who has been involved with higher education in the last twenty-five years will tell you there is a change underway in our higher education system. In many ways, the transformation mirrors that of the economy as a whole. Universities now compete for faculty and students on a global scale, much like the alumni they produce who will compete globally for attractive jobs. No longer can a college or university isolate itself from the outside world, nor should it.

Institutes of higher education are becoming fully integrated members of their communities and environments in ways large and small, contributing to the physical environment through campus architecture and the cultural environment by fostering creativity and expression. Universities and their communities have become inextricably linked through economic and geographic ties. This evolving relationship, of course, presents both sides with opportunities and challenges, and many are realizing that a spirit of cooperation can yield mutually beneficial results for all parties; a college may need to expand its campus, and a city may be looking to revitalize a former industrial zone, or a small business may be looking to expand its sales, while a university needs a new vendor. Trani and Holsworth show, through extensive case studies, that maintenance of positive relationships between colleges and universities and their publics add value to the school and the communities they serve.

I was particularly pleased that *The Indispensable University* offers an extensive look at the rapidly evolving role of community college systems, especially as it relates to economic competitiveness. More people are using the community college system to find their way into the higher education system or acquire new skills and knowledge to remain competitive in an increasingly crowded job market. Virginia has recognized the tremendous potential of the community college system and has initiated a transformation to make it the center of our workforce development efforts. When I became governor, twenty-six separate agencies and secretariats had workforce development obligations, with no centralized leadership or structure. I thought so highly of the community colleges and their limitless potential that I made the chancellor of the community college system the head of our workforce development efforts. As Gene and Bob rightly note, the community college is a uniquely American institution that has long enjoyed a mutually beneficial relationship with its communities; whether through job training or college credit for high school students, they offer an abundance of opportunities for people of all ages and from all walks of life.

The presence of a university can have both a direct and indirect impact in bringing economic development and opportunity to a region. I have found that the quality of an area's educational system, particularly higher education, can be the difference-maker when negotiating economic development deals. When I was a mayor working to attract a private sector prospect to open a business in my city, I found the make-or-break factor was usually the tax incentive package. These days, the number-one thing that companies ask about is the educational system and opportunities for higher education partnerships. Virginia recently secured a large aircraft engine manufacturing facility due in large part to the site's proximity to world-class research and engineering schools that can help to supply the facility with highly skilled workers. In exchange, schools can then hold out their relationships with private sector partners as an enticement to high-quality students and faculty.

A great challenge of the twenty-first-century educational system and economy will be maintaining global competitiveness in the face of emerging powers. One would be remiss to ignore the higher education systems of other nations, and *The Indispensable University* boldly examines the developments in some of the biggest emerging players in the international economy—Israel, Qatar, China, Russia, and India. Higher education systems serve unique purposes in these nations, whether fostering creativity, empowering women, or developing human capital. It is important to remember that while the higher education system in the United States is still the envy of the world, there are plenty of nations completely engaged in the effort to overtake us. That is why it is so important to make serious investments in our institutions of higher learning to make sure that America produces the scientists, engineers, architects, and researchers that will keep our economy vibrant. In Virginia in 2008, we made a record capital investment of $1.5 billion in our higher education capacity, ensuring that the campuses of our colleges, universities, and community colleges can continue to offer opportunities to our best and brightest.

While my career has taken me to some places I didn't necessarily expect, I have never forgotten the lessons I learned as a lawyer, small-businessman, and a local government official. I have seen firsthand the transformative effect that higher education can have on an individual and a community. *The Indispensable University* does a fine job of tracking the evolution of higher education, assessing its current state, and showing opportunities for growth and improvement in the future. I am happy to say that my friends Gene and Bob have created a thorough and thoughtful work that will be of value to anyone with an interest in the economic well being of their community—be they a university administrator, business leader, or government official.

Both of these dedicated educators have much more to offer the world of higher education and I look forward to their continued contributions.


*The Honorable Timothy M. Kaine has just completed his four-year term as governor of the Commonwealth of Virginia. Prior to being elected governor, Mr. Kaine served as lieutenant governor of the Commonwealth of Virginia from 2002 to 2006. Governor Kaine entered political life in 1994 and was elected to four terms on the city council of Richmond, Virginia, including two terms as mayor.*

# Preface

Both of us have had the good fortune to spend a substantial part of our careers at an urban research university in the latter part of the twentieth century and the beginning of the twenty-first. We came to believe that higher education institutions located in the cities and metropolitan areas of the United States were essentially the land-grant colleges of contemporary times. We provided access to advanced learning for the majority of Americans; we were inextricably involved with partnering with our communities in addressing major social issues; and, in many cities, university hospitals were both a health care destination for patients with challenging medical conditions and the major provider of indigent care where access was an enduring and troubling issue in the larger system. At Virginia Commonwealth University (VCU), we were engaged in a determined effort to have an impact on our area—to promote the economic development of the greater region and to address the difficult challenges of community development. In time, we recognized that we were part of a larger effort to demonstrate that universities that knew how to build the right kind of partnerships and collaborations could develop innovative instructional programs and cutting-edge research agendas, and enable their own communities to flourish and compete in the global economic environment.

This conception of an urban research university struck a resonant chord in both the Richmond metropolitan area and the Commonwealth of Virginia. Business leaders approached VCU with ideas (and pledges of support) for a School of Engineering and a biotechnology research park. Community organizations increasingly tapped university expertise in responding to matters such as neighborhood economic deterioration, youth violence, school dropouts, and public safety challenges. We were personally asked as representatives of the university to help lead major community groups and initiatives such as the greater Richmond Chamber of Commerce and Richmond Renaissance (Trani) and to lead studies on the future of the regional infrastructure and the city schools (Holsworth). The overwhelming majority of political officials responded favorably to the vitality and energy evident at the university. And students voted with their admissions applications, increasing the size of the university more than 50 percent in about fifteen years.

During this period, we also had the benefit of visiting, teaching, and conducting research at other universities around the world. It became clear that what we were trying to accomplish in Richmond was part of a trend that extended far beyond urban universities in the United States and was actually related to a conception of the university's role in contemporary society that was global in scope. Universities all over the world—in both developed and developing nations—were responding to the economic and social challenges coursing through the wider society. Leading European universities, emergent schools in China, and an entirely new system of higher education in Qatar were all engaged in seeing how they could better promote the economic and social development of their regions. In Cambridge and Oxford, for instance, two of the oldest and greatest universities in the world were engaged in a deliberate reinvention that would permit them to utilize their enormous human and intellectual capital to partner with external entities that would simultaneously enhance the capacity of business and government and increase the practical relevance of the universities.

The transformation efforts were so striking that, after spending mini-sabbaticals at Cambridge and University College–Dublin, one of the authors (Trani) composed two extensive reports and distributed these to the university community, to the major private-sector actors in the Richmond region, to the political leadership in Virginia, and to members of national groups such as CEOs for Cities. The first report, "Richmond at the Crossroads: The Greater Richmond Metropolitan Area and the Knowledge Based High Technology Economy of the 21st Century," drew on the Cambridge experience to illustrate the lessons that our region could draw upon to realize our goals more successfully.[1] The second report, "Dublin Diaries: A Study of High Technology Development in Ireland," drew upon interviews with seventy individuals in academia, government, and business to understand the economic boom of the "Celtic Tiger" and the factors that had contributed to the phenomenon that were relevant to our own conditions in the Richmond area and throughout Virginia.[2]

There has, of course, been a large-scale macroeconomic reversal that has occurred on a worldwide basis in the last two years. This has reduced overall investment in universities, put tremendous stress on institutions that are serving more students with reduced resources, often placed higher education leadership in an adversarial relationship with political officials, and made it more difficult to support new research ventures. The economic downturn in Ireland has been almost as dramatic as the boom that preceded it and is widely considered to be one of the worst in the Euro-zone. Reductions in support for higher education will be painful and have the potential to impact negatively matters such as access, diversity, the working relationship between universities and the state, and construction of research facilities. In an odd way, however, the worldwide recession will hasten the implementation of some of the trends in higher education that we have been describing. There will be elevated interest in linking university discoveries to commercial applications. There will be increased attention to collaborations between university and industry and between university and university. And there will be heightened attention to the outcomes of higher education and its relevance to regional economic success. Universities will remain indispensable to both economic recovery and growth, though there will be more directed efforts to ensure that they are operating to accomplish these aims.

## NOTES

1. Eugene P. Trani, "Richmond at the Crossroads: The Greater Richmond Metropolitan Area and the Knowledge Based High Technology Economy of the 21st Century" (Richmond: Virginia Commonwealth University, 1998).

2. Eugene P. Trani, "Dublin Diaries: A Study of High Technology Development in Ireland" (Richmond: Virginia Commonwealth University; Dublin: Keough-Notre Dame Center, 2002), 2.

# Acknowledgments

This book has been nearly twenty years in the making, as we implemented many of the points made in this volume in our administrative positions at Virginia Commonwealth University—Eugene Trani as president from 1990 to 2009 and Robert Holsworth as chair of political science, director of the L. Douglas Wilder School of Government and Public Affairs, and dean of humanities and sciences from 1991 to 2008. During those years, we also visited and studied many universities in the United States and around the world that were also dealing with the same issues, and from many examples selected a series of case studies that became the major focus of this book.

We want to thank many colleagues in higher education who have read our manuscript or chapters of the case studies and made valuable and helpful suggestions that have improved our study. These individuals include a number who have reviewed chapters of case studies, including Steven Sample, president, University of Southern California; Ira Harkavy, associate vice president, University of Pennsylvania; Katherine Lyall, president emeritus, University of Wisconsin System; Joseph Corry, formerly assistant vice chancellor, University of Wisconsin–Madison; Howard Martin, formerly dean of continuing education, University of Wisconsin–Madison; Robert Bruininks, president of the University of Minnesota, and his colleagues; Gordon Gee, president, Ohio State University; Glenn DuBois, chancellor of the Virginia Community College System; Eduardo Padrón, president, Miami Dade College; Rufus Glasper, president, Maricopa County Community College; Chris Johnson, formerly senior bursar, St. John's College, Cambridge; Ralph Waller, principal, Harris Manchester College, Oxford; Kevin Whelan, director, University of Notre Dame

Center, Dublin; Shlomo Mor-Yosef, director general, Hadassah Medical Organization, Jerusalem, Israel; Chen Yinznang, vice president, Fudan University, Shanghai; and Sergei Karpov, dean, history faculty, Moscow State University. The following colleagues provided valuable comments on the entire manuscript: Roderick M. McDavis, president, Ohio University; John Casteen, president, University of Virginia; David Perry, professor at the University of Illinois–Chicago; Nancy L. Zimpher, chancellor of the State University of New York System; and Paul Temple, director of the Higher Education Program at the Institute for Education, London. Their comments and suggestions proved invaluable.

Our editors, Susan Slesinger and Paula Moore, of the American Council on Education, and Patti Belcher of Rowman & Littlefield Education, offered wise counsel and encouragement during the preparation of this volume. Susan Slesinger, in particular, spent countless hours helping us throughout the whole process, from initial discussions about the idea to final editing. We also want to thank our colleagues at Virginia Commonwealth University, Sue Ann Messmer, vice president for outreach and chief of staff in the President's Office at VCU, and Kelly Myles, Kathy Honsharuk, and Shannon Foley, for their thorough, diligent help in researching, drafting, editing, and organizing the final manuscript. In particular we would like to thank Kelly Myles, who did extensive work on the research and drafting of a number of chapters of the book. We would also like to thank Joseph McCarthy, formerly senior associate dean of the John F. Kennedy School of Government at Harvard University for arranging Dr. Trani's appointment as a summer 2008 visiting scholar in the Kennedy School's Taubman Center for State and Local Government to work on this manuscript. Though the visit was shortened by health concerns, the atmosphere was first-rate and the ability to focus on research and writing without parallel.

# Chapter 1

# Basic Premise: Colleges and Universities Indispensable to Economic and Community Development

The basic premise of this book is simple: higher education is in the midst of a major transformation that is fundamentally redefining the relationship of colleges and universities to the broader community. This transformation is occurring at every level of higher education, from community colleges, to comprehensive undergraduate schools, to research-intensive doctoral universities. And it is becoming an increasingly global phenomenon as universities around the world seek to redefine themselves in ways that will enable them to become significant actors in the modern, knowledge-based economy.

In recent years, there have been various efforts to characterize the transformation that is taking place across universities. An emerging literature speaks about entrepreneurial universities and how the practices associated with the private sector have increasingly been adopted by forward-looking leaders in higher education. Scholars point to the development of strategic planning inside universities, the recruitment of university presidents from outside the traditional pipeline of provosts and deans, the development of benchmarking and the use of accountability measures in assessing instructional and research performance, and the increasing importance of private fundraising as evidence of the entrepreneurial tendencies in higher education today. Other authors have emphasized the extent to which universities are becoming engaged with their communities as a characteristic feature of what is occurring today.[1] Scholars note how traditional "town-gown" relationships and tensions are being reconfigured around mutually beneficial partnerships where universities assist community development through the efforts of their faculty and students, by the utilization of university resources for real estate development, or through the contribution the university makes to the community as an employer.

Universities are clearly more engaged and more entrepreneurial than ever before, and, overall, these developments have been generally positive. But the nature and scope of the transformation of higher education are more far-reaching and have a greater impact than discussions of entrepreneurialism and engagement normally describe. Colleges and universities have become indispensable actors in the social and economic development of modern society, at almost every level and in almost every venue.

Higher education is a key actor in the revitalization of urban communities, in the development of responses to declining economies in rural areas, and to the competitive strategies of regions, states, and nations. This is true if we are talking about the school system in Richmond, Virginia, tobacco farmers in North Carolina, the revitalization of the Irish economy, or the attempt by China to take advantage of its enormous population resources.

The recent success of American higher education in the broader marketplace has been nothing short of phenomenal. The surge in the number of applications for admission has been widely discussed. In 2008, Harvard had more than 27,000 applications for approximately 1,600 slots and many of the elite Ivy League schools were accepting students at record low rates—some at a rate of less than 10 percent of applications, down from approximately 90 percent fifty years previously.[2] But it is not only the Ivy League that has experienced the surge, as similar trends are evident at state universities.

At Virginia Commonwealth University (VCU), we have seen first-year applications rise from approximately 5,000 in 1993 to more than 17,500 in 2008. A good portion of the rise in applications can be attributed to a demographic bubble that will begin to subside in a few years. But the increased relevance of a college education to economic success and the global appeal of American colleges and universities account for much of the increase as well.

The admissions boom also has resulted in the success of any number of spin-off businesses surrounding the application process. Test-preparation companies and publishers, coaching services, application specialists, and other service providers have flourished by targeting teens and, most especially, anxious parents with products regarding almost every aspect of the admissions process. And while a demographic shift in the number of college-age students in the United States during the next few years will obviously mute the admissions boom, the underlying dynamic pointing to the growing importance of higher education for personal success will continue unabated.

The recognition of the indispensability of higher education has extended far beyond the universe of students seeking admission to the university. The knowledge economy has fundamentally transformed town-gown relationships from an uneasy coexistence to a wide-ranging, constantly reinvented set of partnerships aimed at enhancing the experience and opportunities of students and faculty while addressing the concrete challenges that face communities, regions, and states on a daily basis.

Although debates over campus expansion can still roil local communities, these encounters do not begin to define the day-to-day relationships that most university administrators experience with the surrounding areas. Today, most localities spend very little time worrying about where their local university is expanding because they are much too busy beating down the door to the university asking it to come their way. Similar to the surge in the number of students seeking admission, we have also witnessed an increase in the number of companies who want to employ our students and utilize the intellectual capital of our faculties, while governments and nonprofits find new ways of enlisting the university in addressing societal challenges.

It is, of course, nothing new for students to serve as interns and for faculty to become consultants. What is different today is the extent of these activities, the range of universities that are engaging with their communities, and the altered nature of partnerships that bear little resemblance to traditional consulting contracts.

First, the sheer number of the relationships between colleges and universities and the external community is rapidly multiplying. At VCU, there is hardly an industry group, government agency, or nonprofit that has not approached us about establishing a closer relationship, ranging from business leaders in the early 1990s who wanted to establish a School of Engineering, to a technology community that was interested in the establishment of a research park, to dozens of state agencies seeking leadership training, all the way to advocates of midwifery who were hoping that the Women's Studies Department had expertise that could be utilized in the legislative and regulatory processes.

Second, the creation of ties between the university and the broader community is by no means limited to higher education institutions that were established with this particular mission in mind. Across the spectrum of higher education institutions, deeper and better relationships with the community are becoming more prevalent. One of the most interesting features in recent years is how both prominent and aspiring private institutions have reoriented their mission to emphasize their connection to the broader community. For example, the University of Pennsylvania is often viewed as a national model for the work that it has undertaken in partnering with the city of Philadelphia and the community organizations in West Philadelphia to enhance the neighborhood. In Los Angeles, the University of Southern California (USC) is widely acknowledged for its success not only in attracting increased numbers of applicants, but also in helping to revitalize the surrounding neighborhoods. In fact, private universities have often faced fewer constraints in developing innovative ways of partnering with their communities than public ones. They operate in a different legal and regulatory environment and, as a result, may not always face the same type of constituency pressures that public universities do.

Third, the nature of the relationship between universities and their relevant communities tends to be far richer than the one captured by the nature of a consulting arrangement. More and more, universities are entering into mutually beneficial partnerships with their relevant communities. And while consulting may be part of the partnership, it is less frequently the defining characteristic. Instead, individual faculty members and university-based centers tend to form partnerships in which academic expertise and practical experience are focused on addressing a significant societal challenge.

The indispensability of universities has elevated both the attractiveness of higher education across a spectrum of constituencies and stakeholders and simultaneously elevated the attention that higher education receives not only from students and parents, but also from legislators, business people, and community groups. Because higher education is so vital to fulfilling their aspirations, they pay far more attention to what occurs within it.

This has certainly benefited colleges and universities to a remarkable extent inasmuch as any number of donors and funders find it easy to make the connection between their contribution and the general progress of society. But it also has raised the stakes for the internal organization and governance of the university. Boards that choose university presidents, for example, are coming to realize that the traditional career path in higher education—from chair to dean to provost—may not necessarily provide the skill set or the range of experiences that are absolutely necessary for an effective college president. And this has made it important that universities develop internal processes that enable them both to be responsive to opportunities and to address abuses in a timelier manner than may have always been the case in the past.

This chapter outlines the nature of the transformation that is occurring across modern universities. We illuminate the kinds of partnerships that universities are now developing with the broader community and we show how these developments are occurring on a global as well as a national scale. The chapter also examines what these changes mean for the leadership of universities. And we conclude by assessing key criticisms that have been made of these trends within contemporary higher education.

In 1982, Derek Bok published *Beyond the Ivory Tower: Social Responsibilities of the Modern University.*[3] The book offers a set of reflections on one basic issue: to what extent should modern universities depart from the tradition of being autonomous institutions in pursuit of fundamental truths in order to fulfill social responsibilities that either internal or external constituencies define as important?

Although the volume was written, to some extent, in response to the political debates that roiled universities in the 1960s and 1970s in regard to accepting funding from federal agencies implicated in the Vietnam War, Bok also examines a set of issues that are still relevant today. He studied the role of technology-transfer operations inside universities. He addresses the potential conflict in faculty roles when the faculty members become entrepreneurs running start-up companies. He looks at the potential for universities to assist communities in developing what we might call today "social capital." And he asks what responsibilities universities have in the admissions process to address the social inequities that persist in American society.

Bok's overall approach is to maintain that it is crucial that universities do not abandon their role as places where scholars can pursue truth in a disinterested way; yet he applies this criterion to the particular controversies he addresses pragmatically and sensibly. He is relatively comfortable with the use of affirmative action in the admissions process as a means of diversifying the university. He believes that conflicts of commitment by faculty members may be a product of a new entrepreneurial climate, but suggests that these can be managed by a set of rules that universities should be able to formulate. He is, however, less sanguine about the university's capabilities as an engine of social reform. While he acknowledges, for instance, that urban universities may have a special service responsibility, he does not believe that university faculty members possess the requisite skills, especially political ones, to offer genuinely effective assistance to social and governmental agencies that address the most challenging conditions.

Bok's work remains today one of the most comprehensive treatments of a matter that has become increasingly important. Since this volume in 1982, he has continued to explore a similar set of issues in recent books examining the commercialization of higher education and the quality of learning that takes place within it.[4] His arguments, throughout the corpus of his published work, are ultimately grounded in a distinction that implies that the disinterested pursuit of truth and the institutional commitments to commercial innovation and societal betterment are inherently in tension if not outright conflict.

We do not necessarily believe that the framework fully captures the evolution of modern intellectual challenges. Bok is clearly worried about how the pursuit of academic truth can be undermined and contaminated by external forces. This may be true in particular instances. But what Bok rarely considered in 1982 is the way that academic research can itself be enhanced by the kind of engagement with the community that the modern university can provide.[5] Indeed, there are many areas of serious intellectual endeavor where engagement with the broader society enriches and enhances the capacities of researchers to conduct basic work and answer crucial questions.

A good way of illustrating this difference is to examine three common types of partnerships in which universities commonly engage with their communities and external partners. It is our sense that these activities have increasingly become part of the fabric and definition of modern universities and are not merely useful appendages to be undertaken if possible.

## UNIVERSITIES AS DEVELOPERS OF SOCIAL CAPITAL[6]

There is little doubt that many universities, especially urban research universities such as VCU, have become more involved and engaged with their communities than they may have been three or four decades ago.[7] Today, urban-based universities are themselves extraordinarily diverse. They range from private institutions generally considered to be at the pinnacle of American higher education, such as Yale, Columbia, and the University of Pennsylvania, to universities such as the University of Alabama–Birmingham and the University of South Florida, which combine access for a general population with world-class programs in the biomedical arena, to colleges where the primary mission remains undergraduate instruction for a population of modest economic means, including America's large system of community colleges. One common thread across all these institutions, however, is their commitment to enhance the capacity of their surrounding neighborhoods, local community organizations, and school systems. This commitment cuts across the public-private divide, the prestige differential, and even the nature of the current student body.

There are many different reasons that urban-based universities made this commitment originally. Some public universities may have done so as a result of legislative mandates contained in their articles of original formation. And some have done so out of a sense of enlightened self-interest when university leaders came to understand that the reputation and attractiveness of their own universities were at risk if they could not find a way to improve the conditions of their surrounding environment to make it more secure and appealing to prospective students and employees. But whatever the original rationale for the commitment, it has today frequently become embedded in the core mission and identity of the institution. And this is the case regardless of the source of funding, prestige, or mission of the university. The social responsibility of urban universities is seen more and more as an integral feature of university identity.

This commitment has not been embraced by every university located in an urban venue. The Los Angeles area, for example, has two world class universities in USC and the University of California–Los Angeles (UCLA). Yet USC has made a far more extensive commitment to partnering with the community than UCLA. In a number of others cities, one could point to institutions—both public and private—that have either refused to make a commitment to working closely with their surrounding community or have done so fitfully, awkwardly, and not very successfully. But we think that the trend and trajectory is clear. Even as universities become more and more involved in the global arena, they are simultaneously developing strategies and dedicating resources to enhancing the social and economic development of their neighborhoods, community, and region.

The University of Pennsylvania's commitment to West Philadelphia is often discussed as a prototype of how an urban-based institution of higher education relates to its surrounding neighborhood. Most descriptions of the origin of Penn's exemplary approach note that it began, at least in part, out of a calculus of self-interest when university leaders noted that the reputation of the university was suffering from the perception that it was located in an inhospitable area of the city where crime and other social disorder had a negative impact on the appeal of the university itself.[8] Today, however, the strength of the community ties at the university and its broad-based commitment to enhancing the social capital of West Philadelphia is a well-developed and highly visible element of the university's core identity. Materials produced by the university note that this commitment is perfectly consistent with American democratic norms and Benjamin Franklin's vision of a university that could simultaneously be a scientific leader while contributing to the advance of the broader society.

In 1982, Bok suggested that enhancing social capital was unlikely to be an effective part of the core mission of an effective contemporary university, in part because of a mismatch between what might be needed to accomplish this and the normal skill set of a university faculty member. He noted that working with community organizations, negotiating the perilous shoals of local political conflicts, and maintaining a long-term commitment to the practical implementation of ideas were unlikely to be skills that faculty members who excelled in basic research were likely to possess. In the ensuing twenty-five years, policy research has itself begun to focus on the collaborative skills that are necessary to develop successful urban policy at both the neighborhood level and at the level of citywide institutions. And while there are certainly faculty who can perform important research while maintaining a level of detachment, most researchers themselves believe that on-the-ground experience with school systems, nonprofits, community organizations, and city agencies is inherently a positive contributor to basic research.

## UNIVERSITIES AS HEALTH CARE PROVIDERS

A similar dynamic can be traced in the commitment of universities to provide medical care to the surrounding populations. In many urban areas, university medical centers occupy an extremely important role. They often serve as destination centers for a regional, state, and sometimes national patient base. The capacity of university-based medical centers to bring together state-of-the-art research with the highest-quality clinical care enables them to be hospitals of choice for the most challenging medical conditions. At the same time, their location—frequently in the heart of downtown areas—has also made them hospitals of choice for urban residents who have had limited access to health care and limited means of paying for it. University-based urban hospitals thus play crucial roles in providing health care to indigent patients in communities across the nation. In addition, a university-based hospital is often the lead institution within a region for the provision of trauma care—whether as a result of auto accidents, fires, or gunshot wounds.

The very experience of providing these types of services has raised a set of questions that have had a substantial impact on the kind of research that is needed to address issues regarding the organization of health care. Administrators, physicians, and nurses in university hospitals have become acutely aware of what occurs when a population does not have regular access to health care, but relies on hospitals to address problems after they have already become emergencies. This awareness has catalyzed a set of administrative actions and new research directions that take place within university medical centers and in academic departments that are affiliated with them.

Hospital administrators have begun to think of better ways to serve patients who are likely to wind up in the emergency room for primary-care services. For example, at VCU we ultimately established a partnership with community primary-care providers in which our medical center reimbursed the physicians at rates higher than Medicaid rates for taking care of patients at their offices. The partnership enabled patients to receive appropriate care in a timelier manner; and, despite the costs to the medical center, the treatment was less expensive than utilizing emergency resources for primary-care delivery.

The experiences of a university medical center also have opened up very creative lines of research, not only in the technology of new medical advances but also for the host of political and cultural issues that are involved in matters such as the provision of primary-care services, the use of medical and alternative practitioners, the nature of physician-patient interactions, and issues that promote compliance with medical treatment. These are not minor incidental issues, or simply applied matters, but are challenges that go to the heart of the successful provision of medical care in modern urban society. Moreover, these are matters that only universities, with their interdisciplinary teams and their capacity to assemble a group of physicians, specialists in language and culture, social workers, and medical anthropologists, can adequately address.

## UNIVERSITIES AS PARTNERS IN REGIONAL DEVELOPMENT

The set of task-oriented partnerships we have described does not fully capture the extent to which universities have become indispensable to their broader communities. Besides the specific partnerships that have been designed to achieve defined objectives, there is a more general role that universities have assumed that has gone relatively unnoticed and unexamined. Today, universities are often invited to take a leading role in the formulation and implementation of the broad development strategy of a community, region, or state. Community and state leaders have recognized that demands of competition in a knowledge economy have placed a premium on those venues that can provide a high-quality workforce for knowledge-specific industries and a "creative class" that enhances the overall quality of life for an entire community.[9] For this reason, university presidents and other key officials at the university are often asked to assume responsibilities in development-based organizations because of the importance of the university to the overall strategy of a community or region.

A national organization such as CEOs for Cities is an excellent illustration of this new role that universities have assumed.[10] The organization, founded in 2001 by Paul Grogan, the president of the Boston Foundation, is dedicated to seeing cities as an asset base that make significant contributions to innovation and economic progress in America. At its inception in 2001, CEOs asked each member city to bring together a mayor, a private-sector CEO, and a university president as its permanent delegation to the organization (it has since added a foundation or nonprofit official). The organization conducts state-of-the-art research designed to discover major urban trends and to illuminate replicable innovations that can address common challenges and develop new opportunities in urban America. How can cities foster entrepreneurship? How can cities attract and retain talent? How can cities connect to the global economy? The importance of active and engaged university leadership has become a core component of the practices and innovations that the organization has endorsed.

CEOs for Cities is illustrative of the changing social position of the university within a much larger set of American communities. The university is indispensable, not simply for the specific expertise it possesses but for the overall contribution that it can make to the future of the community and its capacity to compete globally for business, talent, and culture. It would be irresponsible for community-based leadership in a knowledge economy not to consider how it could leverage university resources and assist the university in achieving its aims within the community's overall strategy for economic progress. It would be equally irresponsible for a university not to respond to the community's expectations.

## THE NEW GLOBAL UNIVERSITY

About five years ago, VCU decided to revamp the strategy and methods it was employing in its international programs. The faculty had become very interested in expanding the university's global activities, both in terms of their research and the opportunities available to students. Many of these activities had become quasi-formalized through a set of agreements that typically took place among schools, departments, and centers. In fact, we had developed well over one hundred such agreements. But when we started to assess the institutional impact of the individual agreements, a number of questions were raised that led us to alter our approach. A significant portion of the signed agreements were more an expression of good intentions than a genuine plan of work between institutions. Some agreements that had produced interesting collaborations or valuable student opportunities became dormant when one of the active faculty members on either side retired or departed from the institution. And we had no way of prioritizing the agreements that had the best prospect for furthering the core mission of the institution.

As an alternative to the proliferation of agreements with highly variable impacts and minimal mechanisms for accountability, we decided to establish a much smaller set of international partnerships with sixteen universities around the world. The essence of the new approach was to select a set of relatively comparable universities and to establish institution-to-institution collaborations that were officially endorsed at the presidential level. The elements of these collaborations would include faculty research collaborations; student opportunities ranging from study abroad programs of variable length to joint seminars and even joint degree programs; and administrative partnerships where ideas could be shared about facility planning, research administration, and other operational details.

We succeeded in establishing the institution-to-institution collaborations: four of the partnerships are in Europe or the British Isles, and eleven have been formalized with institutions that are primarily in highly populous nations that are experiencing significant population growth and social transformation.

## CONVERGENCE OF INTERESTS

When the administrative teams of our partner institutions visit and discuss common issues, the issue to which our visitors constantly return is how we have organized our university to foster economic development and promote regional goals. It has become clear that no matter where one goes around the globe, thinking about the manner in which universities can help to foster broad societal development initiatives is of vital importance. Our partners from the University of Cordoba, for example, tell us about the importance of that issue to higher education in Spain. When we speak to our university partners in Russia at Moscow State University and St. Petersburg State University, they are extremely interested in how we developed a research park adjacent to the university to foster new start-up companies and generate high-tech employment for the local area. The challenges of higher education are often culture- and country-specific, but we have come to understand that the relationship of universities to the global knowledge economy is quickly transcending nation-specific concerns.

Throughout the globe, university leaders and policymakers are grappling with the full meaning of this development and are thinking about how to better harness the intellectual capital of universities for their broad social purposes.[11] In many countries, the need for highly skilled individuals has opened up access to universities to individuals who may have previously been excluded. Admissions policies are being rethought to the extent that there is a greater need for more university-trained individuals and less justification for highly restrictive access policies. In addition, the allocation of students across majors has become a major item of concern in many nations. In some places, this can mean thinking about how the government can provide incentives to encourage students to enter economically relevant math- and science-related fields where there is a substantial shortage of qualified individuals.

The development of closer linkages between universities and societal economic progress has fostered a set of actions that extend beyond the reorientation of admissions criteria. In a number of countries, there have been explicit efforts to revisit the metrics by which institutions of higher education are judged to ensure that their contribution to the wider society is related to the budgetary allocations received. It often means developing better vehicles for promoting collaboration with the private sector. And, in some areas of the world such as the Middle East, it actually means asking respected U.S. institutions of higher education to establish branch campuses in other countries. But there is hardly a forward-looking country around the globe where the organization of the university system and its attendant policies is not the object of intense consideration.

The evidence for this development is extensive. We have seen it with entire nations. During the 1980s and 1990s, Ireland essentially reinvented itself as an information technology capital and, in the process, skillfully used its universities as an incubator for talent and for the establishment of collaborations between the academy and the best-known multinational corporations.[12] The "Celtic Tiger" demonstrated that government policies with a supportive academic climate could enable nations to make significant progress within the global economic structure, as Irish gross domestic product, flat for decades, saw a remarkable increase.[13]

Elite institutions such as Cambridge and Oxford also have been involved in the process of reinvention. In the 1980s and 1990s, the "Cambridge Phenomenon" represented a major change in the way the university conducted itself and related to its external stakeholders.[14] Entrepreneurial department chairs built long-term relationships with major companies such as Microsoft, bringing significant resources into the university and helping to establish the so-called Silicon Fen in the surrounding region.[15] At Oxford University, activities such as Enterprising Oxford have developed innovative ways of linking the business acumen of the faculty to the particular challenges faced by British companies in the emergent global economy.[16] And while these trends have occasionally engendered significant internal criticism, the practices that have been developed have been the object of widespread imitation.

The interest in connecting universities with larger societal interests in economic development also has become prevalent in the Middle East. For decades, governments in a number of the Gulf countries have been concerned that the indigenous university systems were not directed at meeting the long-term economic needs of their societies.[17] Many students were sent to American and European universities, where they obtained a practical education that enabled them to perform scientific and administrative tasks more effectively when they returned home. More recently, there has been a notable shift in strategy, one that has focused on bringing U.S. universities to physical locations within the regions.[18]

Eleven years ago, VCU was the first American higher education institution to establish a campus within Education City in Qatar. Since that time, five other institutions have followed suit as the Qatari government has attempted to provide state-of-the-art opportunities to its citizens in a variety of academic areas.[19] In recent times, the effort to establish branch campuses in the Gulf countries has proliferated. While some American universities have declined opportunities based on concerns about academic freedom or gender equality issues, many institutions of higher education see the opportunity as beneficial to their own interests and as a fascinating experiment in the capacity to bring U.S.-style higher education to other populations around the world.[20]

In pointing to a similar response from universities to the global economic environment, we do not mean to suggest that there are not very significant differences in how these responses are organized and manifested. In countries such as the United States, entrepreneurial universities are often just that—universities that have ample freedom in deciding how to reinvent themselves and in defining both their core missions and the strategies for achieving their stated aims (though public universities are very dependent on the values embraced by the political leadership in their states).

At the other pole, there are countries where higher education institutions and their capacities are essentially extensions of the political state and where movement into activities that promote economic development is part of a coordinated government plan or explicit policy initiative. Scholars have often pointed to universities in countries such as China and Singapore in this vein. In between, there are universities in countries such as the United Kingdom that are focusing on economic development initiatives as a combined result of their own internal evolution and an evolving system of governmental incentives.

Efforts to describe best practices and to understand what is or is not transferable need to be sensitive to the broader administrative, social, and governmental contexts in which a given system of universities operates. This will apply to the nature of university leadership, the kind of administrative structures that will be built within universities, the preferred modes of partnering with private-sector or external institutions, and the manner in which accountability will be measured and promoted. At the same time, it is worthwhile to note the near universality of the trends that are impacting higher education and the near universality of the expectation that higher education will be a vital player in the promotion of economic progress.

Two major interrelated themes have often been voiced in popular and academic writing about university leaders, particularly college presidents, in the last ten years. The first describes the increasing complexity of the position and the demands that it places on the individuals who occupy it and on the governing boards that seek to find excellent leaders for their own institutions. The second theme examines how the ever-expanding position requirements combined with the challenging internal political culture of universities have made the job not only more difficult, but also more precarious. In this description, the half-life of a university president starts to resemble the situation of coaches in big-time athletic programs under a mandate of "win or get out."

## THE EXPANDING PRESIDENCY

Descriptions of the increasing complexity of a university president's role typically begin with a description of the proliferating range of con-stituents and stakeholders to which presidents have to respond. In these accounts, college presidents are no longer solely responsible to students, faculty, and alumni, but have to manage relationships with legislative bodies; political officials at the state, federal, and local levels; local com-panies; school systems; various regulatory bodies; and anyone who may contribute financially to the institution or influence the environment in which it operates. In this new milieu, the skills required for successfully performing the job cannot be assumed to have been obtained through the usual set of preparatory jobs that college presidents have held. In essence, the job requirements have outpaced the standard training regimen for the position. For example, time spent as a provost or a dean may or may not be a useful indicator of the success that a president will have raising funds or representing the university externally.

Many observers of the modern college presidency have connected its growing complexity to what they perceive to be its elevated level of dif-ficulty. At the most minimal level, it is evident that the model of a univer-sity president as chief executive officer rarely meshes perfectly with the existing culture of academic organizations, particularly those that have long-standing traditions of faculty autonomy. Reports note that the range of relationships that have to be managed by university presidents always contains the potential for initiating job-threatening crises.

In addition, many observers of the internal culture in contemporary academia have noted that its internal politics can be exceptionally drain-ing and destructive. High-profile faculty-administration conflicts such as the tension between former Harvard president Larry Summers and the arts and sciences faculty of Harvard College are often seen as typical of the kind of energy that is directed from the faculty toward administra-tors. From this perspective, the tension between faculty interests and institutional interests is unrelenting. It is no wonder then that university presidents are perceived to have relatively short tenure in the position.

Descriptions of the growing complexity and difficulty of a college presidency do often describe the day-to-day challenges that can occur in the job. But we should be careful not to take these as a complete depiction of the position and its appeal. In the first place, almost every high-level executive position in the country, whether in the public, private, or non-profit sectors, requires a far more complex set of skills today than thirty years ago. Nor is it atypical for leaders, even of privately held companies, to have far more responsibilities with regulatory bodies, political officials, and the media than they did thirty years ago. How many private-sector companies, for example, now provide their chief executives with various forms of media training and political education? This is not a condition to be deplored, but a simple recognition of the growing interrelationship between various sorts of institutions.

Even more importantly, there is little indication that either the complexity or the precariousness of the job is preventing good people from seeking college presidencies or being satisfied with the job if they are fortunate enough to obtain it. A recent survey of university presidents published by the *Chronicle of Higher Education* showed that job satisfaction among the highest-level university leaders is uniformly very high. About 94 percent said that, if they had it to do all over again, they would still become a college president.[21] The inherent challenge and complexity of the job is one important reason individuals like it so much.

We suspect that another reason that university presidents experience such high job satisfaction is related to the potential impact their activities can generate. In the modern university environment, the opportunities for creative leaders to make a difference in their own institutions and in relating their institutions to the external world are very substantial. In addition, it is currently possible for institutions across the range of colleges and universities to make a very substantial impact.

## PRESIDENTIAL OPPORTUNITY

One point of view holds that colleges and universities may not look very different today than they did fifty years ago. According to some reputational surveys, for example, there has not been that much movement in and out of the list of top fifty universities. The institutions that had the greatest reputation in the 1950s are, by and large, the same institutions that hold that reputation today. However true this may be, the statement does not capture some of the relevant changes that are occurring in contemporary higher education.

A number of institutions may not be included in the top-fifty reputational rankings, but they have managed to make enormous progress nonetheless. In addition, some universities that may not be on everyone's top-twenty list can have absolutely first-rate programs in specialized but crucially important areas. For example, neither the University of Pittsburgh nor the University of Washington is generally rated as one of the twenty best universities in the nation, but each of these excellent institutions is in the top ten universities in the area of National Institutes of Health (NIH) funding for biomedical research. And there are any number of areas where universities have fostered concentrations of strength that enable them to outpace universities that are more highly esteemed overall in their particular areas of focus.

Setting the rankings aside, it also is evident that in the knowledge economy, the need for what colleges and universities provide is so extensive that college presidents and other administrators have a far broader field in which they can make an impact. Throughout the country, successful community college presidents have fostered regional economic development, responded creatively to dislocations in regional economies caused by shifting trends in manufacturing and industry, and have become important leaders in public-private partnerships geared to addressing their community's future. Presidents of doctoral research institutions have an ever-expanding set of opportunities to provide medical services, to link academic programs to the long-term needs of a community and state, and, if they are located in a midsize city, to be a key component of any regional economic development strategy. There simply is no possible way that the elite twenty institutions in the country could provide the number of students and effective partnerships that external entities need from higher education today.

This is not to say that the standard paths for developing university presidents or fostering the kind of university administration that can take best advantage of the new environment could not be improved. For some time, it has been apparent that the representational and fundraising experience of university presidents is not always best acquired through the demanding duties of an internal chief academic officer. It is evident that the boards that govern many universities are not very content with simply considering the experience of being a chief academic officer sufficient background for performing the duties of a university president. Governing boards have adopted a variety of strategies to find the individuals best suited for positions: at times, they have looked through the range of academic administrative positions and selected individuals from ranks other than the provostship; on other occasions, they have looked to individuals with considerable financial expertise and fundraising experience; and, at other times, they have searched for individuals with experience in the political arena because of the importance of the representational aspects of the position.

This trend is likely to continue for some time. While higher education institutions have shown increasing flexibility in determining how they will recruit top leaders, they have not been equally innovative in reorienting their own practices to do a better job of developing the kind of leaders who can flourish in an environment where the expectations placed on university presidents (and many other administrators) are considerably different. The kind of succession planning that is an integral part of private-sector companies is rarely evident in academia, and it is probably far more common for universities than for most major corporations to believe that they cannot find the best leaders from within the organization. In addition, although it has become apparent that other leadership positions besides that of the president require skill sets that extend beyond administration of the academic enterprise, universities have only begun to think about how they can ensure that they have a talented staff who possesses the requisite administrative talents.

It may not, of course, be possible to fully institutionalize entrepreneurialism or to find easy substitutes for the administrative vision that often drives university transformation today. But it certainly should be possible to specify the kind of talents that enable institutions of higher education to progress and to find better ways of developing these capacities more broadly throughout an institution by providing opportunities for individuals committed to the organization to acquire these talents. This has often been a difficult task for higher education, given the fact that many of a university's most talented individuals have little interest in administrative tasks. But if it is the case that universities have a unique capacity to shape and reshape their own identities, leadership matters perhaps more today than at any other time. And while governing boards will continue to seek leaders drawn from the external world with a unique set of talents and attributes, it is crucial that they also begin to work within their own colleges and universities to find more successful ways of institutionalizing these outlooks and skills among a wide array of individuals who have administrative interests or the potential to be successful leaders at all levels of the institution.

## THE MODERN UNIVERSITY AND ITS CRITICS

The vision of modern universities as more fully linked to external institutions and choosing leaders based, in part, on their capacity to execute this new structure has generated critical as well as supportive commentary.

### The Traditionalist Critique

The traditionalist criticism of trends in the contemporary university focuses on what it considers to be the devaluing of the liberal arts for a more pragmatic, training-oriented educational process. From this vantage point, universities have historically provided an opportunity for individuals to study subjects such as history, languages, literature, and philosophy in an environment removed from the pressing day-to-day demands of making a living. At the same time, this intensive experience with the liberal arts ultimately imparted certain traits and attributes—namely, judgment, discernment, adherence to scientific evidence, respect for the past, ethical treatment of others, an understanding of the complexity of human development, and a capacity for self-expression—that made university graduates capable of assuming responsible roles in the public and private sectors. Critics of the contemporary university often believe that the cultivation of these attributes has been overtaken by an interest in skill development in areas such as business and engineering—a process that is important but is not the ultimate objective of a college education.

A second feature of the traditionalist critique contends that the core purpose of the university is being damaged by the ongoing shift in the dynamics of governance as administrative power and discretion have been expanded at the expense of faculty self-governance. Again, a distinctive feature of the university—the governance of the institution by those who work within it and are closest to the students being educated—has been replaced by a system modeled on the leadership of a corporation, where administrative leaders and a board of governors detached from the faculty define the core mission and allocate resources for the university. In this setting, administration itself becomes a career and not a task that a faculty-scholar assumes for a limited period for the good of the institution. The emergence of careerist administrators is seen as undermining the principle of collegiality that enables universities to offer a distinctive educational experience.

### Criticism from the Left

A politicized version of these criticisms is often advanced by the political left. This vantage point emphasizes the university's role as an autonomous institution that has often functioned as a critic of societal norms. Faculty members, who possess academic freedom through their teaching and research, have raised fundamental questions about the assumptions that drive social and political priorities and have served to advance alternative notions of the common good. From this perspective, universities have been one of the crucial institutions within which societies engage in self-reflection and self-criticism. But to the extent that universities become dependent on outside funding for support of building, endowments, and faculty salaries, there is pressure—both implicit and explicit—to abandon or at least de-emphasize the university's role as conscience of the broader society and to mute potential criticisms. In essence, the university has traded its autonomy and lowered its voice for the financial support it might receive for its scientific research from the government and for partnerships with corporations that may not have the public interest at heart.

The picture of a university that has put a "for sale" sign on its conscience has become standard portraiture by the political left. This point of view was commonly voiced during the war in Vietnam, when university-based critics accused their own institutions of supporting an unjust war by seeking and accepting government grants for activities that could be employed by the military. The perspective is regularly advanced by groups that have become involved in various divestment campaigns, demanding that university endowments not place monies in companies or funds that profit from business relationships that are socially irresponsible or politically advantageous for those committing unethical acts. And this point of view has been voiced in recent times by critics of what are presumed to be excessively cozy relationships between universities and the pharmaceutical industry, who argue that science has been compromised by research funding from industry in general or from particular companies. In many of these arguments, the entanglement of the university with external institutions carries the potential of inflicting considerable damage on the institution itself.

## Responding to the Critics

The critics of modern universities correctly identify some trends that have emerged in higher education. We certainly recognize that scientific and mathematical disciplines have become increasingly prestigious. Nor would we argue with the contention that more universities around the globe today have placed a very high premium on administrative vision and managerial competence than may have been the case at one time, even if the contemporary critics fail to acknowledge the impact that visionary leaders have exercised at world-class universities such as the University of Chicago and Harvard University. But we disagree fundamentally with the critics of modern universities who assert that these trends inherently devalue traditional modes of understanding or who contend that collaborations and partnerships with external institutions inherently undermine the sanctity of academic values.

In many ways, the approaches, values, and skills that are traditionally associated with the humanities may be more relevant today in a global society than in any previous era. Language skills, the capacity to communicate across cultures, and the ability to understand how a particular society adopted the worldview it possesses are crucial to successful interaction at almost every level of society. These traits are necessary to the establishment of diplomatic relationships between nations that teeter on the brink of conflict. These attributes are also crucial to professional interactions at the interpersonal level. For example, a capacity to communicate across cultures may enable a patient and a physician from vastly different backgrounds to create a bond that results in an accurate diagnosis and a productive course of treatment for an illness or disease. In addition, we might also look at the elevated role that ethical considerations play in the emergent controversies of the twenty-first century. For example, we cannot assess the practice and implications of genetic testing or the advisability of allowing private-sector companies to utilize the information that could potentially be collected about us without understanding the ethics of privacy and how far it should be protected in a technologically advanced society.

A similar case can be made regarding the continued and enhanced relevance of the arts. Music, performance, painting, sculpture, film, and dance function, as modern science does, as a global language that can be understood across very different cultures. The arts always have been a significant vehicle for understanding both the dominant tendencies and the internal tensions evident in any society. Again, universities have been indispensable in fostering this capacity of the arts. In recent decades, for example, proliferating film and cinema studies curricula have been an important means by which universities have examined popular culture in a variety of national settings. Beyond curricular innovations, universities have been vital participants in funding arts programs, promoting global arts exchanges, nurturing international film festivals, and providing a home (and a paycheck) for artists, enabling them to continue their work even when it is not fully supported by the commercial marketplace. And, to the extent that the author Richard Florida is correct, the emergence of a hip and vibrant arts community is often an integral component of economic growth in the contemporary metropolis.[22]

In speaking about the continuing relevance of traditional areas of the humanities, it also is useful to note the increasing emphasis in fields such as medicine and public health on how matters such as social disparities and cultural norms impact the capacity of the system to deliver effective services. Unequal access to health information, medical facilities, and preventive care has a significant and continuing influence on the overall health outcomes of a society. Moreover, there are issues that cannot be solved by medicine itself, but need policies at the macro and micro levels that link the provision of care to other important related activities. NIH-funded cancer centers require that the recipients of funding not only have active research and onsite clinical programs, but also develop innovative and effective ways of reaching out to populations and communities that might not have sought a cancer center on their own. Successfully addressing these concerns requires psychologists, medical anthropologists, religious studies scholars, and sociologists.

There is a certain irony to the contention that contemporary universities have systematically devalued the humanities and the cultural sciences. According to many conservative critics of the university, the opposite has occurred. In their opinion, universities have essentially been captured by the political agenda of the academic left who staff the humanities and social departments—Roger Kimball's "tenured radicals"—and, most importantly, set the cultural and political tone for the university as an institution.[23] According to conservative critics, humanists and social scientists have entirely rewritten the curriculum of the university to align with their own political beliefs, are shameless in their efforts to foist their own political views upon the students, and have established the parameters for the viewpoints that are and are not acceptable to articulate the university. They contend that anyone who has the temerity to oppose this agenda, such as Harvard president Larry Summers, does so at grave risk to career and reputation. From this perspective, the problem is not the lack of influence of the humanities, but the perversion of its traditional purpose for narrowly political aims.

Our purpose here is not to attempt to settle or even to take sides in the more ideologically driven debates about contemporary higher education. In the twenty-first-century world, universities will invariably dedicate considerable resources to instruction in the sciences and other technologically driven areas. But as institutions of higher education become more engaged with external institutions and more committed to promoting regional development, we will invariably need to address matters of fairness, allocation of resources, the role of minority communities, intercultural communication, and ethical concerns about privacy. For this reason, the argument that the liberal arts and social sciences have become irrelevant to the contemporary university seems terribly misguided. In the twenty-first century, universities must make very substantial investments in science and technology. But the concerns and values of traditional subject areas will be equally needed. To use a political analogy, contemporary universities are big tents that function best when the various factions within are not at war internally but work cooperatively to address a common set of problems.

## NOTES

1. William Talcott, "Modern Universities, Absent Citizenship? Historical Perspectives" (CIRCLE working paper 39, University of Maryland, College Park,

2005). Stephen L. Percy, Nancy L. Zimpher, and Mary J., Brukardt, eds., *Creating a New Kind of University: Institutionalizing Community-University Engagement* (Boston: Anker, 2006).

2. Jacques Steinberg and Tamar Lewin, "For Top Colleges, Economy Has Not Reduced Interest (or Made Getting in Easier)," *New York Times,* March 29, 2009, Blog: The Choice: Demystifying College Admissions and Aid, http://thechoice .blogs.nytimes.com/2009/03/29/for-top-colleges-economy-has-not-reduced -interest-or-made-getting-in-easier/?hpw (accessed April 20, 2009). Ivy Success, "Harvard Admits 7.1 Percent," *IvySuccess.com: Admission Stats 2013,* http://ivy success.com/harvard_2013.html (accessed April 20, 2009).

3. Derek Bok, *Behind the Ivory Tower: Social Responsibilities of the Modern University* (Cambridge, MA: Harvard University Press, 1982).

4. Derek Bok, *Universities and the Future of America* (Durham, NC: Duke University Press, 1990). Derek Bok, *Universities in the Marketplace: The Commercialization of Higher Education* (Princeton, NJ: Princeton University Press, 2003).

5. Michael Gibbons, Camille Limoges, Helga Nowotny, Simon Schwartzman, Peter Scott, and Martin Trow, *The New Production of Knowledge* (Newbury Park, CA: Sage, 1994).

6. Robert D. Putnam, *Bowling Alone: The Collapse and Revival of American Community* (New York: Simon & Schuster, 2000).

7. David C. Perry and Wim Wiewel, eds., *The Urban University as Urban Developer: Case Studies and Analysis* (Armonk, NY: M.E. Sharpe, 2005).

8. Samuel Hughes, "The West Philadelphia Story," *The Pennsylvania Gazette* 96, no. 2 (1997), http://www.upenn.edu/gazette/1197/philly.html (accessed May 15, 2007). Center for Community Partnerships at Penn, "History," University of Pennsylvania, http://www.upenn.edu/ccp/history.html (accessed May 15, 2007).

9. CEOs for Cities and Joseph Cortright, *City Vitals: A Detailed Set of Statistical Measures for Urban Leaders to Understand Their City's Performance in Four Key Areas, Talent, Innovation, Connections and Distinctiveness, in Comparison to the Fifty Largest Metropolitan Regions in the United States* (Chicago: CEOs for Cities, n.d.).

10. Initiative for a Competitive Inner City and CEOs for Cities, *Leveraging Colleges and Universities for Urban Economic Revitalization: An Action Agenda* (Boston: Initiative for a Competitive Inner City and CEOs for Cities, 2002).

11. Joel Spring, *Education and the Rise of the Global Economy* (Mahwah, NJ: Lawrence Erlbaum Associates, 1998). Holger Daun, *Educational Restructuring in the Context of Globalization and National Policy* (New York: Routledge Falmer, 2002). Jean Larson Pyle and Robert Forrant, eds., *Globalization, Universities and Issues of Sustainable Human Development* (Cheltenham, UK: Edward Elgar, 2002). Hugh Lauder, Phillip Brown, Jo-Anne Dillabough, and A. H. Halsey, eds., *Education, Globalization, and Social Change* (Oxford: Oxford University Press, 2006).

12. Eugene P. Trani, *Dublin Diaries: A Study of High Technology Development in Ireland* (Richmond: Virginia Commonwealth University; Dublin: Keough-Notre Dame Center, 2002). Jon Marcus, "The Celtic Tiger," *National Crosstalk* 15, no. 1 (2007): 14–16.

13. Trani, *Dublin Diaries.*

14. SiliconFen.com, "The Silicon Fen Story," http://www.siliconfen.com/sfstory .php (accessed September 10, 2007). Tom Worthington, "The Cambridge Phe-

nomenon: Summary of the Report," Net Traveller, http://www.tomw.net
.au/nt/cp.html (accessed September 10, 2007). Ian Kitching, "The Cambridge
Phenomenon: Cambridge—Past, Present and Future," http://www.iankitching
.me.uk/history/cam/phenomenon.html (accessed September 10, 2007).

15. Barry Moore, "Silicon Fen—the Cambridge Phenomenon as a Case-
History of Present-Day Industrial Clustering," The Diebold Institute for Public
Policy Studies, http://www.dieboldinstitute.org/paper24.pdf (accessed September 10, 2007). Eugene P. Trani, *Richmond at the Crossroads: The Greater Richmond
Metropolitan Area and the Knowledge Based High Technology Economy of the 21st
Century* (Richmond: Virginia Commonwealth University, 1998). SiliconFen.com,
"The Silicon Fen Story."

16. Oxford Economic Observatory, "A New Eye of the High-Tech Economy:
The Oxford Economic Observatory. University of Oxford: Annual Review 2002–
2003," http://www.ox.ac.uk/publicaffairs/pubs/annualreview/ar03/05.html
(accessed September 14, 2007).

17. Nader Fergany, "Arab Higher Education and Development, An Overview,"
Almishkat Centre for Research, Cairo, http://www.worldbank.org/mdf/mdf3/
papers/education/Fergany.pdf (accessed January 16, 2008). Amel Ahmed Hassan Mohamed, "Distance Higher Education in the Arab Region: The Need for
Quality Assurance Frameworks," *Online Journal of Distance Learning Administration* 3, no. 1 (2005), State University of West Georgia, Distance Education Center,
http://www.westga.edu/~distance/ojdla/spring81/mohamed81.htm (accessed
January 16, 2008).

18. Zvika Krieger, "Saudi Arabia Puts Its Billions behind Western-Style Higher
Education," *The Chronicle of Higher Education* 54, no. 3 (2007): A1.

19. Otto Pohl, "Getting a Foreign Education," *New York Times*, March 25, 2005,
http://www.nytimes.com/2005/03/24/world/africa/24iht-schools.html?_r=1
(accessed June 4, 2007).

20. Katherine S. Mangan, "Qatar Courts American Colleges," *The Chronicle of
Higher Education* 49, no. 2 (2002): A55. New York University, "NYUAD—the Vision," NYU, http://nyuad.nyu.edu/about/ (accessed March 31, 2009).

21. Jeffrey Selingo, "A Chronicle Survey: What Presidents Think—Leaders'
Views about Higher Education, Their Jobs, and Their Lives," *The Chronicle of
Higher Education* 52, no. 11 (2005): A26.

22. Richard Florida, *The Rise of the Creative Class: And How It's Transforming
Work, Leisure, Community & Everyday Life* (New York: Basic Books, 2002).

23. Roger Kimball, *Tenured Radicals: How Politics Has Corrupted Our Higher Education* (Chicago: Elephant Paperbacks, 1998).

*Chapter 2*

# The New Role of Higher Education: Economic and Community Development

In 1978, when Robert Holsworth joined Virginia Commonwealth University (VCU) as an assistant professor of political science, the university was involved in a major "town-gown" controversy. Residents of Oregon Hill, a working-class neighborhood at the south edge of campus, were objecting to a proposed expansion of the university that they argued would negatively impact their community. With dozens of citizens protesting outside the president's office, which was itself located on a main thoroughfare to downtown Richmond, the residents of Oregon Hill portrayed themselves as the powerless victims of a large university's insatiable appetite for space.

Although VCU was effectively landlocked and could barely service a growing student population within its existing space, it had even less capacity to make its case to the public and, at a minimum, to explain the possible connection between the university's interests and the long-term well-being of the broader community. The media had adopted the analytical framework of the protesters. Even more telling, there was not a single individual or organization with power or influence not connected to the university that was endorsing the plan and detailing the contribution that VCU made to the Richmond region.

In 1990, when I, Eugene Trani, became president of VCU, I inherited the second chapter of the Oregon Hill expansion saga. The outgoing VCU president had reformulated the university's master plan and once again included expansion southward into Oregon Hill as an integral component. Opponents of the proposal quickly dusted off the script from 1978 and replayed it one more time. Protesters lambasted the university for its continued aggressiveness and for its inability to learn from past mistakes.

25

The silence of local political figures and business leaders spoke volumes. And the university was stuck in the same dilemma—desperately needing to expand, but having a plan that had zero chance of generating support.

I fully recognized that VCU must expand if it was to serve its students and build state-of-the-art research facilities. But it also was clear that if VCU was to move forward, the Oregon Hill experience was an example of what needed to be changed. It was imperative that the growth of the university be linked to a growth in support of VCU by the local community. The community and the university had to see their fates linked through mutual aspirations and not in a permanently adversarial relationship. Within six months of assuming my position, I announced that the plan would be withdrawn and an alternative developed.

The town-gown controversy that persisted for more than a decade at VCU resembled hundreds of others that occurred across the country as wary neighbors objected to the plans that their colleges and universities had formulated to offer better services and more facilities to their students and faculty. But for many presidents of urban universities, the town-gown relationships were even more problematic. Not only did they have to worry about obtaining support from the community for campus expansion and improvement, but they also had to worry at times about what the problems of the surrounding area might mean for the reputation of their own institutions. To the extent that the encroachment of issues such as homelessness, inadequate security, and decaying neighborhoods impacted campus life, the capacity of universities to attract students, retain faculty, and be an employer of choice for dedicated staff members was jeopardized. And this was true not only of universities that had been established to serve an urban clientele, but also of prestigious institutions such as Columbia, Penn, and Yale.

University administrators came to realize that these controversies were essentially two sides of the same coin. As long as the dominant relationship between the university and its surrounding neighborhoods and jurisdictions was that of wariness and suspicion, the past was destined to be repeated over and over again in a way that was not ultimately beneficial for either the institution or the community. A new breed of university administrators began to promote a different paradigm, one that explicitly noted that the success of the higher education institution and the flourishing of the surrounding community should be pursued as a joint project. Even more importantly, they recognized that the commitment of the university had to extend beyond rhetoric—it needed to represent a substantial and comprehensive commitment of university resources that could, over the long term, substantially redefine the relationship between the university and its surrounding communities. In short, the issue was not one to be solved with a public relations campaign, but was instead a challenge where changing university behavior would result in better public relations.

This chapter describes the manner in which many colleges and universities have gone about redefining their relationships with surrounding communities and regions. We examine how institutions of higher education have developed an increasingly proactive and comprehensive approach to this issue. Colleges and universities have frequently become central participants in responding to many of the most pressing challenges facing communities and regions. They are major players in the formulation of economic development strategies. They are vital to the development of community capacity and social capital in underserved populations. And they may be an indispensable provider of health care and a critical agent in proposing and implementing strategies for health promotion among the general population. We outline the principal techniques and strategies that have been recently employed in these arenas by institutions of higher education. The chapter concludes by analyzing how the sum total of these efforts should lead us to understand that colleges and universities occupy a crucial and somewhat unique role in the overall policy process.

## CATALYZING ECONOMIC DEVELOPMENT

Leaders of higher education institutions have developed in recent years a more sophisticated understanding of their own status as economic entities and the effects that they can exercise on their communities and regions. They recognize that they are major employers in the community, often providing more jobs than some of the most well-known private-sector companies in the area. They understand that the university is a significant purchaser of goods, not only from national vendors, but also from a variety of local suppliers. They are aware that major university-sponsored events, such as football and basketball games, concerts, and lectures by celebrities, can attract significant external dollars from visitors to a community.

They know that university decisions about facility location and construction not only may be important to people involved in the construction trades, but also can shape a neighborhood's or community's sense of identity. And they have come to see that the university is a catalyst for other local business development—just like a major plant, suppliers, service vendors, and others tend to locate near the university to garner the dollars that students, staff, and faculty spend in the normal course of a day. There are probably very few university presidents who have not commissioned an economic impact study to demonstrate the importance of their institution to the overall well-being of the community.

Efforts to understand the role that universities play in local and regional economic development typically focus on a common set of activities that universities must perform in order to accomplish their mission and compete with peer institutions. We have drawn a number of our categories from an excellent study by CEOs for Cities and Michael Porter's Harvard-based Initiative for a Competitive Inner City (ICIC).[1]

### Employer

Colleges and universities often provide significant employment opportunities for a wide swath of the community. While much of the faculty in most institutions is originally hired from outside the region, many employment opportunities are available to local individuals. Moreover, these opportunities tend to range across skill levels. While higher education institutions have tended to follow business practices such as outsourcing and relying on contracted services for many jobs, these services tend to be performed by people in the immediate area. Still, compared with many businesses, colleges and universities provide a substantial number of blue-collar positions in facilities, food services, and security services.

In addition, as a core industry within the knowledge economy, higher education has been on a much higher job growth trajectory than many of the companies in the cities and towns where colleges and universities are located. As universities grow to service an increasing number of students or expand research activities as a means of attracting external support, job opportunities for the well-educated have become plentiful. Besides faculty, high-level technical and scientific skills are often needed in support positions for research programs and administrative areas such as finance. Universities that also include large medical centers provide an even greater range of employment opportunities in medicine and the ancillary health care fields.

Although higher education salaries may be not fully competitive with certain private-sector industries, colleges and universities remain an attractive employer. Salaries, especially for the most successful faculty and highly skilled support staff, are reasonable. Benefits for the full-time staff are normally competitive with private-sector companies. And job security tends to be much higher. In public universities, layoffs are relatively rare, and although private universities are not constrained by the bureaucratic intricacies of state human resource policies, financially solvent universities tend to value long-term loyalty among employees. The bottom line is that in many cities and towns, colleges and universities have experienced significant employment growth and are well thought of as employers by local residents.

## Purchaser

Colleges and universities are extraordinarily important customers for those companies that service other businesses or that have substantial governmental contracting. The day-to-day needs of running large universities require enormous amounts of food, books, paper, computer hardware and software, lab equipment, telephones, and services associated with the upkeep and repair of these purchases. Again, universities with hospitals must buy the entire range of supplies to keep a medical center running. Beyond this, the capital improvements of universities are major sources of revenue for architects, interior designers, steel and fabrication companies, and general contracting businesses. Universities, especially public universities, are bound by a set of tightly drawn procurement rules and often buy goods in the national and global marketplace. But there is still an enormous amount of necessary goods and services to purchase locally. Local companies and entrepreneurs work extraordinarily hard at positioning themselves to obtain university contracts.

## Developer

Universities with substantial student populations and significant research operations have invariably undertaken substantial facility growth in recent decades. The expectations of students regarding meal and housing options, recreational facilities, and leisure opportunities have been driven upward by an environment in which institutions compete for them as businesses do customers. In addition, the costs of performing competitive research, especially that which is federally funded, have skyrocketed—both in terms of the start-up packages that faculty want and the scientific facilities that each university constructs in order to attract and retain top-flight scientists. Facility development has become a critical element in the portfolio of successful college presidents. Increasingly, private-sector players are interested in partnering with the university in these and related activities. Developers want to build dorms, knowing that the university students can fill the rooms; they want to construct research parks associated with the university; and they want to build retail and service operations that can address the needs of the university community.

## Incubator and Innovator

In a knowledge economy, the talent at colleges and universities tends to be a factor driving economic innovation. Specific discoveries result in the expansion of university technology transfer offices or the creation of spin-off companies focused on commercializing creativity and invention. Colleges and universities can be relatively adept at bringing people together across traditional boundaries and in ostensibly eccentric arrangements to collaborate on projects that create new lines of work, inquiry, and products. It is far easier to bring biomedical engineers and artists together or to link chemists with rehabilitation therapists in a university than in many private-sector organizations.

Colleges and universities also can be essential in enhancing a culture of creativity that provides definition and identity to a region across a variety of realms that have an economic impact.[2] University influence can range from incubating research parks that focus on a promising set of new technologies, to recruiting art-school faculty who infuse the local culture with vitality and cutting-edge performances, to providing the creative environment and customer base for contemporary music. The capacity of universities to nurture and foster creativity and export this to the entire community is a highly valued attribute with direct economic impact in the contemporary world.

### Developing a Strategic Presence

Almost all the activities noted previously take place within the normal operation of the university. It certainly makes sense for college and university presidents to have a detailed understanding of the impact of their institutions when they talk to community leaders, political officials, and potential funders. But higher education leaders can make an even more valuable contribution once they come to realize that they have flexibility and control over how these activities are initiated, implemented, and coordinated. It is one thing to understand how many local businesses provide services to the university. It is something else to think about how the university's role as purchaser of services can work to enhance the opportunities for small and women- and minority-owned businesses in a community. It is one thing to understand how the building and rehabilitation of university facilities help to support a range of construction and design services provided by local companies. It is something else to recognize that the placement and design of university facilities can contribute to the overall strategic reconstruction of a retail district, a mixed-use project or an entire neighborhood. While it is worthwhile to understand how a university provides important jobs for the residents of a city, it is something different to see how a university can contribute to the enhancement of high-tech employment through a research park.

In essence, universities that actively promote an economic development agenda will not be content simply to articulate the impact of activities that almost any entity of similar size would have. Nor will higher-education leaders be content with simply promoting a single interesting economic innovation. Instead, these universities will consider developing in an intentional and comprehensive manner a plan for utilizing the tangible and informal economic resources at their disposal for their expressed commitments in the broader community. University leaders will work to position themselves within the broader community and regional discussion about providing for a prosperous future. The most effective universities will develop a presence in their communities that others will acknowledge. At the end of the day, the university will become a true partner because its aims are, in some significant ways, aligned with the broader goals defined by the citizens, the business leadership of the region, and the governmental leadership.

David Perry and Wim Wiewel's volume on *The University as Urban Developer*[3] and the report authored jointly by CEOs for Cities and ICIC[4] provide a fascinating set of studies illustrating the myriad ways that universities have taken the potential embedded in their economic role and become strategic leaders in the economic development strategies of their communities.

At St. Louis University (SLU), administrators were faced with a choice in the late 1960s and early 1970s of moving the entire campus to the suburbs or becoming fully involved in efforts to renew and revitalize the area.[5] At first, the university's involvement in an enormous and controversial urban renewal project ensnared it in the city's heated racial conflicts of the era. Over time, however, SLU officials became leaders of the three major community redevelopment organizations focused on midtown St. Louis, and also provided considerable financial backing. University plans often, though not always, proceeded in alignment with a vision for enhancement of the entire area. And while community visions could still, at times, conflict with the university's sense of its own priorities, SLU has been able to further its own growth and expansion while contributing successfully to the revitalization of its neighborhoods.

Gordon Gee arrived in Columbus, Ohio, as president of Ohio State University in 1992 and soon understood that deterioration in some of the neighborhoods surrounding the university was having a negative impact on both campus priorities and the wider community.[6] Gee believed that it was imperative for the university to refocus the priorities that it traditionally had as a land-grant university on the environment in which the campus actually resided at the end of the twentieth century. At the beginning of 1995, he founded and funded an official community development organization called Campus Partners for Community Urban Redevelopment, which involved community members and ultimately developed a comprehensive revitalization strategy for the neighborhoods surrounding the campus. Under the aegis of Campus Partners, the university worked with the community to upgrade a declining commercial district and to revitalize the housing stock in one of the most distressed neighborhoods bordering the campus. A land-grant university had now assumed a principal role in the planning process for Columbus.

Administrators who use their clout in the ways described here essentially have to redefine their own roles. We are familiar with the idea that the modern presidency in higher education has both internal and external roles. Indeed, much attention has been given to the growing external role of the contemporary president and, in particular, how this relates to the need for raising funds. Our suggestion is that there is an important external role that may ultimately be of tremendous financial assistance to universities, but is not primarily undertaken for this end. In a knowledge economy, university administrators can have a decisive impact on their communities if they organize university resources to do so. A substantial body of literature has emphasized the importance of "regions" and "clusters" in the establishment of successful economic development strategies.[7] Universities are well-positioned to be regional drivers in this new economy, though we have often been reluctant to assume this role. College presidents can become leaders of local chambers of commerce; universities can develop research parks that can link academic research to entrepreneurship.

## BUILDING SOCIAL CAPITAL

University initiatives focused on developing social capital in their communities have undergone a similar evolution from a series of ad hoc efforts primarily undertaken by individual staff and faculty members to a relatively sophisticated set of strategies undertaken within a larger rubric of institutional social responsibility.[8] Historically, members of the university—faculty, staff, and students—have often been very active in their communities and key participants in the leadership of social movements. Whether we are speaking of the civil rights movement in the American South; the antiwar movement of the 1960s; or the efforts to organize poorly paid, predominantly minority workers, there has been an extended tradition of university-based commitment to social justice causes. For this reason, it is not surprising that community-based organizations regularly approach local colleges and universities for assistance in addressing their needs, often seeking individual faculty members who have demonstrated a special commitment, either professional or voluntary, to the subject matter on which they focus.

Moreover, particular institutions within higher education have been charged with enhancing social capital as an integral part of their reason for existence. The formation of land-grant institutions in the nineteenth and twentieth centuries is the most recognizable manifestation of this.

Federal and state governments made a deliberate effort to create a system of colleges and universities that would focus on meeting the needs of an expanding citizenry, especially responding to the challenges that existed in frontier lands regions and in recently settled areas.[9] The invention of a remarkable range of "extension activities," where universities provided expertise to individuals, groups, and entire communities, remains a signature achievement of the American system of higher education.[10]

Similarly, the more recent establishment of universities with distinctive urban missions has often been described as bringing the concept of the land-grant college to the more densely populated regions of the country.[11] In the 1960s and 1970s, state legislatures across the country established or enlarged urban campuses to meet the growing needs of metropolitan higher education. The goals were to provide opportunities to individuals who might not have been able to seek higher education elsewhere; to respond to the educational needs of individuals who needed evening opportunities that they could combine with work; and to seek collaborative ways that urban areas could improve K–12 education, revitalize economies, and restore blighted neighborhoods.

Much of the community college system also serves similar purposes. On the one hand, these institutions provide the background that enables many students to seek a four-year degree who might otherwise have been prevented from doing so by reason of geography, income, high school record, or lack of information about the options available to them.[12] At the same time, these institutions are important actors in both economic development and the formation of social capital. They have been an instrument in the workforce development and business recruitment strategies of regions and states. In addition, localities have often recognized that community colleges can be an unparalleled provider of skills for populations that have had limited educational opportunities.

The particular strategies that have been utilized to develop social capital are the following:

## Convening and Facilitating

One of the major challenges that typically face members of underserved communities is finding venues and the appropriate instruments for articulating their concerns and having their voices included in the arenas where decisions are made. Colleges and universities have the capability of providing the venues where concerns are expressed and taken seriously as policy matters. Through academic conferences that focus on the issues that matter most to poor people, through the formation of advisory groups that include their participation, through service learning projects in which university students enable young people to voice their concerns in the expressive modes with which they are most familiar, universities can help to enable and publicize the issues that are often unheard by large segments of the broader community.

## Analysis

Colleges and universities have traditionally provided their communities with expertise targeted at providing clear information and impartial analysis relating to their concerns. University survey labs and policy centers provide policy makers with scientific evidence about the issues that communities find most important, about their policy priorities, and about their opinions on how to address those priorities. Scholars provide analyses of outcome data, ranging from student achievement issues to job placement programs to efforts to reduce the level of youth violence or teen pregnancy. They provide policy makers with extended studies about the demographics of particular neighborhoods, mobility patterns, and the match or mismatch between community needs and transportation availability. In many instances, university scholars also work directly with neighborhood and community groups, assisting them with analyses of economic development possibilities or crime prevention programs.

## Institutional Agents

University efforts to build social capital in the community have typically proceeded from providing expertise and analysis on a case-by-case basis to the establishment of institutional bodies that are related to community engagement. Higher-education institutions have developed a set of departmentally based and interdisciplinary centers that are focused around a particularly salient issue in the community, such as school improvement, the teaching of math and science, school readiness, youth violence, teen pregnancy, substance abuse, and family economics. A more recent trend is to establish an institution-wide office or center that is the principal coordinator and point of contact for a large range of university-community relations. In this vein, colleges and universities establish centers for community engagement that help put together service learning programs for units across an entire university; they may establish community relations liaison boards that maintain a dialogue between the institution and the relevant community groups; and they may establish an official administrative unit inside the university that serves as an initial point of contact for the outside community and works to coordinate strategically the individual community-oriented efforts of units inside the university.

**Intercultural Communication**

University efforts to promote the development of social capital often place higher education institutions in a relatively unique and fascinating role as an intermediary between grassroots, neighborhood-based cultural institutions, such as community action agencies and faith-based groups, and a community's business and cultural institutions where the membership is drawn primarily from the elite.

From the perspective of community-based groups, faculty and professional staff at colleges and universities can serve as advocates for a variety of their needs in the broader community. The university is itself a source of multiple resources, ranging from facilities to hold meetings to financial support for joint initiatives. In addition, higher education can provide an entire set of urgently needed services. Faculty can provide advice about how to obtain resources and in many settings can work jointly on grant proposals for doing so. Faculty members can provide the kind of leadership training that will enable members of community-based groups to participate more actively and successfully in advocating for their own needs before governmental agencies and philanthropic organizations. Members of higher education institutions often have an understanding of larger social dynamics that can assist community-based groups in obtaining a hearing.

From the perspective of a community's elite institutions, university-based groups and individual faculty members can assist citizens and leaders in understanding the changing dynamics of their community and what they should be doing in response. Research centers at colleges and universities describe the changing composition of a community and use geographic systems analysis to plot geographical trends and to provide coherent and usable data about school achievement, crime patterns, public transportation gaps, and housing needs. Higher education institutions have outreach organizations that may address issues of cultural competence, explaining to human resource managers the cultural and religious backgrounds of potential employees and providing translation skills for institutions, such as hospitals and courts, that may be dealing with new populations. And they may work closely with the community relations departments of corporate organizations, advising them about major community needs and evaluating the effects of their efforts to respond to these needs.

**Innovation and Incubation**

Community-based problem solving takes place today in a national context. A growing body of scholarship within the academy addresses the kind of challenges that minority and underserved populations often confront at a local level. This is particularly true of fields such as urban planning, education, social work, community ecology, and sociology. In conjunction with this emphasis, the major national foundations in the United States have become intensively focused on the response to social problems in local communities, especially those in urban areas. This focus has resulted in the distribution of extensive sums to communities across the country.

The impact of that funding is analyzed in sophisticated and highly technical ways. Foundations typically have a very clear mission driving what will and what will not be funded. They have professional staff who interact extensively with prominent scholars in their fields of activity, using the best thinking to inform their approach and to understand their successes and failures. In multisite programs, national foundations regularly convene participants at the ground level and have them meet with academic researchers to discuss lessons learned, consider new strategies and generate best practices. They work diligently to examine interventions that can be "brought to scale" and be relevant in multiple locales. In addition, the federal government, through organizations such as the National Science Foundation and the National Institutes of Health (NIH), has started to fund projects that provide more than basic scientific understanding about communities, projects that explicitly link theory and practice.[13]

One of the more fundable sets of projects in the last decade has examined how to build community capacity and address enduring social and economic challenges in creative and innovative ways, especially when these projects can have a broader application. This has provided a way that university researchers interested in the development of social capital can have opportunities that resemble the incubation initiatives that take place with respect to the establishment of cluster industries or new technologies.[14] University-based schools and university initiatives in the schools can, for example, target some of the most pressing issues in urban education. They may be involved in new ways of engaging young people in defining and responding to the challenges they face in building a productive future in difficult circumstances. They may work to inspire cooperation and participation in public safety efforts in communities that are driven by crime but also permeated by a historical distrust of police and local government. In all these ways, the effort to develop social capital goes beyond particular assistance to enabling communities to reinvent themselves around a future of their own conception and choosing.

## MEETING HEALTH CARE NEEDS

For many Americans, obtaining and retaining affordable and high-quality health care is one of the most important quality-of-life issues that they confront. It is an issue that has affected individuals across the spectrum of American life. With a changing economy, many American workers have found it more difficult to find employers willing to shoulder much of the cost of obtaining health insurance. For individuals in a number of under-served communities—both rural and urban—obtaining access to providers who can offer routine treatments and guidance on health promotion behaviors may be a very difficult task for a variety of reasons ranging from the supply of providers to lack of information and knowledge about how to access the system.[15] Even affluent Americans who have medical coverage may struggle when they try to discover the best way to care for aging parents and relatives with debilitating conditions.

Although the discussion of higher education has an unfortunate tendency to cordon off medical education and medical centers as separate entities, more than one hundred universities are involved in these activities. For university presidents, the financial health of their medical centers, the research productivity and clinical successes of the faculty, and the role of the enterprise in health promotion and policy formation are critically important and not incidental questions. Moreover, as we think about the entire issue of community engagement, the role of academic medical centers is central to any university that possesses one. These are typically very large units that have an enormous impact on a community and a vital cultural role.

### Economic Impact

To some extent, the impact of university-based medical centers is described in terms similar to those employed to assess the contribution of the overall university. In the last decade, most major medical centers—university- and nonuniversity-based—have contracted for an economic impact study and in a number of instances have employed the same consultant. Many of the categories utilized in the reports are the same used to assess the impact of universities in general. The published reports describe the number of employees and average wages of medical centers; compare employment trends to the trajectory in the wider community and in the larger university; evaluate the medical center's role as purchaser of goods; estimate the impact of spending by staff and students; total the number of patient visits; and estimate the dollar impact on the community of visits to patients from relatives and friends from outside the immediate area. Considerable attention is given to the economic impact of facility development and the role that medical centers play in the real estate market.

Invariably, these reports demonstrate a broad and wide-ranging economic impact by university health care centers. In fact, the employment data contained in these reports, which indicate that university medical centers have as many or more employees than the major corporate employers of a region, are nearly always a surprise to everyone, including individuals who pride themselves on their detailed knowledge of their communities. The Ohio State University Medical Center (OSUMC), for example, would rank as the fifth-largest employer in the Columbus, Ohio, metropolitan statistical area (MSA) if it were a separate corporate entity.[16] Two of the four larger employers are the state of Ohio and the U.S. government.[17] Only two private-sector companies in the entire region have more workers—J. P. Morgan Chase and Nationwide Insurance; the difference between the number of employees at Nationwide and at OSUMC is fewer than five hundred.[18] During the last six years, however, OSUMC had the largest amount of employment growth in absolute numbers than any other employer in the region.[19]

### Health Care Provision

University medical centers are integral and often unique providers of medical care in the broader community. On one hand, the powerful research base of these institutions has a direct and positive influence on their clinical capabilities. University medical centers attract researchers and scientist-clinicians who not only are at the cutting edge of their fields, but who are also committed to translating this knowledge into state-of-the-art patient care. There is widespread recognition that for certain diseases, including highly prevalent ones such as cancer, the outcomes associated with treatment at an NIH-recognized cancer center are likely to be more positive than at smaller hospitals unaffiliated with a university center. Some institutions emphasize particular specialties. Not only can local residents go there for treatment, but, because of a national and international reputation as destination medical centers, relatively affluent individuals who are knowledgeable consumers of medical care can also go there for assistance. Team-oriented collaborations that mark the treatment of complex medical conditions within university medical centers often provide unparalleled opportunities for considering and assessing treatment plans from multiple perspectives.

At the same time, many university-based medical centers provide a high percentage of their region's care to the uninsured, the underinsured, and those who do not receive regular medical care. Outreach to rural populations with minimal access to health care personnel and facilities is part of the mission of medical centers associated with the traditional land-grant institutions. It tends to be an even larger part of the portfolio of the urban-based university medical centers, which may provide an absolute majority of the area's care for the uninsured and underinsured.[20]

As a part of its core mission, the VCU Health System has served as the predominant provider of care to the uninsured and underinsured in the Commonwealth of Virginia throughout its history. Our role is to ensure that there is timely access for the medically indigent to quality medical services that include emergency, primary, and specialty care. Our health system dedicates nearly 49 cents of every dollar spent to meeting the needs of the uninsured and underinsured and provides care to roughly one-third of the state's medically indigent. In 2000, the health system launched the Virginia Coordinated Care (VCC) for the Uninsured program to enhance coordination of health care services for vulnerable populations. The goal of the VCC program is to demonstrate the positive impact of establishing a medical home for the uninsured on the cost and utilization of health care services at an academic medical center. Eight years after implementation, the program provides services to over 20,000 patients annually. In addition, the VCC program has provided the VCU Health System with an opportunity to develop relationships with community physicians and safety net providers who are also committed to providing care to the uninsured in the greater Richmond and tri-cities communities. University-based medical centers occupy a distinctive role in the overall health care system. They are committed to providing the most advanced treatments for the most complex diseases, and, at the same time, they are probably the most familiar with the entire set of issues that may compromise the medical conditions and long-term health outcomes of the individuals and groups that have the least access to or are the least comfortable with the health care system as it is currently organized.[21]

## Health Promotion

In addition to direct provision of care, university medical centers help formulate and implement efforts at health promotion among the general population and in selected at-risk groups. National Cancer Institute (NCI)-designated cancer centers are required, for example, to establish significant outreach efforts to assist high-risk communities in engaging in prevention activities and taking the necessary steps that might enable them to avoid some of the cancers with which they have been historically afflicted. The Centers for Disease Control and Prevention (CDC) funds university-community collaborative centers where researchers work with local organizations to achieve better health outcomes. Schools of public health at many universities are committed to applying knowledge for health promotion, but also work to address the underlying health disparities that generate differential outcomes. Steve Woolf, a family medicine scholar at VCU, has contended that making progress on addressing health disparities would actually have a greater impact on health outcomes than many of the major technological advances that have been made.[22] Over time, there has been increased emphasis on the translation of scientific knowledge to a broader public in a manner that can impact health outcomes.

The interest in translating medical knowledge into usable practices for health promotion resonates powerfully in many developing nations. It has been our experience that government officials from developing countries who attend international conferences on university engagement are keenly interested in its implications for the long-term health of their public. Countries in Africa that are faced with a plague-like HIV-AIDS crisis, for example, have an immediate need to discover the best means of enabling its men and women to alter behavior, which will help them avoid contracting the disease. They are looking for the kind of partnerships they can develop with university medical centers not only for treatment of the disease, but also for meeting the long-term policy challenge that it represents for the nation's officials.

Overall, we see the same trend in the efforts of university medical centers to meet the health needs of local populations that we observed in their initiatives on economic development and social capital. University medical centers have taken a responsibility that they have long embraced—meeting the health needs of underserved populations—and have attempted to develop methods for meeting this obligation in a more proactive and strategic way. Today, university medical centers are not content with simply providing care to those who might come through the doors of the emergency room because they have no other place to go. Instead, they are devising better ways of providing access to primary care in the community, either through partnerships with existing providers or outreach efforts in which practitioners from the medical center are located in underserved communities. In addition, university medical centers are far more engaged in the health promotion aspects of medical care than previously, utilizing schools of public health as an institutional mechanism for engaging with populations in a manner that can enable them to make more informed choices that will influence their own health outcomes.

University medical centers also have undertaken a greater role in the advocacy and formation of health policy. Part of this is related, of course, to financing questions, reimbursement issues, and matters regarding the education of physicians, nurses, and other providers that impact the long-term interests of the institutions themselves. But a significant part of policy advocacy, in both this country and abroad, is directly related to matters that impact general issues such as access to care and the affordability of care. Moreover, medical centers may be key strategists in developing regional and national approaches to coping with disease and other conditions that are especially problematic in specific locales. As key actors in the fight against cancer and in almost every other major research area, in the development of strategies for health promotion, and in the provision of medical care to underserved communities, university medical centers also have an important contribution to make to debate about and formulation of relevant policy issues.

## UNIVERSITIES AS POLICY ACTORS

### Becoming a Player

This chapter has described the extent to which colleges and universities have become involved in crucial social, economic, and health issues in their localities and states and in the nation. It also has described the principal techniques that have been employed to do this. Taken individually, these efforts are impressive and have often, albeit not always, made a significant impact. While every college and university has not become involved in this arena at the same level of commitment and sophistication, it is clear that institutions of higher education have become more strategic, more proactive, and more comprehensive in their approach to community and economic development issues.

Taken together, we believe that the impact of these activities amounts to something more than just the sum of the parts. When we consider the full impact of the range of activities that institutions of higher education are involved with in terms of economic development, social capital formation, and health care, a more general conclusion is warranted. In essence, colleges and universities are becoming indispensable actors in the policy arena. If the influence of higher education were removed from regional efforts to create an attractive business climate, from a state's commitment to indigent care and health promotion among underserved populations, or from a locality's effort to promote a sense of community and cross-cultural communication, it is almost inconceivable that the remaining strategies and actors would be as creative and effective.

Policy making is centrally concerned with the mobilization of resources around particular areas of concern. The term points to the importance of accumulating and targeting a set of assets that can respond successfully to a specific challenge. These assets can be people or groups; institutions and organizations; financial or in-kind support; and "soft assets" such as communication skills, cultural competence, and media influence. Successful policy makers must be able, at a minimum, to identify the range of assets available in a community, to find ways of mustering these assets even when they are not all under the direct control of government, and, ultimately, to channel these assets in an effective way that can improve the quality of life in a community.

Political leaders and governmental administrators who understand the commitment that many colleges and universities have to their communities and who are able to recognize the extraordinary array of resources that universities can mobilize are likely to find themselves in a position where they are able to leverage assets that extend well beyond those they directly control. Indeed, it is becoming clear that perceptive elected officials are doing just this. Recent reports on Atlanta, Columbus, and Philadelphia, for example, note the role that university presidents at Georgia State, Ohio State, and Penn have played in heading mayoral transition teams, participating in downtown development organizations, and starting public-private partnerships.[23] The personal role of the university president is often only the initial step in recruiting the university as a full-fledged partner in a region's policy agenda. Elected officials and public administrators want to work in partnership with a university's efforts to assist underserved communities and with activities designed to strengthen educational systems.

In a knowledge economy, it is appropriate that the most capable and visionary political leaders be interested in mobilizing the resources of the very institution that is built around developing talent in all realms of human endeavor. Leaders of colleges and universities need to recognize that this is an expectation that is likely to grow and not recede in the foreseeable future. It will become very difficult for higher-education institutions to tell policy makers and community leaders that their mission of educating students and conducting research is only indirectly or secondarily involved with the challenges those leaders face. University boards will have to ensure that the leaders they select are comfortable with this role. And, inside the university, administrators will have to create the infrastructure that will enable their institution to become effective as this responsibility becomes more prominent. How should instruction be organized to make these possibilities relevant for students? How should relations with the community be coordinated and managed? And how can this commitment be sustained through the kinds of transitions that so often occur in university leadership teams?

### The Unique Role of the University

Scholars of urban politics have developed a convenient dichotomy to characterize the tensions that are typically manifested between competing visions of urban development. In their description, urban leaders normally choose between enhancing downtown and revitalizing neighborhoods.[24] The competing foci emerge from the coalitions that normally compete for power in large American cities. The emphasis on neighborhood development reflects a political orientation in which grassroots organizations;

issue-specific, community-based organizations; and neighborhood voter mobilization are necessary to obtain and retain political power. Leaders who are elected with this base often express views that are populist in style and content, rarely have deep roots or strong ties to the business community, and usually speak in terms that emphasize empowerment, social equity, and economic justice. The focus on downtown enhancement as the signature of a city's identity occurs when political power reflects the capacity of elite coalitions to utilize their resources to nominate and elect candidates. These leaders speak about the necessity of collaboration and the importance of revitalizing the business climate of the city, and they view economic growth as a necessary if not sufficient condition for enabling the prosperity of neighborhoods.

We do not believe that the goals of downtown development and neighborhood revitalization are inherently incompatible. It is difficult to think of a great city that has wonderful neighborhoods but a decrepit downtown where no one wants to live and work. Conversely, it is hard to imagine that anyone really thinks that cities can be vibrant and successful if they have an attractive downtown but are without livable neighborhoods with distinctive identities. Even in practice, we think, the purported dichotomy between downtown and neighborhoods as absolute priorities is likely to be moderated by the complexities of political power. Elections are rarely absolute in their implications, and even where one side wins office, its opponents may still exercise a measure of influence on governmental priorities. At the same time, it is often true that the contest for political power does mobilize very different constituencies around individuals who are often quite disparate in background, political orientation, and voter support.

What is fascinating about the role of colleges and universities in the policy process is that they are some of the few institutions that are actually invested in both sides of the traditional urban political divide and are not easily pigeonholed as having chosen sides in these perennial disputes. In the knowledge economy, universities are linchpins for downtown redevelopment in many urban areas, because of the role that the institutions may play as real estate developers and, often more importantly, because of how important higher education is to the supply of an educated workforce and a culturally vibrant social environment. At the same time, the commitment of colleges and universities to enhancing social capital is frequently unmatched by any other mainstream, relatively elite institution. They assist in program development and implementation for neighborhood revitalization, they provide much of the medical care for the poor and place-bound, they formulate plans for microeconomic development, and they provide advocacy and translation skills for communities unfamiliar with acting in the broader policy arena.

The capacity of colleges and universities to bridge (at least potentially) this historical line of division provides a unique platform for higher education institutions in the community. It also furnishes university leaders, especially public-spirited presidents, with an enviable opportunity to cultivate an enormously wide range of community supporters. Universities not only may assist scientifically driven economic development, promote healthy behavior, and empower citizens in distressed neighborhoods to invent a better future, but also can find ways of encouraging the entire community to envision a common and more inclusive future. In this respect, civic engagement for colleges and universities extends beyond the practical projects that they assist or develop to a more general concern for the well-being of the entire community. Universities have the capacity to be neutral facilitators of dialogue across opposition lines, framing discussion in a way that will enable common aspirations to be more important than simply re-airing old anxieties.

Let us be clear. Colleges and universities pursue their own interests and are not simply altruistic institutions. Nor is the decision by institutions of higher education to become fully committed to civic engagement an activity without considerable risk in its own right. University interests can obviously conflict with the interests of other major players in the policy arena. Scott Cummings and his colleagues, for example, argue that the University of Louisville was assigned at least partial blame for the failure of the city to land an NBA basketball team either because the university was uninterested in fostering competition for its own nationally ranked collegiate squad or because the university leadership wanted the NBA facility on its campus and not downtown.[25] University presidents who enter the roiling waters of urban politics or the highly charged partisan air in many state capitals do so at considerable peril to both their own reputation and their institution's well-being. The political arena is a complex, competitive, and combative venue that is often not kind to less skillful practitioners, no matter how well-intentioned they may be. And while academic politics are notoriously vicious, many academic leaders can find themselves unprepared to negotiate the political terrain.

But none of these potential pitfalls is sufficient to justify neglecting to utilize the full range of opportunities placed before colleges and universities. The penalties for remaining aloof and uninvolved are likely to be far more punitive for most universities than the risks associated with partnership and engagement. The expectation of citizens and leaders about the institutions of higher education in their midst has changed, and institutions that do not recognize this are likely to experience diminished support, at least from their surrounding neighborhoods and localities. Universities that refrain from an engagement ethos may put themselves at a competitive disadvantage with their peers as well. In the scientific community today, high priority is given to "translational research" of all kinds, inquiries that eventually help to move from the basic building blocks of science to technological development and clinical application. And in the applied social sciences, foundation and governmental funding is invariably tied not only to the development of new concepts and approaches, but also to the capacity to enlist community groups and underserved populations in defining and helping to address their own challenges.

## NOTES

1. Initiative for a Competitive Inner City and CEOs for Cities, *Leveraging Colleges and Universities for Urban Economic Revitalization: An Action Agenda* (Boston: Initiative for a Competitive Inner City and CEOs for Cities, 2002).

2. CEOs for Cities and Joseph Cortright, *City Vitals: A Detailed Set of Statistical Measures for Urban Leaders to Understand Their City's Performance in Four Key Areas, Talent, Innovation, Connections and Distinctiveness, in Comparison to the Fifty Largest Metropolitan Regions in the United States* (Chicago: CEOs for Cities, n.d.).

3. David C. Perry and Wim Wiewel, eds., *The Urban University as Urban Developer: Case Studies and Analysis* (Armonk, NY: M. E. Sharpe, Inc., 2005).

4. Initiative for a Competitive Inner City and CEOs for Cities, *Leveraging Colleges and Universities*.

5. Scott Cummings, Mark Rosentraub, Mary Domahidy, and Sarah Coffin, "University Involvement in Downtown Revitalization: Managing Political and Financial Risks," in Perry and Wiewel, *The Urban University*, 147–74.

6. David Dixon and Peter J. Roche, "Campus Partners and the Ohio State University—a Case Study in Enlightened Self-Interest," in Perry and Wiewel, *The Urban University*, 268–84.

7. Michael E. Porter, "Location, Clusters, and Company Strategy," in *Oxford Handbook of Economic Geography*, ed. Gordon L. Clark, Meric S. Gertler, and Maryann P. Feldman (Oxford: Oxford University Press, 2000). Michael E. Porter, "Location, Competition, and Economic Development: Local Clusters in a Global Economy," *Economic Development Quarterly* 14, no. 1 (2000): 15–34. Christian H. M. Ketels and Olga Memedovic, "From Clusters to Cluster-Based Economic Development," *International Journal of Technological Learning, Innovation and Development* 1, no. 3 (2008): 375–92.

8. Stephen L. Percy, Nancy L. Zimpher, and Mary J., Brukardt, eds., *Creating a New Kind of University: Institutionalizing Community-University Engagement* (Boston: Anker, 2006).

9. U.S. Department of State, "Backgrounder on the Morrill Act," USINFO. STATE.GOV, http://usinfo.state.gov/usa/infousa/facts/democrac/27.htm (accessed April 30, 2007). Association of Public and Land-Grant Universities, "What Is a Land-Grant College?" The Land-Grant Tradition: NASULGC, http://www.nasulgc.org/publications/Land_Grant/land.htm (accessed September 8, 2006).

10. Cooperative State Research, Education, and Extension Service, "CSREES overview. About Us," United States Department of Agriculture, http://www.csrees.usda.gov/about/background.html (accessed January 29, 2008).

11. Percy et al., *Creating a New Kind of University*, 126–27.

12. American Association of Community Colleges, "CC STATS home," AACC, http://www2.aacc.nche.edu/research/index.htm (accessed February 18, 2008).

13. Percy et al., *Creating a New Kind of University*, 164–66, 192.

14. Initiative for a Competitive Inner City and CEOs for Cities, *Leveraging Colleges and Universities*, 26–28.

15. Percy et al., *Creating a New Kind of University*, 192.

16. Bill LaFayette, "Impact of OSU Medical Center's Growth on the Columbus Region," Columbus Chamber, http://medicalcenter.osu.edu/pdfs/osu%20medical%20center%20impact%20(2).pdf (accessed May 18, 2009).

17. LaFayette, "Impact of OSU Medical Center's Growth," 2.

18. LaFayette, "Impact of OSU Medical Center's Growth," 2.

19. LaFayette, "Impact of OSU Medical Center's Growth," 1.

20. Laurence D. Hill and James L. Madara. "Role of the Urban Academic Medical Center in U.S. Health Care," *Journal of the American Medical Association* 294, no. 17 (2005): 2219–20.

21. Hill and Madara, "Role of the Urban Academic Medical Center," 2219.

22. Steven H. Woolf and Robert E. Johnson, "The Health Impact of Resolving Racial Disparities: An Analysis of U.S. Mortality Data," *American Journal of Public Health* 98, suppl. 1 (2008): S26–S28.

23. Lawrence R. Kelley and Carl V. Patton, "The University as an Engine for Downtown Renewal in Atlanta," in Perry and Wiewel, *The Urban University*, 131–46. Dixon and Roche, *Campus Partners*, 281. Elizabeth Strom, "The Political Strategies Behind University-Based Development: Two Philadelphia Cases," in Perry and Wiewel, *The Urban University*, 116–30.

24. Perry and Wiewel, *The Urban University*.

25. Cummings et al., "University Involvement," 161–62.

# Chapter 3

# U.S. Higher Education: The Emergence of Urban Universities

Leaders of urban universities have often described the mission of their institutions as analogous to the role performed by land-grant universities in the nineteenth and twentieth centuries. The tendency of urban-based universities to become engaged with some of the most pressing challenges of our time has a precedent in the formation of the land-grant schools that applied the core competencies of the academy to the issues confronting the country as it engaged in its full expansion and settlement. Today, urban universities assist metropolitan police forces with public safety issues. They sometimes run model schools at the elementary, middle, and secondary levels that incubate new approaches to achieving success in urban settings. And they partner as real estate developers with the private sector to revitalize distressed neighborhoods. As a result of the changes that have occurred over time in Columbus, Ohio, The Ohio State University avers that it must apply its obligations as a land-grant school to addressing the challenges of its urban environment.

The route by which urban universities have become engaged in their communities has differed considerably from institution to institution. Some universities were established with the express mission of serving the educational needs of the region's citizens and have been explicitly charged with helping to build social capital and promote economic development. Yet many universities came to the mission of civic engagement by a far different path. For example, in the 1960s and 1970s, many universities in American cities began to worry that the ramifications of emerging urban problems—declining neighborhoods, increases in crime, unsuccessful school systems—were impacting their ability to compete effectively in the higher education marketplace for students and faculty.

They recognized that efforts to wall themselves off as ivory tower institutions were ultimately self-defeating and that engagement was the only way they could stop the encroachment of urban social problems into their institutions. Social responsibility was not simply an altruistic commitment, but a matter of survival.

One of the more unique features of the civic engagement practices created by American universities has been the prominence that privately run institutions have assumed in this development. Any list of universities that have contributed the most to their communities inevitably includes as many private universities as public ones in the top echelon. Yale, the University of Pennsylvania, the University of Southern California, and Marquette have all been routinely cited for the contributions that they have made to their own cities. The discipline imposed by a competitive marketplace has clearly taught private universities that their own appeal is at least partially dependent on building an attractive environment in their own neighborhoods. In addition, private universities have often possessed the resources and the regulatory flexibility that have enabled them to respond quickly and innovatively to the challenges of their environment.

This chapter examines three very different universities—the University of Pennsylvania, the University of Southern California, and Virginia Commonwealth University—that have pursued different paths to a similar end, a practical and comprehensive approach to engagement with their community. Penn is often viewed as the quintessential model of urban engagement, and rightfully so. Its current practices have emerged from a multidecade process of trial and error that originated in a concern that the problems of West Philadelphia were threatening to make Penn a far less competitive university. Today, Penn sees this commitment as a manifestation of the philosophy of its founder, Benjamin Franklin. The University of Southern California utilized its commitment to Los Angeles as a way of enhancing its own reputation as a cutting-edge university, enhancing the quality of its student body, and taking advantage of its location as a cultural capital. Virginia Commonwealth University utilized its commitment to the city of Richmond and economic development in the region as a means of imparting a clear identity to a university that was known more for its potential than its accomplishments.

## A PRACTICAL VISION: THE UNIVERSITY OF PENNSYLVANIA

Tracing its origins to the 1740s, the University of Pennsylvania was founded on a visionary premise. At the time of its inception, the four other schools in existence in the English colonies were Harvard, William and Mary, Princeton, and Yale.[1] Each of these schools was primarily designed for the education of the clergy. Breaking from colonial tradition, Benjamin Franklin endorsed a broader concept of higher education. Franklin wanted Penn not only to teach the "ornamental" disciplines such as the classics, but also to offer instruction in the sciences and training in the practical skills necessary for citizens to make a living.[2] His proposed program of study became the nation's first liberal arts curriculum.[3]

At critical points in the institution's history, Franklin's inventiveness and practicality have helped Penn face its major challenges and move the institution forward. In the late nineteenth century, Penn reinvented itself as a modern research university, based on the German model of higher education that had swept across Europe.[4] After World War II, a massive infusion of federal research dollars further enabled Penn's ascent among modern universities.[5] By almost any measure of quality, Penn has clearly attained national prominence as one of the country's most highly respected institutions. It regularly ranks as one of the top six or seven undergraduate institutions in the annual *U.S. News & World Report* rankings. The Wharton School ranks at or near the top of any international ranking of business schools. And any number of Penn's departments are rated among the top ten or twenty graduate programs in both peer and reputational rankings.

Yet Penn also has faced considerable challenges in the last fifty years, many of these related to the school's urban environment. As a thriving university in a major urban center, Penn has faced the challenge of expanding its facilities and programs. Penn has a single campus situated on 269 acres in the University City neighborhood of West Philadelphia.[6] All of Penn's twelve schools, including the medical center and law school, are within walking distance of one another. Penn's leaders have often referred to its geographical unity as "one university" as a key feature of its interdisciplinary approach to education, scholarship, and research.[7] But geographical unity has not always been accompanied by community support. At various times, Penn's approach to campus expansion has earned it a reputation of being "in but not of the community."[8] During a growth spurt after World War II, Penn was accused of going on "colossal building binges, ripping up whole neighborhoods like some crazed Eastern European dictator, [and] displacing residents and business for its own high minded imperial aims."[9]

At the same time, Penn has consistently worried that declining conditions in the surrounding neighborhood would have a negative impact on the university's future and its ability to attract the very best students. As early as 1920, a group of alumni urged the university to flee the economically struggling West Philadelphia area for greener, safer pastures such as Valley Forge.[10] In the ensuing decades, conditions in the neighboring environment became even less attractive. Commercial development declined, buildings became abandoned and turned into sites for criminal activities, and middle-class residents exited the area. Penn developed a large group of commuting students who used a trolley system to live in a more appealing environment while obtaining an Ivy League education.

Beginning in the 1950s, Penn began a multidecade effort to reverse the situation, grounded in the premise that the university needed to find a better way of integrating its needs with those of the surrounding community. In 1956, Martin Meyerson, then professor of urban planning (and later university president from 1970 to 1981), proposed a "vigorous program of planning, redevelopment and rehabilitation" in West Philadelphia in which Penn would provide leadership and funding for "an area wide organization specifically devoted to neighborhood improvement."[11] This resulted in the formation of the West Philadelphia Corporation (now the West Philadelphia Partnership), which included Penn, Drexel, the Philadelphia College of Pharmacy and Science, Presbyterian Hospital, and the Philadelphia College of Osteopathy. Soon after its establishment, the corporation concluded that a central research center was needed to complement West Philadelphia's academic and medical institutions.[12] In 1963, the University City Science Center was established to "create good jobs and lure high tech businesses to the area."[13] In relatively short order, the Science Center achieved what its founders had intended. In fact, more than forty years later, the Science Center continues to play an important role in the neighborhood's economic revitalization.

Despite its original mission to combat community deterioration, the origins of the Science Center were not without controversy or destruction.[14] More than six hundred residents of the neighborhood were displaced and scores of buildings were torn down.[15] While the West Philadelphia Corporation assisted many of the uprooted residents in finding new homes, the damage to neighborhood relations was already done. Conspicuously absent from the list of corporation members were any neighborhood, civic, or community groups. This was a key and especially egregious omission. Ira Harkavy is today an associate vice president at Penn and the founding director of its nationally recognized Netter Center for Community Partnerships (formerly, the Center for Community Partnerships).[16] In the 1960s, however, he was a student protester allying with community groups attempting to block Penn's expansion. Despite the corporation's best intention, the result was directly contrary to this purpose. Penn's poor relationship with the community worsened, and the university became described as "the institution its neighbors love to hate."[17]

By the 1980s, however, Penn had begun to develop a more nuanced and effective approach to community relations that was consistent with the institution's own "enlightened self-interest."[18] In 1983, it created the West Philadelphia Partnership, the successor to the West Philadelphia Corporation with an expanded membership that included equal numbers of directors from neighborhood organizations and institutions. The same year, Penn created the Office of Community-Oriented Policy Studies to promote research-based assistance to the neighborhood. In 1985, four enterprising undergraduate students created a summer job training corps for an honors seminar class that was eventually institutionalized as the West Philadelphia Improvement Corps (WEPIC). Several years later, WEPIC's after-school program at a local elementary school became a national model for how higher education could assist community schools. In 1992, this set of initiatives culminated in Penn's creation of the Center for Community Partnerships to focus the entire university's efforts in a more proactive and coherent manner.

Under the leadership of President Judith Rodin from 1994 to 2004, Penn continued the process of expanding and institutionalizing the approach to community development that it had embraced in the 1980s. Rodin established "The Urban Agenda" as one of Penn's six official academic priorities, worked to enhance the neighborhood economy, revitalized its housing, enhanced the security of the area, and utilized Penn's expertise to promote local commercial development. By the end of the decade, any university that was considering how it could enhance its efforts to build better community relations had to look at Penn as a potential model.[19]

### Social Capital

Penn has established and institutionalized numerous efforts to promote social capital in its West Philadelphia neighborhood. The Netter Center for Community Partnerships, for example, coordinates a wide range of engagements on the part of Penn students, faculty, and staff. Three principal types of activity fall under its rubric: academically based community service, direct traditional service, and community development.[20] Each year, thousands of students, faculty, and staff participate in hundreds of volunteer and community service programs. In fiscal year 2006 alone, more than 6,500 students, faculty, and staff took part in more than three hundred programs, representing thousands of hours invested in time and talent.[21] Penn has developed a model array of service learning programs for students that provide benefits to the community while recognizing that the city provides an ideal real-life setting for professional and clinical training.

The Netter Center has been a national leader in the university-assisted community school approach to education reform. A recent annual report of the Center defines community schools as

> both a place and a set of partnerships that bring the public school together with other community resources. Schools become hubs for their neighborhood, in which an integrated focus on academics, health and social services,

youth development, community development and community engagement
leads to improved student learning, stronger families, and healthier communities.[22]

The theory undergirding the university-assisted community school approach maintains that the application of university resources can help engage and empower an entire neighborhood and simultaneously provide
universities with an unparalleled vehicle for nurturing civic development
among students and enabling faculty to conduct research with genuine
social significance. Established fifteen years ago, the Netter Center now
partners with eight university-assisted community schools in which Penn
students provided over fifty thousand hours of service. It has also become
a model for school engagement for other universities, both nationally and
internationally. The opportunities made available by the Netter Center
are a key reason that Penn was ranked first in service learning by *U.S.
News & World Report* in 2002.[23]

In recent years, Penn has highlighted the Center for Community Partnerships' work as a way of recruiting potential students and promoting a
distinctive university identity.[24] In terms of recruitment, urban universities have flourished in the last decade as many teens find the excitement,
opportunity, and diversity of these locations far more preferable than
they did a decade earlier. Amy Gutmann, Penn's current president, has
frequently linked Penn's service learning programs and its commitment
to the West Philadelphia neighborhood as an essential feature of Penn's
academic identity. According to Gutmann, a noted political theorist, civic
engagement is not merely a pragmatic instrument for responding to the
challenges of an urban environment, but also a means of embodying the
practical vision of the school's founder in its daily activities.[25]

We noted earlier that Penn's leaders recognized that perceptions of
campus and neighborhood safety were extraordinarily important to its
capacity to attract and retain the kind of faculty and students consistent
with its academic stature. Soon after arriving as president, Judith Rodin
recognized that crime and blight in some areas surrounding the campus had reached levels entirely unacceptable to the university and the
citizenry.[26] In response, Penn took the initiative in convening a group
of families, community groups, businesses, and other local institutions
to develop a multipronged approach to the problem. They made visible
improvements in the environmental design of the neighborhood, planting
trees and enhancing street lighting. They worked with the city to increase
the number and visibility of the police, and they recruited and trained
volunteer neighborhood safety ambassadors. The impact of the safety
efforts has been noticeable. Overall crime has dropped by more than 36
percent in five years, with auto thefts down 74 percent, robberies down
62 percent, and assaults down 54 percent.[27] The changes in environmen-

tal design have served as a catalyst for improving storefronts and home fronts. And there is far more walking traffic on the streets as residents and students feel much safer.

Penn has been a genuine leader in developing institutional and collaborative ways of bringing a sense of permanence to its community involvement. A key for establishing and sustaining its commitment to building social capital in the neighborhood has been the development of the University City District (UCD), a public-private partnership that Penn helped to found in 1997, along with community groups, government agencies, and partner institutions such as Drexel University.[28] Today, financial support for the UCD comes from a wide array of stakeholders, including Penn, Drexel, Amtrak, Children's Seashore House, Children's Hospital of Philadelphia, the U.S. Postal Service, the Veterans Affairs Medical Center, and the West Philadelphia Partnership. The UCD has elevated ad hoc and single-institution efforts in the neighborhood to an enduring, community-wide initiative. As Rodin's executive vice president, John Fry, noted, "Penn's role is very much that of a catalyst. Penn can't by itself make everything work."[29]

### Economic Development

Penn's initiatives to build social capital in the area have been accompanied by extensive efforts to promote the economic development of its surrounding community. In 1995, the university launched a "Buy West Philadelphia" and "Hire West Philadelphia" campaign. Between 1995 and 2006, Penn's spending on goods and services in West Philadelphia increased by more than 400 percent.[30] The university identifies and purchases products from West Philadelphia vendors and also has utilized its expertise to assist small businesses in forging partnerships with major national firms such as IKON Office Solutions, Fisher Scientific, and Staples. This effort has been a substantial boost to minority businesses in the area. In fiscal year 2006, Penn purchased more than $70 million in goods and services from neighborhood businesses, with more than $49 million going to minority vendors.[31]

Penn is now the largest private employer in the city of Philadelphia and the fourth-largest private employer in the state.[32] Under the university's Community Advisory Committee for Economic Inclusion, community participation in campus employment and employment generated by university investment has increased sharply. For instance, in 1999 Penn converted a parking lot into a $90 million University Square retail and hotel development site. The project was the largest single commercial investment in West Philadelphia history.[33] More than 150 West Philadelphia residents and 559 other Philadelphia residents worked on the project, with more than $18 million or 20 percent of the construction dollars awarded to minority- and women-owned businesses.[34] Today, West Philadelphia residents fill more than half of the permanent jobs created by the University Square merchants.[35]

The University Square project is also indicative of how Penn has emerged as a major real estate developer in the West Philadelphia area. In The Left Bank project, for example, Penn worked with a private developer and invested $55 million to transform a vacant General Electric factory into an apartment, retail, and office complex.[36] Appealing to potential renters and retailers because of its proximity to a major Amtrak station and city transportation hubs, The Left Bank provided housing opportunities to an area that had been essentially bereft of residential life. As Judith Rodin put it, "The transformation of this vacant warehouse into University City's first new large-scale rental housing in decades is truly significant. It demonstrates once again that University City is on the move. Expanding the range of quality housing choices in University City is an integral part of our broader efforts to enhance the quality of life in our community."[37]

Penn's stature as a leading research university makes it a major contributor to the intellectual capital of its neighborhood and Philadelphia more generally, and the university provides a competitive advantage for firms in the emerging life sciences economy. As a key shareholder in the University City Science Center, Penn is a major contributor to the innovation and entrepreneurialism that emerge from the incubator and that serve as a "powerful economic engine for the regional economy."[38] Penn is a key participant and contributor to the life sciences economy in Philadelphia. The region includes headquarters for eight pharmaceutical firms, employs 53,000 individuals in the life sciences and 312,000 people in industries that support the life sciences, and has the highest rate of life sciences industrial research and development funding per capita in the nation.[39]

Penn's Wharton School is internationally recognized as one of the world's premier business programs. It draws students from around the world, and its faculty consults widely for companies on a global basis. In recent decades, Penn has worked to apply the faculty and student talent of Wharton in ways that can directly benefit local and neighborhood organizations as well. For example, Wharton has created a Certificate of Professional Development geared to the needs of local organizations. The certificate program provides a menu of short, focused courses that can enhance the specific competencies that an organization needs to tackle its immediate and long-term challenges such as mergers, negotiations, building new businesses, and profiting in competitive markets.[40] It enables local companies to draw upon the national and global expertise of Penn faculty in bringing a fresh perspective to their challenges with the intent of creating a real-time solution that can be immediately tested.

Over the last forty years, Penn has fully redefined its relationship with the West Philadelphia community. And its most recent president, Amy Gutmann, has continued that process. Gutmann has explicitly connected Penn's commitment to the community to the democratic vision embodied in the views that Benjamin Franklin articulated when the university was founded.[41] In Gutmann's view, Penn's dedication to partnering with its community while enhancing its stature as a global research university is not contradictory but a perfect manifestation of Franklin's belief that the highest levels of scientific learning can be utilized for practical benefits. This is, in part, what makes Penn distinctive among the Ivies. In short, what was a practical necessity to save the university in the 1960s has become a distinctive virtue at the outset of the twenty-first century.

## A PIONEER: THE UNIVERSITY OF SOUTHERN CALIFORNIA

Throughout its more than 125-year existence, the University of Southern California (USC) has defined itself as a pioneer. Quite literally, its establishment helped settle a new geographic territory, Los Angeles, which was nothing more than a frontier town in 1870 when a group of public-spirited citizens envisioned the establishment of a university in the region.[42] Ten years later, when USC opened its doors to fifty-three students and ten teachers, L.A. still lacked paved streets, electric lights, and a reliable fire alarm system.

As a budding university in the early twentieth century, USC blazed new trails in the international arena. In 1914, a group of international students founded the Cosmopolitan Club at USC to promote friendship among students from Asia, Latin America, and Europe.[43] A decade later, USC established the first school of international relations in the United States; only six years later, USC had more than seven hundred foreign students, which represented 10 percent of the student body, ranking the university third in the country in international enrollment.[44] Today, students from more than one hundred nations seek the opportunity to study at USC.[45] For the 2006–2007 academic year, total university enrollment stood at approximately 16,500 undergraduate students and approximately 16,500 graduate and professional students, out of which an estimated 5,600 were international students.[46] In the latter half of the twentieth century, USC continued the tradition of defining itself by its commitment to cutting-edge intellectual pursuits such as the life sciences and biotechnology. In 1952, USC's Health Sciences Campus opened. In the early 1980s, USC's path-breaking Neurological, Informational and

Behavioral Sciences program (known as NIBS, and later reorganized as the Neuroscience Research Institute) began training graduate students. With the 1988 establishment of the Institute for Molecular Medicine (later renamed the Institute for Genetic Medicine), USC positioned itself as a leader in biotechnology. USC continued to build its reputation as a leader in the life sciences throughout the 1990s, receiving a $112.5 million donation in 1998 to establish the USC Alfred E. Mann Institute for Biomedical Engineering and $110 million in 1999 for its medical school, which was renamed the Keck School of Medicine of USC.[47] The opening of the Health Sciences Campus office of the USC Stevens Institute for Innovation in 2007 has positioned USC to continue to chart new intellectual territory in the life sciences over the years ahead.[48]

USC also has attempted to capitalize on its location in the home of American culture's biggest export—Hollywood films—by developing leading programs in all areas of communication studies relevant to an information age. In 1929, USC established the country's first filmmaking program.[49] Since then, it has expanded its offerings into a widely sought-after array of programs, geared to developing students proficient in all forms of cultural communication in a digital age. USC's Robert Zemeckis Center opened as the country's first and only fully digital filmmaking training facility in 2001. George Lucas's $175 million gift in 2006, the largest gift in USC's history, was earmarked for the building of new facilities at the university's film school and for an endowment to support it.[50]

The Lucas gift punctuated another major development that had occurred at USC during the last few decades—its entrance into the major leagues of academic fundraising. USC's 1961 Master Plan for Enterprise and Excellence in Education included the ambitious goal of doubling the university's endowment.[51] Then, in the 1970s, USC launched its "Toward Century II" fundraising campaign, which brought in more than $309 million in five years.[52] By 1990, the university's next effort, "The Campaign for USC," had raised $641.6 million.[53] Over the course of the 1990s, USC tripled its endowment to $1.5 billion.[54] By 2000, the seventh year of a fund-raising campaign, the university's endowment had quadrupled.[55] At the close of the "Building on Excellence" campaign in 2002, USC had set a record in higher education by conducting the most successful fundraising effort ever, raising $2.85 billion in nine years.[56] In 2004, USC reported that its strong financial base had been bolstered by "the largest fundraising campaign in the history of higher education," indicating that the university's endowment had nearly quintupled over a dozen or so years.[57] As of June 30, 2006, USC's endowment stood at $3.1 billion.[58]

Since 1991, USC's rise has been led by Steven Sample, who arrived in L.A. after bringing the State University of New York at Buffalo into the upper echelon of American research universities, as signified by its election to the Association of American Universities.[59] At USC, Sample established a vision that the university would "be widely regarded as one of the very best universities in the United States. And not only regarded as that, but, in fact, to be one of the very, very best."[60] Sample has raised student selectivity while increasing diversity, has been a prodigious fundraiser (he was the first university president to bring in five gifts of more than $100 million each), and has used the dollars from the campaigns to support new facilities and recruit world-class faculty.

USC has become one of the "hottest" schools in the nation for students who want to make films, participate in the business side of the entertainment industry, establish new forms of Internet communication, and cover these industries as journalists and broadcasters. Its entrepreneurialism program ranks first in the country, and the list of recognitions has continued to grow. USC was ranked forty-second on the *U.S. News & World Report* list of best national universities in 2000.[61] In 2001, the Kaplan/ *Newsweek* "How to Get into College" guide named USC one of America's nine "hottest schools," and the Association of American Colleges and Universities singled out USC as one of sixteen "leadership institutions."[62] Once seen as a fallback school for the wealthy, USC has shed its image as a "university of second choice" or a "university for spoiled children."[63]

### Enhancing Social Capital

Not only has USC set itself apart nationally, but it also has been a pioneer in fostering strong relations in its own backyard, paving the way for America's urban universities in the area of community outreach. In 1934, USC debuted its "University on the Air," an educational outreach program broadcast on radio.[64] In 1968, USC launched The Urban Semester, a program that sends students out of the classroom and laboratory and into the city streets and halls of power. A few years later, USC established the Joint Academic Program, one of the first service learning programs in the United States. In 1994, USC inaugurated its comprehensive Good Neighbors Campaign; it launched its Friends and Neighbors Service Day the following year.

One of USC's most successful community outreach programs is the Neighborhood Academic Initiative (NAI). Opening its doors in 1991, NAI is a six-year, comprehensive, educational outreach program that prepares low-income, minority students living in the neighborhoods surrounding USC for success in college.[65] At NAI's core is the Pre-College Enrichment Academy, which provides accelerated curriculum in math and language arts to students drawn from three local schools, each of which has up to 90 percent of its student population qualifying for the free federal school lunch program.[66] Going beyond similar types of programs at other universities,

NAI's goal for its scholars is not merely acceptance to, but rather success at and graduation from four-year universities, leading to the enrichment of individual lives, families, and communities.[67] Scholars who complete the NAI program in good standing and meet all requirements for admission to USC are eligible for a full four-and-a-half-year financial aid package to the university.[68] To date, over 33 percent of NAI scholars have attended or are currently attending USC, and other NAI scholars have been accepted to universities such as Stanford, the Massachusetts Institute of Technology, Rutgers, Boston University, the University of California at Berkeley, the University of California at Santa Cruz, and the University of California at Los Angeles.[69]

Another aspect of USC's transformation has been improving its location, both in reality and perception. In addition to several new capital projects in the area, improved safety is among the real improvements USC has helped bring about in its neighborhood. Creative efforts to enhance safety are excellent examples of how it is possible to address matters that are vital to the success of the institution and equally significant to the citizens in the surrounding locale.

In the early 1990s, USC hired a veteran L.A. police officer to work out an agreement with the city police force to allow campus officers to patrol the surrounding community.[70] USC Campus Police then expanded the size of its force to patrol an area sixteen times larger than the campus.[71] In addition, USC organized the Kid Watch Program to ensure children's safety as they walked to and from school; it has become a model for other cities. Working in partnership with the L.A. Unified School District and the L.A. Police Department, USC helps train and organize nine hundred neighborhood Kid Watch volunteers.[72] USC also launched a program to remove graffiti from the neighborhood within twenty-four hours of its appearance; the program later received funding from the city. Such efforts have contributed to a decrease in the crime rate in USC's neighborhood that is far more dramatic than in the rest of the city. In turn, improved safety has helped allay parents' concerns about sending their children to college in the inner city, contributing to an increase in the number of applicants to the university.

USC's real estate development enterprise has created community-oriented projects such as the USC Neighborhood Homeownership Program. Started in 1995, the program now offers subsidies of $50,000 or 20 percent of the purchase price (whichever is less) to USC employees who buy homes in the neighborhoods surrounding the University Park and Health Sciences campuses.[73] The home-buying initiative was established by President Sample shortly after he arrived at USC as part of his strategy to strengthen the university's ties with its communities. According to the program's administrator, Maxine McNeal, the program's main objectives are "to allow employees to purchase homes, to live near work and have a vested interest in their community."[74] USC is one of only a handful of institutions that offer such subsidies to employees (Yale University is among the others with a similar program). USC's program helped 109 university employees purchase homes from 1995 to 2006.[75] More than seventy of the local employees hired as part of USC's targeted recruitment efforts have been aided by the Neighborhood Homeownership Program.[76]

In addition to addressing neighborhood problems in a tangible, measurable way, USC has played a larger role in its surrounding community as it has, over time, enabled the neighborhood to become a genuine player in enhancing the economic and cultural identity of Los Angeles. The new California Science Center and other improvements to Exposition Park near USC's University Park Campus have enabled the university to start marketing itself as one of the bookends of a thriving arts and cultural corridor that runs down Figueroa Street to downtown, thereby transforming its long-held image as a school located in a depressed area of South Central L.A.[77] Northwestern University's new president, Morton Owen Schapiro, said, "Steve [Sample] has managed to relocate USC from the ghetto of South-Central Los Angeles to the edge of vibrant downtown L.A.—without moving an inch."[78] Having created "one of the most ambitious social-outreach programs of any university in the nation" over the latter part of the twentieth century, USC was named by *Time* and the *Princeton Review* as "2000 College of the Year."[79] The *Princeton Review* again acknowledged USC in 2005, selecting it as one of eighty-one "Colleges with a Conscience" based on the university's outstanding record of community involvement.[80] In 2006, Evan Dobelle, president of the New England Board of Higher Education, released a list of twenty-five "best neighbor" urban colleges and universities that had "dramatically strengthened the economy and quality of life" of their communities, earning them Dobelle's title of "Saviors of Our Cities."[81] Topping Dobelle's list was USC because of its community and economic development efforts, which will be discussed in more detail later in this chapter.

## Economic and Community Development

To illustrate the growing economic importance of urban universities such as USC, Sample has often cited the fact that L.A.'s largest private employer is "not a defense firm, not a movie studio, but the University of Southern California."[82] And he has been quick to note that "unlike other major private employers, USC won't be sold, merged or moved to Phoenix."[83] USC has deliberatively and extensively attempted to use its economic might to promote the growth of the university and the prosperity of the surrounding community.

USC retained Economics Research Associates (ERA) to evaluate the economic impact of the university's operations for fiscal year 2006.[84] The report assessed the overall economic impact of USC as an institution. It also examined its role as employer, workforce developer, real estate developer, attracter of financial capital, and producer of intellectual capital. And, in most of these areas, it reviewed how USC's economic impact was directly related to the well-being of the surrounding community.

In determining the overall economic impact of USC, ERA limited its calculations to all USC spending associated with university operations, along with indirect and induced economic impact, within Los Angeles County.[85] Based on the USC-related economic activities documented in the 2006 report, ERA determined that for every dollar spent by USC in Los Angeles County during fiscal year 2006, an additional 39 cents of output was created elsewhere in the regional economy.[86] Also, every dollar of earnings that workers were paid for USC-related expenditures supported an additional 36 cents of wages elsewhere in the county.[87] Every $1 million spent by USC in the region supported more than ten and a half full-time equivalent jobs.[88] Based on ERA's direct and indirect and induced economic impact calculations, it was determined that the total economic impact of USC operations in fiscal year 2006 within Los Angeles County was close to $4 billion in total output, with earnings of more than $1.4 billion that in turn supported more than 42,700 jobs.[89] USC was estimated to have accounted for 0.42 percent of the city's estimated total gross product.[90]

Approximately 31 percent ($22.2 million) of the university's fiscal year 2006 nonpayroll spending within the city occurred in the immediate neighborhoods of the Health Sciences Campus and the University Park Campus.[91] USC has worked to direct a growing proportion of its considerable purchasing power to nearby businesses through the USC Local Vendor Program (LVP).[92] Firms participating in the LVP are given an opportunity to bid on USC projects open to competitive bidding. In addition, participating businesses are included in the USC Small Business Directory, which is used by more than nine hundred senior USC business officers, staff, and faculty members, as well as two hundred off-campus organizations.

In 2000, $7 million out of a total of $248 million (3 percent) worth of goods and services was bought from vendors within a five-mile radius of both the University Park Campus in South Central L.A. and the Health Sciences Campus in East L.A.[93] USC also has targeted its purchasing power toward small, minority-, women-, and disabled veteran–owned suppliers, and it did more than $45.4 million in business with such suppliers in 2002, the last year for which data are available.[94] In addition, from 1987 to 2000, USC's Business Expansion Network helped more than six thousand businesses, 80 percent of which were minority-owned, with business planning services, resulting in the businesses' receipt of some $20 million in loans and $15 million in government contracts.[95]

USC's efforts as a property and real estate development enterprise have been transformative for the university and for the neighborhood. USC has developed facilities such as the Galen Center Arena and the Norris Research Tower, which provide a first-class venue for athletic events and a state-of-the-art research facility for faculty.[96] But the cumulative effects of USC's building program, the development of the California Science Center, and improvements to Exposition Park near the heart of the University Park Campus have been far more substantial.[97]

In recent years, the establishment of the USC Stevens Institute for Innovation (USC Stevens) is a perfect example of how the university is working to marry the production of intellectual capital with its broader economic and community development missions. The purpose of USC Stevens is to support the university's students and faculty in the translation of inventions and discoveries into practice, not only to position USC at the forefront of creative research, but also to enable USC to make a meaningful difference in the health and welfare of society.[98] USC Stevens owes its creation to entrepreneurship—that of USC and the man whose firm helped bring such innovators as YouTube and Google to the marketplace, venture capitalist Mark Stevens, who along with his wife, Mary, contributed $22 million to create the institute.[99] Evolving out of the USC Stevens Institute for Technology Commercialization in the USC Viterbi School of Engineering, the USC Stevens Institute for Innovation opened for business on March 28, 2007.[100] According to Stevens, a USC alumnus and trustee and a general partner in Sequoia Capital, "We envision USC as a powerful engine for making a better world in the 21st century. To realize this vision, we must have faculty and students who are capable of engaging in research of the highest caliber and of connecting with colleagues in industry and venture capital to address real-world problems."[101]

Representing much more than merely a name change and a new executive director, USC Stevens signified a departure from its predecessor institute, as well as from most innovation institutes at other universities. This was the first time a major research university had consolidated technology transfer (the former Office of Technology Licensing was folded into USC Stevens), educational and cocurricular programming, and innovator development in a university-wide, centralized hub based in the office of the provost.[102] Emphasizing the advantages of being centrally positioned organizationally, as opposed to being an offshoot of one or a limited number of disciplines, Stevens executive director, Krisztina Holly, noted, "We have a huge commitment from the provost to be a university-wide resource. . . . [W]e're not just working with our engineering school and with the School of Medicine, but also with a top-notch cinematic arts school and music school, and a school of communications."[103] In keeping with USC's public-minded approach to economic development, USC Stevens differentiated itself from the pack by pairing its innovation and commercialization enterprise with its community outreach mission.

USC Stevens positions the university to strengthen and leverage L.A.'s robust life sciences industry.[104] According to the Southern California Biomedical Council, the Los Angeles–Orange County metro area has a 36 percent higher concentration of biosciences employment than other metro areas in the United States. Most notably, the L.A. region is first among U.S. metropolitan areas in medical device sector employment and second in biosciences research, testing, and labs. The *Money Tree Report* by PricewaterhouseCoopers indicated that the Los Angeles–Orange County metropolitan area is tenth in the nation for biotechnology venture capital funding.[105]

In looking to the future, USC has acknowledged that conditions in the world are changing at an increasingly rapid rate, requiring the development of flexible strategies for accelerating the university's progress.[106] Therefore, in engaging in planning processes that cast its focus ten to twenty years ahead, USC has opted to identify strategic capabilities that can position it for "unknowable challenges," rather than opting to outline a detailed road map.[107] For instance, USC has identified the expansion of its research capabilities as one of the key elements of its ongoing success. In turn, USC has identified distinguishing features upon which to expand its research capabilities.

Two of the distinguishing features related to achieving its research vision are its urban location and its close ties to the community.[108] Related to the university's urban location, USC's 2030 Master Plan notes:

> USC is one of the most enduring institutions in the city of Los Angeles. While others have forsaken the city, USC has recommitted itself to Los Angeles, serving as an economic engine and stirring civic pride with the success of its sports teams, its academic accomplishments and the contributions of its alumni.[109]

Related to the university's close ties to the community, the 2030 Master Plan states, "Working closely with its neighbors in 'respectful partnership,' USC is helping create better schools, safer streets and a greener, more beautiful environment."[110]

As the twenty-first century unfolds, USC's urban location and community outreach features will become inextricably linked. As stated in the university's plan for increasing academic excellence, "The histories of USC and the region it serves are closely linked, and both evolve together. USC considers its commitment to being a great university as one of the most important contributions it can make to its region."[111]

## CREATING AN IDENTITY:
## VIRGINIA COMMONWEALTH UNIVERSITY

In 1990, Virginia was experiencing its worst recession in decades, and state support for universities had been reduced considerably.[112] At the same time, it was also clear that people at Virginia Commonwealth University (VCU) and in the broader community believed that VCU's untapped potential was substantial. Community organizations, the business community, and local and state government agencies were coming to the realization that having a strong collaboration with a research university could be extremely beneficial to the long-term interest of their organizations, the region, and the commonwealth of Virginia. Yet it was also clear that the collaborations that did exist were often ad hoc, related to the particular interests of an individual faculty member and a specific organization, agency, or business, and were not driven institutionally. As an institution, VCU did not have a large footprint or a clear identity in the minds of people in almost any segment of the Richmond community.

Over the last twenty years, VCU has worked assiduously to rectify this. It has creatively partnered with community organizations and assumed leadership positions in the region's major initiatives. In doing so, it has become an essential contributor to the future of its region.

### Building Social Capital

In the early 1990s, VCU initiated a Community Service Associates Program that enabled community organizations to tap faculty members' expertise for a semester on a part-time basis.[113] Faculty members worked with schools, nonprofit organizations, and state and local agencies on projects of mutual interest—improving child care, enhancing infant health, revitalizing neighborhoods—while the president's office reimbursed their academic departments for their time. An official request-and-approval process was developed whereby organizations would identify a specific need, the need would be matched with the expertise and interest of particular faculty members, and a project of a semester or year's length would be established. From 1990 to 2008, more than three hundred community projects were supported by the expertise of the university's faculty.[114]

VCU has worked in a number of other ways for almost two decades to promote social capital and capacity building in the larger community. While VCU and its neighbors once had an "unpeaceful" coexistence, since 1990 the university has assumed the role of facilitator—helping to bridge the divisions that existed in the community in the early 1990s by bringing together groups and organizations that did not have a good history of working cooperatively.[115] Like Penn, VCU has involved its community partners in helping to shape major university-wide initiatives, such as master site planning. VCU reaffirmed its ongoing institutional commitment to university-community partnerships by including outreach as one of the key themes in the "VCU 2020: Vision for Excellence" strategic plan that was adopted in 2006.[116] Key community partnerships include the Carver Neighborhood-VCU Partnership, VCU Community Solutions, Lobs & Lessons, FIRST Robotics, and the Community Nursing Organization.

These initiatives have encompassed a wide array of purposes. VCU has used campus police to promote school safety, faculty members have designed neighborhood housing initiatives, and the university regularly brings children from disadvantaged neighborhoods to campus to experience the possibilities of college life firsthand. And VCU has increasingly utilized the expertise of the VCU Medical Center to promote health and wellness in the broader community.

Another strategy that has been instrumental in strengthening VCU's capacity to support community development has been the personal involvement of the university president in a variety of community organizations, ranging from arts boards to regional development efforts. In the mid-1990s, the Greater Richmond Chamber of Commerce asked me, Eugene Trani, as VCU's president to serve as chair of the chamber board. From 2001 to 2004, the major organization promoting downtown revitalization, Richmond Renaissance, asked me to serve as chair. These requests were indicative of the new identity that VCU was daily creating in the Richmond area. The university was increasingly seen as an indispensable partner in all aspects of the community's future, one whose expertise, energy, and dedication were enabling the Richmond area to reach a potential that had been deferred for too long.

VCU has received national recognition from the Carnegie Foundation for the Advancement of Teaching for its initiatives within the community.[117] In 2006, VCU was selected for Carnegie's Community Engagement Classification, which recognized VCU and seventy-five other U.S. colleges and universities for promoting community engagement as a central focus of their missions. In addition, the Carnegie Foundation selected VCU as one of sixty-two institutions of higher learning nationwide that demonstrated a commitment to community engagement in the classroom and to partnerships and outreach beyond the boundaries of campus. These awards confirmed VCU's belief that it is a campus without walls that seeks to integrate itself within the community.[118]

The partnerships that VCU established during the punishing recession of the 1990s and into the twenty-first century have served the university well internally—enhancing its instructional, research, and public-service missions. They have brought resources to the university at times when the state could not possibly provide them. They have energized faculty members, students, and administrators during challenging times, and helped shape a sharpened sense of university identity, both internally and externally. VCU has worked across disciplines to develop innovative approaches to important scientific and societal issues, has translated research from basic findings to benefits for patient care and social justice, and has used its urban location as an opportunity for scholarly work and student learning.[119]

Today, VCU continues to create partnerships that enhance the university's instructional, research, and public-service missions.[120] For instance, of the more than $20 million in annual grant and contract support for VCU's College of Humanities and Sciences, almost half is for community-based research projects. With the help of a grant from the Centers for Disease Control and Prevention, VCU's Psychology Department now works with the Richmond public schools to reduce the level of youth violence in the community. In the spring of 2008, VCU's School of Education and its Department of Psychiatry in the School of Medicine developed a collaborative partnership with a local elementary school that specializes in educating children with autism. The elementary school benefits from the educational and treatment programs provided by VCU's faculty members, graduate students, and medical-school residents, who in turn receive hands-on training that would be almost impossible to obtain otherwise.

### Economic Development

VCU has recognized that, simply because of its sheer size, it has had an impact on the economic development of its community through its roles as purchaser, employer, and real estate developer.[121] These are roles VCU has taken very seriously. But what VCU also has recognized is that emerging trends linking universities ever more closely to economic development have provided an opportunity to define the university's role in ways that have gone beyond its traditional economic impact. VCU made a deliberate decision to adopt a leadership role in economic development in the region. Since the early 1990s, the university has developed strategies for linking its knowledge base to cutting-edge business development in the Richmond area, for promoting business development in a way that could physically restore and revitalize parts of downtown Richmond, and for bringing disparate elements in the community together around a shared vision.

A prime example of how VCU has consciously linked its knowledge base to the promotion of cutting-edge economic development in the region is the establishment of the School of Engineering. In 1990, the Richmond region was one of the largest metropolitan areas in the nation that did not have a school of engineering in its environs.[122] The business community was very concerned about this deficiency, and the 1991 regional strategic plan that was undertaken under the auspices of the Greater Richmond Chamber of Commerce noted that developing a school of engineering should be a priority.

Working together, we were able to develop state support for the school in a recessionary economic climate. We were able to do so because we developed a strong partnership with the business community and obtained real financial support from the local governments in the region (which did not have a strong history of cooperation); also, the planned school became a linchpin in the state government's effort to woo Motorola to locate major facilities in Richmond.[123] Ultimately, Motorola did not develop the presence in Richmond that had once seemed imminent, but a joint venture between Motorola and Siemens (later named White Oak Semiconductor and then Qimonda AG) resulted in what was a $2 billion computer memory-chip plant, before it was closed amid the current global economic recession.[124] The more than decade-long symbiotic relationship between Qimonda and VCU in the Engineering School's establishment and ongoing development—as well as in the region's economic development—served as a universal model of industry-university partnerships.[125] However, VCU's choice not to rely solely on Qimonda also serves as a model of industry-university partnerships. While the engineering program will have to undergo some reconfiguring, its other industry partnerships, such as with Micron Technology and BAE Systems, and its array of other types of partnerships and revenue streams will ensure its ongoing success amid current and future economic ferment.[126]

About the same time that VCU established its engineering program in the 1990s, it also became the major player guiding the development of the Virginia BioTechnology Research Park.[127] Forward-looking members of the business community had recognized that capitalizing on VCU's Medical Center could be instrumental in the twenty-first-century economic progress of the region. The mission of the park (a joint initiative of VCU, the City of Richmond, and the Commonwealth of Virginia) and its governing authority (a political subdivision of the commonwealth) is to create jobs and business in the biotechnology industry for Virginia and to position the state to compete in this industry.[128] The park, which is situated on thirty-four acres adjacent to the VCU Medical Center in downtown Richmond, is home to a unique mix of more than fifty biosciences companies; research institutes affiliated with the medical center; and major state and national medical laboratories and organizations involved with forensics, testing of biotoxins, and management of the nation's organ transplantation process.[129]

The park works hand in hand with VCU, other academic institutions, businesses, government, and not-for-profit organizations to facilitate technology transfer and business development.[130] Its business accelerator—the Virginia Biosciences Development Center—is the state's first incubator focused exclusively on the life sciences; it assists bioscience start-ups in the park's incubator with everything from legal and financial services to business planning.[131] From the time it opened in 1995 until 2007, the incubator helped sixty-three companies get started—nineteen from VCU or from the Richmond area, and forty-four that were attracted from outside locations.[132] In just over ten years, the park's incubator program successfully graduated thirty-one companies, three of which have been publicly traded, and helped raise more than $155 million in federal and equity funding for its tenants.[133] The 1.2-million-square-foot park contains nine buildings representing more than $525 million in capital investment, and has more than two thousand engineers, technicians, and researchers employed by almost sixty companies, VCU institutes, nonprofits, and state labs.[134]

The contribution that the Virginia BioTechnology Research Park has made to economic development actually transcends the number of people employed, the capital invested, and the square footage built out.[135] The park has become an instrument by which VCU can link its world-class health sciences with entrepreneurial innovations. It also became the principal means of bringing high-tech business with high-paying jobs to downtown Richmond. In fact, the entities in the park as a group have been the largest generator of high-tech jobs in the region in recent years. Moreover, the park has transformed the gateway to the city from Interstates 95 and 64 from a collection of gravel parking lots to an architectural expression of the economic vibrancy to which Richmond aspires.

During the last twenty years, VCU's commitment to both its own growth and the economic development of its surrounding neighborhoods has resulted in considerable investment in physical capital. Capital projects completed from 1981 to 2007 totaled more than $2 billion. VCU's current master site plan, "VCU 2020," includes approximately $1 billion more in projects.[136] In addition to a $228 million combined engineering and business facility, key projects have included a $185 million state-of-the-art critical-care hospital; a $17 million center for nursing; and a 200,000-square-foot, $160 million School of Medicine building currently under construction.[137] These types of projects not only help improve the physical environment of the city, but also provide facilities where innovation can thrive in the region, provide the necessary infrastructure for the university's growing enrollment so the area's workforce can remain vital, and foster opportunities for productive university-community partnerships. They also offer an opportunity for VCU to strategically target its resources to important businesses, including minority contractors. For instance, about 20 percent of the contracts for the critical-care hospital were awarded to minorities.[138]

In addition to investing enormous and strategically directed amounts of resources into physical improvements throughout the city, VCU has learned how to connect the physical growth of the campus to the university's interest in revitalizing its immediate neighborhood, including a predominantly African American community contiguous with VCU's campus where the university has worked with residents on their concerns about education and public safety.[139]

For decades, the West Broad Street commercial corridor near VCU's Monroe Park Campus stood as a stretch of run-down shops, shuttered windows, and empty sidewalks.[140] No one was willing to bet on a turnaround on Broad—until, that is, VCU committed more than $105 million to an expansion of the campus there. That expansion, which included a new recreation and convocation center, a fine-arts building, administrative information technology facilities, a bookstore, a parking deck, and student residences, has spurred an additional $100 million in private investment.[141] A major national grocery chain has moved to the area, and a big-box home repair store opened up, something residents had long sought.[142] Developers have rehabilitated formerly underused and abandoned buildings for a variety of residential and commercial purposes. As a result, VCU has become a more attractive environment for the growing number of students who want to study in a vibrant urban culture, and the city of Richmond is creating a more welcoming and hospitable downtown.

## CONVERGENCE ON THE COMMUNITY

USC, Penn, and VCU are very different universities, with varying missions, histories, and venues. Penn is an Ivy League school that traces its ancestry to Ben Franklin. USC's programs are uniquely shaped by its location in one of the world's most important centers of communication and entertainment. And VCU is a relative newcomer, a forty-year-old institution in the process of completing its own self-definition. Yet in recent years, all of these institutions have approached the general issue of how to relate to their neighboring communities in similar ways. Each institution has viewed its location in a central urban area as an ultimate asset. As urban-based universities have become more appealing to young people who value metropolitan energy and diversity, all of the institutions have experienced significant increases in applications. USC, Penn, and VCU have worked in similar ways to leverage their own assets to revitalize their environs—understanding how a real estate portfolio can improve local housing, revitalize neighborhoods, and serve as a spur to retail development. And each university has understood that developing social capital in its city is a necessary complement to the physical transformation that the university is abetting.

These efforts do not always proceed without tensions. Memories of a time when university-community relationships were characterized by institutional initiatives formulated without citizen consultation still linger. Moreover, consultation and dialogue will not always resolve differences where strongly held views about university expansion are in conflict. In addition, the "community" itself is often not a monolithic body. Communities have their own competing perspectives, historical tensions, and leadership struggles that make any effort to reach agreement with the community impossible. On a case-by-case basis, even a model university such as Penn can find itself in a conflict over expansion that can resemble previous disputes.

But what university leaders can do is to ensure that the case-by-case disputes are overshadowed (or at least balanced) by a broader pattern of collaboration, community development, and mutual goal setting that casts town-gown relations in a very different light. All of the universities described in this chapter have been able to accomplish this. They have developed a wide-ranging set of efforts with the community that has been successful in elevating the level of popular support for the institution. And they have made a positive impact on their neighborhoods that will endure for decades. In each of these cases, presidential leadership assumed that utilizing university talent and resources to promote community development was essential to the long-term interests of the institution and their own personal success. There is no other individual at a college or university who can mobilize the array of resources—real estate development, procurement and employment policies, allocation of faculty time, and student service learning projects—that a president can. Academic leaders cannot accomplish this alone, but they must develop a vision that sees how an entire university can contribute to the goal of community enhancement.

## NOTES

1. Steven Morgan Friedman, "A Brief History of the University of Pennsylvania," University of Pennsylvania, http://www.archives.upenn.edu/histy/genl history/brief.html (accessed May 15, 2007), 1.

2. Friedman, "A Brief History," 1, 3.

3. University of Pennsylvania, "Penn's Heritage," University of Pennsylvania, http://www.upenn.edu/about/heritage.php (accessed May 16, 2007), 4.

4. Friedman, "A Brief History," 6.

5. Center for Community Partnerships at the University of Pennsylvania, "History," University of Pennsylvania, http://www.upenn.edu/ccp/about/history.html (accessed May 15, 2007), 2.

6. University of Pennsylvania, "Penn's Heritage," 4.

7. University of Pennsylvania, "Introduction to Penn," University of Pennsylvania, http://www.upenn.edu/about/welcome.php (accessed May 11, 2007), 4.

8. Center for Community Partnerships, "History," 2.

9. Samuel Hughes, "The West Philadelphia Story," *The Pennsylvania Gazette*, 96, no. 2 (1997), http://www.upenn.edu/gazette/1197/philly.html (accessed May 15, 2007).

10. Hughes, "The West Philadelphia Story."

11. Hughes, "The West Philadelphia Story."

12. Hughes, "The West Philadelphia Story."

13. Hughes, "The West Philadelphia Story."

14. Hughes, "The West Philadelphia Story."

15. Hughes, "The West Philadelphia Story."

16. Ira Harkavy, Associate Vice President and Director, Netter Center for Community Partnerships, University of Pennsylvania, e-mail message to Eugene P. Trani, July 30, 2009.

17. Hughes, "The West Philadelphia Story." Another good description of the 1960s, which reports that, "Penn did not work as integrally with the community in the 1960s, but instead flexed its muscles to restruce itself for its own benefit with little regard for the community's benefit," is found in *Anchor Instructions Toolkit: A Guide for Neighborhood Revitalization* prepared by The Netter Center for Community Partnerships at the University of Pennsylvania (2008), p. 30.

18. Initiative for a Competitive Inner City (ICIC) and CEOs for Cities, *Leveraging Colleges and Universities for Urban Economic Revitalization: An Action Agenda* (Boston: Initiative for a Competitive Inner City and CEOs for Cities, 2002), 8.

19. Hughes, "The West Philadelphia Story," 7–8, 65. ICIC and CEOs for Cities, *Leveraging Colleges and Universities,* 3, 9, 13, 17, 28, 29. See also Lee Benson, Ira Harkavy, and John Puckett, *Dewey's Dream: Universities and Democracies in an Age of Education Reform, Civil Society, Public Schools and Democratic Citizenship* (Philadelphia: Temple University Press, 2007), and Judith Rodin, *The University and Urban Revival: Out of the Ivory Tower and into the Street* (Philadelphia: University of Pennsylvania Press, 2007).

20. University of Pennsylvania, "Penn—'05–'06 Annual Report: Tercentennial Anniversary of the Birth of Penn's Founder," University of Pennsylvania, http://www.finance.upenn.edu/comptroller/accounting/AnnualRpt/Financial_Report_06.pdf (accessed May 17, 2007), 19.

21. University of Pennsylvania, "Penn—'05–'06 Annual Report," 19.

22. 2007–2008 Annual Report, Netter Center for Community Partnerships, University of Pennsylvania, 11, Center for Community Partnerships at Penn, "Center Awards," http://www.upenn.edu/ccp/awards.html (accessed May 21, 2007), 6.

23. 2007–2008 Annual Report, Netter Center for Community Partnerships, 6.

24. University of Pennsylvania, "Penn and Philadelphia," University of Pennsylvania, http://www.upenn.edu/campus/penn_philadelphia.php (accessed May 21, 2007), 1.

25. University of Pennsylvania, "Introduction to Penn," 2.

26. University of Pennsylvania, "Penn's West Philadelphia Initiatives—Clean and Safe Streets," University of Pennsylvania, http://www.upenn.edu/campus/westphilly/streets.html (accessed May 17, 2007), 1.

27. University of Pennsylvania, "Penn's West Philadelphia Initiatives—Clean," 2.

28. University of Pennsylvania, "Penn's West Philadelphia Initiatives—Clean," 4.

29. Hughes, "The West Philadelphia Story," 18.

30. University of Pennsylvania, "Penn's West Philadelphia Initiatives—Creating New Jobs and Economic Growth," University of Pennsylvania, http://www.upenn.edu/campus/westphilly/economic.html (accessed May 17, 2007), 4.

31. University of Pennsylvania, "The Penn Compact—Engaging Locally," University of Pennsylvania, http://www.upenn.edu/compact/locally.html (accessed May 11, 2007), 19.

32. University of Pennsylvania, "Penn's West Philadelphia Initiatives—Clean," 1.

33. University of Pennsylvania, "Penn's West Philadelphia Initiatives—Clean," 3.

34. University of Pennsylvania, "Penn's West Philadelphia Initiatives—Clean," 3.

35. University of Pennsylvania, "Penn's West Philadelphia Initiatives—Clean," 3.

36. University of Pennsylvania, "Penn's West Philadelphia Initiatives—Improving Housing and Home Ownership," University of Pennsylvania, http://www.upenn.edu/campus/westphilly/housing.html (accessed May 17, 2007), 14.

37. University of Pennsylvania, "Converting the Former G.E. Building," *Almanac* 45, no. 20 (1999), 1.

38. The Science Center, *Sc21—The Science Center: Powering Commercialization* (Philadelphia: The Science Center, 2006), 1.

39. The Science Center, *Sc21—The Science Center*, 1.

40. The Wharton School, University of Pennsylvania, "Executive Education—Certificate of Professional Development," University of Pennsylvania, http://executiveeducation.wharton.upenn.edu/cpd/index.cfm (accessed May 22, 2007), 3.

41. University of Pennsylvania, "Introduction to Penn," 2.

42. University of Southern California (USC), "History," University of Southern California—About USC, http://www.usc.edu/about/history/ (accessed November 1, 2007), 1.

43. USC, "History," 26.

44. USC, "History," 38.

45. USC, "USC's Plan for Increasing Academic Excellence: Building Strategic Capabilities for the University of the 21st Century," USC, http://www.usc.edu/private/factbook/StrategicPln_12_10_04.pdf (accessed November 1, 2007), 1.

46. USC, "USC at a Glance," USC—About USC, http://www.usc.edu/about/ataglance/ (accessed November 1, 2007), 4.

47. USC, "USC at a Glance," 88 and 89.

48. Elisa Wiefel and Sally Stewart, "The USC Stevens Institute for Innovation Opens Shop on USC Health Sciences Campus," *PR Newswire,* http://www.prnewswire.com/ (accessed October 26, 2007), 1. Article can be found at http://stevens.usc.edu/read_release.php?press_id=31.

49. USC, "History," 27.

50. Audrey Williams June, "$175-Million Gift Goes to Film School," *The Chronicle of Higher Education* 53, no. 6 (2006): A37.

51. USC, "History," 59.

52. USC, "History," 69.

53. USC, "History," 81.

54. Margot Hornblower, "The Gown Goes to Town," *Time Magazine* (2000): 70–78.

55. Kenneth R. Weiss, "No Longer the University of Second Choice," *Los Angeles Times Magazine* (September 17, 2000), 6.

56. USC, "History," 92.

57. USC, "History," 92.

58. USC, "USC at a Glance," 9.

59. USC, "USC at a Glance," 3. Weiss, "No Longer the University of Second Choice," 29. Association of American Universities (AAU), "Association of American Universities," AAU, http://www.aau.edu/ (accessed November 5, 2007).

60. Weiss, "No Longer the University of Second Choice," 17, 49.

61. Weiss, "No Longer the University of Second Choice," 34.

62. USC, "History," 91.

63. Weiss, "No Longer the University of Second Choice," 4.

64. USC, "History," 40.

65. USC, "Neighborhood Academic Initiative Program: Education—Opportunity—Community" (Los Angeles: USC, no date), 2, 3.

66. USC, "Neighborhood Academic Initiative Program," 2.

67. USC, "Neighborhood Academic Initiative Program," 2.

68. USC, "Neighborhood Academic Initiative Program," 2.

69. USC, "Neighborhood Academic Initiative Program," 2.

70. Weiss, "No Longer the University of Second Choice," 46.

71. Margot Hornblower, "The Gown Goes to Town," 73.

72. USC, "USC and Its Neighborhood," USC—Galen Center, http://www.usc.edu/community/galencenter/neighbors.html (accessed October 30, 2007), 7.

73. Allison Engel, "Owning Your Home, Sweet Home," USC: USC News, http://www.usc.edu/uscnews/stories/12611.html (accessed November 27, 2007), 1, 2.

74. Engel, "Owning Your Home, Sweet Home," 5.

75. Engel, "Owning Your Home, Sweet Home," 6, 7.

76. USC, "USC and Its Neighborhood," 11.

77. Weiss, "No Longer the University of Second Choice," 48.

78. Weiss, "No Longer the University of Second Choice," 48.

79. Hornblower, "The Gown Goes to Town," 71, 72.

80. USC, "History," 95.

81. Evan Dobelle, *Saviors of Our Cities: Twenty-five Urban Colleges Noted for Positive Economic and Social Benefit to their Communities* (Boston: New England Board of Higher Education, 2006), 1.

82. Steven B. Sample, "Southern California's Hidden Economic Engine," *Los Angeles Times* (May 22, 1994), USC, http://www.usc.edu/president/speeches/1994/economic_engine.html (accessed November 6, 2007), 4, 6.

83. Sample, "Southern California's Hidden Economic Engine," 8.

84. Economics Research Associates (ERA), *Economic Impact Analysis of the University of Southern California—Annual Operations, Fiscal Year 2005–2006: Prepared for University of Southern California (ERA Project No. 16668)* (ERA: Los Angeles September 2006), 1.

85. ERA, Economic Impact Analysis, ES-3.

86. ERA, Economic Impact Analysis, 54.

87. ERA, Economic Impact Analysis, 54.

88. ERA, Economic Impact Analysis, 54.

89. ERA, Economic Impact Analysis, ES-3, 55.

90. ERA, Economic Impact Analysis, ES-1.

91. ERA, Economic Impact Analysis, 41. USC, "MAP 17: Los Angeles City Council Districts and USC Neighborhood Outreach Boundaries (2005)," USC, http://www.usc.edu/ext-relations/ccr/private/atlas/vol_2/MAP17.pdf (accessed October 30, 2007).

92. Hornblower, "The Gown Goes to Town," 75. USC, "Business and Economic Development," USC—Community Building, http://www.usc.edu/neighborhoods/community/programs/business.html (accessed November 28, 2007), 7.

93. Hornblower, "The Gown Goes to Town," 75.

94. USC, "USC and Its Neighborhood," 8.

95. USC, "USC and Its Neighborhood," 8.

96. USC, "Galen Center—Fact Sheet: The Galen Center at USC," USC, http://www.usc.edu/neighborhoods/galencenter/ (accessed October 31, 2007), 1. Monika Guttman, "USC Breaks Ground on Harlyne J. Norris Cancer Research Center," *HSC Weekly* 9, no. 20 (2003): 1, USC Health Services, Public Relations, http://www.usc.edu/hsc/info/pr/1volpdf/pdf03/920.pdf (accessed October 30, 2007).

97. Weiss, "No Longer the University of Second Choice," 48.

98. USC, "About Us," USC—Research, http://www.usc.edu/research/about/ (accessed November 28, 2007), 4.

99. USC, "Mission," USC–USC Stevens, http://stevens.usc.edu/about_mission.php (accessed October 26, 2007), 8.

100. USC, "Our History," 2. Helen Walters and Kerry Miller, "USC's New Institute for Innovation," *BusinessWeek*, March 29, 2007, 1, http://www.businessweek.com/innovate/content/mar2007/id20070329_553215.htm (accessed October 26, 2007).

101. USC, "Our Approach," USC–USC Stevens, http://stevens.usc.edu/about_approach.php (accessed October 26, 2007), sidebar.

102. USC, "Our Approach," 6. USC, "Our History," 3.

103. Walters and Miller, "USC's New Institute for Innovation," 10.

104. Wiefel and Stewart, "The USC Stevens Institute for Innovation Opens Shop," 5.

105. Wiefel and Stewart, "The USC Stevens Institute for Innovation Opens Shop," 6.

106. USC, "USC's Plan for Increasing Academic Excellence," 1.

107. USC, "USC's Plan for Increasing Academic Excellence," 1–2.

108. USC, "USC's Plan for Increasing Academic Excellence," 3.

109. USC, "About," USC—University Park Master Plan, http://www.usc.edu/community/upcmasterplan/about/ (accessed November 1, 2007), 2.

110. USC, "About," 2.

111. USC, "USC's Plan for Increasing Academic Excellence," 3.

112. Eugene P. Trani, "Even in Hard Times, Colleges Should Help Their Communities," *The Chronicle of Higher Education* 54, no. 36 (2008): A36.

113. Trani, "Even in Hard Times," 3.

114. Trani, "Even in Hard Times," 6.

115. Eugene P. Trani, "The Capital Corridor: A New Vision for the Region" (PowerPoint presentation given at various locations in Richmond, Virginia, 2008), 26. Eugene P. Trani, *The Role of Universities in Economic Development* (Richmond: Virginia Commonwealth University), 3.

116. Mike Porter, "VCU Receives National Recognition for Community Initiatives," VCU—VCU News Center, http://www.news.vcu.edu/vcu_view/pages .aspx?nid=1897 (accessed December 21, 2006), 5.

117. Porter, "VCU Receives National Recognition," 1.

118. Porter, "VCU Receives National Recognition," 3.

119. Trani, "Even in Hard Times," 7.

120. Trani, "Even in Hard Times," 8.

121. Eugene P. Trani, "Virginia Commonwealth University: A Partner in Richmond's Revitalization," *Economic Development America* (Winter 2004): 9.

122. Trani, *The Role of Universities in Economic Development*, 2.

123. Trani, *The Role of Universities in Economic Development*, 2.

124. Trani, *The Role of Universities in Economic Development*, 2. Emily C. Dooley, "Area to Feel Qimonda Demise," *Richmond Times-Dispatch* (February 4, 2009), http://www2.timesdispatch.com/rtd/business/local/article/B-QIMO04_ 20090203-%20222213/197474 (accessed March 25, 2009), 1, 2. Emily C. Dooley, "Staff Reports: VCU Engineering School Loses Ally in Qimonda," *Richmond Times-Dispatch* (March 1, 2009), http://www2.timesdispatch.com/rtd/business/ local/article/QIMO01S_20090228-222430/218693 (accessed March 25, 2009), 10.

125. Dooley, "Area to Feel Qimonda Demise," 29. Dooley, "Staff Reports," 1, 4.

126. Dooley, "Staff Reports," 12, 13.

127. Trani, *The Role of Universities in Economic Development*, 2

128. Trani, *The Role of Universities in Economic Development*, 2. Virginia Commonwealth University (VCU), "Virginia BioTechnology Research Park," VCU, http://www.vcu.edu/biotech/ (accessed May 29, 2008), 1.

129. VCU, "Virginia BioTechnology Research Park," 1, 2. Jeffrey Kelley, "Richmond's Technology Stars Honored," *Richmond Times-Dispatch* (May 10, 2007), http://www.inrich.com (accessed May 10, 2007), 4.

130. VCU, "Virginia BioTechnology Research Park," 3.

131. VCU, "Virginia BioTechnology Research Park," 3. Kent Jennings Brockwell, "Odds and Ends: The Va. BioTech Park Wins an Award," *The Richmond Times-Dispatch* (June 8, 2007), http://www.richmond.com (accessed June 11, 2007), 1.

132. Brockwell, "Odds and Ends," 1.

133. Brockwell, "Odds and Ends," 1.

134. Kelley, "Richmond's Technology Stars Honored," 4. Trani, "The Capital Corridor," 20.

135. Trani, *The Role of Universities in Economic Development*, 2.

136. VCU, *Innovation Is Our Tradition* (Richmond: Virginia Commonwealth University, 2006), 22.

137. VCU, *Innovation Is Our Tradition*, 23.

138. Alan Bjerga, "Richmond's Rising Tide Lifts Minority Boats, Too," *The Wichita Eagle*, September 14, 2006, 2.

139. Trani, "Even in Hard Times," 9.

140. VCU, *Innovation Is Our Tradition*, 21.

141. VCU, *Innovation Is Our Tradition*, 21. Trani, "Even in Hard Times," 9. Trani, "The Capital Corridor," 22.

142. Trani, *The Role of Universities in Economic Development*, 3.

# Chapter 4

# U.S. Higher Education: The Reinvention of the Land-Grant University

The mission, first articulated in colonial times and given life in the Morrill Act of 1862, of providing education to all citizens is, today, both enduring and changing. The philosophical principles and lofty goals remain. The audience, the programming, and the geographical reach of the institutions are changing. The world is a much more complex place than it was in 1862.[1]

## THE EVOLUTION OF LAND-GRANT UNIVERSITIES

### Origins

As far back as colonial times, education has been a central tenet of American democratic thought.[2] Education has been viewed as a means of inculcating ideals of citizenship from the very formation of the American Republic.[3] Over time, publicly funded primary education became a staple in the belief system of democracy and individual advancement in the United States. Education also came to be seen as a societal good as well as an individual benefit. James Sherwood points to Thomas Jefferson's hope of seeing an "aristocracy of achievement rising out of a democracy of opportunity" as the epitome of the American belief in education's transforming power.[4]

The actual practice of early American higher education was often in tension with the ideals of access, utility, and social mobility. Until the first half of the nineteenth century, U.S. universities were greatly influenced by the European model in which higher education was designed to serve the upper ranks of a sclerotic class system and not the needs of an emerging, dynamic democratic society.[5]

Initially, American higher education institutions functioned in much the same fashion as European institutions, offering primarily classical and professional curricula.[6] Some American institutions had begun to expand upon the traditional curricula, but higher education was still largely unavailable to many agricultural and industrial workers.[7] By the middle of the nineteenth century, however, widespread demands for more agricultural and technical education emerged from a society in the midst of an enormous geographical expansion and economic transformation.

In 1860 and 1861, the political events that made the Civil War necessary also made possible the passage of landmark higher education legislation that would transform American society. The secession of southern states from the Union set in motion a chain of events that forever changed the course of U.S. history.[8] Without southern opposition, northern states could pass a number of bills that the South had blocked before 1860, and many of these measures helped to spur economic growth in the western territories. One such initiative was the Morrill Act of 1862 (also known as the Land-Grant Act), which made it possible for western states to establish colleges for their citizens.

Sponsored by Justin Morrill, a Vermont congressman, the act gave every state that had remained in the Union a grant of thirty thousand acres of public land per member of the state's congressional delegation, the proceeds from which the state was to use to establish colleges in engineering, agriculture, and military science, reflecting the demand for such training that emerged in the nineteenth century. The intent of the Morrill Act was to provide a broad segment of the population with a practical education that had direct relevance to the students' daily lives. At least three movements were furthered by the 1862 Morrill Act:

1. The protest against the dominance of the classics in higher education
2. The desire to develop college-level instruction relating to the practical realities of an agricultural and industrial society
3. The interest in preparing those belonging to the "industrial classes" for the "professions of life"[9]

The language used in the Morrill Act stating the legislation's purpose was as follows:

The leading object shall be, without excluding other scientific and classical studies, and including military tactics, to teach such branches of learning as are related to agriculture and mechanic arts, in such manner as the legislatures of the State may respectively prescribe, in order to promote the liberal and practical education of the industrial classes in the several pursuits and professions in life.[10]

The Morrill Act was signed into law by President Abraham Lincoln on July 2, 1862.[11] Sixty-nine colleges were funded by the land grants called for in the act. In 1887, the Hatch Act was passed, mandating the creation of agricultural experiment stations for scientific research.[12] Also in 1887, the National Association of State Universities and Land-Grant Colleges, now known as the Association of Public and Land-Grant Universities (APLU), was founded to support excellence in teaching, research, and public service, a mission it has upheld since that time, earning it a prominent role in the evolution of land-grant institutions for more than 120 years.[13] In 1890, the second Morrill Act was passed, providing further endowment for colleges, including funding for institutions for black students, which led to the creation of seventeen historically black land-grant colleges.[14] Legislation contributing to the expansion of land-grant institutions continued to be enacted in the twentieth century. In 1914, the Smith-Lever Act was passed, providing federal support for cooperative extension efforts with state and local communities.[15] The Bankhead-Jones Act was approved in 1935, adding annual appropriations for land-grant institutions.[16] The 1944 Servicemen's Readjustment Act (GI Bill), Public Law 346, dramatically increased the enrollment of such institutions as land-grant universities and colleges by providing for the higher education of veterans.[17] In 1994, legislation was passed that led to the establishment of twenty-nine Native American tribal colleges, all of which are located on or near reservations.[18]

Over the course of the nineteenth and twentieth centuries, many of the established land-grant colleges grew, with additional state aid, into large public universities, educating millions of Americans who otherwise might not have been able to afford college.[19] Today, there are more than one hundred land-grant institutions.[20] Many of the land-grant institutions have joined the ranks of the nation's most distinguished public research universities, and millions of students have been able to study every academic discipline and explore fields of inquiry far beyond the scope that was envisioned in the original land-grant mission. Land-grant institutions have not only broadened higher education access and opportunities for the general population, but they also have opened doors to specific segments of previously unserved and underserved populations. For instance, the network of American tribal colleges has become the most important provider of higher education opportunities for Native Americans and has been notably successful in retaining students and sending them on to four-year colleges and universities.[21] The tribal colleges also have provided a variety of community services, such as family counseling, alcohol and drug abuse programs, job training, and economic development. In addition, the Historically Black Colleges and Universities (HBCUs), which trace their roots to the second Morrill Act, now stand eighteen strong in number and continue to produce the greatest number of degrees awarded to African Americans in this country.[22] In 2002, President George W. Bush established the President's Board of Advisors on HBCUs, to develop measures to ensure that HBCUs remain a vital part of the nation's history and educational system.[23] Complementing the land-grant mission of educating "the people" is the extension function these institutions perform. Since the Smith-Lever Act was passed in 1914, the federal government's Cooperative State Research, Education, and Extension Service (CSREES) has grown within the U.S. Department of Agriculture, helping to advance knowledge about agriculture, the environment, human health and well-being, and communities.[24] CSREES accomplishes this by supporting research, education, and extension programs at land-grant universities, as well as by partnering with other organizations. CSREES helps states identify priorities of public concern that affect agricultural producers, small-business owners, youth and families, and others, and provides annual formula funding and competitively awarded grants to land-grant universities. A network of state, regional, and county extension offices is staffed by educators and other personnel who respond to public inquiries and conduct informal, noncredit workshops and other educational events. Now ninety-five years old, the land-grant system of extension services disseminates helpful information that addresses commonly encountered problems through educational materials (print, video, CD), the Internet, the telephone, and other means, helping to extend the outreach impact of land-grant universities.

## Shaping a Contemporary Mission

During the last half of the twentieth century, the distinctiveness of land-grant institutions progressively eroded. Colleges and universities that had grown up as "ag schools" became far more comprehensive universities, in terms of both course offerings and diversity of student population.[25] As these institutions began to reflect larger trends altering the higher education landscape, the shifting emphasis between teaching and research inside universities resulted in less time for public service, and an increase in private and corporate research sponsorship resulted in less public disclosure and dissemination of research results, thereby diminishing two functions that had long been central to the role of land-grant institutions. In some states, the demise of the family farm, which caused the traditional "customers" of cooperative extension programs to disappear, left the outreach mission of land-grant schools more uncertain.

Moreover, many of the land grants were now actually located in thriving metropolitan areas and the notion of having an exclusively or even primarily rural mission became increasingly anachronistic.

According to Sherwood, by the 1990s some leaders of land-grant institutions were becoming increasingly concerned over what they saw as abandonment or at least a shift in emphasis away from the principles upon which their institutions were founded.[26] In 1995, convinced that structural changes "as deep and significant as any in history" were besieging the entire country, including the nation's state and land-grant institutions, APLU turned to the W. K. Kellogg Foundation for support in examining the future of public higher education.[27] The Kellogg Foundation awarded a grant of $1.2 million to APLU to fund a twenty-five-member presidential commission through March 2000.[28] The following series of reports was issued, documenting the commission's findings:

- "Renewing the Covenant: Learning, Discovery, and Engagement in a New Age and Different World" (March 2000)
- "Returning to Our Roots: Toward a Coherent Campus Culture" (January 2000)
- "Returning to Our Roots: A Learning Society" (September 1999)
- "Returning to Our Roots: The Engaged Institution" (February 1999)
- "Returning to Our Roots: Student Access" (May 1998)
- "Returning to Our Roots: The Student Experience" (April 1997)[29]

Five reports addressed campus issues and called for public universities to join the Kellogg Commission in "returning to our roots," becoming once more the "transformational" institutions they were established to be.[30] The sixth report called for a renewal of the "covenant" (or partnership) between the public and "the public's universities."[31] That final report also addressed learning, discovery, and engagement in a new age and a different world, noting:

> The dawning of a new millennium is the perfect time to renew the educational commitment that has spawned so many of the intellectual, material, and economic benefits enjoyed by citizens of the United States. It is the right time to reclaim that heritage and, in so doing, to renew the faith of Justin Morrill and Abraham Lincoln, the fathers of American public higher education, that our institutions would truly be the "public's universities."[32]

This chapter examines the manner in which three major land-grant universities—the University of Wisconsin, the University of Minnesota, and The Ohio State University—have redefined their historic mission for the challenges of the twenty-first century. We explore how the University of Wisconsin has modernized "the Wisconsin Idea" to respond to the economic challenges that face a state that has had a growth rate below the national average for the last twenty-five years. Our discussion of the University of Minnesota and The Ohio State University focuses on two traditional land-grant universities that are located in what have become rapidly changing urban areas and that have adapted the philosophy of the land grant in framing their interaction with their surrounding communities. Promoting economic development, enhancing social capital, addressing community health care needs, and continuing to bridge theory and practice are the key ways that the traditional land-grant schools remain indispensable to the aspirations of their states and citizens, even if the conditions that gave rise to these institutions have dramatically changed.

## MODERNIZING THE WISCONSIN IDEA:
## THE UNIVERSITY OF WISCONSIN AT MADISON

In 1848, the same year that Wisconsin achieved statehood, a constitutional clause set forth a provision for "a State University, at or near the seat of state government."[33] On February 5, 1849, seventeen students convened to attend the first class of the university. In 1864, just two years after the passage of the Morrill Act by the U.S. Congress, the University of Wisconsin (UW) obtained a designation as the state's land-grant institution, making it one of the nation's first land-grant universities.[34] That university, located in the state's capital, later became known as the University of Wisconsin at Madison, the flagship school of the UW system.

Since the establishment of UW in 1848, the Madison campus has regularly refocused its activities to meet the changing needs of the state.[35] In the late 1800s, UW saw the economic benefits of adopting the German model of integrating research into the university's instructional mission. In 1904, UW president Charles Van Hise crystallized the university's commitment to public service in coining the term "the Wisconsin Idea," which mandated that "the beneficent influence of the university [be] available to every home in the state."[36]

For more than one hundred years, the Wisconsin Idea has been a catalyst to UW's growth and prosperity, reflecting the university's unique approach to fulfilling its land-grant mission. The Wisconsin Idea also has been the galvanizing force behind UW's unwavering commitment to meeting the ever-changing needs of the state of Wisconsin. The managing director of UW's Office of Corporate Relations (OCR), Charles B. Hoslet, noted, "A century ago, the challenge facing Wisconsin and the nation was to produce enough food to feed a growing population. We met and surpassed that challenge, in part by putting the UW to work for the public good in a grand endeavor known as 'The Wisconsin Idea.'"[37] As the twentieth century unfolded, Wisconsin's agricultural needs were joined by statewide business and industry needs, prompting UW to refocus its activities on supporting the growth of the industrial sector. UW's agricultural and industrial foci have continued to this day.

The reinvention of the Wisconsin Idea for the twenty-first century has occurred in four key areas:

- Developing intellectual capital relevant to twenty-first-century needs
- Developing technology transfer functions that can help transform Wisconsin's economy
- Creating "Wiscontrepreneurs" who possess skills to parlay innovative ideas into sustainable enterprises
- Modernizing its public service commitment through the creation of collaborative partnerships to replace unidirectional service delivery

Over the last thirty years, chancellors Irving Shain, Donna Shalala, David Ward, and John Wiley have worked to reinvent the Wisconsin Idea while working to maintain UW's stature as a globally competitive research university. They have done so in the context of a system-wide focus of economic development established by the Board of Regents that multiplied the efforts of the flagship institution at Madison with aggressive regional initiatives as well.

### Developing Intellectual Capital

According to a 2003 economic impact study conducted by NorthStar Economics, Wisconsin has had a mature, slow-growth economy based on manufacturing and agriculture, while high-growth economies are built on brainpower, new ideas, research, new technology, and high-paying jobs.[38] The NorthStar report added that research universities such as UW are critical to developing the critical components of a high-growth economy, concluding that "the university's real impact is the economic benefits from new ideas and research. . . . New ideas and research create high-growth business clusters that will drive economic prosperity in the 21st century."[39]

UW has occupied a leading position among research universities in the country for many decades. In 2006, UW ranked third in research expenditures, fifth in federally funded research, second in non–federally funded research, and second in doctorates granted.[40] For 2005 to 2006, UW's total sponsored funding awards equaled almost $900 million.[41] UW libraries are ranked eleventh among research libraries in North America, according to a survey by the Association of Research Libraries in 2002 and 2003.[42]

In recent years, UW has attempted to shape its historical research strength in ways that would enable it to modernize the Wisconsin economy. Take agriculture, for instance. The Morrill Act of 1862, which created a program of agricultural experiment stations, was visionary for its time. UW continues to promote agricultural education, research, and development in support of Wisconsin's agricultural industry, but the university has reinvented the way it does that to become a twenty-first-century leader in agricultural innovation. The Center for Dairy Research focuses on developing lower-fat cheeses, specialty cheeses, and quality and safety issues. The Center for Dairy Profitability explores new strategies to help Wisconsin dairy farms thrive, including an innovative online program for start-up dairy farms. That center is critical to the future of the industry in a state that now faces significant challenges from California and other southwestern states.

Also, UW research and development has moved well beyond traditional agricultural research to support modern biotechnology. The Biotron, for example, is a state-of-the-art facility at UW that provides controlled-environment research rooms and chambers for plant, animal, and materials experiments. Within the building, almost any environmental condition occurring on Earth can be simulated. Projects include the development of a genome initiative to create one hundred thousand lines of knockout plants and the growing of potatoes with a protein that will induce resistance to hepatitis B if the potatoes are eaten raw. Helping Wisconsin farmers harvest UW's agricultural intellectual capital are the university's thirteen agricultural research stations, which support the state's $51.5 billion agriculture industry.

UW has also established a wide array of interdisciplinary research centers that bring scholars together from multiple disciplines to advance knowledge in ways that make practical contributions to advancing science and addressing social problems. Many of these are science-based, such as its Genetics-Biotechnology Center, McArdle Laboratory for Cancer Research, and Space Science and Engineering Center. Others focus on building social capital, such as its Institute on Aging, Institute for Research on Poverty, and Waisman Center, which is dedicated to research that benefits people with developmental disabilities and their families. One recent example is the Department of Energy Great Lakes Bioenergy Research Center. This center, along with a $125 million research grant to support it, is intended to allow UW to concentrate its research focus and speed the advent of promising science, engage private partners in Wisconsin and the Great Lakes region, and enable the Midwest to become a nexus for the emerging bioenergy market.[43]

Today, UW has twenty schools and colleges, including the state's only public schools of law, medicine, and veterinary medicine.[44] UW is one of only two state-supported schools to offer doctoral degrees, with UW–Milwaukee being the other. UW students may choose from 136 undergraduate majors, 155 master's degree, and 110 doctoral degree programs. The June 2006 issue of *U.S. News & World Report* ranked UW's academic programs thirty-fourth among all of the nation's universities and eighth among the nation's public universities.

Like other top-ranked public research universities across the country, UW's growth in size and prestige has had an economic ripple effect. An inherent part of running any university is certain operational functions, such as purchaser, employer, and real estate developer, which can have positive economic impacts, especially when they are carried out on a relatively grand scale, as they are with UW. Therefore, as UW's campus and course offerings have expanded, it has become an even greater contributor to the regional and state economies.

Not only do major research universities pump money into economies and employ a considerable number of workers, but they also have become real estate developers in their own rights, as they put in place the physical infrastructure required to be a leader in training a competitive workforce, offering innovative ideas to society and the marketplace, and building stronger communities. For example, in addition to more than nine hundred acres of university and community buildings, UW's University Research Park (URP) has thirty-four buildings and spans 255 acres.[45]

Certainly, UW is like other major research universities in how its organizational operations inherently spur on economic development. However, UW has remained loyal to—while at the same time reinventing—its land-grant mission to strategically capitalize on today's knowledge-based economy for the benefit of the state of Wisconsin.

### Technology Transfer

While UW faculty and leaders began appreciating the economic benefits of integrating research into the university's core instructional mission in the late 1800s, it was not until after the turn of the twentieth century that UW started making a concerted effort to translate its research activities into private-sector applications. In the 1920s, the Wisconsin Alumni Research Foundation (WARF) was founded as a partner institution to UW to transfer inventions arising from university research to the private sector, beginning with Harry Steenbock's discovery of the role of ultraviolet irradiation in the production of vitamin D.[46] The establishment of the Office of University-Industry Relations in 1963 was the next major step in UW's budding technology transfer enterprise. Then the URP's establishment in

1984 provided the physical environment and other resources to put companies in close contact with university researchers.

In 1992, the University–Industry Review Committee determined that a significant portion of useful university-generated technology was not being transferred to the private sector and that the full potential for industrial support of university research remained critically unrealized.[47] Throughout the 1990s, UW implemented several changes that helped position the university's technology transfer enterprise to reshape Wisconsin's economy. For instance, in 1999 WARF became the exclusive patent management organization of UW, centralizing and harnessing resources for that function.

Next, the UW strategic plan for 2001–2009 included goals and initiatives to gear up the university's tech transfer function. Within the strategic priority to "Amplify the Wisconsin Idea," the goal of fostering technology transfer was listed.[48] Under that technology transfer goal, example initiatives included:

1. Develop long-range technology transfer strategy, including facilities, process, and people
2. Create environment supportive of faculty, students, and staff committed to technology transfer
3. Increase funding for research ideas leading to technology transfer
4. Provide opportunities that encourage high-tech businesses and employees to locate in Wisconsin
5. Link business with technology initiatives
6. Extend UW technology transfer connections regionally and globally

In 2003, newly inaugurated Wisconsin Governor Jim Doyle, along with other government, business, and education leaders, such as UW Chancellor John Wiley, turned their attention to finding a long-term budget solution for the state of Wisconsin.[49] Within this context, Wiley created the Chancellor's Task Force on University-Business Relations to study the relationship between UW and the business community and to recommend ways that the university could better serve the needs of that community. Wiley's task force made several recommendations to better position UW to build Wisconsin's economy, including that the university place special emphasis on technology transfer in its efforts to create and strengthen university-industry relationships. Wiley stated in a task force report, "Embedded in the UW–Madison Strategic Plan's priority of 'Amplifying the Wisconsin Idea' is the goal of creating a state-university partnership to develop critical mass for growing technology transfer in Wisconsin."[50]

Key features of UW's tech transfer efforts include the WARF. According to *Chronicle of Higher Education* reporter Goldie Blumenstyk, "Among technology-transfer offices, WARF is considered an innovator."[51] Not only is WARF an innovator among innovators, but its endowment of $1.6 billion makes it the richest and most independent university-related patent foundation in the country. Having introduced the notion of patenting ideas from university inventors almost a century ago, WARF has become the model upon which more than three hundred universities draw in providing patenting and licensing services.[52] WARF played a role in negotiations that in 1968 allowed UW to become the first university in the country to win the right to own patents on inventions financed with federal money, an arrangement that eventually became the basis for the Bayh-Dole Act of 1980, which has contributed to today's major focus in higher education on the commercialization of research.[53]

In 2005, WARF received the National Medal of Technology, the highest honor granted by the president of the United States for innovation in using technology to better the economy and the lives of citizens.[54] The same year, the National Institutes of Health designated WARF's nonprofit subsidiary, WiCell Research, as the National Stem Cell Bank.[55] It was a UW pathologist, James A. Thompson, who first isolated and cultivated stem cells from human embryos. Today, aside from holding a key U.S. patent in the promising field of stem cell research, WARF's claims to fame include bringing to market the blood thinner warfarin, which prevents strokes, and key technologies used in PlayStation 2 video game machines. The latter owes its invention, in part, to UW Chancellor Wiley, who helped invent a chip in the game's patented circuit design.

WARF's ongoing mission to make inventions created by UW faculty available to private industry has fueled state economic development. Since its founding, WARF has processed approximately 5,600 inventions created by UW faculty and staff, obtained more than 1,800 U.S. patents on these inventions, and completed more than 1,500 license agreements with various companies.[56]

### University Research Park

Another UW-affiliated entity that fosters tech transfer is the University Research Park. URP was established not only to endow research programs, but also to encourage tech transfer.[57] The URP hosts the Madison Gas & Electric Innovation Center, which has helped more than forty fledgling technology business ideas take flight since opening in 1999.[58] Demand was so strong in 2006 that the center was planning to double its capacity. In its discussion of the positive economic impacts UW has on Wisconsin's economy, NorthStar observed that URP is creating a high-technology products cluster that will be an economic engine for the entire state.[59]

### Office of Corporate Relations

In addition to forging external partnerships, UW reorganized itself internally to establish the tech transfer function as a key priority. One simple step was to create an Office of Corporate Relations to provide a more visible "front door" for companies interested in working with the university.[60] OCR helps to facilitate commercialization of university technologies and discoveries by connecting potential investors with early-stage companies, hosting activities such as a First Look Investor Forum and a CEO Breakfast Series.

### Workforce Development

Workforce development initiatives have become an increasingly important means of reinterpreting the Wisconsin Idea for the twenty-first century. This is especially important to a state that currently ranks twenty-first in per capita income, but where the rate of income growth lagged behind the national average from 1973 to 1998 and where current projections hold that the slippage in relative rank may continue.[61] NorthStar concluded that to raise per capita income to the national average, Wisconsin needs to create 140,000 "high paying" ($50,000 or higher annual salary) jobs.[62]

UW operates, as do many land-grant schools, a relatively traditional set of statewide outreach programs that meet the public's continuing education needs and interests. Approximately 139,000 people take advantage of more than three thousand professional development and personal enrichment continuing education programs through UW each year.[63] In striving to support the professional development of Wisconsin's workforce, UW provided 1,022 evening and weekend courses, which enrolled 26,824 students and totaled 62,288 student credit hours in 2005–2006 alone.[64]

UW cultivates corporate leadership through its campus-based Fluno Center, which is one of the largest executive education programs in the country.[65] Each year, the Fluno Center offers more than 220 public programs covering eighty business topics, as well as numerous custom programs for companies worldwide. In 2005, the Fluno Center served more than five hundred Wisconsin companies, and nine thousand Wisconsin business leaders benefited from Fluno executive programs.

One of the unique ways that UW is developing Wisconsin's workforce is its effort to groom a new generation of Wiscontrepreneurs, Badger State residents who organize, operate, and assume the risk for a business venture.[66] Key to UW's efforts to develop Wiscontrepreneurs is the university's selection as one of twenty-two institutions to receive a grant from the Ewing Marion Kauffman Foundation of Kansas City, Missouri, to help build the spirit and skills of entrepreneurship among all students. UW is the only Kauffman campus with a "Wisconsin Idea" component built into its plan. The $5 million, five-year grant will help educate students about the principles and practices of entrepreneurship, and will connect them and others with technology and ideas that can evolve into ventures. Once honed at UW, the program will be expanded to work with campuses and communities statewide.

## Community Involvement

The tradition of community involvement at UW spawned by the Wisconsin Idea has had a distinguished history. UW has been a central contributor to policy ideas and policy debate on major social issues since the turn of the twentieth century. Contemporary programs such as its Family Impact seminars have been widely replicated across the state. And work at the Institute for Research on Poverty has had a major influence on national as well as state policy. In recent years, UW's commitment to the public service component of its land-grant mission has become more expansive than ever, encompassing local community outreach, continuing education programs, health promotion, small-business development, and international initiatives.[67] The university carries out its community outreach mission through a variety of venues, including the Community Partnerships Center, Speakers Bureau, and Morgridge Center for Public Service.

Extending UW's community outreach to the local, national, and global levels, the Morgridge Center for Public Service (Morgridge Center) was created in 1994 though an endowment by John and Tashia Morgridge to advance the Wisconsin Idea.[68] The center has become a leader in:

- Engaging students in learning and leadership through service to local, regional, national, and international communities
- Assisting faculty and other teaching staff in the design of service learning and community-based research experiences
- Creating sustainable partnerships with community organizations, citizen groups, and local coalitions to meet identified community needs
- Promoting a lifelong commitment to active citizenship in a diverse democratic society

UW's outreach efforts in medicine and the health sciences are a good example of how its community outreach activities today combine its historical rural focus with a more recent commitment to addressing Wisconsin's urban challenges. Over the years, the UW School of Medicine and Public Health has established a statewide campus extending to every corner of

Wisconsin, for bringing better health care to all of the state's communities.[69] More recently, the school has developed an urban medicine training program, Training in Urban Medicine and Public Health, in response to a documented shortage of physicians in urban areas of the state.[70]

## University-State Tensions

UW's efforts to modernize the land-grant mission for the twenty-first century have not proceeded without significant friction between the university and its funders in the state legislature. On leaving the chancellorship in 2008, John Wiley asserted in an article for Madison Magazine that "Wisconsin has lost its way. We've lost touch with our traditions and values. Our politics has become a poisonous swill, and the most influential voice for the business community has been taken hostage by partisan ideologues."[71] In a remarkably blunt and bitter piece, Wiley argued that Wisconsin's political system had lost its capacity to operate in a bipartisan way and had become obsessed with cultural issues such as abortion, arming of teachers in the classroom, and the definition of marriage, while not providing the funding necessary to reverse the state's economic decline. Wiley maintained that the university was losing its competitiveness and that Minnesota, Wisconsin's neighbor, was outpacing Wisconsin by almost every important yardstick. In essence, he argued that UW's effort to reinvent itself was stymied by a politics that had replaced a pragmatic and progressive outlook with a debilitating focus on culturally divisive but economically irrelevant matters. These statements notwithstanding, the relationship between the UW and the State of Wisconsin remains very close as Wisconsin works to modernize its economy in the twenty-first century.

Wiley's exit rhetoric could have been voiced by public university presidents in a number of states who have become concerned by what they consider to be a reduction of support for higher education and an effective privatization of their universities. Yet these kinds of broadsides are unlikely to have the desired effect. Wiley's commentary is reflective of a larger cultural problem emerging between higher education and political leaders—how to respond to the environmental changes of the twenty-first century in a manner that simultaneously enables universities to compete in a global environment and to address the highest priority needs of their own states. This is a challenge that will not be successfully resolved by the simple exchange of argumentative briefs about funding and accountability between higher education administrators and political officials. It is likely to require the formulation of a "new bargain" between the leadership of states and their higher education institutions in which states recognize the legitimate research needs of their institutions and, in turn, the institutions respond to the emergent needs of the twenty-first century in their own environments.

## THE LAND GRANT IN THE CITY:
## THE UNIVERSITY OF MINNESOTA

### A Mega-University and the Community

The University of Minnesota (U of M) was started as a preparatory school in 1851, before the territory of Minnesota was established as a state in 1858.[72] After U of M's brief closure for financial reasons, Minneapolis entrepreneur John Sargent Pillsbury, who was a university regent, state senator, and governor, used his influence to reopen it in 1867 through support from the Morrill Land-Grant Act. About fifteen years later, two students received the university's first Bachelor of Arts degrees.

Today, U of M has more than 65,000 undergraduate, graduate, professional, and other students; more than four thousand full-time faculty members; and around four hundred thousand alumni. It has five campuses and a statewide network of regional Extension offices, research and outreach centers, and other important university locations.[73] Ranked among the top public research universities in the world with $612.2 million in sponsored research awards, U of M has made life-changing discoveries, such as the recent creation of a beating heart in the laboratory.

True to its land-grant heritage, U of M remains committed to helping its students afford tuition, housing, and books; agriculture is still an important focus of its teaching, research, and outreach.[74] At the same time, the university has adapted its historic land-grant mission to fit the challenges of a new economy and the needs of its immediate surroundings, including focusing on cutting-edge genomic research and health care research and addressing the complex urban issues of a multicultural community.

Because of its land-grant mission, U of M has always felt a duty and desire to be an integral part of the economic vitality of the communities it serves.[75] Like other universities, U of M's sheer size and main campus location in a large metropolitan area enable it to assume a number of influential economic development roles, including employer, purchaser, workforce developer, and real estate developer. Yet, like the universities that have defined themselves as specifically urban in focus, U of M has developed major initiatives that carry its economic development mission beyond the ones dictated by its size alone.

### Economic Development, the Community, and the State

U of M's Office for Business and Community Economic Development was established in 1999 to advance the university's interests in promoting economic development and employment and training opportunities for historically underserved communities.[76] Since its establishment, this effort has grown from a single program to a university office with nine programs and four units. It has doubled the university's purchases from emerging small businesses; created more than 1,300 employment opportunities for women, people of color, and people with disabilities on university construction projects; and offered management and technical assistance services that have helped small businesses build capacity. One of the office's most exemplary initiatives is its partnership with Comcast Cable, a ten-year program that provides scholarships and internships for students of color. The partnership also provides major funding for leadership training and other business development initiatives that support emerging small businesses.

Another effort by U of M to strategically and deliberately promote economic development is its Academic and Corporate Relations Center (ACRC). The university created ACRC to increase the opportunities for collaboration and connection in support of U of M's and the business community's shared goals of attracting and retaining quality people, expanding knowledge, and enhancing research and innovation.[77] ACRC's concierge service, Web interface, and relationship managers help ensure that the business community can readily access U of M's vast economic development assets.[78]

One of ACRC's most potent economic development tools is connecting businesses with world-class resources, such as the Initiative for Renewable Energy and the Environment (IREE).[79] The mission of IREE is to promote statewide economic development, sustainable, healthy, and diverse ecosystems, and national energy security through the development of bio-based and other renewable resources and processes. Research and collaboration with the business community are key to IREE's fulfilling its mission; in turn, IREE provides a wealth of opportunities for the community's businesses. ACRC helps ensure that these reciprocal benefits are realized.

One of U of M's most groundbreaking economic engines is the Minnesota Partnership for Biotechnology and Medical Genomics. Announced in 2003, the partnership among U of M, the Mayo Clinic, and the state of Minnesota leverages the state's two renowned research institutions using state resources.[80] Minnesota Partnership funding is being used to place the state at the forefront of advanced research and development capability in several bioscience technology fields, including genetics and genomics, proteomics, bioinformatics, x-ray crystallography, and therapeutic protein production.[81] In addition, more than $20 million has been invested in building research facilities and $8 million has been allocated to develop a BioBusiness Development Center adjacent to the partnership facilities. The partnership has leveraged in-state funding with further federal funding and other external funding, including corporate and philanthropic support. A very high level of research productivity and high levels of patent generation efficiency have already been achieved by the partnership, with many papers published by fewer than twenty full-time equivalent personnel and one patent generated for every $1.07 million in research expenditures. In addition to producing new patentable technologies and commercialization products, the partnership's research initiatives are likely to drive more patients to U of M's Academic Health Center (AHC) and the Mayo Clinic, generating further economic benefits for the state, because many of those treated will be coming from outside Minnesota. Also, the partnership's leading-edge research infrastructure, technology, and associated support services create a powerful mechanism for recruiting top-quality professionals to Minnesota for research and development projects. And the partnership's infrastructure investments provide Minnesota bioscience commercial enterprises with contracted access to state-of-the-art equipment and services that would not be cost-effective for companies to individually acquire and operate.

## Building Social Capital in the City

In tandem with its efforts to promote economic development, U of M offers a wide range of programs, initiatives, and other opportunities for enhancing social capital. These connect the university's ideas, discoveries, and resources to citizens in communities neighboring its campuses and throughout the state.[82]

U of M's Office for Public Engagement works to enhance the university's activities and stature as a publicly engaged university, overseeing a wide array of programs.[83] These include:

- America Reads Challenge
- Career and Community Learning Center
- Center for Transportation Studies
- Center for Urban and Regional Affairs
- Children, Youth and Family Consortium
- College of Continuing Education
- Community Engagement Scholars Program
- Institute on Community Integration
- Regional Sustainable Development Partnerships Program

Also, given U of M's land-grant status, an integral and long-standing element of U of M's public engagement enterprise is its extension service. Since 1909, extension faculty have extended the reach of the university into every corner of the state, providing Minnesotans with access to practical, research-based information and high-quality, relevant educational programs to help improve their lives.[84] U of M's Extension Service target areas include agriculture, community vitality, the environment, family, gardening, and youth.[85] In addition to spinning a statewide web of outreach through its extension services, U of M's outreach efforts target specific neighborhoods in its urban surroundings. In 2006, the University Northside Partnership was established to bring together community organizations based in North Minneapolis with city and county representatives, faith leaders, and university faculty and staff.[86] The goal of the partnership is to realize a strong urban vision of community revitalization, provide improved education and training, and support effective business development in North Minneapolis. Since 2006, the university has invested $120,000 in the Northside Seed Grant Program, administered by the Center for Urban and Regional Affairs, to support proposals from community organizations that operate programs that serve residents of the Northside community.

Over the past several years, the university has been working to create the first Urban Research and Outreach/Engagement Center (UROC) as the delivery mechanism to interface with the Northside partnership.[87] The efforts of the UROC work groups have been funded by a three-year, $750,000 (total) grant from the federal Fund for the Improvement of Post-Secondary Education, to document the process of community engagement around the themes of out-of-school time, healthy foods, and youth entrepreneurship. Renovations to UROC's building are scheduled for completion in fall 2009.

To be located in the UROC building, the Center for Innovation and Economic Development, which received a $300,000 Empowerment Zone grant from the city to support programs for youth entrepreneurs, will serve as a business incubator and offer a computer refurbishing program, along with other technical assistance and support for Northside businesses and nonprofits.[88] Multipurpose space in the facility will create opportunities for other university services to come into the Northside, as well. While reflecting its one-hundred-year-plus land-grant heritage of community outreach, UROC is poised to anchor the university commitment to urban community engagement and find ways to use its resources to work collaboratively with its local partners to address the enormous challenges of our current times.

## Social Capital and Health Care Outreach

Established more than a century and a half ago, the AHC of the University of Minnesota has grown into one of the most comprehensive health education and research centers in the United States.[89] Today, the AHC comprises six schools and colleges, including the disciplines of medicine, dentistry, nursing, pharmacy, public health, and veterinary medicine. Augmenting the AHC's broad range of professional health education and research efforts are strong interdisciplinary centers and programs in bio-ethics, cancer, genomics, infectious disease, drug design, animal health, food safety, and spirituality and healing.

The AHC's schools educate 70 percent of Minnesota's health care professionals.[90] The AHC also serves as an economic engine driving Minnesota's leading industry, health care services and products. In addition to developing new health technologies independently, the AHC works in collaboration with Minnesota biomedical companies in making cutting-edge discoveries.

Beyond its workforce and economic development roles, the AHC operates an expansive patient care enterprise. In 1997, the University of Minnesota Hospital and Clinics merged with Fairview Health Services, a system of seven hospitals and thirty clinics, to become University of Minnesota Medical Center, Fairview. The medical center was named among the nation's best in 2008 by *U.S. News & World Report,* ranking among the nation's top fifty hospitals in ten medical specialties.[91] Most of the AHC's faculty physicians (more than 650) and approximately 1,300 health professionals are members of University of Minnesota Physicians, which provides innovative clinical care in more than one hundred specialties and subspecialties and has a primary affiliation with the medical center.

The AHC also is committed to providing outreach to Minnesota through an extensive array of venues, from its Mini Medical School to news columns by the AHC's health experts to continuing education.[92] One of the AHC's most far-reaching and innovative outreach venues is its Community-University Health Care Center (CUHCC).

Originally opening its doors in 1966 as a pilot project for providing pediatric health care to low-income families in South Minneapolis, the CUHCC has expanded to become a comprehensive community-based provider of medical, dental, mental health, legal, literacy, and other related services.[93] It also serves as a training site for AHC students and residents, with the partnerships between AHC departments and the clinic providing students with a community health orientation, as well as allowing the clinic to enhance its services to the community. The CUHCC provides in-clinic programs targeted to specific groups of patients, as well as specialized outreach programs for patients in collaboration with other community agencies.

The CUHCC's menu of programs is too extensive to present in its entirety here. A few of the more innovative programs that reflect the clinic's commitment to keeping pace with contemporary health care outreach opportunities include:

- Culturally Specific Adult Mental Health Rehabilitative Services Program—for Laotians, Hmong, Vietnamese, Cambodians, Somalis and

Latinos who have a diagnosis of serious mental illness and could benefit from learning independent living skills, discussing mental health symptoms, participating in activities that include crafts and food preparation, and being connected to other needed community resources.[94]

- Sexual Assault Program for East African Women—Culturally appropriate advocacy services for East African immigrants and refugees who have experienced rape or assault in the United States or in their homelands during civil war.
- Culturally Specific Diabetes Program—Facilitated by an interdisciplinary health team, patient education groups are available in six languages to support the effective management of diabetes through sharing dietary information and information about how to monitor diabetes, as well as through the provision of general care for diabetes-related medical problems.
- Reach Out and Read Program—Volunteers read to young children in the clinic's waiting room to encourage literacy. The children choose high-quality, developmentally appropriate books to bring home with them after their medical appointments, and staff members give four thousand to five thousand books annually to children at the clinic.[95]

U of M has not received the same kind of attention that other urban-based universities have for its commitment to developing social capital. But it is obvious that it has been engaged in a creative interpretation of the land-grant mission for the benefit of urban Minnesota. Moreover, this reinterpretation has been comprehensive, embracing the activities of not only the helping professions and the applied social sciences, but also the university's world-class medical centers and programs. It is one more example of how a major, internationally known research university has become centrally involved in the economic and cultural development of its own community.

## THE OHIO STATE UNIVERSITY

Like UW and U of M, The Ohio State University (OSU) is a land-grant institution whose mission has helped support, as well as respond to, changes to the communities it serves. Made possible through the Morrill Act, the school was originally established as the Ohio Agricultural and Mechanical College in 1870. It was renamed The Ohio State University in 1878.[96] Classes began in 1873 with twenty-four students meeting at "the old Neil farm" about two miles north of Columbus; in 1878, the first class of six men graduated.

OSU has now granted more than six hundred thousand degrees.[97] In the fall of 2008, OSU's enrollment stood at 61,568 students, and its multiple campuses and other university locations and facilities covered almost sixteen thousand acres. In fiscal year 2009, OSU's budget was $4.22 billion. Its fiscal year 2008 research expenditures were $706.2 million, and its endowment stood at more than $2 billion as of June 30, 2008. OSU's total employee head count stood at just under forty thousand in the fall of 2008.

OSU's original land-grant outreach mission has expanded significantly in scope and stature in response to changing economic and social trends that have presented formidable challenges to Ohio and to OSU's increasingly urbanized environs in Columbus. The state's economy has been lagging behind the nation since the 1960s, with population growth, job growth, and income growth falling below national averages.[98] In addition, overall educational attainment trends in Ohio have raised serious concerns for its position in an emerging knowledge-based economy.[99] While Ohio has experienced a recent increase in the number of high school graduates, similar gains have not been experienced at the college level, with an overwhelming majority of Ohio's counties falling below the national average for higher education attainment in 2000.

Closer to home, Columbus is a dynamic metropolitan area that has the full range of urban opportunities and challenges. In recent years, OSU experienced a number of the same concerns that were felt by the University of Pennsylvania in Philadelphia. The social and economic dislocation of neighborhoods surrounding the university impinged on the quality and appeal of campus life. And while Penn embraced the commitment of its founder, Ben Franklin, to making knowledge practical as the basis of its new commitment to community revitalization initiatives, OSU asserted that the land-grant tradition was directly applicable to its embrace of neighborhood renewal. We observed in chapter 2 how OSU responded to declining conditions in its neighboring communities by taking a lead role in promoting housing revitalization, including making a financial commitment on the part of the university that was well beyond what almost any other institution was willing to assume.

## Building Social Capital

As a land-grant university, OSU has long-established partnerships for outreach and engagement that take a variety of forms—from focused, short-term partnerships to address immediate local needs to broader, long-term partnerships to address more far-reaching, enduring needs.[100] To help leverage, integrate, and increase the impact of such partnerships, OSU created and staffed the Office of University Outreach and Engagement in 2001. The office has overseen the awarding of millions of dollars in grants to sustain and extend collaborative solutions to community issues.[101] It has supported the launching of a nationally groundbreaking, comprehensive approach to urban revitalization in Columbus, Ohio. It has supported a unique collaboration—originally established by the College of Engineering—between OSU and Honda of America, which spans education, research, and public service for a variety of audiences and beneficiaries. For these two and the many other outreach efforts OSU operates, the Carnegie Foundation for the Advancement of Teaching recently recognized the university for its community outreach efforts and for its community-engaged curriculum.[102]

The OSU Medical Center (OSUMC) is also a key player in the institution's effort to build social capital. OSUMC harnesses its vast resources to build social capital through central Ohio, across the state, and throughout the world, by helping to break down various barriers to quality health care, such as access, education, transportation, literacy, and fear.[103] It does this through a variety of approaches, including:

- Community education, public speaking, classes, and student mentoring
- Outreach activities, sponsored events, and collaboration with schools and other community organizations
- Preventive screenings and support-group leadership
- Free and reduced-cost clinics
- Consultation to, or representation on, community boards and committees by community relations professionals
- Medical education and research that stimulate job growth and economic prosperity
- Monetary contributions, including subsidized health services
- A host of community outreach programs that build social capital in targeted urban areas and rural areas, as well as on statewide and global levels[104]

For instance, in a rural southeastern area of the state, OSUMC is playing an important role in the delivery of personalized health care through a community-based, participatory research study that looks at the significant health problems that affect disadvantaged groups such as women in the Appalachian region, where there is a high rate of cancer (especially cervical cancer), heart disease, and lung disease.[105] With funding from the National Cancer Institute, the study seeks to directly improve the health of women in the region by empowering them to take charge of their well-being, such as through participation in a smoking cessation program, and to reduce the economic burden on society caused by tobacco use. And, in rural northwest Ohio, OSU physicians, medical residents, and students travel to Amish homes to meet with groups of women to increase their awareness of and participation in prenatal care. The OSU medical teams bring modern equipment, such as a laptop computer, fetal Doppler monitor, electronic blood pressure cuff and portable scales, to an Amish family home, where pregnant women arrive in horse-drawn buggies to receive prenatal care and listen to a guest speaker with specialized experience.

OSUMC also reaches out to underserved populations in urban areas. For instance, the medical center has teamed up with the Mount Vernon Avenue District Improvement Association to enrich the economic and cultural vitality and the health of residents in Columbus' Near East Side, through programs developed collaboratively by OSU and local business leaders.[106] Even more far-reaching is OSU's Urban Residency Program, one of the first programs in the country to gear resources specifically to an urban population. OSUMC physicians are trained to care for the unique needs of people living in urban areas who might otherwise have to travel out of their community to obtain medical treatment.

In addition, many of the OSUMC community outreach efforts are statewide in scope. For example, OSUMC staff members chair the Ohio Asthma Coalition, which created a statewide asthma plan.[107] The group provides advocacy for asthma programs, as well. OSUMC also strives to improve communities through global missions, such as Project EAR. The nonprofit organization, which involves OSU surgeons and audiologists and is headed by an OSU neurotologist, has helped improve the hearing and health of more than one thousand of some of the poorest people in the Caribbean nation of the Dominican Republic.[108] Project EAR volunteers coordinate the collection and transport of supplies, while a native Dominican Republic otolaryngologist screens patients and prepares them for the surgical care that the OSU Project EAR team provides on-site.

### Promoting Economic Development

A key outreach arm of OSU that works closely with the Office of the Senior Vice President for University Outreach and Engagement is OSU Extension. In response to the previously mentioned challenges facing Ohio as well as challenges not detailed here, OSU Extension, which has thrived for more than a century, has expanded its partnerships beyond the traditional agricultural, veterinary medicine, and human ecology sciences to also include those that help shape economic development, expand appreciation of the arts, tackle issues of community health, and address the needs of small businesses.[109] OSU Extension now has offices in all eighty-eight counties of Ohio. In 2005, OSU Extension had almost 760,000 direct contacts with Ohioans; more than 34,000 volunteers, working with Extension faculty and staff, contributed almost 1.5 million hours to delivering educational programs.

An economic impact study of OSU Extension was conducted in 2005 by Battelle, a global science and technology institute adjacent to the university that conducts more than $3.4 billion in annual research and development.[110] Battelle determined that, beyond the benefits of its transfer of scientific knowledge and functional expertise, OSU Extension generates a significant economic impact for the state of Ohio.[111] OSU Extension receives funds from the federal government, extramural funding sources, capital resources, and infrastructure to benefit the state. In turn, expenditures by Extension faculty and staff in Ohio then become a significant generator of economic impact. Battelle's analysis of OSU Extension's direct and indirect expenditure impacts shows that OSU Extension generates the following economic benefits for Ohio on an annual basis:

- $159 million in total economic output (sales)
- 1,918 jobs
- $64 million in personal income for Ohio residents
- $4.8 million in tax revenues

Clearly, OSU Extension—which is just one component of OSU's comprehensive, award-winning program of outreach and engagement—is playing a key role in improving the overall quality of life in Ohio and transforming the state's economy.[112] Battelle predicts that university Extension activities will grow in their central importance to economic progress, as knowledge and intellectual capacity become the foremost drivers of modern economies.

## SUMMARY

Land-grant colleges and universities are one of the United States' greatest education inventions. These institutions have enabled the United States to imbue its entrepreneurial, exploratory spirit with the knowledge generated in the world's most successful research laboratories. These colleges and universities combine theory and practice in a manner that gives a distinctive identity to mass higher education in America. Over time, a number of these institutions have become world-class universities, in almost every way that "world class" could be measured.

Today, many of these institutions want to demonstrate that they are as indispensable for the twenty-first century as they were for the nineteenth. In a number of places, such as Ohio, Minnesota, and Wisconsin, land-grant colleges and universities have to apply their expertise to the challenges of states that are declining, not increasing, in population and in economic competitiveness. Often, they have had to do this in environments where funding is limited and even, in some places, where legislators need to be convinced of the continuing utility of higher education to the pressing challenges of their states.

But it is clear that many land-grant universities are working to be central players in state economic development policies intended to restore competitiveness. And they are reinterpreting the land-grant tradition to assume new responsibilities in the provision of health care and the creation of social capital in areas far removed from their traditional rural clientele. We have seen this with universities located in metropolitan areas such as OSU and U of M. But it is also the case for universities such as Virginia Tech, which has a main campus in relatively rural Blacksburg but has expanded its higher education offerings in northern Virginia, the multicultural capital of the state. And it is also true for the University of Georgia, which now looks to Georgia's urban areas as a major laboratory for its expertise.[113] The reinvention of the land-grant tradition is an integral feature of the contemporary commitment of American universities to their communities and states.

## NOTES

1. James E. Sherwood, "The Role of the Land-Grant Institution in the 21st Century," *Research & Occasional Paper Series*: CSHE.6.04 (August 2004), Center for Studies in Higher Education, University of California, Berkeley, repository http://repositories.cdlib.org/cgi/viewcontent.cgi?article=1034&context=cshe (accessed January 9, 2008), 8.

2. U.S. Department of State, "Backgrounder on the Morrill Act," USINFO.STATE.GOV, http://us.infostate.gov/usa/infousa/facts/democrac/27.htm (accessed April 30, 2007), 2.

3. Sherwood, "The Role of the Land-Grant Institution," 2.

4. Sherwood, "The Role of the Land-Grant Institution," 2.

5. Association of Public and Land-Grant Universities (APLU), "Development of the Land-Grant System: 1862–1994," APLU—the Land Grant Tradition, http://www.nasulgc.org/publications/Land_Grant/Development.htm (accessed April 30, 2007), 2.

6. APLU, "Development of the Land-Grant System," 3.

7. APLU, "What Is a Land-Grant College?" APLU—the Land-Grant Tradition, http://www.nasulgc.org/publications/Land_Grant/land.htm (accessed September 8, 2006), 5.

8. U.S. Department of State, "Backgrounder on the Morrill Act," 4; APLU, "What Is a Land-Grant College?" 5.

9. APLU, "Development of the Land-Grant System," 13.

10. U.S. Department of State, "Backgrounder on the Morrill Act," 10.

11. The Library of Congress, September 21, 2007, "Morrill Act," *Primary Documents in American History*, The Library of Congress, http://www.loc.gov/rr/program/bib/ourdocs/Morrill.html (accessed December 12, 2007), paragraph 1.

12. APLU, "A Chronology of Federal Legislation Affecting Public Higher Education," APLU—the Land-Grant Tradition, http://www.nasulgc.org/publications/Land_Grant/Chronology.htm (accessed April 30, 2007).

13. APLU, "Welcome to NASULGC Online," APLU, http://www.nasulgc.org/NetCommunity/Page.aspx?pid=183&srcid=-2 (accessed January 10, 2008).

14. APLU, "A Chronology of Federal Legislation."

15. APLU, "A Chronology of Federal Legislation."

16. APLU, "A Chronology of Federal Legislation."

17. APLU, "A Chronology of Federal Legislation."

18. APLU, "What Is a Land-Grant College?" 6; APLU, "Development of the Land-Grant System," 28.

19. U.S. Department of State, "Backgrounder on the Morrill Act," 5.

20. APLU, "The 105 Land-Grant Colleges and Universities," APLU—the Land-Grant Tradition, http://www.nasulgc.org/publications/Land_Grant/Schools.htm (accessed April 30, 2007), 1.

21. APLU, "Development of the Land-Grant System," 28.

22. Wendi A. Williams, "History & 1890 Land-Grant Institutions," *Metro News: Making Extension Connections* 1, no. 5 (2002), Alabama Cooperative Extension System, http://www.aces.edu/urban/metronews/vol1no5/history.html (accessed January 22, 2008), 6.

23. Williams, "History & 1890 Land-Grant Institutions," 6.

24. Cooperative State Research, Education, and Extension Service (CSREES), "CSREES overview," United States Department of Agriculture—About Us, http://www.csrees.usda.gov/about/background.html (accessed January 29, 2008), 4.

25. Sherwood, "The Role of the Land-Grant Institution," 4.

26. Sherwood, "The Role of the Land-Grant Institution," 5.

27. Kellogg Commission on the Future of State and Land-Grant Universities, *Returning to Our Roots: Executive Summaries of the Reports of the Kellogg Commission on the Future of State and Land-Grant Universities* (Washington, DC: APLU, 2001), preface.

28. APLU, "Kellogg Commission on the Future of State and Land-Grant Universities," APLU—University Engagement, http://www.nasulgc.org/NetCommunity/Page.aspx?pid=305&srcid=751 (accessed January 9, 2008), 2.

29. APLU, "Kellogg Commission," 2, 3.

30. Kellogg Commission, *Returning to Our Roots*, preface.

31. Kellogg Commission, *Returning to Our Roots*, preface.

32. Kellogg Commission, *Returning to Our Roots*, preface.

33. University of Wisconsin (UW), "Almanac," UW—University Communications, http://www.uc.wisc.edu/docs/2006_almanac.pdf (accessed December 12, 2007), 1, 4.

34. John D. Wiley, "Report of the Chancellor's Task Force on University-Business Relations (April 21, 2003)," UW, http://www.chancellor.wisc.edu/businessrelations.html (accessed January 31, 2008), 1.

35. Wiley, "Report of the Chancellor's Task Force," 1.

36. UW, "Almanac," 1.

37. Office of Corporate Relations (OCR), "The Office of Corporate Relations: Annual Report for 2006–2007," UW, http://www.ocr.wisc.edu/images/OCRar0607.pdf (accessed December 13, 2007), 5.

38. UW, "Study: UW–Madison's Essential to State's Economic Growth," Board of Regents of the University of Wisconsin System—News, http://www.news .wisc.edu/8573 (accessed December 14, 2007), 6.

39. NorthStar Economics, Inc. (NorthStar), "The New Economy and the University of Wisconsin–Madison," NorthStar Economics, Inc., http://www.news .wisc.edu/misc/EIS/eis.pdf (accessed December 14, 2007), 33.

40. UW, "Research," UW, http://www.wisc.edu/research/ (accessed December 14, 2007), sidebar.

41. Academic Planning and Analysis, Office of the Provost and the Office of Budget, Planning, and Analysis (Academic Planning et al.), "Data Digest 2006–2007," UW, http://www.bpa.wisc.edu/datadigest/DataDigest2006-2007 .pdf (accessed December 12, 2007), "Quick Facts."

42. UW, "Almanac," 9.

43. OCR, "The Office of Corporate Relations," 2.

44. Academic Planning et al., "Data Digest 2006–2007," "Quick Facts"; UW, "Almanac," 1.

45. NorthStar, "The New Economy," 37.

46. Wiley, "Report of the Chancellor's Task Force," 2; UW, "Almanac," 15.

47. Wiley, "Report of the Chancellor's Task Force," 2.

48. UW, "Strategic Plan: Goals and Initiatives (Revised)," UW, http://www .chancellor.wisc.edu/strategicplan/2005-2006.pdf (accessed January 31, 2008), 9.

49. Wiley, "Report of the Chancellor's Task Force," 4.

50. Wiley, "Report of the Chancellor's Task Force," 3.

51. Goldie Blumenstyk, "A Tight Grip on Tech Transfer," *Chronicle of Higher Education* 53, no. 4 (2006): A31.

52. UW, "Almanac," 11.

53. Blumenstyk, "A Tight Grip," A30.

54. UW, "Building Wisconsin's Economy," 7.

55. Blumenstyk, "A Tight Grip," A32.

56. Wisconsin Alumni Research Foundation (WARF), "Quick Facts," WARF, http://www.warf.org/about/index.jsp?cid=27&scid=36 (accessed January 7, 2008), 1.

57. University Research Park (URP), "About the Park," UW—University Research Park, http://universityresearchpark.org/about/ (accessed December 11, 2007), 2.

58. UW, "Building Wisconsin's Economy," 11.

59. NorthStar, "The New Economy," 38.

60. OCR, "The Office of Corporate Relations," 2; Wiley, "Report of the Chancellor's Task Force," 23–25.

61. NorthStar, "The New Economy," 14.

62. NorthStar, "The New Economy," 15.

63. UW, "Almanac," 6.

64. Academic Planning et al., "Data Digest 2006–2007," 103.

65. UW, "Building Wisconsin's Economy," 8.

66. OCR, "The Office of Corporate Relations," 16.

67. UW, "Outreach," UW—Outreach, http://www.wisc.edu/outreach/ (accessed December 12, 2007), 1, 2–6.

68. UW, "About Us—Morgridge Center for Public Service," UW—Morgridge Center for Public Service, http://www.morgridge.wisc.edu/about.html (accessed December 13, 2007), 1.

69. UW School of Medicine and Public Health, "About the UW School of Medicine and Public Health," UW School of Medicine and Public Health, http://www.med.wisc.edu/about/main/35 (accessed April 23, 2009), 1.

70. UW School of Medicine and Public Health, "About Urban Medicine," UW School of Medicine and Public Health—Urban Medicine, http://www.med.wisc.edu/education/md/urban/about.php (accessed April 23, 2009), 1.

71. John D. Wiley, "From Crossroads to Crisis," *Madison Magazine* (September 2008), http://www.madisonmagazine.com/madison-magazine/september 2008/from-crossroads-to-crisis/ (accessed May 27, 2009), 1.

72. Regents of U of M, "History and Mission," Regents of U of M—About the U, http://www1.umn.edu/twincities/hist.php (accessed February 19, 2009), sidebar.

73. Regents of U of M, "Welcome to the U of M," Regents of U of M—About the U, http://www1.umn.edu/twincities/about.php (accessed February 19, 2009), sidebar; Regents of U of M, "Community Engagement," Regents of U of M, http://www1.umn.edu/twincities/community.php (accessed February 19, 2009), sidebar.

74. Regents of U of M, "Welcome to the U of M," 4.

75. Regents of U of M, "Community Engagement," sidebar.

76. Regents of U of M, "About Us," Regents of U of M—Office for Business & Community Economic Development, http://www.ced.umn.edu/About_Us.html (accessed February 19, 2009), 1.

77. Regents of U of M, "Academic and Corporate Relations Center—Home," Regents of U of M—ACRC, http://www1.umn.edu/urelate/acrc/index.php (accessed February 19, 2009), 1.

78. Regents of U of M, "About ACRC," Regents of U of M—ACRC, http://www.business.umn.edu/aboutacrc.cfm (accessed February 19, 2009), 2.

79. Regents of U of M, "Utilizing Our Resources," Regents of U of M—ACRC, http://www1.umn.edu/urelate/acrc/about.php (accessed February 19, 2009), 2.

80. Regents of U of M, "U of M–Mayo Partnership," Regents of U of M—Academic Health Center, http://www.ahc.umn.edu/research/u-mayo/home.html (accessed February 19, 2009), 2.

81. Mayo Foundation for Medical Education and Research and Regents of U of M, "Economic Impact Study," Mayo Foundation for Medical Education and Research and Regents of U of M—Minnesota Partnership for Biotechnology and Medical Genomics, http://www.minnesotapartnership.info/economic_impact/eqs.cfm (accessed February 19, 2009), 2.

82. Regents of U of M, "Programs & Initiatives," Regents of U of M—the Office for Public Engagement, http://www.engagement.umn.edu/programs/index.html (accessed February 19, 2009), 1.

83. Regents of U of M, "Community Engagement," sidebar.

84. Regents of the University of Minnesota, "100 Years Old and Counting," Extension Centennial 1909–2009, http://blog.lib.umn.edu/extmedia/centennial/ (accessed February 19, 2009); Regents of U of M, "Programs & Initiatives," 11.

85. Regents of U of M, "Community," Regents of U of M—University of Minnesota Extension, http://www.extension.umn.edu/Community/ (accessed February 19, 2009), 1, sidebar.

86. Regents of U of M, "About UROC," Regents of U of M—Urban Research and Outreach/Engagement Center, http://www.uroc.umn.edu/about/index .html (accessed February 19, 2009), 5.

87. Regents of U of M, "About UROC," 6.

88. Regents of U of M, "About UROC," 11.

89. Regents of U of M, "AHC Overview," Regents of U of M—Academic Health Center, http://www.ahc.umn.edu/about/overview/home.html (accessed April 23, 2009), 1.

90. Regents of U of M, "AHC Overview," 3.

91. Regents of U of M, "AHC Overview," 4; University of Minnesota Physicians, "University of Minnesota Physicians," http://www.umphysicians.umn .edu/ (accessed April 24, 2009).

92. Regents of U of M, "Outreach," Regents of U of M—Academic Health Center, http://www.ahc.umn.edu/outreach/home.html (accessed April 23, 2009), 1.

93. Regents of U of M, "About CUHCC," Regents of U of M—Community-University Health Care Center, http://www.ahc.umn.edu/cuhcc/aboutcuhcc .html (accessed April 23, 2009), 1; Regents of U of M, "Healthcare Services," Regents of U of M—Community-University Health Care Center, http://www.ahc. umn.edu/cuhcc/healthcareservices.html (accessed April 24, 2009), 5; Regents of U of M, "History and Milestones," Regents of U of M—Community-University Health Care Center, http://www.ahc.umn.edu/cuhcc/aboutcuhcc/history.html (accessed April 24, 2009), 1.

94. Regents of U of M, "Programs," Regents of U of M—Community-University Health Care Center, http://www.ahc.umn.edu/cuhcc/aboutcuhcc/ programs.html (accessed April 23, 2009), 2.

95. Regents of U of M, "Programs," 10; Regents of U of M, "Healthcare Services," 4.

96. The Ohio State University (OSU), "Ohio State History and Traditions," OSU—News Room, http://www.osu.edu/news/history.php (accessed February 20, 2009), 1, 2.

97. OSU, "Statistical Summary (2008)," OSU—The Ohio State University, http://www.osu.edu/osutoday/stuinfo.php (accessed February 20, 2009).

98. Mark D. Partridge and Jill Clark, *Our Joint Future: Rural-Urban Interdependence in 21st Century Ohio,* Brookings Institution, http://www.brookings.edu/ events/2008/~/media/Files/events/2008/0910_restoring_prosperity/Partridge .pdf (accessed February 20, 2009), 1.

99. Ayesha Enver, Mark D. Partridge, and Jill Clark, *Growth and Change: Closing Ohio's Knowledge Worker Gap to Build a 21st Century Economy,* The Ohio State University, Department of Agricultural, Environmental, and Developmental Economics, Extension, http://exurban.osu.edu/growthandchange08/educ.pdf (accessed February 20, 2009), i, ii.

100. OSU, *Time and Change: A Decade of Progress at The Ohio State University— Re-accreditation Self-Study Report for the Higher Learning Commission of the North*

*Central Association of Colleges and Schools*, OSU, http://oaa.osu.edu/reaccredita tion/documents/OhioStateSelfStudyReport.pdf (accessed February 20, 2009), 114.

101. Office of University Outreach & Engagement, OSU, *Building the Future: The Impact of Engaged Partnerships*, Office of University Outreach & Engagement, http://outreach.osu.edu/pdf/OEimpact2008-web.pdf (accessed February 20, 2009), executive summary.

102. OSU, "Ohio State's Outreach Efforts Gain National Recognition," OSU— Ohio State News, http://www.osu.edu/news/newsitem2315 (accessed February 20, 2009), 1, 2.

103. The Ohio State University Medical Center (OSUMC), "Serving Our Community," OSUMC, http://medicalcenter.osu.edu/aboutus/community_ benefits/Pages/index.aspx (accessed April 27, 2009), 1.

104. OSUMC, "Serving Our Community," 1; OSUMC, *Changing the Face of Medicine . . . One Person at a Time: Community Impact Report 2007*, OCUMC, http:// medicalcenter.osu.edu/pdfs/about_osumc/Community_Benefit_Report.pdf (accessed April 27, 2009).

105. OSUMC, *Changing the Face of Medicine*, 5.

106. OSUMC, *Changing the Face of Medicine*, 20.

107. OSUMC, *Changing the Face of Medicine*, 20.

108. OSUMC, *Changing the Face of Medicine*, 10.

109. OSU, *Time and Change*, 103.

110. OSU, *Time and Change*, 115.

111. Battelle, *Ohio State Extension: A Generator of Positive Economic Impacts for Ohio*, OSU, http://extension.osu.edu/about/executive_summary.pdf (accessed February 20, 2009), vi.

112. Battelle, *Ohio State Extension*, v.

113. Karin Fischer, "Reimagining the 21st-Century Land-Grant University," *Chronicle of Higher Education* 55, no. 42 (2009): A14–A15.

*Chapter 5*

# U.S. Higher Education: Community College—a Uniquely American Institution

Community colleges are a uniquely American institution with a long tradition of supporting their local communities.[1] At the start of the twentieth century, growing international economic competition called for a more skilled workforce, which in turn made obtaining postsecondary education an increasingly valuable credential for the marketplace. However, three-quarters of high school graduates were choosing not to further their education, in part because of their reluctance to leave home for a distant college. Around the same time, the nation's rapidly growing public high schools were looking for new ways to serve their communities. It became common for them to add a teacher institute, a vocational education component, or a citizenship school to their standard diploma programs, with the high-school-based community college becoming the most successful type of add-on program.

In 1907, California passed legislation permitting state high schools to offer college-level work.[2] By 1915, the number of junior colleges across the United States had jumped to seventy-four. With the return of soldiers from World War I, the number of public and private two-year colleges reached more than two hundred by 1921.[3] The next surge in the number of two-year colleges came after World War II, when the total climbed to around three hundred. Helping to boost the acceptance of two-year colleges around that time was the 1947 President's Commission on Higher Education, better known as the Truman Commission, which introduced the term "community college."[4]

Then, a series of events in the 1950s and 1960s combined to form what is now considered the nation's major community college movement. In 1952, the original GI Bill of 1944 was extended to Korean War veterans;

in 1953, the Selective Service granted student deferments to all draft-age men enrolled as full-time students. By 1960, there were more than four hundred two-year public colleges.[5] Around this time, Jesse R. Bogue became the executive secretary of the American Association of Junior Colleges; he helped to popularize the term *community college* through his 1950 book, *The Community College.*[6]

The launching of sputnik and the ensuing National Defense Education Act highlighted the need for a technological education.[7] Also, the large cohort of offspring of World War II veterans (baby boomers) hit college age in the early 1960s. Helping to make the community college option more appealing to the wave of baby boomers was B. Lamar Johnson, who in 1968 put together a task force that gave rise to the League for Innovation in the Community College, to promote the community college concept. By 1970, the number of public two-year colleges had reached 847.[8]

Today, there are almost 1,200 public, independent, and tribal community colleges.[9] Community college enrollment stands at 11.5 million, with 6.5 million students enrolled in for-credit programs and 5 million students in noncredit programs. Part-time enrollment stands at about 60 percent. The average age of community college students is twenty-nine years, with close to 60 percent of students older than twenty-two. Minorities make up 35 percent of all community college students, with non-U.S. citizens making up 8 percent. Nearly 40 percent of community college students are the first in their families to attend college, and 17 percent are single parents.

Among the nation's total enrollment of undergraduates, community college students constitute almost half (46 percent) of all U.S. undergraduates, 55 percent of all Native American undergraduates, 55 percent of Hispanic undergraduates, and 46 percent of Asian/Pacific Islander and African American undergraduates.[10] Approximately 77 percent of full-time community college students are employed on a full-time or part-time basis, while 83 percent of part-time community college students are employed on some basis. Almost half (47 percent) of community college students receive some form of financial aid. Each year, community colleges award 555,000 associate degrees and 295,000 certificates; ninety-five community colleges are now awarding baccalaureate degrees.

These numbers are nothing short of astounding, especially when compared with the commonly held views of what the college and university experience is like in the United States. With almost half of all the undergraduates in the United States and with about half of all the minority students enrolled in higher education, community colleges occupy a crucially important role in American higher education. But it is a role that is often mentioned as an afterthought and rarely given an adequately high profile in discussions of American higher education. Moreover, with the additional role that community colleges have played in workforce development through job training and skill enhancement, in industry recruitment through their willingness to tailor specific programs to workplace needs, and in their crucial importance to many regions throughout the nation, the true significance of these institutions becomes increasingly apparent.[11]

The evolution of community colleges in the latter half of the last century and into the first decade of the twenty-first century directly relates to a number of the themes that we have developed about contemporary higher education in general.

Community colleges are essential institutions in the development of social capital in the contemporary world. They provide access to education for individuals, especially those from disadvantaged groups who might not otherwise have had the opportunity to benefit from higher education.[12] Moreover, they often provide this opportunity to individuals who need a second chance—who for a variety of reasons were not able to acquire the skills in high school that would enable them to flourish in higher education.

In addition, community colleges have often wholeheartedly embraced the role of contributing to a region's economic development.[13] In region after region, community colleges are vital players in the effort to nurture economic prosperity in an extraordinarily competitive environment. They help to attract industry; they tailor job training programs to regional needs; and, if a region loses its competitive edge, community colleges are invariably a vital component in the strategy for revitalization.[14] In fact, our changing economy has made the workforce training component of community college an even more significant contributor to regional economic success.

This chapter examines in detail the role that community colleges play in building social capital. We begin by describing how community colleges are providing access to the nation's diverse learning pool, how these institutions are venues of continuing opportunity, and how community colleges are promoting regional economic aspirations. We then provide three brief case studies—Miami Dade College in Florida, Montgomery College in Maryland, and Maricopa County Community College District in Arizona—that are models of access provision, continuing opportunity, and innovative regional development.

## ACCESS, CONTINUING OPPORTUNITY, REGIONAL ECONOMIC DEVELOPMENT

### Providing Access in Multiple Ways

A growing number of students are making community colleges their starting point on the path of lifelong learning that is required in today's knowledge-based economy, and that number is expected only to increase.

Enrollment at community colleges has grown by about 20 percent in the past decade, with no signs of tapering off, according to the American Association of Community Colleges.[15]

Today, community colleges are the top choice for more and more students of all abilities who want to be relevant to today's workforce.[16] Even high school students with academic credentials strong enough to gain admission to reputable four-year colleges (referred to as "students with choice") are more frequently opting to start their collegiate careers at one of the nation's community colleges.[17]

A core and enduring way in which community colleges support access is through their proximity to the community members they serve. The convenient location of community college campuses makes it easier for local residents to attend.[18] Convenient scheduling of classes also supports access. Evening classes are held at various campus locations, with almost as many students attending at night as do during the day.

More recently, community colleges have redefined access in response to demographic shifts in the general population and an interest in serving the working population.[19] Recognizing that proximity to campuses and evening classes are no longer adequate to ensure access for many of today's learners, community colleges have become leaders in employing new, more diverse, and innovative instructional strategies, such as:

- Short-term courses that teach specific skills and begin at various times throughout the year
- Open-entry/open-exit courses, which a student can enter any day or night of the week and exit as soon as mastery is attained
- Computer-assisted instruction, which makes it possible for a student to learn non-computer-related content, as well as how to use computers to accomplish a myriad of tasks, with a minimum of faculty lecture
- Online courses, which make it possible for a person to complete courses on any Internet-connected computer

In addition to launching innovative instruction delivery techniques to make their programs more physically accessible, community colleges continue to make their programs more financially accessible.[20] The original founders of the community college movement intended to make higher education affordable to everyone.[21] Although most community colleges initially required students to pay very little or no tuition, they have had to increase tuition in recent years. The entire higher education financing system has been adversely affected by declining state subsidies and a faster increase in cost per student than inflation or family income. However, while average tuition and fees rose 36 percent at private four-year colleges and universities and rose 51 percent at public four-year institutions from 1995 to 2005 (after adjusting for inflation), they rose only 30 percent (and from a lower initial base) at community colleges over the same period.[22] Even with the rise in tuition for a community college education, it remains a tremendous bargain, at just over one-third of the cost for public four-year institutions.[23]

According to a 2008 article in the *New York Times*, more and more nontraditional students are returning to school to improve their job skills during the current economic downturn.[24] Because these students cannot afford or are not willing to pay the cost of four-year colleges, many community colleges are experiencing record enrollments.

In addition to having lower average tuitions than four-year colleges, community colleges help with affordability through dual enrollment programs. For more than twenty-five years, community colleges have been successful with dual enrollment programs in which high school students meet graduation requirements by taking college courses and, after completing high school, matriculate at a community college for employment preparation or to complete the first two years of a baccalaureate degree.[25] A new development in dual enrollment programs is the establishment of formal alliances, which coordinate high school, community college, and university curricula so that students can progress without duplication of time, energy, or expense. Dual enrollment programs also ease the transition to postsecondary education from high school.[26]

Even outside of dual enrollment programs, community colleges offer a less challenging entry point for many students through easier application and admission processes than most traditional four-year colleges. In fact, open admission has long been a hallmark of the community college movement.[27]

As centers of lifelong learning, community colleges also provide students with easier access to higher education once they complete their two-year degree. Community colleges serve as a good on-ramp for students in pursuit of a four-year degree.[28] University transfer education, which enables students to transition to four-year colleges and universities, has long been an important part of the community college mission.[29] In the past, the transfer function happened in a more linear way, with high school students going on to a community college and from there to a university. Today, it happens in a more circuitous fashion, with many college students attending the institution of higher education that most cost-effectively meets their needs in a less sequential manner.

To better facilitate transfer education, community colleges have assembled Articulation Task Forces to develop programs that enable their students to transfer to a public state university as a full junior as if they had completed their first two years on the four-year institution's campus.[30]

Another new trend is that most vocational courses will transfer to a university, and many community college graduates who earn an associate degree in a vocational track can transfer to a four-year university as a full junior. Consequently, many vocational students are transferring to a university and working on a baccalaureate degree. Today, most two-year colleges are highly respected within their local communities for providing transfer credits that are recognized by brand-name universities as equal to their own.[31] The value of the transfer credits is now recognized by students, as well.

Looking to the future, growing community college enrollment trends are expected to continue. In the 2006 report of the Commission Appointed by U.S. Secretary of Education Margaret Spellings (Higher Education Commission), "A Test of Leadership: Charting the Future of U.S. Higher Education," one of the commission's stated goals is the creation of a higher education system that is accessible to all Americans throughout their lives.[32] Community colleges, with their physical, financial, and flexible accessibility, are poised to play a leading role in achieving this goal for the twenty-first century's increasingly diverse, lifelong learners.

## Continuing Opportunity

The second prominent theme in the current community college movement is its contribution to the creation of continuing opportunity for those who may not have exited high school with the level of knowledge or the capacity to learn that would enable them to become either successful college students or employed at a desirable level within a knowledge-based economy.

In contemporary society, the educational level necessary for most kinds of success has been increasing.[33] And there has been a growing concern in the United States that young people, as a group, may not compare well with their counterparts around the globe. In 1970, tests of high school seniors in seven industrial countries found that Americans ranked last in math and science.[34] More than thirty-five years later, America's youth sometimes do well on international tests, but U.S. rankings drop as students get older. A 2003 study of fifteen-year-olds in thirty-nine countries placed the United States twenty-fourth in math and nineteenth in science.[35]

The 2006 Higher Education Commission report expressed grave concern over the future of the nation, given the fact that many students never make it to postsecondary education or arrive at postsecondary education without being adequately prepared.[36] The commission's report states, "We are losing some students in our high schools, which do not yet see preparing all pupils for postsecondary education and training as their responsibility."[37] It went on to say that "among high school graduates who do make it on to postsecondary education, a troubling number waste time—and taxpayer dollars—mastering English and math skills that they should have learned in high school."[38] The Higher Education Commission's report noted that inadequate college preparation is compounded by poor alignment between high schools and colleges, often creating an "expectations gap" between what colleges require and what high schools produce.[39]

In their 2007 report, "Innovation America: Investing in Innovation," the National Governors Association and the Pew Center on the States attributed the decline of the United States as one of the world's innovation leaders, in part, to weaknesses in K–12 education.[40] Similarly, The New Commission on the Skills of the American Workforce of the National Center on Education and the Economy (NCEE) released a 2007 report that examined a number of issues with America's K–12 education system and that echoed others in concluding that the educational system was not successfully preparing graduates for a twenty-first-century workforce.[41]

While commissions such as the one appointed by the U.S. secretary of education and the one assembled by the NCEE point to troubling conditions with the K–12 system, others point to social issues in explaining why so many students are not prepared or destined for postsecondary education. Decline in two-parent families, the number of children in poverty served by our high schools, and the increasing number of students who arrive in school without basic English language skills are said to account for some of the poor outcomes that are routinely seen.

Universities nationwide began talking about remediation in the 1970s, with students who graduated from high school arriving on campus not prepared for college.[42] Today, community colleges have essentially been tasked with the responsibility of providing the twenty-first-century skills—both academic and job prep—that many people did not obtain in high school. They are vehicles for offering a second chance or continuing opportunity to a wide swath of the population that, for whatever reason, comes to postsecondary education with identifiable learning gaps. In recent decades, the provision of remedial education in the community college system has increased dramatically. Modern community colleges are now accepting responsibility for the education of even greater numbers of citizens who lack basic academic skills.[43] Community colleges spend $1.4 billion annually on remedial courses for recent high school graduates, according to a 2006 report by the nonprofit group Alliance for Excellent Education.[44]

*Washington Post* columnist, Robert Samuelson, observed in 2006 that "we're often teaching kids in college what they should have learned in high school."[45] He added that good community college remedial education should not be "an excuse for not trying to improve our schools. We would certainly be better off if more students performed better. Nor should it inspire complacency."[46] However, the current reality is that community colleges are in the business of getting students ready for advanced education, as well as getting them equipped to immediately enter the twenty-first-century workforce from high school.

In this respect, the nation's community colleges are assuming an increasingly important role in building social and human capital in contemporary America. While it would certainly be preferable to have an educational system that could ensure more seamless transitions between levels and into the workforce, the role of the community college in keeping opportunity alive for individuals is providing an extraordinary social benefit.

## Economic Development

The third prevalent theme in the current community college movement is the increasingly vital and innovative contribution these institutions are making as potent catalysts for regional economic development, particularly through their workforce training function.[47]

In today's global economy, the need for a skilled American workforce is greater than it ever has been, especially because—as noted previously—other countries are educating their citizens to more advanced levels than the United States is.[48] With the majority of new jobs that will be created by 2014 requiring some postsecondary education and the demographics of the workforce changing, employers increasingly rely on the very students who currently are least likely to complete their education. Without community colleges, millions of students and adult learners would not be able to access the education they need to be prepared for further education or the workplace.

One of the reasons ongoing workforce development has become more necessary is the rapidly changing functions within jobs.[49] When community colleges first became widespread, jobs tended to change little from year to year. However, modern job functions have a volatility that requires workers to constantly learn new skills. With the current requirement for lifelong learning, even those who are in the workforce after completing a two-year degree, four-year degree, or graduate program, as well as those who enter the workforce straight from high school, will require education and training throughout their careers. Community colleges are uniquely positioned to meet the continuing education imperative over the spectrum of today's careers.

The increased focus on information in most of today's industries makes workforce development a never-ending need for employees. Workers now need to be more knowledgeable than their predecessors.[50] For example, in 1965 an automobile mechanic who had read 5,000 pages of technical manuals could fix any automobile on the road, while today the same technician would have to decipher 465,000 pages of technical text to do the same job. Community colleges teach the needed knowledge for today's broad range of jobs in traditional and emerging industries.[51]

In addition, workforce development is more necessary to economic development because the U.S. workforce has gotten smaller.[52] The large numbers of people born immediately after World War II have become middle-aged, and they had fewer children than did their parents, resulting in a smaller number of workers seeking employment. Further diminishing the number of workforce-bound high school graduates is the fact that while about 80 percent of all American high school graduates sought full-time employment immediately upon graduation from high school in 1960, more than 60 percent of high school graduates now defer full-time employment and elect postsecondary education instead. Consequently, most of the young people who have just left high school and are interested in full-time employment today are either dropouts or from the lowest quartile of academic achievement, which has prompted employers to align themselves with community colleges as a way to obtain the training services needed to upgrade the skills of these employees.

This alignment has provided a big push for "tech prep," which is becoming increasingly more important to the U.S. economy. Less than 30 percent of all high school graduates earn baccalaureate degrees, and, in fact, most good jobs do not require a baccalaureate degree, even in today's information age.[53] However, in the twenty-first-century global, knowledge-based economy, the traditional high school diploma no longer prepares students for the workplace—additional education and training are required. Community colleges help compensate for this lack of preparation by bridging the gap between the K–12 education and workforce training communities through a variety of tech prep models.[54]

On the other side of the spectrum of preparing high school dropouts and graduates for their entrée into the workforce is the continuing education of older workers and retirees. According to the *New York Times*, the nation's community colleges are preparing for a wave of baby boomers who are already enrolling in community colleges to earn credentials for a second career as well as to expand their horizons.[55]

Not only are community colleges the choice for more and more learners, they also are becoming the top choice for more and more businesses that want to be competitive in today's global, knowledge-based economy.[56] Postsecondary institutions can serve an invaluable role for the private and public sectors in their geographical region by providing various types of training to employees, as well as partnering with employers to support their recruitment and retention efforts, personnel planning, and other workforce development functions.[57] While different types of higher education institutions bring unique competencies to different workforce development roles, community colleges have the proven track record to provide skills training. And, in the twenty-first century, community colleges have become even more job-oriented, providing training for local firms and offering courses to meet market demands.[58]

Contemporary economic development theory emphasizes the importance of creating successful regional economies as integral to a nation's overall success. These economies typically develop concentrated focus areas of related industries, what Harvard's Michael Porter labeled as clusters.[59] To support these industries, regions must create effective workforce development entities that are dedicated to nurturing the success of the regional economy through job training programs, the establishment of partnerships between industry and the educational system, initiatives that increase the supply of knowledgeable workers by tapping nontraditional recruitment sources, and various other efforts. Regions that are successful in creating these specialized economies will experience higher growth rates, higher income, and an overall quality of life better than those regions that do not execute a thoughtful and comprehensive strategy.

Looking to the future, community colleges are poised to continue to be major factors in the development of successful regional economies. This tends to be broadly recognized in the emerging literature about regional economic development. In response to the unprecedented workforce development needs of the twenty-first century, the New Commission on the Skills of the American Workforce recommended the creation of regional competitiveness authorities that blend regional economic development with regional workforce development to make the United States more competitive.[60] Toward that end, the commission proposed that the federal government authorize governors and state legislators, together with local elected officials, to align workforce areas, economic development areas, and community college districts into common regions based on labor markets, economic activity, and other objective criteria. In including community colleges as a key partner in developing regional economic competitiveness, the commission noted that community colleges are the primary providers of postsecondary education and training in most states and local areas. Under the commission's planned system, community colleges (where they exist) would be designated as the primary adult education providers, in order to connect adult and career-related learning and to encourage continued learning.

The perspective of the New Commission on the Skills of the American Workforce is not the only national perspective that recognizes the critical role of community colleges for the future of the U.S. economy. The National Governors Association and the Pew Center on the States, recognizing that "Ideas and innovation are the most precious currency in the new economy," cited in their 2007 report examples of community colleges that are fueling America's innovation pipeline.[61]

Community colleges are likely to continue to have a tremendous impact on the economic development of regions across the country, through their workforce development role. For instance, of the many community college offerings, the five most popular programs nationwide address key twenty-first-century workforce needs, including nursing, law enforcement, radiology, and computer technologies.[62] Also, 95 percent of businesses and organizations that employ community college graduates recommend community college workforce education and training programs.[63] And, with the average expected lifetime earnings for a graduate with an associate degree standing at about $.4 million more than a high school graduate earns, economic incentives continue to drive up community college enrollment.[64]

## CASE STUDIES

We have selected three community colleges that have addressed the issues of access, continuing opportunity, and economic development in interesting ways. We describe how Miami Dade College in southern Florida has become a model of access for lifelong learners. We show how Montgomery College, just outside Washington, DC, has responded to the challenge of providing continuing opportunity for those who did not acquire the skills necessary for success in their primary and secondary education. And we describe how the Maricopa County Community College District ("Maricopa Community Colleges") in the greater Phoenix area has developed model economic development programs in a system that serves more than a quarter of a million students.

### "Democracy's College": Miami Dade College

In 2006, William Frey, a Fellow with the Metropolitan Policy Program of the Brookings Institution, conducted an analysis of Census Bureau population estimates to determine the distribution of racial and ethnic groups within and across U.S. metropolitan areas since Census 2000.[65] Based on Frey's work, the Brookings Institution reported that Hispanics, Asians, and African Americans remain more likely to reside in large metropolitan areas than the population as a whole. The study also observed that almost one-third of the nation's 361 metropolitan areas registered declines in the white population from 2000 to 2004, with economically stagnant parts of the country among those metropolitan areas experiencing some of the greatest declines. During the same period, minorities contributed the majority of population gains in the nation's fastest-growing metropolitan areas and central metropolitan counties. Frey's analysis also illustrated that this trend was far from complete. The nation's child population is more racially diverse than its adult population. And less than half of all people younger than fifteen are white in nearly one-third of all large metropolitan areas.

President George W. Bush delivered the commencement address at the spring 2007 graduation ceremonies of Miami Dade College (MDC), the largest institution of higher education and one of the most highly regarded colleges in the country.[66] Addressing MDC's graduates, Bush stressed the importance of academic pursuits, telling them:

> Today you are leaving this fine college with a degree with your name on it, and a promise of a better future. . . . You enter a world of unbounded opportunity . . . and new possibilities are opening every day. And the key to unlocking those possibilities is a good education.[67]

He highlighted the importance of academic pursuits for the more than half of MDC students who were raised speaking a language other than English, noting, "Over the years, this school has helped open the door to opportunity to hundreds of thousands of immigrants—and that is why MDC proudly calls itself Democracy's College."[68]

MDC has been "Democracy's College" since it opened its doors to 1,428 students in 1960 as Dade County Junior College, amid the strain of desegregation and the influx of thousands of Cuban refugees.[69] At the time, the college was open to any county resident who had graduated from high school, including the seven black students who made Dade County Junior College the first integrated junior college in Florida, along with the many Cuban refugees seeking to better their lives.[70] By the mid-1960s, enrollment had grown to more than fifteen thousand students.[71] By 1967, it was the largest institution of higher education in Florida and the fastest-growing college in the nation, with more than twenty-three thousand students; it enrolled more freshmen than the University of Florida, Florida State University and the University of South Florida combined.

In the 1970s, the college elevated its expectation of students, setting a new standard for community colleges throughout the nation.[72] K. Patricia Cross, a visiting professor at Harvard's Graduate School of Education during that time, called MDC "the most exciting institution of higher education in the country."[73] Part of the excitement was MDC's diversity, with minorities constituting more than 65 percent of its student body and women constituting more than 55 percent.

The 1980s were years of maturation and recognition for the college.[74] At the close of the 1980s, the college's place in education was nationally recognized: the prestigious University of Texas Community College

Leadership Program identified MDC as the "Number One" community college in America, demonstrating how complementary excellence and diversity can be. The 1990s marked an era during which MDC prepared for a new world economy by launching comprehensive academic and administrative reform.[75] It revamped the academic core and elective courses, modernizing the curriculum to meet the needs of a changing world. In 2006, MDC welcomed its 1.5 millionth student. MDC now has more than 170,000 students, eight campuses, and numerous outreach centers.[76]

Bob McCabe, who was president of Miami-Dade from the late 1970s through 1995, played a significant role in the growth and transformation of Miami-Dade. He was the first community college president to receive a MacArthur Foundation "Genius Award" for his commitment to building the institution and demonstrating the impact that community colleges could have on the future of individuals and the broader community. On his retirement, Senator Bob Graham commended him to Congress for personifying the fundamental precept of American education that knowledge is "not bounded by race or class or religion, that in a truly free society all people have access to learning."[77]

MDC has not lost sight of its urban mission amid its own and the city's enormous growth and change. Simply stated by President Bush in his 2007 commencement address, "This college serves the city of Miami."[78] In a community of 2.3 million people, MDC's role remains central to the region's economic and educational growth.[79] MDC is a leading provider of postsecondary education to its community, with 96 percent of credit students hailing from Miami-Dade County.

About one-third of all minority students attending Florida community colleges are enrolled at MDC.[80] According to the U.S. Department of Education, MDC enrolls more minorities than any other college or university in the country, including the most Hispanics and the second-most African Americans and non-Hispanics. As of fall 2007, MDC's ethnic mix was as follows:

- 9 percent white non-Hispanic
- 19 percent African American non-Hispanic
- 67 percent Hispanic
- 4 percent other

The U.S. Department of Education also reports that MDC graduates more minorities than any other college or university in the country, including the most Hispanics and the most African Americans.

MDC has taken a number of steps to ensure that local populations throughout the sprawling South Florida area have adequate and convenient access to its programs and opportunities. It has developed a multipronged approach that addresses a range of barriers that could otherwise prevent individuals from obtaining the benefits of higher education.

First, MDC has developed convenient campus locations. Until recently, South Florida has been one of the fastest-growing areas in the nation and MDC's campuses required extensive travel from one part of the region to another. Today, while each of MDC's campuses has its own distinct identity and specialties, they also offer a broad base of general education courses, allowing students to take first-year classes at any of the campuses (except the Medical Center Campus).[81] This has given the student body flexible options relevant to the entire region that it serves. For example, students can take their entire set of first-year classes at one location, but if it is more convenient to take some courses near a place of employment and others closer to home, this can be easily arranged. Ensuring access to programs has also entailed utilizing innovative approaches to distance education. In the 1990s, MDC introduced multimedia classrooms and the Virtual College, placing it on the Internet map by allowing students to "attend" class via the World Wide Web.[82] "Democracy's College" also has placed special emphasis on overcoming the language barriers faced by many students. Given the huge immigrant population in Miami-Dade County, MDC's Department of English as a Second Language and Foreign Languages integrates the latest linguistic methodologies in grammar, writing, reading, and speech, which are taught by highly qualified and experienced faculty.[83] Students also have access to state-of-the-art laboratories: the Audio Labs, where students learn to master pronunciation and speaking skills; and the Computer Labs, where students reinforce their grammar, reading, and writing skills. Further supporting MDC's accessibility for immigrants is the college's bilingual studies program. Bilingual studies became a full-fledged division in 1979, with more than two thousand students enrolled in outreach centers in the Little Havana area. The centers soon became the InterAmerican Campus, the nation's largest bilingual facility in higher education.

Yet another way that MDC excels at providing access to postsecondary education is by offering a wide range of for-credit higher education programs that are designed to respond to the education and career needs of the diverse and populous metropolitan Miami-Dade County community.[84] MDC offers the following four-year degrees:

- Bachelor of Science in:
  - Exceptional student education
  - Secondary mathematics education
  - Secondary science, with specialties in biology, chemistry, earth science, and physics
- Bachelor of Applied Science in public safety management
- Bachelor of Science in nursing

MDC's associate degree programs include:

- Associate in Arts (university transfer programs)
- Educator Preparation Institute
- Associate of Applied Science (two-year degree that leads to employment)
- Associate in Science and College Credit Certificates (two-year degrees, college credit and certificate programs in occupational areas, several of which are transferable to the upper division)

MDC's professional programs are offered via twelve schools that include the schools of allied health technologies, architecture and interior design, aviation, business, community education, computer and engineering technologies, education, entertainment and design technology, fire and environmental sciences, funeral services education, justice, and nursing.[85]

According to the U.S. Department of Education, MDC is first in the country among colleges in awarding the most:

- Associate degrees to Hispanics
- Associate degrees to African Americans
- Associate degrees in all disciplines to minorities
- Associate degrees in all disciplines[86]

Approximately nine out of ten MDC students stay in the region and contribute to the local economy after they leave the college.

MDC also facilitates access to postsecondary education by serving as the on-ramp to four-year institutions. More than 76 percent of students with an Associate in Arts degree continue their education at a four-year college or university in Florida immediately upon graduation.[87] MDC has transfer agreements with all of the state universities, as well as numerous agreements with top colleges and universities across the country, including the University of Wisconsin–Madison, Georgia Tech, Smith College, and the University of Texas.

MDC performs on an extraordinarily large scale a task that community colleges across the nation have assumed: providing access to higher education that would not be available to many members of our communities. The services that these institutions perform for the existing and emergent minority communities in the country are often not widely acknowledged. Yet, when one considers that MDC alone serves more than one hundred thousand Hispanic students and more than thirty thousand African American students, the crucial nature of these institutions is easily discerned. So much of the debate about minorities in higher education has focused on the admissions policies of elite universities. However important this question might be, finding even more effective ways of building a ramp to upward mobility through the community college system will impact far more families in the short term.

### Providing Continuing Opportunity: Montgomery College

Besides providing access to higher education to underserved groups, community colleges have become an important vehicle for addressing educational goals that were not successfully met in the K–12 education system. This is the case everywhere, but it is especially true for many of the urban and metropolitan populations that are served by many community colleges. In almost every major American city today, there is an ongoing political struggle about control of the schools. There is hardly a big-city mayor who has not attempted to gain greater influence over the schools in order to improve their outcomes. Washington, DC, Chicago, Philadelphia, Los Angeles, Detroit . . . the list goes on. And, in a number of places, the relevant state government has attempted to exercise extraordinary powers over selected metropolitan school districts, at times even placing systems in effective receivership. In almost every case, the ostensible reason for the effort is the stated belief that the K–12 school system is failing students in some important way, either in not preparing them for four-year institutions or in not providing them with the skill sets necessary for productive employment.

Community colleges have increasingly been tasked with the responsibility of offering the remedial courses that will enable individuals to have continuing opportunities even if they did not succeed in high school. Few would argue that this is an ideal situation, and, in a better world, there would not be so many students who require remedial education. But one of the great values of the community college system is that it flexibly and creatively responds to the needs of the students who come their way and not to an idealized conception of what high school graduates should be. In many instances, community colleges have assumed the role of providing continuing opportunities innovatively and with great determination.

Montgomery College (MC) in Maryland exemplifies best practices among urban colleges in preparing underserved, at-risk students for postsecondary education and training.

Based in Maryland, about twenty miles north of the nation's capital, Montgomery College began offering classes in 1946; those classes took place in the evenings at a local high school and were attended by approximately two hundred men and women.[88] Today, MC has become a multicampus institution with more than twenty thousand for-credit students and fifteen thousand continuing education students.[89] Over the past sixty years, more than half a million men and women have attended MC's campuses in Takoma Park, Rockville, and Germantown, Maryland, in addition to those who have come to its numerous training centers and continuing education sites, to take individual courses for skill building and personal interest or to complete the first two years of traditional college degree programs.[90] In 2007, the *New York Times* cited MC among ten or so community colleges across the country that are frequently named models of success by scholars who were interviewed for the article.[91]

According to fall 2006 enrollment data for MC, 39.8 percent of students are white, 28.1 percent are black, 15.8 percent are Hispanic, and 15.6 percent are Asian.[92] A majority of students are twenty-one or older (58.7 percent), female (54.9 percent), and taking classes on a part-time basis (61.6 percent). MC serves approximately one-quarter of Montgomery County's graduating high school students, with almost 90 percent of the college's students coming from Montgomery County.

Until the close of the twentieth century, Montgomery County had a reputation for affluence, more than double the national percentage of adults with post–high school degrees, and a nationally recognized public school system.[93] However, like MC, Montgomery County Public Schools (MCPS) now have significant diversity within the student body, including diversity in income, college preparation level, race, ethnic background, native language, and cultural attitudes toward education. While MCPS had a 94 percent white student body in 1968, by the mid-1990s the system had grown to 125,000 students in twenty-one high schools, twenty-six middle schools, and 123 elementary schools; the student makeup was 57 percent white, 19 percent African American, 12 percent Asian, and 12 percent Hispanic.

In 1994 the first state-mandated Student Outcome and Achievement Report (SOAR) indicated that 57 percent of MCPS graduates enrolling in MC required math remediation and almost 40 percent were not reading at college level.[94] Not only did the statistics stun local educators and residents, but they also generated intense interest and questioning from the local media, including the *Washington Post*, *Montgomery Gazette*, and *Montgomery Journal*, which wanted an explanation for how a highly acclaimed school system with a $900 million budget could graduate large numbers of students assessed as underprepared according to the local community college.

At that time, MC already offered extensive developmental services to its students who were not academically prepared for college-level work.[95] However, up until the release of the 1994 SOAR data, the relationship between MC and MCPS was cordial but distant. In response to the newly prominent achievement gap between local high school graduation and college requirements, close communication and collaboration began to occur between all levels of MC and MCPS, from college and school staff on up to the college's trustees and the school system's board of education. In 1996, a well-attended press conference was held to announce the Partnership Initiative, a collaboration between MC and MCPS that would include testing, research, follow-up professional development, and curriculum sharing to increase the college readiness of MCPS graduates. The Partnership was launched at three pilot high schools.

Today, the MC/MCPS Partnership Initiative consists of more than thirty joint projects for the benefit of students.[96] Partnership projects help identify and monitor college readiness through PSAT and assessment testing and support, and accelerate student success by easing the transition from high school to college through curriculum development, summer programs, early placement programs, and school-based intervention programs. MC and MCPS also work together to extend outreach to parents and the community through the *Prep Talk* newsletter and television show, parent information meetings, and an annual leadership breakfast that brings all MCPS principals together with MC and MCPS administrators for discussions of present and future partnerships.

One of the key initiatives of the partnership, the Gateway to College program at MC, serves at-risk youth, sixteen to twenty years old, who have stopped attending Montgomery County public high schools or who are not on course to graduate.[97] The Gateway to College program was developed at Portland Community College in Oregon, which selected MC as one of the first two community colleges nationwide to replicate the program.[98] The MC/MCPS collaborative program provides students with the opportunity to simultaneously accumulate high school and college credits, earning their high school diploma while progressing toward an associate degree or certificate. Support for the program comes from Portland Community College, a national intermediary of the Bill and Melinda Gates Foundation and the Gates Foundation's partners (the Carnegie Corporation of New York, the Ford Foundation, and the W. K. Kellogg Foundation); the program is funded through MC and MCPS.

Sharing resources and establishing common goals have begun to change the lives of students in Montgomery County.[99] Boundaries between MC and MCPS curricula and instructional objectives have started to dissolve into a more seamless effort that is yielding measurable progress. Demonstrating the effectiveness of MC/MCPS collaboration are test results from a recent cohort from MCPS's Seneca Valley High School. After the group of around sixty students participated in MC-led preparatory sessions, their college readiness jumped from 29 percent to 51 percent in reading and from 40 percent to 46 percent in sentence structure.[100] For math, their college readiness rose from 37 percent to 51 percent. In addition to the prestige of their accomplishment, the students deemed "College Ready" collectively saved $37,500 by avoiding remedial courses if they chose to attend MC.[101] Beyond the MC/MCPS Partnership Initiative, the college offers a broad spectrum of developmental supports for students, including:

- Assessment services to determine students' college readiness
- Remedial courses in reading, English, and math
- Credit courses that support academic success, ranging from a class on developing strong study habits to a class on building confidence in math
- An Online Student Success Center, including a Virtual Counseling and Advising Center
- Campus-based Learning Centers dedicated to giving students the tools, skills, and confidence they need to succeed in college and beyond
- TRIO Student Support Services, a federally funded grant program that provides intensive academic assistance, including remedial instruction, to help qualifying low-income students stay in college and, eventually, pursue their baccalaureate degrees
- Project SUCCESS, a program that is open to all MC students and offers mentoring, study groups, tutoring sessions, workshops, counseling, and social, cultural, and educational activities
- Boys to Men mentoring program, aimed specifically at the retention of black male students
- Study skills and strategies resources aimed at improving time management, studying habits, test-taking abilities, learning styles, goal setting, memory development, and stress management
- The Student Success Center, which provides one-to-one and group tutoring sessions
- The Medical Learning Center, which provides state-of-the-art computers, books, and videos, as well as two instructional assistants, to support the learning needs of health science students[102]

### Urban Economic Development: Maricopa Community Colleges

Across the United States, the traditional workforce training function of community colleges has assumed an even greater role in driving regional economic development in the twenty-first century.[103] That is especially true in economically depressed urban areas. In addition to the growing demographic diversity and the scarcity of infrastructure resources that suburban sprawl has created in inner cities, another consequence has been the movement of employment and economic activity from the center of the metropolitan region to the periphery; this has lowered opportunities for gainful employment for low-income residents of central cities and inner-ring suburbs, especially those residents with a substandard education.[104] Therefore, urban community colleges have had to assume a more prominent role in regional economic development by striving to build the human capital of some of the most economically stagnant cities in the country.

A 2002 joint study by the Initiative for a Competitive Inner City (ICIC) and CEOs for Cities looked at the role that postsecondary institutions can play in urban and regional economic growth.[105] To encourage city leaders to leverage the assets of colleges and universities, they developed a strategic framework that included workforce development. The ICIC/CEOs for Cities study cited several ways that urban colleges and universities can assist their regions with workforce development, including:

- Recruiting, training, retaining, and promoting workers, especially workers who need their skills upgraded or adults who are entering the workforce for the first time
- Conducting research on labor supply and demand, as well as workforce development best practices
- Program design and capacity building for workforce development partners
- Facilitating workforce development partnerships and programs through outreach to local and regional businesses

Urban community colleges are beginning to adopt innovative versions of these strategies, as the following case of the Maricopa Community Colleges (MCCs) in the Phoenix, Arizona, metropolitan area illustrates.

The MCCs are dedicated to meeting the workforce and economic development needs of the businesses and citizens of the greater Phoenix area.[106] With more than 260,000 students taking credit and noncredit courses each academic year, the MCCs and Centers are one of the largest higher education systems in the world, the largest community college district in the United States, and the largest provider of higher education and job training, including the largest provider of health care workers, in the state of Arizona.[107]

MCC has assigned a high priority to more contemporary economic development roles, in response to the emerging knowledge-based economy. With the greater emphasis on information access and utilization skills in the workplace today, MCC has stepped up its service to local residents and industries by providing more responsive workforce development services, in tandem with business support services. The MCCs serve as a major resource for business and industry, as well as for individuals seeking education and job training.[108]

Serving as a general resource for local businesses is the MCC Small Business Development Center (SBDC), which is one of the bases for the

Arizona Small Business Development Center Network.[109] SBDC provides a roster of vital support services to area businesses to help them succeed, such as:

1. Confidential, one-on-one counseling by diverse business professionals at no charge
2. Referrals to industry-specific business information and educational resources
3. Low-cost seminars and workshops
4. Online seminars (self service 24/7)
5. Live webinars[110]

Another economic development resource, the MCC Center for Workforce Development, connects the programs, resources, and services of the ten MCCs and two skill centers with employers in the greater Phoenix region.[111] As the recognized leader in greater Phoenix in fulfilling the job training needs of diverse employer communities throughout Maricopa County, the center brings together industry and education for discussions on curriculum and faculty training. The Center for Workforce Development is an active partner with the greater Phoenix employer community around workforce training, economic development initiatives, and industry data availability in the following key sectors: architecture and construction; bioscience; business services; education; health services; information technology; manufacturing; public safety; transportation, distribution, and logistics; and sustainability and green technologies.[112] To highlight just one of those key sector areas, MCC's workforce development enterprise has been instrumental in helping to create a biosciences niche in Arizona.[113] Since the late 1990s, Arizona has strategically focused on developing its existing and emerging clusters of strength to build an innovation-oriented research enterprise. In support of this goal on a regional level, in 1994 the MCCs targeted more than $100 million of a voter-approved bond package for biosciences and health care training. More recently, MCC's GateWay Community College (GateWay) raised $6 million from the Department of Commerce, the Economic Development Administration, and the City of Phoenix for the design and construction of a bioscience incubator on its campus in a downtown redevelopment area.[114] The new incubator will help strengthen the bioscience industry in the state of Arizona by addressing an identified shortage of affordable lab space, growing new companies, marketing new technologies, and supporting workforce training needs.

In addition to targeted economic development units and initiatives, MCC's ten colleges help fulfill the community college district's workforce development role by specializing in career and job training programs for area residents.[115] Whether just out of high school, beginning or reentering college, or seeking lifelong education, citizens of Maricopa County have a wide range of opportunities through the MCCs, which offer approximately one thousand occupational programs (degrees and certificates), and thirty-seven academic associate degrees.[116]

Classes are highly affordable, easily accessible and offered in a variety of formats, including online, televised, traditional classroom, hybrid, mail, accelerated, evening, weekend, and open-entry/open-exit choices.[117] Also, transfer agreements with public and private colleges and universities enable seamless transitions to four-year institutions.

Another way that MCC supports workforce development in the greater Phoenix area is through its efforts at reaching underserved populations. According to the 2000 U.S. Census, nearly half a million adults in Maricopa County were neither enrolled in high school nor had a high school credential.[118] One way MCC is helping to address this issue is through Adult Basic Education (ABE) classes offered by Rio Salado College. In 1979 when the ABE program was established, it enrolled seven hundred students.[119] Today, over thirteen thousand students are utilizing the ABE program, with Rio Salado now serving not only adults who did not complete high school, but also non-English speaking adults, incarcerated individuals, adults with physical and mental challenges, and other adults considered "at risk" in the general population.[120] Classes are funded by the Arizona Department of Education, Adult Education Division. After completing an ABE program, 85 percent of participants were successful at improving their employment, increasing both their skills and pay level.[121]

One more MCC workforce development initiative aimed at underserved populations is the GateWay Early College High School. In 2004, GateWay Early College High School was one of only fourteen schools in the United States to be awarded a Tech Prep Demonstration Program grant.[122] GateWay received almost $700,000 to help design and implement a Tech Prep program for incoming high school juniors who focus their academic studies in one of five technical or vocational areas of study:

- Automotive technology
- Hydrologic technology
- Nursing
- Web development
- Networking, including networking administration and security and networking technology

GateWay's Tech Prep program offers a high school education that facilitates a seamless transition into community college courses leading to a certificate of completion or an associate degree. Each of the occupational areas is aligned with industries that are in great need of qualified employees, making Tech Prep graduates highly employable.

## CONCLUSION

The United States must ensure that a broad cross-section of its citizens receives postsecondary education and workforce training, in order for the country (1) to remain competitive in the twenty-first-century global, knowledge-based economy; and (2) to provide today's emerging communities with an acceptable quality of life. While four-year institutions of higher education will continue to play an important role, community colleges—especially in the nation's highly and diversely populated urban regions—will be central to achieving these two missions. Innovation and responsiveness will need to be the hallmarks of community college initiatives related to accessibility, continuing education, and economic development, as regional and global conditions continue to change rapidly and often in unexpected ways. The three cases presented here epitomize how urban community colleges can continue to honor their long tradition of supporting local economies, while keeping pace with shifting demographic, educational, and economic trends.

## NOTES

1. John Bradley, "The Community College Movement," http://www.emc.maricopa.edu/faculty/bradley/organizational_leadership/edu250/comcol.htm (accessed February 19, 2008), 1; American Association of Community Colleges (AACC), "Historical Information," AACC—About Community Colleges, http://www.aacc.nche.edu/aboutCC/history/pages/default/aspx (accessed May 7, 2007), 1.

2. Harold A. Geller, *A Brief History of Community Colleges and a Personal View of Some Issues (Open Admissions, Occupational Training and Leadership)*, George Mason University, http://www.eric.ed.gov/ERICDocs/data/ericdocs2sql/content_storage_01/0000019b/80/19/95/c3.pdf (accessed March 3, 2009), 4.

3. Geller, *A Brief History of Community Colleges*, 5.

4. Geller, *A Brief History of Community Colleges*, 6.

5. Geller, *A Brief History of Community Colleges*, 6.

6. AACC, "Significant Events," AACC—Historical Information, http://www.aacc.nche.edu/AboutCC/history/Pages/significantevents.aspx (accessed March 3, 2009).

7. Geller, *A Brief History of Community Colleges*, 7.

8. Geller, *A Brief History of Community Colleges*, 7.

9. AACC, "CC STATS Home (2008)," AACC, http://www2.aacc.nche.edu/research/index.htm (accessed September 18, 2008).

10. AACC, "CC STATS Home (2008)."

11. AACC, "CC STATS Home (2007)," AACC, http://www2.aacc.nche.edu/research/index.htm (accessed February 18, 2008), 2.

12. AACC, "CC STATS Home (2007)," 2.

13. AACC, "CC STATS Home (2007)," 2.

14. Initiative for a Competitive Inner City (ICIC) and CEOs for Cities, *Leveraging Colleges and Universities for Urban Economic Revitalization: An Action Agenda* (Boston: ICIC and CEOs for Cities, 2002), 33.

15. Gary Robertson, "Community College First Choice for Many," *Richmond Times-Dispatch* (June 25, 2007), http://www.inrich.com (accessed June 25, 2007), 5.

16. David Pluviose, "More High-Achieving Students Are Choosing Community Colleges First," *Community College News* (February 21, 2008), Diverse Online, http://diverseeducation.com/artman/publish/article_10714.shtml (accessed February 21, 2008), 3.

17. AACC, "CC STATS Home (2007)"; Pluviose, "More High-Achieving Students," 1.

18. Bradley, "The Community College Movement," 14.

19. Bradley, "The Community College Movement," 18.

20. U.S. Department of Education, *A Test of Leadership: Charting the Future of U.S. Higher Education* (Washington, DC: U.S. Department of Education, 2006), xi.

21. Bradley, "The Community College Movement," 13.

22. U.S. Department of Education, *A Test of Leadership*, 10.

23. Bradley, "The Community College Movement," 13.

24. Sam Dillon and Tamar Lewin, "Pell Grants Said to Face Shortfall of $6 Billion," *New York Times*, September 18, 2008, http://www.nytimes.com/2008/09/18/education/18grant.html (accessed September 18, 2008).

25. Bradley, "The Community College Movement," 51.

26. Pluviose, "More High-Achieving Students," 16.

27. Bradley, "The Community College Movement," 11.

28. "A Conversation with the *Times-Dispatch*: The Presidents of Virginia Commonwealth University and J. Sargeant Reynolds Community College Sat Down for a Discussion with Members of the *Times-Dispatch*'s Editorial Staff and Newsroom," *Richmond Times-Dispatch*, January 20, 2008, http://www2.richmond.com/cva/ric/search.apx.-content-articles-RTD-2008-01-20-0114.html (accessed January 22, 2008), 27.

29. Bradley, "The Community College Movement," 6.

30. Bradley, "The Community College Movement," 25.

31. Pluviose, "More High-Achieving Students," 3.

32. U.S. Department of Education, *A Test of Leadership*, xi.

33. National Center on Education and the Economy (NCEE), *Tough Choices or Tough Times: The Report on the New Commission on the Skills of the American Workforce* (San Francisco: Jossey-Bass, 2007), xviii.

34. Robert J. Samuelson, "How We Dummies Succeed," *Washington Post*, September 6, 2006, A15.

35. Samuelson, "How We Dummies Succeed," A15.

36. U.S. Department of Education, *A Test of Leadership*, x.

37. U.S. Department of Education, *A Test of Leadership*, x.

38. U.S. Department of Education, *A Test of Leadership*, x.

39. U.S. Department of Education, *A Test of Leadership*, 8.

40. National Governors Association (NGA) and Pew Center on the States, *Innovation America: Investing in Innovation* (Washington, DC: NGA Center for Best Practices, 2007), 9, introduction.

41. NCEE, *Tough Choices or Tough Times*, xix–xx.

42. "A Conversation with the *Times-Dispatch*," 43.

43. Bradley, "The Community College Movement," 10.

44. Joe Smydo, "Remedial Courses Used by Many to Adjust to College," *Pittsburgh Post-Gazette*, September 1, 2008, http://www.post-gazette.com/pg/08245/908603-298.stm (accessed September 19, 2008), 18.

45. Samuelson, "How We Dummies Succeed," A15.

46. Samuelson, "How We Dummies Succeed," A15.

47. AACC, "CC STATS Home (2007)," 2, 4.

48. AACC, "CC STATS Home (2007)," 3; U.S. Department of Education, *A Test of Leadership*, x.

49. Bradley, "The Community College Movement," 27.

50. Bradley, "The Community College Movement," 36.

51. Bradley, "The Community College Movement," 36.

52. Bradley, "The Community College Movement," 37.

53. CORD, "The ABCs of Tech Prep," *The Cornerstone of Tech Prep Series* (Waco, TX: CORD, 1999), 7.

54. CORD, "The ABCs of Tech Prep"; Margaret Terry Orr, "Community College and Secondary School Collaboration on Workforce Development and Education Reform," *The Catalyst* (Spring 2004), National Council for Continuing Education & Training, BNET.com (accessed March 4, 2008); Debra D. Bragg, "Emerging Tech Prep Models: Promising Approaches to Educational Reform," *Centerfocus* 5 (1994), National Center for Research in Vocational Education, University of California at Berkeley, http://vocserve.berkeley.edu/CenterFocus/CF5.html (accessed March 4, 2008).

55. Robertson, "Community College First Choice for Many," 7–9.

56. Pluviose, "More High-Achieving Students," 3.

57. ICIC and CEOs for Cities, *Leveraging Colleges and Universities*, 33.

58. Samuelson, "How We Dummies Succeed," A15.

59. Michael E. Porter, *Location, Clusters, and Company Strategy*, ed. Gordon L. Clark, Meric S. Gertler, and Maryann P. Feldman (Oxford: Oxford University Press, 2000); Michael E. Porter, "Location, Competition, and Economic Development: Local Clusters in a Global Economy," *Economic Development Quarterly* 14, no. 1 (2000): 15–34.

60. NCEE, *Tough Choices or Tough Times*, 142.

61. NGA and Pew Center on the States, *Innovation America*, 5.

62. AACC, "CC STATS Home (2007)."

63. AACC, "CC STATS Home (2008)."

64. AACC, "CC STATS Home (2008)."

65. William H. Frey, *Diversity Spreads Out: Metropolitan Shifts in Hispanic, Asian, and Black Populations Since 2000*, The Brookings Institution, http://www

.brookings.edu/reports/2006/03demographics_frey.aspx (accessed September 17, 2008), 1.

66. George W. Bush, "President Bush Delivers Commencement Address at Miami Dade College," speech presented at the graduation ceremonies of Miami Dade College—Kendall Campus, Miami, Florida, April 28, 2007, Office of the Press Secretary, http://www.whitehouse.gov/news/releases/2007/04/20070428-3.html (accessed February 19, 2008), 1; MDC, "About Miami Dade College," MDC, http://www.mdc.edu/main/about/default.asp (accessed February 19, 2008), 1.

67. Bush, "President Bush Delivers Commencement Address," 5, 8.

68. Bush, "President Bush Delivers Commencement Address," 12.

69. Bush, "President Bush Delivers Commencement Address," 12.

70. MDC, "History," MDC, http://www.mdc.edu/main/about/history.asp (accessed February 19, 2008), 1.

71. MDC, "About Miami Dade College," 3.

72. MDC, "About Miami Dade College," 4.

73. MDC, "About Miami Dade College," 4.

74. MDC, "History," 5.

75. MDC, "History," 9; MDC, "About Miami Dade College," 5.

76. Eduardo Padrón, president, Miami Dade College, personal communication to Eugene P. Trani, July 17, 2009.

77. U.S. Congress, *Congressional Record*, vol. 141, August 1, 1995, p. S11124.

78. Bush, "President Bush Delivers Commencement Address," 16.

79. MDC, "History," 18.

80. MDC, "Facts in Brief (January 2008)," MDC—About MDC, http://www.mdc.edu/main/about/facts_in_brief.asp (accessed February 19, 2008).

81. MDC, "About Miami Dade College," 2.

82. MDC, "About Miami Dade College," 5; MDC, "History," 10.

83. MDC, "ESL & Foreign Languages," MDC, http://mdc.edu/wolfson/academic/ArtsLetters/esl/ (accessed February 29, 2008), 1.

84. MDC, "Developing a Tutor Training Program for Six Campuses," paper presented at 40th Annual CRLA Conference, Portland, OR, Oct. 31–Nov. 3, 2007, http://www.pvc.maricopa.edu/~sheets/CRLA2007/presentations/1hr_CC_88_Lemons_Dixie.html, (accessed February 29, 2008), 8.

85. Eduardo Padrón, president, Miami Dade College, personal communication to Eugene P. Trani, July 17, 2009.

86. MDC, "Facts in Brief (January 2008)."

87. MDC, "Facts in Brief (January 2008)."

88. MC, "History of Montgomery College," MC, http://cms.montgomerycollege.edu/edu/plain.aspx?id=2496 (accessed September 22, 2008), 1.

89. Beth Frerking, "For Achievers, a New Destination," *New York Times*, April 22, 2007, http://www.nytimes.com /2007/04/22/education/edlife/bestccs.html (accessed September 22, 2008), 25; MC, "History of Montgomery College," 1.

90. MC, "History of Montgomery College," 3; MC, "Courses and Programs," MC, http://cms.montgomerycollege.edu/EDU/tertiary2.aspx?urlid=9 (accessed September 22, 2008), 1.

91. Frerking, "For Achievers, a New Destination," 11, 21–25.

92. MC, "Student Enrollment Profile (Fall 2006)," MC—Office of Institutional Research and Analysis, http://www.montgomerycollege.edu/Departments/inplrsh/Fall%202006/Complete_Fall_2006_Student_Enrollment_Profile.pdf (accessed September 22, 2008), i.

93. Charlene R. Nunley, Mary Kay Shartle-Galotto, and Mary Helen Smith, "Working with Schools to Prepare Students for College: A Case Study," *New Directions for Community Colleges* 111 (Fall 2000): 10.

94. Nunley et al., "Working with Schools," 10.

95. Nunley et al., "Working with Schools," 12.

96. MC, "Academic Initiatives and the MC/MCPS Partnership at Montgomery College," MC, http://www.montgomerycollege.edu/Departments/mcmcps/ (accessed September 22, 2008), 2.

97. MC, "Academic Initiatives," 5.

98. MC, "FAQ," MC—Gateway to College Program at Montgomery College: An MC/MCPS Partnership Initiative, http://www.montgomerycollege.edu/Departments/mcmcps/gateway/faq.htm (accessed September 22, 2008), 8.

99. Nunley et al., "Working with Schools," 36.

100. Janet Johnson and Jeff Baker, "Getting a Jump on College: Winning Secondary-Post Secondary Partnership Programs," PowerPoint presentation on June 17, 2008, Montgomery College Montgomery County Public Schools Partnership, http://www.montgomeryschoolsmd.org/departments/cte/conf/strand_c/Rigor%20through%20Relevancy%20Conference.Getting%20a%20Jump%20on%20College.ppt#1 (accessed September 22, 2008), 20.

101. Johnson and Jeff, "Getting a Jump on College," 22.

102. MC, "Assessment & Placement," MC, http://www.montgomerycollege.edu/departments/AssessCtr/assessment-placement.html (accessed September 22, 2008); MC, "Academic Support," MC, http://www.montgomerycollege.edu/Departments/studev/support.html (accessed September 22, 2008); MC, "Online Student Success Center," MC, http://www.montgomerycollege.edu/Departments/studevgt/onlinsts/ (accessed September 22, 2008); MC, "Learning Centers," MC, http://www.montgomerycollege.edu/exploremc/learning centers.html (accessed September 22, 2008); MC, "Montgomery College Student Success Stories," MC, http://www.montgomerycollege.edu/news/studentsuccess/rosettanesbitt.html (accessed September 22, 2008); MC, "Project SUCCESS," MC, http://www.montgomerycollege.edu/Departments/studevrv/Project-Success.html (accessed September 22, 2008); MC, "Boys to Men (BTM) Mentoring Program," MC, http://www.montgomerycollege.edu/Departments/studevrv/mentoring.html (accessed September 22, 2008); MC, "Student Success Center—Tutoring," MC, http://www.montgomerycollege.edu/Departments/studevgt/ssergt/tutoring.html (accessed September 22, 2008); MC, "Medical Learning Center Overview," MC, http://www.montgomerycollege.edu/Departments/medlearntp/index.html (accessed September 22, 2008).

103. AACC, "CC STATS Home (2007)," 2.

104. The Urban Institute, *Sprawl, Smart Growth and Economic Opportunity* (The Urban Institute, 2002), http://www.urban.org/UploadedPDF/410536_Sprawl andEquity.pdf (accessed February 28, 2008), 2.

105. ICIC and CEOs for Cities, *Leveraging Colleges and Universities*, 2.

106. MCC, "Discoveryourself," About Us: Maricopa Community Colleges, http://www.maricopa.edu/about/index.php (accessed July 13, 2009), 1.

107. Beth Hunt Larson, in an e-mail message to Kelly Myles, August 6, 2009.

108. MCC, "Discoveryourself," 2.

109. MCC, "Small Business Development," About Us: Maricopa Community Colleges, http://www.maricopa.edu/about/index.php?sbdc (accessed July 13, 2009); Bradley, "The Community College Movement," 42.

110. Arizona Small Business Development Center Network, "Maricopa Community Colleges SBDC—Central Phoenix," AZSBDC Network, http://www.azsbdc.net/center.aspx?center=93010&subloc=0/ (accessed July 13, 2009).

111. MCC, "Workforce Development," About Us: Maricopa Community Colleges, http://maricopa.edu/about/index.php?workforce_development (accessed July 13, 2009); MCC, "A Force That Works," Maricopa Community Colleges Center for Workforce Development, http://www.maricopa.edu/workforce/ (accessed July 13, 2009).

112. MCC, "A Force That Works."

113. NGA and Pew Center on the States, *Innovation America*, 52.

114. MCC, "Mayor Gordon to Announce $6 Million Bioscience Incubator Project," Maricopa Community Colleges: Press Room, http://maricopa.edu/press/releases.php?nr=949 (accessed July 14, 2009), 1, 2.

115. MCC, "Discoveryourself," 2.

116. MCC, "Discoveryourself," 3.

117. MCC, "Discoveryourself," 4; MCC, "Continuing Education—Non-credit Programs," About Us: Maricopa Community Colleges, http://maricopa.edu/about/index.php?continuing_education (accessed July 13, 2009), 2.

118. Rio Salado College Online, "Adult Basic Education," Maricopa Community Colleges, http://www.riosalado.edu/programs/abe/Pages/default.aspx (July 13, 2009).

119. Rio Salado College Online, "Adult Basic Education."

120. Rio Salado College Online, "Adult Basic Education."

121. Rio Salado College Online, "Adult Basic Education."

122. GateWay Community College, "Early College High School," MCC, http://highschool.gatewaycc.edu/Information/TechPrep/ (accessed July 13, 2009), 1, 2, 4.

*Chapter 6*

# British and Irish Higher Education: Ancient but Thoroughly Modern

This chapter begins by describing the changes that occurred, albeit with considerable resistance, at Cambridge and Oxford that enabled the institutions to link faculty research with external needs and to assume a leading role in global economic development. It then moves to discuss how higher education in Ireland became an essential component of the national revitalization strategy that created the "Celtic Tiger." The chapter concludes by showing why the economic downturn of recent years will place considerable strain on higher education institutions (HEIs), but is unlikely to reverse the reform thrust that calls for greater integration of colleges and universities with the economic development strategies of the United Kingdom, Ireland, and the European continent.

## FROM COLLEGIALITY TO NATIONAL POLICY

Traditionally, British universities used a system of collegiality to govern their institutions that limited both the power of the institution's central administration to control the various units and the power of the state to control the institutions. Collegiality could be seen as a federal system in which the local units retained considerable power and autonomy. Within universities, individual colleges were often self-governing, legally independent, corporate bodies. The colleges maintained control of key institutional goals and the ability to make choices about how to achieve them. In this system, the government exercised little direct control of the colleges and universities, other than providing necessary legal and financial support that enabled them to carry out their missions. In the ideal university, academics engaged in the disinterested pursuit of knowledge, unencumbered by either state direction or the dictates of their own central administration.

The conception of the liberal ideal of the university began to change in the United Kingdom in the 1960s. In 1964, the University Grants Committee and Research Councils were placed under the Department of Education and Science. This movement placed funding decisions regarding the universities in the political and ideological realm. It essentially recognized that a modern state should have an explicit higher education policy, that it should coordinate its resources to achieve its policy aims, and that states without higher education policies were not utilizing all the policy tools at their disposal. The creation of polytechnics in 1965 to provide vocational, professional, and industrially relevant courses was a clear example of how the state could influence the overall direction of higher education. These policies created a role for the university in addressing societal needs and legitimized the authority of the government over the institutions.

In the 1980s, the Conservative government, headed by Margaret Thatcher, set out to apply concepts of "new public management" to the government in general, but also to universities. A new discourse of governance began to emerge where the language of economics and management sought to replace that of "professionalism," "administration," and the "public interest." The idea was to apply private-sector management techniques to produce an increase in efficiency, effectiveness, and economy. The new public management valued, for example, outputs over inputs. It was more important to know how many graduates universities were producing in areas of critical societal need than whether this year's budget represented an increase over last year's. In essence, universities would be held to accountability goals that were imposed externally and were not entirely of their own design.

The norms of new public management were not very compatible with the traditional system of collegiality and created significant tensions. Collegial governance, which seeks consensus through a committee structure, produces a slow decision-making process and is inherently suspicious of external efforts to say what the academic process should value and how it should be implemented. Moreover, there was, at least initially, a sense that the new public management was a narrowly political and ideological agenda associated with Thatcherite conservatism. Maybe when Thatcher went away, it would go away too.

The reality turned out to be very different. While the Labour government that eventually took power was to initiate policies that were far different from Thatcher's in many regards, it had little interest in returning to a laissez-faire state with respect to higher education. Modern governments were increasingly viewing the higher education system as essential to national economic goals and the United Kingdom was no exception, regardless of the ideological orientation of the party holding power. Ideas about aligning higher education to national priorities, accountability for taxpayer dollars, and developing specialized responsibilities for different kinds of colleges and universities transcended political boundaries. Traditionalists who disliked the modern conception of higher education could no longer think that their opponents were concentrated in a single ideological camp.

What was happening in the United Kingdom was not, in fact, very different from what was occurring on the European continent. As Michael Shattock has observed, while systems of higher education have been evolving in accord with their country's particular economic, organizational, and constitutional framework, one thing is consistent throughout Europe—a new agenda for higher education is emerging.[1] Much of the literature about these changes focuses on the "market mechanisms" that have been applied to higher education. But it may well be more accurate to note that what has happened has been the application of market-based criteria to the formulation of national and, in some cases, international higher education policy. Although the pace and path of change vary among (and, to some degree, even within) countries, Europe's systems of higher education are going in the same general direction—toward the alignment of a higher education system with explicit policy goals, toward greater overall accountability, and toward increased specialization and differentiation.

The United Kingdom has moved strongly in this direction, with the government setting priorities, but with measures that explicitly align funding decisions and allocations with performance measured against accountability goals. To some degree, Oxford and Cambridge actually continue to be set apart from other British universities from a governance perspective, remaining steadfast in the collegiality system. A 2003 Treasury-commissioned report remarked on trends among UK HEIs since the end of the twentieth century, noting, "In the last ten years, there has been a gradual movement towards a more executive style of management, already common among post-1992 institutions," and adding, "Oxford and Cambridge have a unique set of governance and management issues."[2] But significant changes have occurred at these two universities, enabling them to become more responsive to the needs of their external constituencies.

## CAMBRIDGE

Cambridge has undertaken a number of steps that have enabled the institution to become more proactive in contributing to economic and regional development priorities. Some of the changes have directly impacted the governing structure of the university. Others have involved the creation of new administrative entities that have enhanced the ease of interaction between the university and commercial enterprises. In addition to the formal changes, there has been the emergence of an informal culture that promotes increased interaction between faculty and business and involvement of the university in regional economic development efforts.

## Building Administrative Capacity

The enhancement of the responsibility, authority, and capacity of the central administration is one of the major governance changes that have taken place at Cambridge. The vice-chancellor's office has been strengthened by the appointment of five pro-vice-chancellors, who oversee planning and resources, education, research, personnel, and special responsibilities.[3] The pro-vice-chancellors work in partnership with senior administrators to help drive strategy and policy development. The financial function also is being enhanced and rationalized, with the roles of the treasurer and the secretary general being subsumed into the finance director's office.[4] In addition, a centralized electronic financial management system is being utilized to assist with sound planning and budgeting decisions.[5]

One of the largest actions to shift power to the central authority was increasing the number of votes required to call a ballot at the Regent House.[6] The Regent House is the governing body and principal electoral constituency of the university. It has more than 3,800 members, comprising university officers, Heads and Fellows of Colleges, and certain other categories defined by Ordinance.[7] This procedural change increased administrative discretion and made significant movement toward decreasing the ability of the individual colleges and faculty to block administrative decision making. In addition, two external members have been added to the university's governing council, moving the internal governance system a step toward the model that exists in many American states.[8]

## New Vehicles for University-Business Collaboration

The creation of a stronger executive team at Cambridge University has enabled the university to spend more time tackling big-picture industry-relation issues.[9] Enormous effort has been devoted to developing a faster-moving, more industry-friendly, and more entrepreneurial organization. With more than four thousand academics in more than one hundred departments, faculties, and schools, Cambridge possesses a wealth of expertise that it now strategically exchanges internally and with industry in order to foster innovation and the commercialization of promising discoveries.[10]

One of the most controversial steps toward modernization was the university's initiative to reform its intellectual property (IP) rights policy. It became necessary to create an administrative structure to facilitate moving knowledge outside the university.[11] Initially, the faculty and the administration were at odds about the form the policy should take.[12] The IP proposal underwent several revisions before a compromise was reached.[13] The new policy provides the university with a claim to ownership of registrable IP, but the individual inventor may have ownership of other residual IP rights, including the right to assign or license them.

Cambridge has established a sophisticated and well-regarded technology transfer office, Cambridge Enterprise.[14] Cambridge Enterprise exists to help university inventors, innovators, and entrepreneurs "make their ideas and concepts more commercially successful for the benefit of society, the UK economy, the inventors and the University."[15] Formed in 2006 as a wholly owned subsidiary of the university, Cambridge Enterprise provides the following services to the university's academics:

- The identification, protection, and licensing of IP
- Support, advice, and mentoring in the creation of new companies
- Provision of seed funds and links to organizations providing further funding
- Costing, contract negotiation, invoicing, insurance, and tax filing support for staff who provide consultancy services to external organizations
- Links to industry through showcasing and networking events

Another example of how Cambridge is becoming increasingly entrepreneurial is the creation of "embedded" institutes, or laboratories, whereby a university department enters into a relationship with a company for mutual benefit. That company may actually co-occupy space inside or close to a department.[16] Designed to secure the benefits of corporate investment and cooperation around shared strategic interests, examples of embedded laboratories include the Glaxo Institute of Applied Pharmacology, the embedded research facility from Rolls-Royce in the Department of Chemistry, and SmithKline Beecham in the Department of Medicine's Clinical School.[17] In addition, Toshiba, Hitachi, Hoechst, Unilever, BP Amoco, Seiko Epson, and Microsoft all have a strong presence. Microsoft Research Cambridge, an early "embedded" institute in the university and initially headed by the late computer systems professor Roger Needham, has become one of the largest computer science research laboratories in Europe, with more than one hundred researchers.[18]

Another way Cambridge has created relationships with industry is through its Research Services Division (RSD). RSD offers outside companies an informed entry point into the university to help prospective partners find the appropriate academic expertise and identify opportunities for collaboration.[19] RSD supports the development of relationships between academics and industry, whether these result in major multifaceted collaborations with global companies or simply in finding experts for specific one-time projects.

Cambridge has also developed an informal culture in which individual faculty members and departments develop closer linkages with firms and business associations. A survey conducted by the university-based ESRC Centre for Business Research indicated that high-tech firms in the city of Cambridge had extensive and wide-ranging links with the university.[20] For example, 28 percent of those surveyed had collaborative projects with the university, 12 percent had academics on their boards, and 24 percent used university staff as consultants. More than half (56 percent) of the respondents emphasized the importance to their firms' success of such links to academia.

## The Cambridge Phenomena

The Cambridge region has experienced two waves of growth and development. The first, during the period from the 1960s through the 1980s, is called the *Cambridge Phenomenon,* and it was concentrated on small, independent high-technology firms.[21] The second, referred to as the *Cambridge Phenomenon Revisited,* occurred in the late 1990s and was based more on telecommunications and biotechnology development. The UK Department of Trade and Industry says Cambridge is one of the three leading locations for biotech research and development (R&D) in the country.[22] It also is the world's second-largest venture capital market outside the Silicon Valley.[23] For this reason Cambridge is sometimes called "Silicon Fen," referring to the boggy fen that lies north of the city.[24] Silicon Fen now hosts approximately one thousand high-tech companies that produce $3 billion in revenue.

The initial Cambridge Phenomenon and its subsequent wave could not have happened without the presence of the university.[25] The capacity of the major technology and pharmaceutical companies to access the intellectual capital of Cambridge was essential to their interest in locating in the region. Access to local knowledge institutions is an important part of the technology strategy of some investors.[26] In the Cambridge region, most investment is linked to collaborative R&D in the university, as well as in other public research institutes. Microsoft, Schlumberger, SmithKline Beecham, Toshiba, and Sony became an integral part of the Cambridge region's high-tech cluster. And once the enterprises were present, the collaborations developed, such as the embedded laboratories, produced synergies that surpassed initial expectations.

Besides Cambridge's formalized collaborations with commercial firms, the indirect effects of the university on the region's economic development are enormous. The university provides a source of high-caliber employees and a remarkably strong regional workforce pool.[27] Around 2,500 postgraduate students provide skilled part-time staff for local high-tech businesses. Also, it is not uncommon for university graduates to stay in Cambridge and either join established high-tech companies or start their own.[28] In addition, approximately half of the teaching and research staff has no tenure and is on short, fixed-term contracts. Many want to remain in Cambridge, but do not foresee long-term careers with the university. Some may wind up starting their own businesses and others provide the staffing for emerging companies.

As an institution, the university has enlarged its ties with the community in terms of commercial links, policy involvement and volunteerism. It works with groups that promote regional innovation such as the Cambridge Network and the Greater Cambridgeshire Partnership.[29] Cambridge also has engaged with the local public sector. The university's Office of Community Affairs coordinates public engagement events, and faculty and staff from the university participate in the formation of public policy by assuming advisory roles with local and national government and with organizations such as the Cambridge University Government Policy Programme.[30] During the 2003–2004 academic year, one in three students and one in four staff members volunteered for one of the university's projects.[31] Cambridge has an Active Community Fund, which helps encourage and coordinate student and staff volunteerism, as well as provide financial resources to projects within the university and to external community organizations.[32]

## OXFORD

Oxford has faced similar challenges as Cambridge with the tensions between the traditional and modern conceptions of the university and how it should be organized and governed. Like Cambridge, it ultimately reached a set of compromises that did strengthen some of the operating powers and capacities of the central administration.

### Building Administrative Capacity

Oxford's vice chancellor, John Hood, announced in 2007 that a report by the Higher Education Funding Council for England (HEFCE) reiterated concerns it had expressed earlier about elements of Oxford's governance that differ from national guidelines, most particularly how Oxford falls short in meeting requirements for "independent scrutiny of outside investors' interests."[33] HEFCE urged Oxford to take measures to make its governing body's membership largely nonexecutive, external, and free of potential conflicts of interest. Oxford was charged by HEFCE to review its current deviation in governance structure from national standards. Ultimately, four external members have been appointed to the governing council of the university, and the council's committees have been restructured.[34]

Oxford has taken a number of steps to improve the internal organization of the university and its operational efficiencies. In 2003, it began installing a university-wide financial management system to greatly improve the process of resource allocation across the university.[35] One significant change indicating the movement toward collaboration and centralization is that Oxford's departments and faculties have been organized into a divisional structure, enabling clear leadership for interaction with industry, especially in the three science divisions, but also with the social sciences and the humanities. The new organization promotes the kind of interdisciplinary collaboration that is increasingly the hallmark of contemporary research.

Oxford has focused on creating structures to facilitate serving the surrounding community, as well. A sabbatical post of vice president for charities and community affairs has been established within the Oxford University Student Union to coordinate and develop student volunteering, as well as connect local charities and community groups with students.[36] These connections provide the basis for community development and utilization of knowledge and research outside of technology transfer. Not only does the community benefit from the work of the students, but students benefit from the hands-on experience and receive greater learning outcomes.

In 2007, Oxford for the first time appointed a director of international strategy, to act as a focal point for Oxford's international relations and global profile.[37] The position was designed to oversee Oxford's many links and collaborations with international institutions and organizations, which exist at the university, the college, and departmental levels, and to ensure that information on the range of these links is made available and a coherent approach is taken to develop them further.

### Building a Culture of Innovation

In response to these and other pressures to modernize, the university has rationalized and updated its approach to the ownership of IP. Essential ingredients of its model are a generous revenue-sharing policy, which brings significant personal benefits to inventors (employees or students), and a hugely successful and well-resourced technology transfer operation. Oxford's IP and technology transfer model is now being copied by other leading universities.

One of the prime examples of Oxford University's growing entrepreneurial culture is its technology transfer company, Isis Innovation Ltd. The company helps university researchers identify, evaluate, protect, and market research with commercial potential.[38] Isis files, on average, one patent application each week and has assisted in the formation of more than forty university spin-out companies since 1997. Overall, the university has produced more than one hundred companies with a combined market capitalization of more than $2 billion.[39] Just three of the university's spin-offs—VASTox, Evolutec, and Physiomics—raised a total of around $290 million.

The university also operates Oxford University Consulting (OUC), a professional service dedicated to finding direct, cost-effective solutions to private entrepreneurs' consulting needs.[40] OUC introduces clients to appropriate experts in the university and manages all aspects of the consultancy process, including due diligence, patent violation, expert witness, data analysis, testing services, and management consultancy.

The Saïd Business School represents another example of how the university as a whole and faculty members individually are embracing an entrepreneurial culture. Saïd, Europe's fastest-growing business school, addresses subjects pertinent to the knowledge economy, such as the politics of global business and the management of innovation.[41] The Saïd Business School is developing a strong reputation for entrepreneurship and innovation research. Entrepreneurship and science and technology studies are core disciplines in the Saïd Business School, which has a research program that looks at some of the major challenges—technological, environmental, and economic—that face businesses in the twenty-first century.

Oxford's Saïd Business School has two major centers for entrepreneurship, the innovative Skoll Center for Social Entrepreneurship, established by eBay founder Jeff Skoll, and the Oxford Science Enterprise Center, which aims to give scientists the vision and skills to deal with the reality of business.[42] The Oxford Centre for Entrepreneurship encourages entrepreneurship in the university's science and technology communities, by providing training and support for early stage businesses.

Further indicating the entrepreneurial culture of faculty, many of the university's top scientists have launched successful enterprises. One is Graham Richards, longtime chairman of the Department of Chemistry at Oxford and the founder of Oxford Molecular Group PLC, now part of Pharmacopeia Inc.[43] Another professor, Sir David Weatherall, established the Institute of Molecular Medicine in 1989 in the Clinical School of the University of Oxford, and it now houses about four hundred scientists working on diseases ranging from cancer to AIDS.[44] In 2000, the facility was renamed the Weatherall Institute of Molecular Medicine.

### Promoting Regional Development

Like Cambridge, Oxford has created strategic external relationships with industry that have enhanced the development of the Oxfordshire region's high-tech sector, specifically through the establishment of research and science parks. For instance, the Oxford Science Park was set up by Magadalen College and Prudential Assurance Company to encourage the formation and development of knowledge-based businesses and other innovative companies.[45] Also, Genetics Knowledge Park was launched from a partnership between the university and Oxford Radcliffe Hospitals NSH Trust to translate advances in genetics research into clinical practice.[46] And Begbroke Science Park was established by the university to enable high-tech start-up companies and university entrepreneurs to work side by side to capitalize on discoveries in materials science.[47]

Another way that modern universities impact the local economy is by providing capital to support regional entrepreneurial efforts. Oxford does this through the Isis Angels Network at Isis Innovation. Through the Isis network, Oxford links potential private investors to companies that spin off from the university.[48] Oxford University works hard in other ways to forge productive relationships with enterprises in its region.[49] It has developed close relationships with numerous local economic development organizations, such as the Oxfordshire Economic Partnership, both City and County Strategic Partnerships, the South East England Development Agency and the Government Office for the South East. The university has a Regional Liaison Office that works in collaboration with university departments and units to develop the university's regional strategy and maximize its contribution to the local economy.

Between 1991 and 2000, Oxfordshire experienced a faster rate of growth in high-tech employment than any of the other forty-five English counties.[50] In the 1990s, Oxfordshire's high-tech sector grew by 40 percent each year, outpacing any other English region.[51] The 2004 estimates of total high-tech activities included about 3,500 businesses and 45,000 employees. In 2005, the county's 82 percent growth rate in high-tech employment was the highest in the UK.[52]

The University of Oxford has played a significant part in developing Oxfordshire into one of the most dynamic business regions in the country, if not all of Europe.[53] Oxford has helped produce the intellectual capital required to fuel "Enterprising Oxford," the regional economic development initiative that refers to Oxfordshire's role as one of Europe's leading centers of innovation-led economic development.[54] For example, in medicine and bioscience the local high-tech economy has benefited tremendously from the medical research expertise contained in Oxford University's hospitals and clinical departments.[55] Oxford University has been awarded five Queen's Anniversary Prizes, most recently in recognition of the Clinical Trial Service Unit's uniquely large randomized trials and epidemiological studies that have led to substantial changes in public health policies and treatment strategies.[56]

Complementing the area's wealth of intellectual capital is its rich supply of human capital, in no small part thanks to Oxford University. In addition to the roughly eighteen thousand students who are enrolled in its world-class undergraduate and postgraduate academic programs, every year some fifteen thousand people take part in courses offered by the university's continuing education department.[57] The CPD Centre (in continuing education) provides part-time courses for industry and individual professionals, with more than 150 courses offered each year through in-company, online or open delivery in a range of subjects, including software engineering, mathematical finance, bioscience and bioinformatics, health care, nanotechnology, public policy, and telecommunications and electronics.[58]

The university's own economic impact is substantial as well. Oxford employs about 8 percent of the local workforce.[59] Overall, sixteen thousand jobs are supported directly and indirectly by Oxford University, the colleges, Oxford University Press, and spin-off companies from the university.[60] Through its combined spending, the university injects an estimated $960 million into the local economy every year and adds about $550 million to local disposable income. The historic university also is a magnet for tourism and tourists' discretionary spending. Surveys that identify important local tourist attractions consistently include ten Oxford University sites among the top seventeen attractions. All told, four million people visit the Oxford area each year, spending around $500 million and creating 5,300 jobs. The activities of Oxford University itself have produced more than one hundred companies with a combined market capitalization of more than $2 billion.[61]

In addition to more fully engaging with industry, Oxford has developed a robust program of community engagement. One area the university targets as part of its program of community engagement is local schools. Each year university students studying for the Postgraduate Certificate in Educational Studies work in the Oxfordshire schools, and local teachers study part time for the university's Postgraduate Diploma in Educational Studies.[62] The university and local schools work together on a range of other projects, as well, such as the Great Oxfordshire Bug Quest, the Oxfordshire Science Writing Competition, and the Nuffield Science Bursary Scheme, which offers students the chance to work alongside practicing scientists. A Museums Outreach Coordinator works with more than 150 staff and student volunteers to extend existing outreach programs to schools and to those who have not traditionally participated in such events.

## THE REPUBLIC OF IRELAND

### A Transformed Economy

Covering about 27,000 square miles, the Republic of Ireland is just slightly larger than the state of West Virginia.[63] With just over 4.3 million people (according to 2008 estimates), Ireland's total population pales in comparison with that of some major metropolitan areas across the globe.[64] Also, the size of its higher education network—with seven universities and thirteen institutes of technology—is modest in comparison with the size of the higher education networks of some of the world's metropolises.[65]

In the years following Ireland's independence after the Anglo-Irish War of 1919–1921, virtually every aspect of the Irish economy—from unemployment to national debt—was a measure of fiscal failure.[66] Even in the 1950s, Ireland's economic growth rate was less than 1 percent annually. But in the 1990s, Ireland began redirecting its faltering economy away from farming and manufacturing and toward technology and services by strategically investing in R&D.[67] Over the ensuing years, Ireland went from being one of the poorest countries in Europe to one of the richest.[68]

Ireland became home to such multinational corporations (MNCs) as Intel, Microsoft, IBM, Gateway, Hewlett-Packard, Dell, and Johnson & Johnson.[69] In all, more than 1,200 MNCs—in areas ranging from electronics to health care products to financial services—had established bases in Ireland by 2000, employing more than 140,000 people.[70] In 2002, MNCs accounted for more than $66 billion worth of exports and spent just over $20 million in the Irish economy. Through their employment at foreign-owned firms, Irish workers amassed experience in such areas as engineering, computer science, and software development, helping to contribute to Ireland's budding entrepreneurialism. Enterprise Ireland (the agency geared to building up indigenous businesses) helped build up Ireland's own multinational sector using this growing base of entrepreneurial experience. In addition, significant increases in R&D funding spurred innovation, as Ireland's R&D in business, higher education, and public research increased threefold in the 1990s.[71] Brian Sweeney of Siemens Ireland described the Celtic Tiger as a story about a transition from "brawnpower" to "brainpower."[72]

Strategic investment in universities was an essential part of the economic development strategy that remade the nation into a high-tech mecca and catalyzed a phenomenal growth spurt. R&D-earmarked funds from the 2000–2006 National Development Plan (NDP) were administered primarily by Science Foundation Ireland (SFI) and the Higher Education Authority through the Programme for Research in Third Level Institutions (PRTLI).[73] The total earmark under the 2000–2006 NDP for SFI grants was around $897 million, through a variety of programs supporting both individual researchers and joint research efforts. Complementing SFI's direction of funds toward research projects was PRTLI's provision of funds for R&D infrastructure needs. PRTLI funds also supported research partnerships, a major need in the expansion of Ireland's R&D base.

One such partnership, the Dublin Molecular Medicine Centre, was established by Trinity College Dublin's Institute of Molecular Medicine and University College Dublin's Conway Institute for Biomolecular and Biomedical Research.[74] Considered an unprecedented coming together of researchers and their institutions, the project helped to establish the all-important critical mass of researchers working in an interdisciplinary fashion on the processes occurring at the molecular level—a level of collaboration critically needed in Ireland to enable discoveries to be made in such areas as new therapies and diagnostic tools.

## The Evolution of Higher Education

Equally as vital to Ireland's global integration and economic ascension as its new public-private R&D enterprise was its increased commitment to educational attainment at the undergraduate and graduate levels. Tuition for undergraduates was eliminated in Ireland in 1995, and the number of students ages nineteen to twenty-four in college ballooned from 11 percent in the mid-1960s to 56 percent in 2007.[75] Also, with an increased emphasis on upper levels of the third-level sector, enrollment in graduate programs increased by more than 20 percent from the 2001–2002 academic year to the 2005–2006 academic year, and the total number of graduates (from both undergraduate and graduate programs) increased by 19 percent during the same period.[76] The number of graduates specifically from Ph.D. programs increased by 7.5 percent from the 2004–2005 academic year to the 2005–2006 academic year. Ireland's universities also have transformed their governance structures. Ellen Hazelkorn, director and dean of the Faculty of Applied Arts and director of the Higher Education Policy Research Unit at Dublin Institute of Technology, noted that, in response to the pressures of higher education's greater role in economic development, HEIs around the world have adopted market-influenced behaviors.[77] Hazelkorn cited Ireland as one of the countries that had been enforcing changes in institutional governance, replacing elected rectors with corporate CEO-type leadership.

In addition to launching the new higher-education-focused NDP, Ireland has continued to adopt other university-based strategies to drive national economic growth. First, Ireland set up a national steering group to oversee its implementation of the Bologna Process, an initiative designed to establish a European Higher Education Area that would make university education more compatible and comparable across nations.[78] Also, five Bologna promoters were appointed to provide a resource to the wider higher education community in responding to the challenges of the Process. One of the most important outcomes of Ireland's participation in the Bologna Process has been a better system of quality assurance. The Irish Higher Education Quality Network was established as a formal network, comprising the main organizations with a role or significant interest in quality assurance in higher education and training in Ireland.[79]

With the assistance of Enterprise Ireland, Irish universities began implementing a number of important strategies to connect faculty with industry leaders and instill a greater sense of entrepreneurship in their academic cultures.[80] Examples of the innovations that emerged in the third-level sector include University College Dublin's University Industry Programme (UIP); UIP's new innovation center, NOVA; and the Campus Company Development Program, a joint initiative of UIP and Enterprise Ireland. Also, newer universities, such as the University of Limerick and Dublin City University (DCU), developed an entrepreneurial approach to their curriculum and research development. DCU's Invest, the university's commercial arm, represents just one DCU initiative designed to foster university-industry ties.

Providing further evidence of more market-influenced behaviors among Irish HEIs is the increased focus on intellectual capital production. In June 2006, a fund of almost $42.5 million was put in place to improve technology transfer from universities to industry.[81] And, as of 2007, the SFI had awarded more than $353 million for research and had invested more than $59 million in three new centers for science, engineering, and technology to connect Irish universities with communications and biotechnology companies. From 2000 to 2007, other annual government funding for research increased from almost $472 million to over $960.5 million. Higher education's share of that increased spending helped the universities increase their R&D spending by more than 50 percent.

Realizing the need to pool and leverage resources, Ireland has sought ways to promote productive partnerships among HEIs. The Irish government set up the Strategic Innovation Fund, which was originally budgeted at $424 million over five years to promote inter-institutional collaboration within higher education.[82] In December 2006, the government approved the first fourteen projects under the fund, totaling more than $59 million.

Also, some MNCs started working more closely with surrounding HEIs on R&D.[83] For instance, at Wyeth Medica's Wyeth BioPharma Campus at Grange Castle, in the suburbs of Dublin, researchers collaborated with surrounding HEIs, including National University–Maynooth, DCU, Trinity College Dublin, University College Dublin, and the Institute of Technology Tallaght. And Irish-owned Iona Technologies, a Dublin-based multinational software firm specializing in eBusiness, was developed in Trinity College Dublin's mathematics department.

### Higher Education in a Time of Economic Stress

In October 2006, the National Competitiveness Council of Ireland said there were signs that the Celtic Tiger was losing its momentum.[84] By January 2009, the *New York Times* proclaimed, "The Irish economy . . . has collapsed."[85] And property tycoon Sean Dunne pronounced, "The Celtic Tiger may be dead."[86] In a matter of months, Ireland went from the fourth most affluent country in the Organization for Economic Cooperation and Development to falling into a deep recession. Several factors contributed to Ireland's transformation from an economic miracle to an economic catastrophe over the summer of 2008. According to a February 2009 report released by the European Commission, the downturn of Ireland's economy was caused by the crisis in the country's financial sector, the sharp correction in the housing market, and the recessions underway in the United States and the United Kingdom, which are Ireland's primary trading partners.[87]

As a result of the stress on public finances, the government rolled out a series of cutbacks at HEIs. In July 2008, the minister of education, Batt O'Keefe, met with Ireland's seven university presidents to discuss a 3 percent cut in payroll costs from third-level institutions and the vocational educational system.[88] At the beginning of October 2008, Ireland's Department of Education imposed a spending "pause" to the Strategic Innovation Fund, which was being used to fund a series of highly touted initiatives, including cross-university collaborations to reform undergraduate teaching and boost international student recruitment.[89] The proposals were not well received in university circles as the reductions were seen as making it far more difficult to catch up to other European nations in the percentage of gross domestic product allocated to higher education. But the broader economic recovery plan that Ireland developed in the response to the global downturn continued to see higher education as a linchpin to national development.[90]

A key feature of the plan, titled "Building Ireland's Smart Economy: A Framework for Sustainable Economic Renewal," is building the innovation component of Ireland's economy through the utilization of human capital.[91] In striving to create the "innovation island," the plan includes a number of key actions—and funding—in the higher education arena, just a few of which are listed here:

- Continuing substantial investment in R&D, as demonstrated by the launch of a fifth cycle of the Programme for Research in Third-Level Institutions
- Restructuring the higher education system to enhance system-wide performance, by developing a new higher education strategy
- Giving priority to flexible learning initiatives that can be targeted to up-skilling people in the workforce, under the Strategic Innovation Fund (which, as noted previously, had been "paused" months earlier)
- Investing hundreds of millions of euros in third-level capital projects (which stands in stark contrast to the cuts announced less than two months later, as cited previously)
- Using research funding through SFI, Enterprise Ireland, and IDA (Industrial Development Authority) to instill a culture of commer-cialization in third-level institutions to complement the embedded teaching and research culture[92]

Not long after the recovery plan's launch, five new SFI strategic research clusters (SRCs) were established and funded, involving seven academic institutions and twenty-two collaborating companies.[93] Introduced in 2007, the SRC program sets out to link scientists and engineers in partner-ships across academia and industry to address crucial research questions, foster the development of new and existing Irish-based technology compa-nies, and grow partnerships with industry. At the ceremony announcing the new SRCs, Jimmy Devins, the minister for science, technology, and innovation, said, "SRCs bring together academic and industrial expertise to create innovative research and entrepreneurial foresight that, in com-bination, will help to re-shape Ireland's economy, create employment op-portunities, boost our reputation abroad and ultimately act as the engine that sustains all of these in the long-term."[94] National University of Ireland Galway, University College Dublin, Waterford Institute of Technology, and DCU will be the lead principal investigators for the new SRCs.

The consternation in the higher education community about the imme-diate effects of budget cutbacks is understandable. The reductions may, however, be prompting discussions that are long overdue and innova-tions that can generate long-term progress. For example, a serious dia-logue has emerged about the extent to which students and their families ought to pay fees to support higher education, a debate that is probably long overdue. In addition, Trinity College Dublin and University College Dublin have announced a merger at the graduate level, with the intention of scaling up activity that will create jobs. A change of this magnitude, in all likelihood, will precipitate other mergers and consolidations. This is a bold move and one that shows how competitive higher education has become as countries around the world see the linkages between higher education and economic development. Given the argument that higher education can make about the role it will pay in an economic recovery strategy, it is hard to imagine that colleges and universities will not be equally or even more vital to post-recession Ireland.

In fact, it is this indispensability of colleges and universities that should enable HEIs to emerge from the recession in far better long-term shape than institutions such as newspapers, banks, and housing entities. And Ireland's proposed "recovery plan" offers some glimmers of optimism inasmuch as investment in higher education remains a crucial feature of its strategy. There may well be tighter control of spending, even greater momentum toward accountability measures, and interest in developing cross-institutional collaborations that utilize resources more efficiently. But the thrust of all these changes will not be to disengage from universities and defund them, but to make them even more essential partners in the quest for regional and national progress. If Cambridge and Oxford have seen it in their interest to become committed partners with their regions, it is difficult to imagine a recovery strategy that ignores the extraordinary social and economic impact of higher education.

## NOTES

1. Michael Shattock, "Entrepreneurialism and the Knowledge Economy in Europe," in *Entrepreneurialism in Universities and the Knowledge Economy: Diversification and Organizational Change in European Higher Education*, ed. Michael Shattock (Berkshire, England: Open University Press, 2009), 200.

2. Richard Lambert, *Lambert Review of Business-University Collaboration: Final Report* (London: HM Treasury, December 2003), 93.

3. University of Cambridge, "University Governance: Notice," *Reporter* 132, no. 18 (February 6, 2002): annex 2 and section 5.4; University of Cambridge, "Cambridge Governance Reforms," News and Events (June 26, 2002), http://www .admin.cam.ac.uk/news/dp/2002062602 (accessed November 9, 2007), 2; Lambert, *Lambert Review*, 104.

4. Phil Baty, "Cambridge Rebels Hold Up Rejig," *The Times Higher Education Supplement* (THES) (December 13, 2002), http://www.timeshighereducation .co.uk/story.asp?storycode=173593&sectioncode=26 (accessed November 9, 2007), 2.

5. Laura Rohde, "Cambridge May Sue Oracle, KPMG for Failed System," Mossavar-Rahmani Center for Business & Government, John F. Kennedy School of Government: In the News (November 9, 2001), IDG News Service, an InfoWorld affiliate, http://www.hks.harvard.edu/m-rcbg/ethiopia/Publications/Cambr

idge%20may%20sue%20Oracle,%20KPMG%20for%20failed%20system.pdf (accessed November 9, 2007), 1, 3.

6. University of Cambridge, "University Governance: Notice," section 5.4.

7. University of Cambridge, "How the University Works—the Regent House," University of Cambridge—the University & Its Departments, http://www.cam.ac.uk/cambuniv/pubs/works/regenthouse.html (accessed November 9, 2007), 1.

8. University of Cambridge, "Cambridge Governance Reforms," 3; Lambert, *Lambert Review,* 104; University of Cambridge, "How the University Works—the Council," University of Cambridge—the University & Its Departments, http://www.cam.ac.uk/cambuniv/pubs/works/council.html (accessed November 9, 2007), 4.

9. Jim Kelly, "Spin Out Doctors: Is the 'Cambridge Phenomenon' about to Be Revived? And If So, Can the Pitfalls of the Last Boom Be Avoided?" *The Guardian—Education Guardian Weekly* (March 2, 2004), *The Guardian,* http://www.guardian.co.uk/education/2004/mar/02/highereducation.businessofresearch (accessed September 11, 2007), 8.

10. University of Cambridge, "Business Services Guide: Working with the University," University of Cambridge, http://www.cam.ac.uk/cambuniv/business/working.html (accessed September 10, 2007), 1.

11. Gautam Naik, "Cambridge Tries U.S. Model to Make Profits on Patents," *Wall Street Journal* (August 16, 2002), Dow Jones & Company, Inc., http://www.cl.cam.ac.uk/~rja14/Papers/wsjcam.html (accessed November 8, 2007), 5.

12. Ross Anderson, "Analysis of the Vice-Chancellor's Proposal," *Campaign for Cambridge Freedoms,* http://www.cl.cam.ac.uk/~rja14/expropriation.html (accessed November 12, 2007), 1.

13. Mike Clark, *The Cambridge University Policy on Intellectual Property Rights: A Critical Appraisal* (January 26, 2006), http://people.pwf.cam.ac.uk/mrc7/cuipr/ (accessed November 8, 2007), 2.

14. Kelly, "Spin Out Doctors," 12.

15. The Old Schools, "Cambridge Enterprise," University of Cambridge, http://www.enterprise.cam.ac.uk/about/about.html (accessed September 18, 2007), 1.

16. Eugene P. Trani, *Richmond at the Crossroads: The Greater Richmond Metropolitan Area and the Knowledge Based High Technology Economy of the 21st Century* (Richmond: Virginia Commonwealth University, 1998), 3.

17. Barry Moore, "Silicon Fen—The Cambridge Phenomenon as a Case-History of Present-Day Industrial Clustering," The Diebold Institute for Public Policy Studies, http://www.dieboldinstitute.org/paper24.pdf (accessed September 10, 2007), 15.

18. Microsoft Corporation, "Microsoft Research Cambridge," Microsoft Corporation, http://research.microsoft.com/cambridge (accessed September 10, 2007); Rick Rashid, "Roger Needham," Microsoft Corporation, http://research.microsoft.com/users/needham/needham.aspx (accessed September 18, 2007); Microsoft Research, "Roger Needham," Microsoft Corporation, http://research.microsoft.com/users/needham/default.aspx (accessed September 18, 2007).

19. University of Cambridge, "Business Services Guide," 2.

20. Barry Moore, "Silicon Fen," 16.

21. Tom Worthington, "The Cambridge Phenomenon: Summary of The Report," Net Traveller, http://www.tomw.net.au/nt/cp.html (accessed September 10, 2007), 12–13, 29; Ian Kitching, "The Cambridge Phenomenon," Cambridge—Past, Present and Future (April 5, 1999), http://www.iankitching.me.uk/history/cam/phenomenon.html (accessed September 10, 2007), 14.

22. Moore, "Silicon Fen," 8.

23. Excelsior Information Systems Limited, "Cambridge Tourist Information," AboutBritain.com, http://www.aboutbritain.com/towns/cambridge.com (accessed September 4, 2007), 12.

24. SiliconFen.com, "The Silicon Fen Story," SiliconFen.com, http://www.siliconfen.com/sfstory.php (accessed September 10, 2007), 9.

25. SiliconFen.com, "The Silicon Fen Story," paragraph 2.

26. Moore, "Silicon Fen," 14.

27. Worthington, "The Cambridge Phenomenon," 32.

28. Kitching, "The Cambridge Phenomenon," 1.

29. Kelly, "Spin Out Doctors," 12.

30. University of Cambridge, "Cambridge in the Community: Public Engagement," University of Cambridge, http://www.cam.ac.uk/cambforall/public.html (accessed September 10, 2007), 2–4.

31. University of Cambridge, "Cambridge in the Community: University Students and Staff," University of Cambridge, http://www.cam.ac.uk/cambforall/univ.html (accessed September 10, 2007), 1.

32. University of Cambridge, "Volunteering: University Funding for Volunteering," University of Cambridge, http://www.cam.ac.uk/cambuniv/volunteering/activecommfund.html (accessed September 10, 2007), 1.

33. John Hood, "Oration by the Vice-Chancellor," *Oxford University Gazette* Suppl. 3, no. 4818 (2007): 97.

34. Lambert, *Lambert Review*, 104.

35. Lambert, *Lambert Review*, 104.

36. University of Oxford, "Business and Community Liaison," University of Oxford, http://www.ox.ac.uk/aboutoxford/community.shtml (accessed September 14, 2007), 17.

37. University of Oxford, "Oxford Appoints First Director of International Strategy," Media (March 7, 2007), University of Oxford, http://www.ox.ac.uk/media/news_stories/2007/070307.html (accessed January 23, 2008), 1.

38. University of Oxford, "Business and Community Liaison," 5.

39. Saïd Business School, "Entrepreneurship at Oxford," University of Oxford, http://www.sbs.ox.ac.uk/about/Entrepreneurship+at+Oxford.htm (accessed September 14, 2007), 2.

40. University of Oxford, "Business and Community Liaison," 8.

41. Saïd Business School, "Who We Are," University of Oxford, http://www.sbs.ox.ac.uk/about/ (accessed September 14, 2007), 1, 2.

42. Saïd Business School, "Entrepreneurship at Oxford," 3, 5.

43. Department of Chemistry, "Screensaver Lifesaver," University of Oxford, 2005, http://www.chem.ox.ac.uk/cancer/wgrichards.html (accessed September 24, 2007), 1.

44. The Weatherall Institute of Molecular Medicine, "Welcome to the Weatherall Institute of Molecular Medicine," University of Oxford, http://www.imm.ox.ac.uk/ (accessed September 24, 2007), 1.

45. Oxford City Council, "Oxford Science Park," Oxford City Council, http://www.oxford.gov.uk/business/oxford-science-park.cfm (accessed September 14, 2007), 1, 2.

46. Oxford Economic Observatory (OEO), "A New Eye of the High-Tech Economy: The Oxford Economic Observatory," Annual Review 2002–2003, University of Oxford, http://www.ox.ac.uk/publicaffairs/pubs/annualreview/ar03/05.html (accessed September 14, 2007), 5; University of Oxford, "Launch of Oxford's Genetics Knowledge Park," News, April 6, 2004, University of Oxford, http://www.admin.ox.ac.uk/po/news/2003-04/apr/06.shtml (accessed September 21, 2007), 2.

47. University of Oxford, "Business and Community Liaison," 9.

48. University of Oxford, "Business," University of Oxford, http://www.ox.ac.uk/business (September 14, 2007), 1.

49. University of Oxford, "Business and Community Liaison," 3.

50. Helen Lawton Smith, James Simmie, Andrew Chadwick, and Gordon Clark, "Enterprising Oxford: The Growth of Oxfordshire High-Tech Economy," Oxfordshire Economic Observatory, http://oeo.geog.ox.ac.uk/research/eo.pdf (accessed September 14, 2007), 1.

51. OEO, "A New Eye," 2.

52. Saïd Business School, "Entrepreneurship at Oxford," 1.

53. Lambert, *Lambert Review*, 104.

54. Lawton Smith et al., "Enterprising Oxford," 1.

55. OEO, "A New Eye," 5.

56. University of Oxford, "Facts and Figures (2006)," University of Oxford, http://www.ox.ac.uk/aboutoxford/facts/ (accessed September 14, 2007), 3.

57. University of Oxford, "Facts and Figures (2006)," 1.

58. University of Oxford, "Business and Community Liaison," 12.

59. University of Oxford, "Business and Community Liaison," 2.

60. University of Oxford, "Facts and Figures (2006)," 2.

61. Saïd Business School, "Entrepreneurship at Oxford," 2.

62. University of Oxford, "Business and Community Liaison," 13.

63. U.S. Department of State, "Profile (July 2008)," Background Notes: Ireland, Bureau of European and Eurasian Affairs, http://www.state.gov/r/pa/ei/bgn/3180.htm (accessed February 26, 2009), 1.

64. U.S. Department of State, "Profile (July 2008)," 2.

65. Jon Marcus, "The Celtic Tiger," *National Crosstalk* 15, no. 1 (2007): 14.

66. Eugene P. Trani, *Dublin Diaries: A Study of High Technology Development in Ireland* (Richmond: Virginia Commonwealth University, 2002), 5; U.S. Department of State, "Profile (October 2007)," Background Notes: Ireland, Bureau of European and Eurasian Affairs, http://www.state.gov/r/pa/ei/bgn/3180.htm (accessed May 6, 2008), 14, 15.

67. National Governors Association (NGA) and Pew Center on the States, *Innovation America: Investing in Innovation* (Washington, DC: NGA Center for Best Practices, 2007), 49.

68. Jon Marcus, "The Celtic Tiger," 1.

69. Trani, *Dublin Diaries*, 6.

70. Gabriel M. Crean, *The Role of Higher Educational Sector and Its Institutes of Technology in Irish Economic Development*, presented to Congres National du RC-CFC, Winnipeg, Canada, November 1–3, 2007, p. 11.

71. Forfas, *Building Ireland's Knowledge Economy: The Irish Action Plan for Promoting Investment in R&D to 2010—Report to the Inter Departmental Committee on Science, Technology and Innovation* (July 2004), http://www.entemp.ie/publications/enterprise/2004/knowledgeeconomy.pdf (accessed May 6, 2008), 2.

72. Trani, *Dublin Diaries*, 5.

73. Trani, *Dublin Diaries*, 7.

74. Trani, *Dublin Diaries*, 7–8.

75. Marcus, "The Celtic Tiger," 14.

76. Higher Education Authority (HEA), "Higher Education Key Facts and Figures: 05/06," HEA, http://drupal.hea.ie/files/files/file/archive/statistics/2006/Higher%20Education%20Key%20Facts%20&%20Figures%2005-06.pdf (accessed May 6, 2008), 5, 6.

77. Ellen Hazelkorn, "Has Higher Education Become a Victim of Its Own Propaganda?" *Surviving the Construction of Global Knowledge/Spaces for the Knowledge Economy, GlobalHigherEd*, February 14, 2008, http://globalhighered.wordpress.com/2008/02/14/has-higher-education-become-a-victim-of-its-own-propaganda/ (accessed May 6, 2008), 3.

78. Bologna.ie, "Implementation in Ireland," Irish National Information Site on the Bologna Process (2005), http://www.bologna.ie/implement_ireland/default.asp (accessed May 6, 2008), 1.

79. Bologna.ie, "Progress to Date on Bologna Process," Irish National Information Site on the Bologna Process (2005), http://www.bologna.ie/progress/default.asp (accessed May 6, 2008), 1.

80. Trani, *Dublin Diaries*, 8.

81. Marcus, "The Celtic Tiger," 15.

82. Marcus, "The Celtic Tiger," 15.

83. Trani, *Dublin Diaries*, 6.

84. Marcus, "The Celtic Tiger," 14.

85. Landon Thomas Jr., "The Irish Economy's Rise Was Steep, and the Fall Was Fast," *New York Times*, January 4, 2009, http://www.nytimes.com/2009/01/04/business/worldbusiness/04ireland.html?_r=1 (accessed February 19, 2009), 3.

86. Thomas, "The Irish Economy's Rise," 6.

87. Eoin Burke-Kennedy, "EC Warns Ireland Over 'Optimistic' Recovery Plan," *Irish Times*, February 18, 2009, http://www.irishtimes.com/newspaper/breaking/2009/0218/breaking47_pf.html (accessed February 25, 2009), 2, 8.

88. Sean Flynn, "University Heads Warn of Severe Impact of Cutbacks," *Irish Times*, July 28, 2008, http://www.irishtimes.com/newspaper/frontpage/2008/0728/1217013341171.html (accessed February 25, 2009), 2.

89. Sean Flynn, "University Presidents Brace for More Cuts," *Irish Times*, September 25, 2008, http://www.irishtimes.com/newspaper/ireland/2008/0925/1222207743950.html (accessed February 25, 2009), 1; Sean Flynn, "University Presidents Angry at Latest Cuts," *Irish Times*, October 3, 2008, http://www.irishtimes

.com/newspaper/ireland/2008/1003/1222959304916.html (accessed February 25, 2009), 1, 2.

90. Niall Murray, "University Staff Vow to Resist Pay Cuts as Chiefs Outline Financial Difficulties," *Irish Examiner* (January 29, 2009), http://www.examiner.ie/story/ireland/idmhausnkf/rss2/ (accessed February 25, 2009), 1.

91. Government of Ireland, *Building Ireland's Smart Economy: A Framework for Sustainable Economic Renewal* (Dublin: Stationery Office, Government Publications, 2008), 7.

92. Government of Ireland, *Building Ireland's Smart Economy*, 13, 14, 15, 75.

93. Education Ireland, "Tanaiste Announces Establishment of Five New Science Foundation Ireland 'Strategic Research Clusters,'" About Us: Latest News, National University of Ireland, Galway (February 25, 2009), http://www.educationireland.ie/index.php?option=com_content&view=article&id=412%3Ata naiste-announces-establishment-of-five-new-science-foundation-ireland-strategic-research-clusters&catid=1%3Aeducation-ireland-news&Itemid=1 (accessed February 25, 2009), 1.

94. Education Ireland, "Tanaiste Announces Establishment," 4. A good survey of the National Development Plan, 2007–2013, and the role of higher education is included in a speech given by Peter Sutherland, a business leader and former Attorney General of Ireland, at the NUI Centennial Conference, Dublin Castle, December 2, 2008.

# Chapter 7

# Middle Eastern Higher Education: Two Oases in the Desert

Until recently, nations in the Middle East would not have been very prominent in any discussion of global higher education. Despite having increased the numbers of universities significantly, most Arab and Persian states had not been able to develop systems of higher education that were globally competitive or, in a number of instances, could fully meet the emerging needs of their own communities and nations. The overall rate of enrollment growth did not match the gains that were being made in most other nations, and, with a few notable exceptions, this problem was even more glaring for female students.[1] The bias toward the wealthy in college preparatory institutions limited the access of large segments of the population to higher education. And most nations found it extremely difficult to offer the technical and scientific training that Western states provided in order to develop the cadres of skilled engineers, information technology specialists, and others crucial for economic growth in the contemporary world. The output of higher education, in many nations, was mismatched with the emerging needs of a knowledge-based society.

Today, however, two of the most interesting experiments in higher education are taking place in the region. The small nation of Qatar is striving to utilize the wealth it has derived from its natural gas reserves to transform itself into a knowledge-driven economy that can sustain itself when its natural resources are depleted. Qatar has developed a unique set of partnerships with leading universities in the United States, funding them to establish branch campuses in Education City that focus on areas in which the university is internationally renowned. Virginia Commonwealth University (VCU) was the first university to establish a campus in Qatar, but it has been followed by many others, including Carnegie

Mellon, Cornell, Texas A&M, Georgetown, and Northwestern. The Qatar model is now being replicated by other nations.

Israel is another country that has been at the forefront of innovation in higher education. Thirty years ago, it had a small group of excellent, highly selective universities that served a relatively small portion of the population. Since then, a major transformation has occurred. There has been an explosion in the number of colleges and overall enrollment. Israel's policy priority of maintaining a technologically superior defense structure has given an extraordinary impetus to catalyzing a scientific infrastructure that goes well beyond defense and has enabled Israel to become a major player in new fields such as nanoscience and the biosciences. At the same time, local competition to become the chosen sites for new colleges and universities has demonstrated with particular clarity the relationship between colleges and universities and regional success and prosperity.

This chapter focuses on Qatar and Israel as two major models of higher education innovation in the Middle East. It begins with Qatar's effort to utilize its wealth from natural resources to create a new model for higher education in the Arab world. It then examines Israel's higher education transformation, showing how its response to pressing national security concerns has created a higher education system that has enabled the nation to develop a reputation in applied sciences that extends far beyond weapons and security systems. The innovations in both countries are in keeping with the trends occurring in higher education in the United States and Europe and in other parts of the developing world.

## QATAR: THE ECONOMIC BACKDROP

Jutting out into the waters of the Persian Gulf and barely brushing dry land along the borders of Saudi Arabia and the United Arab Emirates lies, according to Qatar's self-description, "one of the most progressive countries in the Arab world."[2] Sheikh Hamad Bin Khalifa Al-Thani has been the head of state of Qatar's emirate form of government since he deposed his father in a bloodless coup in 1995.[3] Considered progressive by regional standards, the Emir has introduced a series of relatively liberal reforms over the past decade or so in a country where the majority of its citizens (roughly 78 percent) are Muslim.[4]

After remaining small and stable until the early to mid-1900s, Qatar's population surged during the last half of the twentieth century, jumping from a reported sixteen thousand residents in 1949 to 111,113 in 1970.[5] Qatar's population growth has continued into the twenty-first century, reaching an estimated 907,229 residents in 2007.[6] Qatar's population growth has been matched and even exceeded by its increased economic output. Qatar was reported to have had the greatest growth in gross domestic product per capita in the world from 1995 to 2002.[7]

Once based on pearl fishing, Qatar's economy was transformed by the discovery of large deposits of oil and gas in the Persian Gulf in the 1940s.[8] No bigger than Connecticut at just over 4,400 square miles, Qatar shares an offshore natural gas reserve of 900 trillion cubic feet—the world's largest purely natural gas reserve, called the North Field—with Iran.[9] Qatar's portion of proved reserves of natural gas constitutes more than 5 percent of the world's total reserves, the third largest in the world.[10] Formerly one of the poorest countries in the Persian Gulf region, Qatar rose to regional economic prominence during the latter part of the twentieth century as a result of its successful and tenacious efforts to find ways to transport its huge reserves of natural gas to distant markets.[11]

The Emir has launched a targeted strategy to place Qatar "on the frontier of the global economy" by more fully capitalizing on Qatar's natural gas reserves, as well as by building and fully capitalizing on the country's intellectual reserves, through deep investments in education and science.[12] By 2012, Qatar is expected to have developed the technology to become the world's largest producer of liquefied natural gas and gas-to-liquid fuels.[13] Without losing sight of its ambitions to become a worldwide energy giant, Qatar also is trying to attract foreign investment in the development of its non-energy projects by further liberalizing the economy.[14] Supported by a five-year investment pipeline of $133 billion and a welcoming climate for foreign investment, major growth sectors in Qatar's economy include petroleum, industrial equipment, health care, utilities, construction, and aviation.[15]

Qatar's effort to sustain the prosperity created by its natural gas reserves by creating a higher education system relevant to a knowledge-based economy may be its most distinctive public policy initiative. Intent on transforming the country into a globally competitive knowledge-based society, the Emir founded the Qatar Foundation for Education, Science and Community Development (Qatar Foundation) in 1995.[16] The initial and ongoing mission of the Qatar Foundation has been, "To prepare the people of Qatar and the region to meet the challenges of an ever-changing world, and to make Qatar a leader in innovative education and research."[17] Attesting to the importance of the foundation's mission to the country's prosperity, the creation of the Qatar Foundation was among the earliest of the Emir's initiatives upon deposing his father.[18] A decade later, in a 2007 announcement on future plans of the Qatar Foundation, Robert Baxter, the foundation's communications adviser, cited the fact that the Emir has set aside 2.8 percent of Qatar's gross domestic product for education and research, highlighting the importance Qatar is giving to developing its human, intellectual, and social capital.[19] The Qatar Foundation is governed by a board of directors made up of internationally recognized leaders and innovators from academia, business, and government.[20] Chairing the board is Sheikha Mozah Bint Nasser Al-Missned, one of the Emir's three wives.[21] The foundation supports a network of centers and partnerships with elite institutions that encompass the education, health, community development, social service, media, corporate, and research sectors. Together, the foundation's affiliates are working to achieve the Emir's quest to raise Qatar's international profile, stimulate social progress, invest in his people's human potential, and diversify an extremely natural gas-dependent economy.[22] The hope of the foundation's leaders is that the Qatar Foundation's initiatives will serve as "an engine of growth and change for the nation."[23] The signature initiative for this aspiration has been the development of Education City, not only the site of the Qatar Foundation's headquarters and many of the foundation's centers and affiliates, but also one of the most interesting contemporary experiments in higher education, creating a national system of universities by partnering with a prestigious set of American universities.

## Education City: A University of Universities

While the presence of American or American-style universities in the Middle East dates back as far as 1866 with the establishment of the American University of Beirut and, a few decades later, the American University in Cairo, Education City has forged new territory in the Middle East and in the broader world of academia.[24] The "pedagogic city" is the first of its kind in the Middle East to host outposts of top-tier U.S. colleges.[25] The project's planners wanted to bring American-style higher education to Qatar and adapt it to Qatari culture, but they desired a more expeditious and convenient route than creating new universities on their turf as was done with the American University of Beirut or the American University of Kuwait.[26] According to a former Qatar Foundation spokesman, "The Emir's idea is that the world moves very fast, that your only real resource is your people, and that your people need to be equipped to adapt to a changing world. The feeling was, why start from scratch when the resources are there to bring great universities here? Why not bring the best of the best and put them together in Qatar?"[27] Thus was born the branch campus model of higher education in the Middle East. The brainchild of the Emir, Education City's branch campus goal is simple, yet unusual: "build a world-class institution comprising parts that are themselves highly regarded universities."[28] In essence, Education City is a "university of universities."[29]

VCU, based in Richmond, was chosen as Education City's pioneering school.[30] Opening its Qatar branch (VCUQ) in 1997, VCU brought four-year programs in arts and design from its prestigious School of the Arts.[31] VCUQ was so successful that the Qatar Foundation recruited the Ivy League's Cornell University in 2002. Cornell duplicated its Manhattan-based Weill Cornell Medical College in offering premed courses, as well as in offering the first American medical degree outside the United States and establishing Cornell's first branch campus overseas.[32] In 2003, Texas A&M University started operating undergraduate engineering programs, building on its Texas-based programs which have been routinely ranked among the best in the United States.[33] Carnegie Mellon University followed in 2004 with its undergraduate courses in business administration, which have been recognized in America for their scientific approach, and its computer science program, which is one of the oldest and most pioneering programs in the world.[34] The next addition, in 2005, was Georgetown University, which opened a branch of its elite School of Foreign Service.[35]

In 2007, Carnegie Mellon University in Qatar teamed up with the Qatar Science & Technology Park (QSTP) to begin offering an Executive Entrepreneurship Certificate Program.[36] Aiming to "transform Qatar's deep investment in research and education into business success stories," the nine-month, part-time program is run by Carnegie Mellon's Tepper School of Business and its Donald H. Jones Center for Entrepreneurship, which is recognized as one of the best in the world and has taught thousands of people to create new businesses, including the founder of iGate Corporation, a global information technology company with nearly $400 million market capitalization.[37] The same year, the Qatar Faculty of Islamic Studies began offering a two-year General Diploma in Islamic Studies, which was followed in February 2008 by an M.A. in Contemporary Fiqh (modern Islamic jurisprudence) and an M.A. in Public Policy in Islam.[38] And, in the fall of 2008, Northwestern University in Qatar began offering programs in journalism and communications.[39]

Before Education City came into existence, it was customary for Qatar's wealthier and more able male students to pursue their postsecondary education overseas, particularly in the United States.[40] Some never returned to Qatar, "apparently having decided that the West suited them better." Certainly, Qatar is not the only Arab country that has felt the pain of "brain drain." According to a study by the United Nations Development Program, more than fifteen thousand Arab physicians left their countries between 1998 and 2000.[41] Also, Arab academics and scientists are often faced with a dearth of job opportunities at home, as well as scant funding for research and development (R&D), which prompts them to search for greener pastures abroad. By importing Western higher education and taking other measures to bolster the country's research infrastructure, the masterminds behind Education

City insist that Qatar will experience "brain gain, not a brain drain."[42] They hope the branch campuses can meet the country's future requirements for engineers, doctors, and other professionals.[43] And they may end up being right. Since the advent of Education City's conglomeration of elite American university programs, fewer young Qataris say they will go abroad after high school.[44] In addition to the appeal of attending top-ranked programs, the prospect of having their tuition covered at highly competitive universities seems to be going a long way in recruiting Qatari residents to Education City.

While the recruitment and retention tool of free tuition requires considerable infusions of cash by the Qatar Foundation, such expenses are clearly only the tip of the mountain of investment that has been plowed into Education City. Precise financial figures are not publicly available.[45] However, a 2005 *Chronicle of Higher Education* article reported that "many billions of dollars" had been pumped into Education City.[46] ABC News reported in 2007 that more than $1 billion had been spent just on building Education City.[47] While none of the American universities with branch campuses comment directly on finances, it is clear that professors at the Education City campus are rewarded at a level "well beyond that of their colleagues in the United States."[48]

The investment in new and expanding university programs in Education City seems to be paying off. In 2005, more than six hundred applications were submitted for sixty spaces in Texas A&M's engineering program and forty students were selected from 170 applicants at VCUQ.[49] According to Robert Baxter (Qatar Foundation communications adviser), approximately seven hundred students attended the university programs at Education City in 2007, about half of whom were Qataris.[50] And enrollment numbers are expected to grow over the years ahead, climbing to eight thousand by 2015.[51]

In addition to quantitative success, Education City's enrollment has enjoyed qualitative success. American universities with campuses in Education City are finding the students "brighter and harder-working" than expected.[52] According to Suresh Tate, a professor of biochemistry at Weill Cornell Medical College in Qatar, "There was a lot of skepticism about the quality of the students we'd get here, but the quality is just unbelievable. More and more of our faculty in New York are asking to come here." Certainly, Qatar's deep pockets are part of what appeals to professors about Education City, but part of the allure undoubtedly is the opportunity to teach top-caliber students. And, professors get to do that using unparalleled educational resources. Marion Tate, a mathematics professor at Carnegie Mellon University in Qatar, described the experience of teaching in Education City's state-of-the-art facilities as "indescribable."

## Connecting to the Global Knowledge Economy

We have seen how the development of university-based research parks has become a common mechanism for connecting higher education research to commercial innovation. The QSTP exemplifies the national commitment to becoming a central participant in the global knowledge economy. With an investment of $600 million in the first phase of its buildings, QSTP includes world-class offices and laboratories designed for technology-based companies.[53] QSTP's Tech Centers are able to accommodate both heavily equipped laboratories and modern offices, and the park's Innovation Center includes a business incubator and offers business services.[54] As a free-trade zone, QSTP provides an easy, attractive setting in which to establish a technology-based company in Qatar.[55] And the Qatar Financial Center located in the park is designed to help attract international financial institutions and firms that provide professional services to the financial sector, further enhancing the park's appeal to established and start-up firms.[56]

Current tenants at QSTP include ConocoPhillips, Microsoft, General Electric, European Aeronautic Defence and Space Company, Cisco, Hydro, and Rolls-Royce.[57] QSTP's physical resources and service infrastructure will foster the types of linkages between academia and industry that can grow Qatar's knowledge economy. As Stephen Brand, senior vice president of Technology for ConocoPhillips (one of the organizations with a research and development center at the park), stated, "At QSTP, we'll be building innovation capability together with other companies, government entities, as well as academia. What's really important is the relationship of QSTP to the Education City that is next door."[58] Similarly, QSTP's operations manager, Salvino Salvaggio, stressed the importance of the higher education underpinnings of the research park: "Qatar has a proud and successful history in economic activities such as oil and gas projects, construction and trading. In the future technology entrepreneurship will be added to this list, as a result of world-class training and support programs of Qatar's universities."[59]

### Enhancing Social Capital

In addition to the obvious outcomes of increased human and intellectual capital, Education City is cultivating significant social capital for Qatar. From the outset, expanding higher education opportunities for Arab women has been one of Sheikha Mozah's main goals for the Qatar Foundation.[60] VCUQ, the first branch campus established by an American institution at Education City, offered its arts and design classes to an exclusively female student body for around a decade, before going coed. "Education City is the best thing ever for women in Qatar," said Dana Ahdad, a 2004 graduate of VCUQ and a graphic designer with Al Jazeera's children's channel, which has headquarters in Doha.[61] According to Ahdad, "Before Education City, higher education for women was not much of an option. Now, more women are becoming convinced bit by bit that they can have their own achievements."[62]

Opening the doors of higher education to women has had a much broader impact than furthering societal reform. It also has had a positive economic impact. With a rapidly expanding business arena, Qatar's workforce needs have dramatically increased, opening up career opportunities for women, especially those with the right training. Women made up an estimated 18 percent of Qatar's workforce in 2002, more than double the rate of neighboring Saudi Arabia.[63] According to a former dean of VCUQ, Christina Lindholm, "We're seeing a greater acceptance of our [female] graduates in Qatar's burgeoning design industry."[64] Going coeducational in the fall of 2007, VCUQ continues to provide all students with the opportunity to "expand their cultural perspectives as well as acquire expertise for the workplace within an energetic and compassionate learning environment."[65]

While Education City represents great social progress for Qatar, providing equal opportunities to male and female students is not always an easy or achievable task. Jacobo Carrasquel, a computer science professor at Carnegie Mellon in Qatar, has men and women participating in roughly equal numbers in his classroom, but men elect to sit on one side of the room, while women sit on the other.[66] According to Dennis Busch, director of student affairs at Texas A&M's Qatar branch, the divide between the genders becomes even more pronounced outside the classroom: "I was not prepared for the extreme gender segregation on a social level." Bridging American and Arab cultures is not without conflict, but foreign professors and administrators are working hard to learn about Qatari culture; and, while Education City's aim in establishing an American university presence in Qatar was to fuel economic growth and social change, American institutions are also adapting to Qatari culture, fostering a process of mutual adaptation.[67]

Such a process of mutual adaptation could not come at a better time in light of the "political minefield" of U.S.-Arab relations.[68] Jim Holste, associate dean for research at Texas A&M in Qatar, said that, at first, Texas A&M officials were "taken aback" when, just months after September 11, 2001, they were approached about creating an overseas campus in a conservative Arab nation.[69] However, Holste said that while university representatives were "very slow to make the first visit," the delegation they finally sent to Qatar was struck by "the sense of opportunity to be a part of a dialogue with the Arab-Muslim world."[70] According to Holste, "As a land-grant institution, part of our thought pattern is, What can we also do for the community? We saw it as a chance to show people in this part of the world how to do things in a progressive way."[71] Similarly, Georgetown's presence in Qatar was embraced as an opportunity to build on "the university's Jesuit tradition of promoting cross-cultural understanding."[72]

More American universities seem to be viewing potential partnerships in the Middle East in the way that those who made the decision to come to Education City see it. But this has not always been or is, even today, the only perspective that has been advanced. In some instances, faculty have been skeptical of the ventures, worrying that the funds derived from the effort were driving university administrators or expressing the belief that the university should not be fully involved in places that may not share its set of beliefs on human rights and cultural freedom. Ultimately, however, the arguments about the benefits of experiencing life in different cultures and the sense that American higher education can be a positive force in the world have carried the day, enabling universities to establish these collaborations without expending much political capital on the home campus.

As for the Qatari perspective on cultural assimilation with Americans, Sheikha Mozah offered a balanced perspective: "Our goal is to do as our ancestors did before us, who believe[d] in the urgency of meeting other civilizations, but not melting into them. And this is why we believe in the power of education to guide us toward this goal."[73] With cultural awareness increasing in both directions, Education City is a place where "bridges are being built, between cultures and to a better future."[74]

## ISRAEL

### Evolution of Higher Education

Even before Israel was established as an independent country, advocates for a Jewish homeland looked to higher education as a basis for cultivating the human capital necessary for a strong economic foundation.[75] In 1924, the Technion—Israel Institute of Technology in Haifa—was opened to train engineers and architects.[76] In 1925, the Hebrew University of Jerusalem (HU) was founded as a center of higher learning for youth in the Land of Israel and to attract Jewish students and scholars from abroad.[77] In 1934, the Daniel Sieff Research Institute (later renamed the Weizmann Institute of Science) was established, originally with two main research branches—organic chemistry and biochemistry.[78]

After Israel became an independent state in 1948, the country's system of higher education expanded incrementally. Bar Ilan University and Tel Aviv University were established in the 1950s.[79] In 1958, the Council for Higher Education (CHE) was established to ensure a coordinated approach to planning and development among higher education institutions (HEIs), and the Planning and Budget Committee (PBC) of the CHE was granted a monopoly on the allocation of public funds to HEIs.[80] The University of Haifa was established in 1963 under the joint auspices of the HU and the Haifa Municipality.[81] In 1972, the university gained academic accreditation as a separate institution from the CHE. Ben-Gurion University of the Negev was established in 1969 with the aim of bringing development to the Negev.

Until the 1980s, Israel's higher education system was dominated by its five full-scale universities, one technological institute, and one research institute, along with Israel's Open University, which was established in the 1970s.[82] Initially, the CHE and PBC assumed a cautious stance toward the expansion of the higher education system, preferring to invest public funds in existing HEIs.[83] However, the 1980s were marked by growing political decentralization and greater economic liberalization in Israel, which led to mounting pressures for change and expansion in higher education.[84] This was reflected in legislation passed in the 1990s that created a more favorable environment for the creation of new colleges and increased competition among institutions of higher education.[85]

The term *college* should be explained, as it has a different connotation in Israel than in the United States. Institutions of higher education in Israel are classified into three major groups by the CHE:

1. Universities and institutes with doctoral degree programs
2. Academic and regional colleges with undergraduate degree programs
3. Teacher training colleges—Colleges of education that grant the B.Ed. degree

Colleges in Israel generally focus on teaching and minimal research takes places at these institutions, unlike universities.

The number of institutions accredited by the CHE went from sixteen in 1980 to sixty-two in 2003.[86] Enrollment more than doubled from 1990 to 1999, increasing from 76,000 students to 180,000, not including Open University attendees. The increased number of institutions of higher education made higher education accessible to individuals who would not have been able to gain entry under the previous system. And rapid population growth, especially that associated with immigration from the former U.S.S.R.[87] helped to fuel the enrollment boom. By 2003, Israel had twenty-three teacher-training colleges, five technical colleges, several regional and specialized colleges, and ten accredited private colleges.[88] In addition, about fifty foreign universities established branches in Israel.[89]

The ultimate impact of this expansion has been a dramatic reorientation of the higher education system, one that has systematically increased accessibility and created the kind of niches and specialized opportunities relevant to a knowledge economy.

They also had an impact on the country as a whole, aiding in the development of various geographical areas, especially in the periphery.

### From National Security to the Life Sciences

Israel's response to its national security concerns has been a defining feature of its evolution as a nation. "Israel has consistently topped any list of developed economies in percentage of national product devoted to defense."[90] At the height of its defense spending in 1976 and 1977, Israel's military expenditures were more than 30 percent of its gross national product (GNP) (the United States spent 5.7 percent, the United Kingdom 4.9 percent, and France 3.85 percent for the same period).[91] Despite significant reductions in the overall percentage of GNP devoted to defense, Israel's defense budget is still today higher in relative terms than that of the United States or European countries.[92]

The development of Israel's military-industrial complex has ultimately been a crucial factor in its prosperity, spurring technological innovation and netting significant export income.[93] The narrative about the domestic impact of Israel's military spending is not unlike the story that has been told in the United States about the civilian benefits that accrued from the space program and from inventions that were initially applied to military purposes. Israel's pursuit of technological superiority in the military sector is widely seen as having a spillover effect in commercial industries, catalyzing the 1990s high-tech boom.[94] Observers have maintained that the entrepreneurial spirit, the problem-solving orientation, and the system-oriented approach, which are characteristic of most of the successful high-tech firms in Israel, originated in Israel's defense industry.[95] In the twenty-first century, the defense sector continues to be a very important source of new technological know-how (intellectual capital) and experienced personnel (human capital) for the civilian high-tech industry.[96]

Israel's universities have occupied an important role in the national effort to develop technological superiority in defense. For more than forty years, leveraging the research capacities of Israel's universities has been crucial to its national security goals. After 9/11, homeland security concerns in Israel became even more urgent. Thirty homeland security companies were launched in Israel in the first six months of 2007 alone, in part because of government subsidies that have provided the means for Israel's universities to serve as incubators for security and weapons start-ups.[97] More recently, Israel's universities have become well-known for their nanotechnology research, an area seen as having significant defense applications. During a 2006 visit to Germany, Israeli president Shimon Peres (vice premier at the time) stated that nanotechnology was the key to Israel's defense in future armed conflicts.[98] "The missiles threatening Israel and the terrorists threatening to hurt the people of Israel should be handled using weapons that will be developed by the technology of the future, nano-technology," Peres said.[99] While in Germany, Peres and Ukrainian president Victor Yushchenko discussed the role of nanotechnology in the fight against world terror.[100]

Israel's scientific output and reputation today extend far beyond the defense arena. In the last two decades, Israel has gained a reputation as a global leader in the knowledge economy. Israel has already been included by the Institute for Science Information among the top fifteen most effective countries in terms of producing nanotech-related knowledge and techniques.[101] Over the last decade, the intellectual property yield of nanoscience and nanotechnology research in Israel has been very high, with more than one hundred patents and about two thousand publications (from 1995 to 2006).[102] Israel is home to six world-class nanoscience and nanotechnology research institutions.[103] Israel's universities accommodate more than 250 nanotech researchers, a figure that is nearly double what it was in 2002. With the announced increase in university-based matching government funds in 2006, Israel's nanotech centers stand to be among the world's best funded, as well as the most respected.[104]

The Israeli effort in nanotechnology is matched by the societal commitment to the life sciences more generally. Israel is leveraging a highly educated workforce, including a talented pool of physicians and biologists, to become a global leader in the life sciences, including the medical devices, biotechnology, and pharmaceutical sectors.[105] As of 2007, Israel was a worldwide leader in patents granted per capita in the life sciences: it had first place in the medical devices arena and fourth place in the biopharmaceutical field.[106] The total number of life sciences patents as percentage of total patents written by Israeli inventors placed the country in first place worldwide.[107] Israel is also at the forefront of embryonic stem cell research.[108]

Israel is headquarters to about nine hundred life sciences companies, approximately half of which were established since the turn of the twenty-first century and only 40 percent of which were generating revenue as of 2007.[109] With an additional 21 percent in the clinical stage of development and the remainder in earlier stages of development, Israel's life sciences industry—a fast-growing, young, innovative industry worldwide—could well become the nation's ticket to even greater global economic prominence in the future.[110] Just in 2005, the Israeli life sciences industry had $3.4 billion in exports and grew by more than 35 percent.[111] Israeli pharmaceutical and biologic sales to the United States alone equaled $1.5 billion in 2005 and an estimated $2.9 billion in 2006, with an additional $480 million in 2005 and $610 million in 2006 in medical devices sales to the United States.[112]

While the life sciences industry is relatively young in Israel, there have already been some remarkable university-driven commercial applications of Israeli biotechnology research, both on its own soil and abroad.[113] Cutting-edge university-based discoveries are fueling Israel's economy, as well as helping to protect the country's security, environment, health, and overall quality of life.

For instance, the Weizmann Institute of Science in Rehovot, which pioneered biotechnology in Israel, is making significant contributions to the international Human Genome Project.[114] Also, the Weizmann Institute's Department of Molecular Genetics was where InterPharm developed its leading product, bulk recombinant human interferon beta-1a for the treatment of multiple sclerosis.[115] One of the contributions of the Bioinformatics Unit in the Department of Molecular Genetics has been the study of mutated genes that cause such disorders as Down syndrome and Alzheimer disease. The Weizmann Institute has its own technology transfer company, Yeda Research.[116] Examples of biotechnology investments include Gamida Cell, developing technologies for ex vivo expansion and manipulation of stem cells in bone marrow, and Balm Pharmaceuticals, developing a proprietary platform technology utilizing diastereomeric peptides. As a result of the Weizmann Institute's enterprising endeavors, the neighboring Kiryat Weizmann Science Park has become the national center of the country's biotechnology industry, with the largest companies based there.

Also, the HU and the affiliated Hadassah University Medical Center allocate major resources to the life sciences.[117] The university's Biotechnology and Fermentation Laboratory is often held up as a model for a new generation of precompetitive industrial research centers, in which industrial and academic scientists work together on problems of scale-up and feasibility testing.[118] Among successes in recent years, a team of HU researchers has created a new material—bioactive sol-gel glass—for immobilizing enzymes and other bio-organic molecules. The immobilized enzymes can even act as biosensors in medical or environmental applications. Another HU success has been in the area of steroids. Researchers in Jerusalem have encapsulated steroids in microscopic vesicles where they are more accessible to chemical interactions. Yissum Technology is the university's technology transfer company. One biotechnology commercial success in the area of bioinformatics based on HU know-how is Keryx. This Jerusalem start-up has developed a mathematical formula that harnesses raw genome data. Based on this, the Jerusalem Bio Park was opened on the Hadassah Ein Kerem Campus with the aim of central-izing all of the commercial activities of Hadassah and the HU.[119]

There are two telling facts that indicate the extent of Israel's commitment to creating a knowledge-based society. First, in 2002, Israel possessed the highest per capita number of scientists in the world, with 135 for every ten thousand citizens (as compared with eighty-five per ten thousand in the United States).[120] Second, in 2007, Israel's total expenditures for R&D as a percentage of gross domestic product topped all industrialized countries at 4.8 percent (the United States was in eighth place at 2.2 percent).[121]

## Higher Education and Regional Development

In addition to the central role that university-based R&D plays in Israel's economic development on a national level, individual HEIs—especially the more recently accredited colleges that have hit Israel's higher education scene over the past decade or so—are playing a key role in the development of the localities and regions where they are located. In much of the rest of the world, the prevailing assumption that HEIs are place-bound and would not relocate because of market forces proves to be true, but Israel is a special case.[122] The documented influence of HEIs on local development, coupled with the rise in new colleges in Israel, has made higher education an arena of competition among local authorities in Israel since the 1990s.[123] Some of the shorter-range effects of HEIs that Israeli localities have competed for are direct employment and the multi-plier effects of HEI expenditures.[124] Longer-range effects largely revolve around improved local human capital.[125] There are also indirect effects, such as the economic growth that results from improved quality of life. Just recently the Israeli Government decided to establish a fifth medical school in the Galilee with the aim of further developing the Galilee.

Until 1980, all accredited HEIs in Israel were located in only six cities: Tel Aviv, Jerusalem, Haifa, Ramat Gan, Rehovot, and Be'er Sheva.[126] By 2003, because localities utilized various marketing and political strategies to recruit new colleges, sixty-two HEIs (excluding foreign branches) were disbursed throughout thirty-three localities.[127] While an HEI presence re-mained most prominent in major metropolitan areas, a transformation in the spatial distribution of HEIs took place as a result of the proliferation of new colleges in metropolitan fringe and peripheral locations, leading to a continued higher incidence in metropolitan centers but a diminishing prevalence.[128] With the increased awareness of the influence of HEIs on economic development, Israel experienced a shift in the role of localities in influencing where new HEIs were established. Despite the continued cen-tralized legal authority over HEIs existing with the CHE, local authorities in Israel have gained substantial informal autonomy since the late 1970s, reflected in the rise of local initiatives around recruiting new HEIs.[129] In the context of a less centralized and more competitive (i.e., open) system of higher education, local governments started making the strategic decision to compete over HEIs and to encourage their development, despite not formally being assigned a role in higher education.[130]

The new publicly funded colleges were intended to meet the growing demand for postsecondary degrees at a price the country could afford, as well as bring higher education to low-income students and geographic regions that lacked easy access to the universities.[131] According to Shlomo Grossman, head of the PBC of the CHE, "Colleges are a success story."[132] Said Grossman, "They have very significantly increased access to higher education. And they have increased the proportion of students in the country's peripheral regions by bringing higher education closer to home."[133]

The enrollment numbers back Grossman's claim, as does the spatial distribution of the new HEIs.[134] In the academic year 1989–1990, Israel had 55,230 undergraduates. By 2003–2004, that number had nearly tripled to 150,150, and less than half of those students were at the universities. At the beginning of the 1990s, there were no institutions of higher education in Israel's northern Galilee region. Today, 6.8 percent of Israel's undergraduates study at the colleges in the north. An additional 15.2 percent study in the southern region, where the substandard schools used to cause people to assume that "only a genius could get a college degree," said Ze'ev Tzahor, president of Sapir Academic College.[135]

Beyond achieving greater accessibility and geographical distribution, the CHE's decision to support the establishment of publicly funded colleges in unserved and underserved geographic regions has served a similar purpose as the government's wide dispersion of military outposts—directing economic activity to less developed parts of Israel.[136] While producing a variety of idiosyncratic benefits, individual HEIs are all generally contributing in four direct ways to their surrounding communities:

1. Human capital development
2. Intellectual capital development
3. Financial capital development
4. Social capital development

An example of this phenomenon is Sapir Academic College, which is located in Sederot, a town that "dangles precariously from the northeast corner of the Gaza Strip," ten miles from the Mediterranean coast in the economically depressed region near the sand dunes of the Negev, Israel's southern desert.[137] Sederot is hardly an idyllic college town, reporting a 19 percent unemployment rate and only a 41 percent high school graduation rate in 2005; it is frequently the target of Palestinian rockets.[138] However, the small green campus of Sapir has put Sederot on the map.[139] With eight thousand students studying in fifteen departments, Sapir is the largest public college in Israel proper, not including the West Bank. Most of the people who live near Sederot cannot afford to relocate to the center of the country to attend any of Israel's major universities.[140] Besides serving the local population, Sapir draws a significant number of students from other parts of the country and, according to Tzahor, "More than 80 percent of our students are the first generation in their families to get higher education."[141]

Beyond opening its doors to a previously unserved cadre of students, Sapir serves the community in a variety of other ways.[142] Its public administration and policy students are required to work in a legal aid clinic in the town. Also, Sapir brought a major high-tech employer to Sederot by tailoring its programs to meet the company's needs. The company, Amdocs, has constructed a facility adjacent to the campus, creating employment opportunities, infusing the town with new financial capital, and fostering the intellectual capital of the region. Sapir also has built a highly regarded film and television department that draws students from central Israel; the department's annual film festival, for which young filmmakers produce works on local and societal issues, has spawned a regional artistic consciousness.[143]

## HIGHER EDUCATION INNOVATION IN THE MIDDLE EAST

In very different ways and for very different reasons, Qatar and Israel are the higher education innovation leaders in the Middle East. Qatar's leadership has undertaken a deliberate and an extraordinarily expensive effort to convert the nation from a small and unusually affluent petrostate to one that can be independently competitive in the global knowledge economy and a commercial leader in the Middle East. It has done so by developing partnerships with a set of Western universities around an area of expertise in which each institution excels. The Western university is funded by the Qatar Foundation to establish a branch campus in Education City, focusing primarily on the identified specialty area. Israel's higher education system has also been transformed in the past twenty-five years. The country's long-standing policy of trying to maintain a defense apparatus that is technologically superior to that of other countries in the region has helped to nurture a university-based science culture that has impacted areas of Israeli society far beyond defense. In addition, Israel's decision to expand the number of colleges and universities has not only increased the number of college and university students, but also created a healthy competition among localities for institutions that contribute to local and regional prosperity.

The Qatar model is, of course, highly unusual inasmuch as it involves taking an entire degree program from a Western university and placing it in Education City. Yet it is an innovation that is becoming widely emulated in the region. In Dubai, Michigan State University (MSU) began operating in 2008 in the emirate's new International Academic City, becoming the first American-run campus to locate in the $3.27 billion, 25-million-square-foot complex designed for universities, colleges, and research centers.[144] MSU Dubai has offered students and professionals from the United Arab Emirates and the wider region bachelor's and master's degree programs as it has phased those programs in over the 2008–2009 and 2009–2010 academic years.[145]

And New York University (NYU) is developing a comprehensive liberal arts campus in a major gateway city to the Middle East, Abu Dhabi.[146] NYU Abu Dhabi will be a full-scale liberal arts college, with select graduate programs driven by advanced research.[147] The first class of students will be enrolled in the fall of 2010. Over time, the campus will have more than two thousand students selected according to the same high standards governing admission to the U.S.-based NYU.[148] NYU's agreement with the Emirate of Abu Dhabi to create NYU Abu Dhabi is the outcome of a shared understanding of the essential roles of higher education in the twenty-first century, including the benefits that a research university brings to the society that sustains it and the public good of preparing students to become true citizens of the world.[149]

Even in places that have not adopted the Qatar model specifically, the nation's renewed investment in higher education is prompting others to do the same. For instance, the budget of Saudi Arabia's higher education ministry nearly tripled from 2004 to 2007, to $15 billion, much of which has been devoted to opening more than one hundred new colleges and universities.[150] And Saudi King Abdullah has invested $10 billion of his own money to establish a graduate-level science and technology university.[151]

Some participants and observers of the Qatar experiment could not be more enthusiastic and believe that the impact will have an irrevocable positive influence on the future of Qatar. The dean of Carnegie Mellon University in Qatar, Chuck Thorpe, envisions his graduates soon starting high-tech companies in Education City using local venture capital.[152] Others have a similar vision: "We are looking forward to the day when a Qatari start-up company with a national as its CEO starts functioning (in QSTP)."[153]

At times, the impact of the experiment is seen as extending far beyond Qatar. Jeffrey Lehman, the former president of Cornell University who was heavily involved with building his university's outpost in Qatar, remarked, "I don't think it's an exaggeration to say that Education City is a glimpse at the future of higher education."[154] Shirley Robinson Pippins, the former president of Suffolk County Community College in New York, was equally impressed. Returning from a visit to Qatar in 2006, she noted, "What I witnessed in Qatar is nothing short of a revolution in education, with major implications for the future of diplomacy, peace in the region and new standards for global competitiveness."[155]

We do not quite know how Qatar's model of importing entire programs from Western universities will eventually evolve. Will the universities in Qatar be able to offer programs of similar quality with similar faculty over time? Will the nation be able to become a successful player in the global knowledge economy? Will the efforts undertaken in Education City such as the establishment of a journalism program under the auspices of Northwestern's prestigious Medill School help to transform the social and political milieu of Qatar, or will it bring Northwestern's graduates into conflict with authoritarian elements in the political culture? But the very fact that these questions are being asked is a testimony to the ambitiousness of the project and the interest with which its outcomes will be observed over the next few years.

The transformation of Israeli higher education has not received anywhere near the attention of that in Qatar. But it has shown that, even for a relatively small nation, it is possible to make significant impacts with higher education policy. The expansion of the college and university system to a far wider range of localities is showing how higher education can have an impact on local prosperity in the twenty-first century. And because Israel has built new colleges and universities, not simply increased enrollments at universities in place, it has provided a demonstration of higher education's economic impact that is not always recognized where institutions already exist. Moreover, the success of Israeli companies in the global economy and Israel's capacity to generate more scientists per capita than most any other nation indicate that the knowledge economy is open to nations of all sizes, if they can find the right niche.

## NOTES

1. Nader Fergany, *Arab Higher Education and Development: An Overview* (Cairo: Almishkat Centre for Research, February 2000), http://www.worldbank.org/mdf/mdf3/papers/education/Fergany.pdf (accessed January 16, 2008), 7.

2. Arabnet, "Qatar: Location," Arabnet, http://www.arab.net/qatar/qr_location.htm (accessed June 4, 2007), 1; Nina Eaglin, "Qatar: Embracing Democracy," CBS News, http://www.cbsnews.com (accessed June 19, 2007), 1.

3. Arabnet, "Qatar: Introduction," Arabnet, http://www.arab.net/qatar/qr_early history.htm (accessed June 5, 2007), 1; Simon Romero, "Qatar Finds a Currency of

Its Own: Natural Gas," *New York Times*, 2005, 1, http://query.nytimes.com/gst/fullpage.html?res=9F07E2D91430F931A15751C1A9639 C8B63; Central Intelligence Agency (CIA), "Qatar: Introduction," *The World Fact Book* (Washington, DC: Office of Public Affairs, Central Intelligence Agency, 2007), https://www.cia.gov/library/publications/the-world-factbook/print/qa.html (accessed June 5, 2007) 1.

4. Katherine Zoepf, "In Qatar's 'Education City,' U.S. Colleges Build Atop a Gusher," *Chronicle of Higher Education* 51, no. 33 (2005): A42; CIA, "Qatar: Introduction," 17.

5. Helem Chapin Metz, "Qatar Population," *Persian Gulf States: A Country Study* (Washington, DC: GPO for the Library of Congress, 1993) http://countrystudies.us/persian-gulf-states/70.htm (accessed June 5, 2007), 1–2.

6. CIA, "Qatar: People," *The World Fact Book* (Washington, DC: Office of Public Affairs, Central Intelligence Agency, 2007), https://www.cia.gov/library/publications/the-world-factbook/print/qa.html (accessed June 5, 2007), 1.

7. Joel F. Colton, "A Middle East Knowledge Economy," *AURP 21st Annual Conference* (Chicago: Qatar Science & Technology Park, Member of Qatar Foundation, October 26, 2006), http://open.nat.gov.tw/OpenFront/report/show_file.jsp?sysId=C09600336&fileNo=011#1 (accessed June 8, 2007), 4.

8. BBC News, "Country Profile: Qatar," BBC News, http://newsvote.bbc.co.uk/ (accessed June 4, 2007), 1; Carl Hilker, *Where Pearls Are Found* (Washington, DC: Trade & Environment Database, American University, 1996), http://www1.american.edu/ted/pearl.htm (accessed June 4, 2007), 1.

9. Romero, "Qatar Finds a Currency," 1.

10. CIA, "Qatar: Economy," *The World Fact Book* (Washington, DC: Office of Public Affairs, Central Intelligence Agency, 2007), https://www.cia.gov/library/publications/the-world-factbook/print/qa.html (accessed June 5, 2007), 1.

11. BBC News, "Country Profile: Qatar," 1; Romero, "Qatar Finds a Currency of Its Own: Natural Gas," 1.

12. Romero, "Qatar Finds a Currency of Its Own: Natural Gas," 1; Colton, "A Middle East Knowledge Economy," 5.

13. Colton, "A Middle East Knowledge Economy," 5, 8.

14. BBC News, "Country Profile: Qatar," 9; CIA, "Qatar: Economy," 1.

15. Colton, "A Middle East Knowledge Economy," 5, 7; IFP Qatar, Ltd., "Qatar Science & Technology Park Announces $130 Million Venture Capital Funds," Industry News, http://www.ifpqatar.com/News_show_news.asp?id=2637 (accessed June 8, 2007), 7.

16. Qatar Foundation, "Qatar Foundation: Our Vision and Mission," Qatar Foundation, http://www.qf.edu.qa/output/page293.asp (accessed May 31, 2007), 2; Qatar Foundation, "Qatar Foundation: History," Qatar Foundation, http://www.qf.edu.qa/output/page294.asp (accessed May 31, 2007), 1.

17. Qatar Foundation, "Qatar Foundation: Our Vision and Mission," 1.

18. Qatar Foundation, "Qatar Foundation: History," 1.

19. "Education City Unveils Expansion Plans," *Gulf Times*, March 27, 2007, http://www.gulf-times.com (accessed March 28, 2007), 8.

20. Qatar Foundation, "Qatar Foundation: Governance—the Board of Directors," Qatar Foundation, http://www.qf.edu.qa/output/page298.asp (accessed May 31, 2007), 1.

21. Zoepf, "In Qatar's 'Education City,'" A42.

22. Qatar Foundation, "Qatar Foundation: Education City," Qatar Foundation, http://www.qf.edu.qa/output/page301.asp (accessed May 31, 2007), 1; Zoepf, "In Qatar's 'Education City,'" A42.

23. Zoepf, "In Qatar's 'Education City,'" A42.

24. Roula Khalaf, "Middle East Still Hungry to Learn the American Way: Arab Enthusiasm for US-Style Education Remains Undimmed Despite Antagonism on the Streets," *FT: Financial Times—World Business Newspaper*, February 11, 2004, www.FT.com (accessed June 20, 2007), 8; AMIDEAST Yemen, "American and American-Style Universities in the Middle East," *Yemen Observer—Opinions* (May 12, 2007), http://www.yobserver.com (accessed June 4, 2007), 1, 3.

25. Reuters, "Qataris Get U.S. Education without Leaving Home," *Washington Post*, April 28, 2004, http://www.washingtonpost.com/wp-dyn/articles/A62294-2004May3_2.html (accessed June 20, 2007), 2.

26. Zoepf, "In Qatar's 'Education City,'" A42.

27. Zoepf, "In Qatar's 'Education City,'" A42.

28. Zoepf, "In Qatar's 'Education City,'" A42.

29. Qatar Foundation, "Qatar Foundation: History," 4.

30. Gary Robertson, "The Art of Expansion," *Richmond-Times Dispatch*, March 16, 2005, http://www2.timesdispatch.com/ (accessed June 4, 2007), 14.

31. Virginia Commonwealth University Qatar (VCUQ), "About VCUQ," VCUQ, http://www.qatar.vcu.edu/output/page139.asp (accessed June 7, 2007), 4.

32. Robertson, "The Art of Expansion," 14; Jim Krane, "Rather Than Study Abroad, Arabs Bring Foreign Colleges to Them," *Richmond Times-Dispatch*, December 1, 2006, 13; Zoepf, "In Qatar's 'Education City,'" A42; Weill Cornell Medical College in Qatar, *Admissions Brochure* (Doha, Qatar: Office of Admissions, Weill Cornell Medical College in Qatar, 2006), 2.

33. Texas A&M University at Qatar, *Chemical, Electrical, Mechanical, Petroleum Engineering Programs* (Doha, Qatar: Office of Admissions, Texas A&M University at Qatar, 2007), 2; Zoepf, "In Qatar's 'Education City,'" A42.

34. Carnegie Mellon Qatar Campus, *Your Future Begins Here* (Doha: Carnegie Mellon Qatar Campus, n.d.), 2; Zoepf, "In Qatar's 'Education City,'" A42.

35. Krane, "Rather Than Study Abroad," 10.

36. Tepper School of Business, Carnegie Mellon University, "Tepper School of Business to Begin Entrepreneurship Program in Qatar," *PR Newswire—United Business Media*, May 24, 2007, FindLaw—Legal News and Commentary, http://findlaw.com (accessed June 8, 2007), 1, 2.

37. Tepper School of Business, Carnegie Mellon University, "Tepper School of Business," 2, 3.

38. Qatar Foundation, "Qatar Faculty of Islamic Studies," Qatar Foundation, http://www.qf.org.qa/output/page284.asp (accessed March 27, 2009), 2.

39. Emily Glazer, "Schools Abroad Try to 'Mirror' U.S. Campuses," *Daily Northwestern*, May 11, 2007, http://www.dailynorthwestern.com/ (accessed June 4, 2007), 2; Qatar Foundation, "Northwestern University in Qatar," Qatar Foundation, http://www.qf.org/qa/output/page283.asp (accessed March 27, 2009), 1.

40. Zoepf, "In Qatar's 'Education City,'" A42.

41. Taieb Mahjoub and Faisal Baatout, "Qatar Seeks to Reverse Arab Brain Drain," *Middle East Times*, March 20, 2006, http://www.metimes.com (accessed June 4, 2007), 2.

42. The Economist Intelligence Unit, Ltd., "Qatar Economy: Investing Big for a New Society," Economist Intelligence Unit—ViewsWire, http://viewswire.com (accessed June 5, 2007), 3.

43. The Economist Intelligence Unit, Ltd., "Qatar Economy," 3.

44. Zoepf, "In Qatar's 'Education City,'" A42.

45. "Arabs Bring Colleges to Them," *Caymanian Compass*, December 4, 2006, http://www.caycompass.com/ (accessed June 4, 2007), 6.

46. Zoepf, "In Qatar's 'Education City,'" A42.

47. Danna Harman, "American Education Thriving . . . in Qatar," ABC News, http://abcnews.go.com/International (accessed February 22, 2007), 18.

48. Harman, "American Education Thriving," 18; Zoepf, "In Qatar's 'Education City,'" A42.

49. Dana Micucci, "Classes Span Cultural Divide," *International Herald Tribune Americas*, October 31, 2005, http://www.ith.com/articles/2005/10/17/news/Redcit.php (accessed June 7, 2007), 16.

50. "Education City Unveils Expansion Plans," 12.

51. Zoepf, "In Qatar's 'Education City,'" A42.

52. Zoepf, "In Qatar's 'Education City,'" A42.

53. Qatar Science & Technology Park (QSTP), "What We Offer," Qatar Foundation, http://www.qstp.org.qa/output/page559.asp (accessed March 27, 2009), 1.

54. QSTP, "What We Offer," 2, 3.

55. QSTP, "What We Offer," 7.

56. QSTP, "What We Offer," 8.

57. QSTP, "Current Members," Qatar Foundation, http://www.qstp.org.qa/output/page54.asp (accessed March 27, 2009).

58. Zawya, "ConocoPhillips Says Qatar Science & Technology Park Will Attract World's Best," Zawya, http://www.zawya.com/Story.cfm/sid ZAWYA20090304115132/ConocoPhillips%20says%20Qatar%20Science%20&%20 Technology%20Park%20will%20attract%20world's%20best (accessed March 27, 2009), 10.

59. Inc.com., "Middle East Entrepreneurship Program Launched," *New York Times*, May 30, 2007, http://www.nytimes.com (accessed June 8, 2007), 2; Lara Lynn Golden, "Entrepreneurship Can Be Learned, Says QSTP: Great Business Innovators Are Made, Not Born, and Qatar Is Setting Up Programs That Will Do Just That," AME Info—the Ultimate Middle East Business Resource, http://www.ameinfo.com/117972.html (accessed June 8, 2007), 6.

60. Zoepf, "In Qatar's 'Education City,'" A42.

61. Micucci, "Classes Span Cultural Divide," 11.

62. Micucci, "Classes Span Cultural Divide," 11, 12.

63. Micucci, "Classes Span Cultural Divide," 9.

64. Micucci, "Classes Span Cultural Divide," 10.

65. John DeMao, e-mail message to Kelly Myles, June 7, 2007; VCUQ, "About VCUQ," 2.

66. Zoepf, "In Qatar's 'Education City,'" A42.

67. Zoepf, "In Qatar's 'Education City,'" A42.

68. Micucci, "Classes Span Cultural Divide," 3.

69. Zoepf, "In Qatar's 'Education City,'" A42.

70. Zoepf, "In Qatar's 'Education City,'" A42.

71. Zoepf, "In Qatar's 'Education City,'" A42.

72. Micucci, "Classes Span Cultural Divide," 3.

73. Qatar Foundation, *Qatar Foundation for Education, Science and Community Development* (Doha, Qatar: Qatar Foundation, n.d.), inside front cover.

74. Qatar Foundation, "Qatar Foundation: Education City—Today," Qatar Foundation, http://www.qf.edu.qa/output/page303.asp (accessed May 31, 2007), 4.

75. Embassy of Israel, "Higher Education: A Strong Foundation," *Israel Update* (Spring 1997), http://www.israelemb.org/highered/index.html (accessed July 13, 2007), 1.

76. Israel Ministry of Foreign Affairs, "EDUCATION: Higher Education," Israel Ministry of Foreign Affairs, http://www.mfa.gov.il/MFA/Facts+About+Israel/Education/EDUCATION-+Higher+Education.htm (accessed July 23, 2007), 1.

77. Israel Ministry of Foreign Affairs, "EDUCATION: Higher Education," 1.

78. American Committee for the Weizmann Institute of Science, "Weizmann Achievements," Weizmann Institute of Science, http://www.weizmann-usa.org/site/PageServer?pagename=abt_achievements (accessed August 9, 2007), 8.

79. Israel Ministry of Foreign Affairs, "EDUCATION: Higher Education," 11.

80. Gillad Rosan and Eran Razin, "The College Chase: Higher Education and Urban Entrepreneurialism in Israel," *Tijdschrift voor Economische en Sociale Geografie* 98, no. 1 (2007): 88, 89. (Haifa University and Ben-Gurion University of the Negev came along in the 1960s. Israel Ministry of Foreign Affairs, "EDUCATION: Higher Education," 12, 13.)

81. Shlomo Mor-Yosef, director general of Hadassah Medical Organization, e-mail message to Eugene P. Trani, July 26, 2009.

82. Rosan and Razin, "The College Chase," 88.

83. Rosan and Razin, "The College Chase," 89.

84. Rosan and Razin, "The College Chase," 89; Nadav Halevi, "A Brief Economic History of Modern Israel," in *EH.Net Encyclopedia*, ed. Robert Whaples (Miami University, EH.Net, and Wake Forest University, 2005), http://eh.net/encyclopedia/article/halevi.israel (accessed July 16, 2007), 21.

85. Rosan and Razin, "The College Chase," 89, 93.

86. Rosan and Razin, "The College Chase," 89.

87. Rosan and Razin, "The College Chase," 89.

88. Rosan and Razin, "The College Chase," 89.

89. Rosan and Razin, "The College Chase," 89.

90. Linda Sharaby, "Israel's Economic Growth: Success without Security," *MERIA—Middle East Review of International Affairs* 6, no. 3 (September 2002): 33.

91. Sharaby, "Israel's Economic Growth: Success without Security," 33.

92. Sharaby, "Israel's Economic Growth: Success without Security," 33.

93. Sharaby, "Israel's Economic Growth: Success without Security," 26.

94. Sharaby, "Israel's Economic Growth: Success without Security," 37.

95. Dov Dvir and Asher Tishler, "The Changing Role of the Defense Industry in Israel's Industrial and Technological Development—Synopsis" (Tel Aviv: The Henry Crown Institute of Business Research in Israel, Tel Aviv University, 1999), http://recanati.tau.ac.il/Eng/Index.asp?ArticleID=695&CategoryID=440&Page=4 (accessed August 7, 2007), 1.

96. Dvir and Tishler, "The Changing Role of the Defense Industry," 1.

97. Naomi Klein, "Laboratory for a Fortressed World," *The Nation,* http://www.thenation.com/doc/20070702/klein (accessed retrieved August 6, 2007), 9.

98. Ronny Sofer, "Peres: Nano-Technology Will Beat Rockets—Vice Premier Concludes Germany Visit, Where He Was Awarded Prestigious Peace Prize, Offers to Promote Negotiations with Palestinians through Financial Endeavors," Ynetnews.com, http://www.ynetnews.com (accessed August 14, 2007), 1.

99. Sofer, "Peres: Nano-Technology Will Beat Rockets," 2.

100. Ronny Sofer, "Yushchenko Offers Technological Aid to Peres—Israeli Vice Premier, Ukrainian President Meet in Berlin, Discuss Collaboration on Nano-Technology in Fight Against Terror," Ynetnews.com, http://www.ynetnews.com/articles/0,7340,L-3310751,00.html (accessed August 14, 2007), 5.

101. "Israeli Nano Centers Receive New Funding Worth $230 Million," Nano-techwire.com, http://nanotechwire.com/news.asp?nid=3791 (accessed August 8, 2007), 14.

102. "Israeli Nano Centers," 14.

103. "Israeli Nano Centers," 15–16.

104. "Israeli Nano Centers," 10.

105. Nechama Goldman Barash, "Facets of the Israeli Economy—Biotechnology," *Israel Ministry of Foreign Affairs* (2002), http://www.israel-mfa.gov.il (accessed July 6, 2007), 1; Israel Life Science Industry (ILSI), "The Israeli Life Science Industry," ILSI, http://www.ilsi.org.il/industry_profile.asp (accessed July 6, 2007), 4.

106. ILSI, "The Israeli Life Science Industry," 14, 15.

107. ILSI, "The Israeli Life Science Industry," 16.

108. Shlomo Mor-Yosef, director general of Hadassah Medical Organization, e-mail message to Eugene P. Trani, July 26, 2009.

109. David Furst, "Ohio—Israel Medical IT Mission: Israel—Pioneer in the Life Sciences Industry," The Israel Export & International Cooperation Institute, http://www.export.gov.il/LS (accessed July 16, 2007), 6, 7.

110. Furst, "Ohio—Israel Medical IT Mission," 7.

111. Furst, "Ohio—Israel Medical IT Mission," 30.

112. Furst, "Ohio—Israel Medical IT Mission," 31.

113. Organization for the Promotion of Trade Israel—Netherlands (OPTIN), "Life Sciences: Universities and Institutes," OPTIN, http://www.optin.nl/ls_uninst.php (accessed July 6, 2007), 1.

114. OPTIN, "Life Sciences," 8.

115. OPTIN, "Life Sciences," 8.

116. Shlomo Mor-Yosef, director general of Hadassah Medical Organization, e-mail message to Eugene P. Trani, July 26, 2009.

117. OPTIN, "Life Sciences," 3.

118. OPTIN, "Life Sciences," 3.

119. Shlomo Mor-Yosef, director general of Hadassah Medical Organization, e-mail message to Eugene P. Trani, July 26, 2009.

120. Sharaby, "Israel's Economic Growth," 25.

121. Jeffrey Kelley, "Va. Opens Door to Israeli Firms," *Richmond Times-Dispatch*, November 4, 2007, http://inrich.com/cva/ric/news/business (accessed November 5, 2007), 30. See also Eugene P. Trani, "Do Not Isolate Israel, Embrace It," *Richmond Times-Dispatch*, September 23, 2007, E6.

122. Rosan and Razin, "The College Chase," 88.

123. Rosan and Razin, "The College Chase," 88, 86.

124. Rosan and Razin, "The College Chase," 88

125. Rosan and Razin, "The College Chase," 88.

126. Rosan and Razin, "The College Chase," 90.

127. Rosan and Razin, "The College Chase," 90.

128. Rosan and Razin, "The College Chase," 90, 92.

129. Rosan and Razin, "The College Chase," 89.

130. Rosan and Razin, "The College Chase," 89.

131. Haim Watzman, "Israel's Regional Colleges, Ambitious but Frustrated, Seek New Role," *Chronicle of Higher Education* 51, no. 34 (2005): A37.

132. Watzman, "Israel's Regional Colleges," A37; Council for Higher Education (Israel), "General," The Council for Higher Education, http://www.che.org .il/template/default_e.aspx?PageId=265 (accessed April 1, 2009).

133. Watzman, "Israel's Regional Colleges," A37.

134. Watzman, "Israel's Regional Colleges," A37.

135. Watzman, "Israel's Regional Colleges," A37.

136. Sharaby, "Israel's Economic Growth," 37.

137. Watzman, "Israel's Regional Colleges," A37.

138. Watzman, "Israel's Regional Colleges," A37.

139. Watzman, "Israel's Regional Colleges," A37.

140. Watzman, "Israel's Regional Colleges," A37.

141. Watzman, "Israel's Regional Colleges," A37.

142. Watzman, "Israel's Regional Colleges," A37.

143. Watzman, "Israel's Regional Colleges," A37.

144. Zvika Krieger, "Dubai, Aiming to Be an Academic Hub, Strikes a Deal with Michigan State," *Chronicle of Higher Education* 54, no. 8 (2007): A33.

145. Michigan State University Board of Trustees, "About MSU Dubai," Michigan State University Dubai, http://dubai.msu.edu/quick-links/about-msu-dubai (accessed March 31, 2009), 1.

146. New York University (NYU), "NYU Abu Dhabi," NYU, http://nyuad .nyu.edu/ (accessed March 31, 2009), 1.

147. NYU, "NYU Abu Dhabi," 1.

148. NYU, "NYU Abu Dhabi," 1.

149. NYU, "NYUAD—The Vision," NYU, http://nyuad.nyu.edu/about/ (accessed March 31, 2009), 1.

150. Zvika Krieger, "Saudi Arabia Puts Its Billions Behind Western-Style Higher Education," *Chronicle of Higher Education* 54, no. 3 (2007): A1.

151. Krieger, "Saudi Arabia Puts Its Billions," A1.

152. Krane, "Rather Than Study Abroad," 24.

153. "Education City Unveils Expansion Plans," 15.

154. Scott Jaschik, "New Era in International Higher Education," *Inside Higher Education*, May 18, 2005, http://www.insidehighered.com/ (accessed June 1, 2007), 10.

155. Shirley Robinson Pippins, "Education Essential as Ever in 'Flattening' World," *Newsday*, May 23, 2006, http://www.newsday.com/ (accessed June 4, 2007), A37.

*Chapter 8*

# Higher Education in Developing Countries: The BRIC Nations

In 2001, Goldman Sachs—a leading global investment banking, securities, and investment management firm—coined the term *BRIC* to describe the expected growing force of Brazil, Russia, India, and China in the world economy over the next fifty years.[1] By 2007, the combined weight of the BRIC economies had already exceeded Goldman Sachs' predictions ahead of schedule, with a combined weight of 15 percent of world gross domestic product (GDP) at that time versus a previously anticipated 10 percent by 2010.[2]

In his 2006 analysis of the Goldman Sachs predictions about the future growth of the BRIC countries, Martin Carnoy of Stanford University made his own forecast about the BRICs' future: "Much of their possibilities for sustained growth in the medium and longer run depend on whether they can develop and utilize high level human capital for the organization and innovation required in today's (and tomorrow's) global information economy."[3] Carnoy's report discussed why higher education policies would be particularly important to the future of BRIC economies.

Predictions also are being made about other global economic subsets. The success of the BRIC nations prompted speculation about the next wave of rising economies. In 2005, Goldman Sachs introduced the concept of the "Next Eleven" or "N-11," referring to a set of countries that could potentially have a BRIC-like impact in rivaling the G7.[4] Included in the diverse grouping are Bangladesh, Egypt, Indonesia, Iran, Korea, Mexico, Nigeria, Pakistan, the Philippines, Turkey, and Vietnam. The N-11's weight in the global economy and global trade has been slowly increasing over the last several years, although it would be ambitious to expect any of these developing countries to ever rival the current major economies or the BRICs.

In its 2008 report, "Accelerating Catch-up: Tertiary Education and Growth in Sub-Saharan Africa," the World Bank drew upon lessons from developing-country success stories, such as those in Asia and other similarly situated regions, that might be applied to sustain and strengthen the economic growth that the sub-Saharan region has experienced since the new millennium.[5] Key among the lessons was the positive impact on economic development when governments consciously seek to foster capacities for "higher-level skills" (human capital) and "problem-solving research" (intellectual capital) and align those capacities with national economic strategy objectives.[6] While the nearly 6 percent economic growth rates in much of sub-Saharan Africa from 2000 through 2008 have been encouraging, the World Bank report posits that tertiary institutions in Africa will need to transform themselves into a different type of educational enterprise—a "21st-century version of the African 'development university'"—in order for the region to be competitive within the new rules imposed by a global knowledge economy.[7]

Recognition of the growing importance of the BRIC nations and other emerging regions of the world has by now seeped into the popular culture. Much has been written about how the enormous resources of these nations—in population, raw materials, and intellectual potential—may vastly outstrip those that could be mustered by the United States alone. Politicians and journalists regularly refer to the number of students enrolled in higher education, the scientists and engineers being produced, and the energy resources at their disposal to evoke an economic threat that could well jeopardize America's preeminent role in the global community.

But it is by no means certain that all or most of these nations will be able to capitalize on the human and financial resources at their disposal. Carnoy is correct in observing that their ultimate success will be, at least in part, dependent on the quality of the higher education systems that they are able to establish and maintain. Moreover, it is by no means certain that all of the BRIC nations will be able to meet the challenge successfully. This chapter reflects on the experiences in three BRIC nations—China, Russia, and India—to illustrate not only the enormous potential of the countries, but also the significant obstacles that are sometimes in the way of developing a globally competitive higher ed system. In each of these countries, we can see a growing acknowledgment of higher education's centrality to national aspiration combined with significant hurdles that hinder fully implementing this recognition. We also look at three of the partner institutions of Virginia Commonwealth University (VCU) in these nations to observe some of the particular strategies being followed to make higher education more relevant to the knowledge economy.

## HIGHER EDUCATION REFORM IN CHINA

### The Economic Backdrop

For centuries, China maintained a distance from much of the rest of the world, especially the West.[8] Over the past quarter century, however, the economic revolution in China has, in large part, reversed this historical tendency. In 2001, China became the 143rd nation to join the World Trade Organization.[9] Today, China is seen by many as the most powerful emergent force in the global market. According to Goldman Sachs, the size of China's middle class could increase by close to ten times by around 2015; China could overtake the United States as the world's largest economy by 2025; and China's GDP could exceed U.S. $44 trillion by 2050, which would place it well beyond the United States and any of the other G8 countries.[10]

One major focus of China's economic reform has been the creation of new enterprises.[11] The Chinese government has increasingly embraced the concept of a knowledge economy and has introduced a series of policies to encourage the development of a venture capital industry to support an economy of innovation.[12] In the mid-1980s, the government decided that it should develop various high-technology industries. In 1999, China's State Council issued the "Decision to Develop High Technology through Innovation and Industrialization," which called for the cultivation of capital markets and a venture capital regime for the further development of high-tech industries.[13] Later that year, the State Council issued "Opinions on Establishing a Venture Capital Regime," which acknowledged that emerging industries and high-tech industries were the key drivers behind the growth of an information-based economy and set out information technology (IT), biotechnology, technologies on new materials, and advanced manufacturing technologies as the priorities of future government investment.[14] Since the time these reports were issued, there has been a substantial influx of venture capital into China's IT industry, particularly in the areas of network and internet infrastructure.

China's "economic revolution" has created unprecedented employment opportunities for university graduates, prompting a greater demand for competency and versatility in skills.[15] China's commitment to developing knowledge-based industries will continue to prompt a rising need for graduates with the requisite skills to spur innovation. According to Ma Wan-hua, education professor at the Graduate School of Education at Peking University and a Fulbright New Century Scholar, "When knowledge and economy are so closely connected, higher education faces a crucial turning point. It is not only expected to provide qualified personnel to fill high-level scientific, technical, professional and managerial positions, it is also expected to be the engine for the country's economic growth."[16]

**Higher Education Investments**

The development of a higher education infrastructure capable of meeting the considerable human and intellectual capital needs of the emerging Chinese economy became increasingly imperative.[17] In 1993, Project 211 was unveiled. When it was implemented in 1995, it provided funding to develop a network of approximately one hundred comprehensive research universities capable of producing world-class research and competing for the world's brightest minds.[18] The first phase of Project 985 was launched in 1998 to provide supplemental funding to a smaller group of elite universities.

According to Michael Crow, president of Arizona State University, the extraordinary investment that China's Ministry of Education is making to qualitatively and quantitatively expand its system of higher education supports China's intention to compete "as a global power—economically, militarily, culturally and every other conceivable way."[19] In 2004, the second phase of Project 985 was launched to widen China's pool of elite universities.[20] Also, China doubled its investment in higher education over the five-year period ending in 2004, while tripling acreage devoted to campuses.[21] By 2006, China had approximately two thousand colleges and universities, up from 392 higher education institutions (HEIs) in 1976.[22]

The number of students attending China's HEIs is soaring, as well. After the Ministry of Education decided to enlarge China's total university enrollment by 30 percent in 1998, the number of students in the country's HEIs jumped from 1.08 million in 1998 to 2.2 million in 2000.[23] By 2004, China had built the largest higher education system in the world, with more than twenty million university students.[24] In 2000, China awarded 11,004 doctoral degrees (along with 47,565 master's degrees).[25] Of the 11,004 doctoral degrees, 42 percent were in engineering, 22 percent in science, 14 percent in medicine, and 6 percent in economics; the remainder were in agriculture, the humanities, and other disciplines.[26]

**The Transformation of Higher Education**

While expanding its production of human capital, China has fostered qualitative changes in the nature and content of higher education that focus on responding to the perceived imperatives of a knowledge economy. New models of higher education continue to emerge in China.[27] In the past, each university specialized in a certain area of study, preventing students from attaining the breadth of knowledge needed to be creative and innovative in the "real world." More recently, specialized colleges have been upgraded to more comprehensive universities, particularly those related to medicine, law, economics, science, and technology. In addition, the Ministry of Education has undertaken multiple reclassifications of disciplines to reflect new market needs for labor. Other initiatives include university-industry partnerships that integrate academic study with work experience in China and abroad and training programs run by multinational corporations based at Chinese universities.[28]

In addition to increasing its quantity and quality of human capital, China has reinvented its concept of higher education to emphasize intellectual capital production, thereby strengthening the role of universities in the country's economic development. From 1952 until the mid-1990s, scientific research was almost completely separated from universities, with most research conducted at the Chinese Academy of Science.[29] With university education highly specialized and research separated from universities, students were deprived of learning how to carry out research and lacked opportunities to apply the knowledge they acquired from books, resulting in a separation of theory from practice. In 1986, the first key national research laboratory was established at Peking University. Early in the twenty-first century, some basic research institutes transferred from the academy to universities.

To further promote the development of research universities after the U.S. model of success for spurring economic development, China has established research-and-development (R&D) funds to support innovative initiatives at universities.[30] In 2003, approximately fifty-five national research laboratories existed under the Chinese Ministry of Education. According to China's minister of education, Zhou Ji, funds for scientific research at HEIs increased by 400 percent from 1998 to 2004, allowing the quality of scientific research to improve and gain greater recognition.[31]

The assumption of a larger role in technology transfer is another example of how China is modernizing the role of higher education, establishing a direct link between university research and knowledge transformation to promote economic development.[32] Higher education has become more entrepreneurial, and commentators have observed that the formation of university-based scientific research and technology innovation parks, such as in Beijing, Shanghai, Harbin, and Jiangsu, are making universities "more like an enterprise than an academy."[33] Indeed, the Chinese university has fundamentally changed its function by transforming research findings and discoveries directly into production. Just after the turn of the twenty-first century, more than five thousand university enterprises existed in China; approximately 40 percent were high-tech-related. Also, universities are collaborating more with industry and research institutes. Even the universities that have not been targeted for significant infusions of government funding have taken extraordinary efforts to raise money on their own through a variety of entrepreneurial activities, such as setting up evening programs, dabbling in real estate, and establishing consulting companies.[34]

Western nations have historically looked at the Chinese market as a potential source of enormous demand. It is certainly the way that entrepreneurial universities are seeing China today. The combination of the size of the Chinese education market with the enormous unmet demand has led to an explosion in the number of foreign colleges and universities in China.[35] China first opened its doors to foreign colleges and universities in 1995; in 2006, more than seven hundred foreign academic programs were operating in China, according to the International Finance Corporation of the World Bank. The increased market for education and the greater reluctance of Chinese students to travel abroad, given the higher costs as well as post-9/11 visa restrictions, have created an entrepreneurial push, which has been likened by college officials to the nineteenth-century gold rush in the American West or Canada's Klondike.[36] So enormous is the demand for higher education that for-profit institutions are entering the Chinese higher education market. CIBT School of Business and Technology Corporation, which is owned by Canadian-based Capital Alliance Group Inc., offers degree programs at three campuses in Beijing; two in Weifang, in Shandong province; and what its website calls "a host of alliance schools spread across China."[37] Foreign nonprofit universities also help China close the gap between demand for and supply of higher education.

Also helping to drive China's economic development in the global knowledge-based market is the increasing practice by Chinese universities of developing international partnerships and fostering international exchanges. Consistent with the worldwide shift of higher education from isolation to collaboration, universities throughout China have reached out to engage with universities from other nations to ensure that their own HEIs generate internationally relevant innovations to address global challenges and develop a globally competitive workforce, in support of China's economic prosperity. As Sichuan University President Xie He-ping said, "In order to be effective knowledge generators and innovation hubs, universities must be both locally active and internationally engaged."[38] The wheels were originally put in motion for strengthening international cooperation and exchanges with Project 211 in 1993, and Project 985 further supported international networking opportunities for Chinese universities with top institutions around the world. Consequently, in the new millennium, dual-degree programs and joint-venture campuses are increasingly common, and foreign institutions are more aware than ever of the need to engage with China and Chinese academia.[39]

## The Fudan Example

At VCU, we established a partnership with Fudan University, an institution that reflects the dramatic changes taking place in Chinese higher education. Fudan University has an international reputation for academic excellence, prompting some to refer to it as "China's equivalent to Harvard."[40] Located in the dynamic city of Shanghai, Fudan University was established in 1905 as the Fudan Public School.[41] Renamed Fudan University in 1917, the institution gradually became one of the most prestigious universities in China over the course of the twentieth century; its goal in the twenty-first century is to become one of the most prestigious universities in the world.

A key boost to Fudan's ascendancy was its inclusion in the elite group of ten universities that were identified by the Chinese Ministry of Education for additional funding through Project 985 in 1998.[42] The increased infusion of resources enabled Fudan to become more intellectually comprehensive and "exert a more positive and profound influence on the world."[43] Another pivotal point in Fudan's expansion and reconceptualization came when it merged with Shanghai Medical University in 2000. The merger led to the expansion of the university's college for medical sciences, Shanghai Medical College.[44] The college has become the nucleus of one of China's premier teaching and research medical centers, which includes approximately twenty national key disciplines, ten key laboratories, four research stations offering postdoctoral fellowships, almost thirty doctoral programs, and eight affiliated hospitals.[45] Today, Fudan has about twenty schools, with dozens of specialties for bachelor's degree candidates, more than two hundred specialties for master's degree candidates, and more than 150 specialties for doctoral degree candidates.[46] Its enrollments stand at more than forty-four thousand students, with around eleven thousand of those students enrolled in graduate studies. Fudan's faculty head count is more than 2,400, with around 160 international faculty members.

In 2007, 95 percent of Fudan's graduates were employed.[47] While Fudan is effective in getting its graduates into the workforce, university officials must contend with complaints by transnational companies looking to do business in China that experience difficulty in finding personnel whose educational background adequately prepares them for job demands.[48] To make their graduates more competitive in today's global market, Fudan has been conducting research into all aspects of American pedagogy with the intention of nurturing creative talent through a more diverse approach to higher education.

One of those more diverse approaches is Fudan's new method of recruitment. Starting in 2006, Fudan stopped looking solely at high school graduates' scores on the notoriously difficult college entrance exam in making admissions decisions.[49] Instead, Fudan has instituted a system similar to that of Harvard University and Yale University, where students sit for a written test developed by the university and attend an interview.

Fudan's goal in modifying its entrance requirements is to provide educational opportunities for a more diverse pool of students, not just those who perform well on standard examinations. Fudan is a trailblazer in experimenting with student enrollment reform, with other Chinese HEIs expected to follow suit if Fudan is successful.

Another departure from the traditional system of Chinese higher education is the establishment of Fudan College, in which freshmen spend a year taking general courses in arts and sciences before moving on to their majors.[50] Typically, Chinese students must choose their college majors before graduating from high school, after which they are divided into liberal arts classes or science classes.[51] That means that each group gets no further grounding in the other disciplines, and it is difficult to switch majors once in college. Fudan College gives students the chance to study those subjects that are unrelated to their majors that they missed out on in high school.

Through Fudan College, students also have the opportunity to take small, seminar-sized classes that are designed to provoke discussion and improve oral and written argumentation skills.[52] This is distinctly different from the standard Chinese educational experience. Most students leave high school and expect to continue listening to teachers and taking notes from textbooks, a model of education that contributes to students' lacking the scope of knowledge, as well as the confidence and initiative, to do independent study and research.[53] According to Dafeng Cai, vice president of Fudan, "Our foundation courses broaden their outlook, encourage analytical and independent thinking and enable today's young intelligentsia to meet the social demands of tomorrow."[54]

In addition to leading the way in responding to China's human capital needs, Fudan has developed an R&D enterprise capable of helping China meet its intellectual capital needs. Fudan has seventy-seven graduate schools, 126 research centers, and twenty-five key laboratories.[55] Fudan's research scope is extensive, including a vast array of burgeoning fields ranging from biodiversity science and ecological engineering to antibiotics and clinical pharmacology. It has also established a thriving biotechnology research park. Fudan also actively transfers that knowledge into market applications, through its incubation and tech transfer roles.[56] In addition, Fudan works closely with industry and government in tailoring its research activities to support China's emergence in the new global knowledge-based economy.

For example, in 2000 the China Center for Venture Capital Investment at Fudan University was established jointly by the university, Science & Technology Fund Development Corporation of Shanxi Province, Tianjin Science & Technology Development and Investment Corporation, Shenzhen Innovative Science & Technology Investment Co. Ltd., and Shanghai

Enterprise Investment Co. Ltd. The academic-based center specializes in research on high-tech start-ups and venture capital investment.[57] Another example of industry collaboration, as well as an illustration of the entrepreneurial spirit that permeates the university, is the Fudan-Lucent Technologies Bell Lab, which is conducting cutting-edge research in such areas as mobile communications, fiber communications, and comprehensive network management.[58]

In addition to collaborating with government and industry, Fudan continues to increase its collaboration with other HEIs, both at home and abroad.[59] Since forging new territory in China in 1950 by becoming one of the first Chinese institutions to enroll foreign students, Fudan has accepted and trained more than ten thousand foreign students from one hundred countries and regions worldwide. Fudan's population of foreign students was ranked second in the country in 2003, and, more recently, international student enrollment stood at 2,200 students.[60] Fudan has established cooperative agreements with more than two hundred universities and research institutions in thirty countries and regions.

### Continuing Challenges

The changes in Chinese higher education in the past few decades have been extraordinary. The level of scholarly productivity in scientific journals has grown significantly, as have other indications of innovation, such as patent activity. Chinese faculty members, especially in the sciences and technical fields, are increasingly judged by international norms. The evolution of relatively elite institutions such as Fudan illustrates the genuine transition that has been occurring in the wider society. Yet considerable challenges remain for the system to realize its ultimate goal of linking higher education policy to the requirements of a knowledge society.

Overall investment as a percentage of GDP is still relatively low, and rising tuition rates at many Chinese institutions are raising considerable problems of access. Changes in admissions policies and curricular reforms that have occurred in universities such as Fudan have not permeated the entire system. There is widespread disenchantment with admissions testing that seems to be unrelated to actual performance in the university. And the curriculum at many schools is still producing graduates unprepared for the job market. In many instances, they are not able to obtain positions commensurate with their education, and they take jobs as housemaids and security guards. Despite the explosion in higher education, multinational companies with a large presence in China still report that skills shortages are one of their largest problems. The problems of access, quality, and market alignment have fostered public concern about higher education policy and illustrated the issues that China must address if its higher education progress is to be effectively sustained.

## RUSSIAN HIGHER EDUCATION

### Economic Backdrop

Throughout much of the twentieth century, a centrally planned, state-owned economic model was in effect under the Union of Soviet Socialist Republics.[61] The country based its economic development on heavy industry, protected from international competition, and its high-technology sector was concentrated in its military complex, with defense spending serving as a considerable driver of the country's economy.[62]

After the fall of the Soviet Union in 1991, natural-resource-sector development was prioritized over diversified manufacturing, particularly over technology-based manufacturing, while many other leading countries in the world were turning their focus to innovation-based economic development.[63] With huge reserves of natural gas and other resources, Russia evolved into a petro-state, becoming heavily dependent economically on natural resource extraction.

In 2004, the ninth in a series of Human Development Reports for the Russian Federation was released. Titled "Towards a Knowledge-Based Society," it stressed that Russia's economy must transition from its reliance on natural resources to reliance on "the most powerful renewable resource known to mankind, which is knowledge."[64] Even with the acknowledgment of its importance, mobilizing knowledge to promote societal innovation remains a continuing struggle in Russia. The rapid and sharp reduction in budget funding (mainly in cuts to government defense spending), along with the inability of the Russian business community to initiate major innovation projects, has had an adverse effect on the nation's innovation activity.

On one hand, there are important features of Russian society vital to innovation that are relatively well-developed. In 2002, the Russian share of R&D expenditure in GDP was ahead of China's and Italy's, although somewhat behind Canada's. And, in 2004, Russia had almost seventy researchers per ten thousand employees, which was seven times more than China, a quarter more than the United Kingdom, and approximately the same as Germany.[65] In essence, a scientific culture with highly trained personnel is already present.[66] Combined with a high level of capital assets and an impending need to modernize a significant portion of its production facilities, there is both a pent-up demand for modernization and resources that can be dedicated to the modernization process. In addition, Russian industry has begun showing signs of growth, and the service sector is continuing to develop.[67] New innovation structures are evolving, evidence of which is the revitalization of research and academic institutes in ways that are making them capable of launching commercially attractive innovation projects.

On the other hand, there are continuing barriers in Russia to the development of an innovation-grounded economy. The scientific culture in Russia has not been complemented by the development of an entrepreneurial infrastructure with personnel who are skilled in the application and marketing of scientific advances. It has been estimated that Russia needs about forty thousand people, at a minimum, to be trained as specialists in innovation-related skills such as IT support, financial and strategic management, international business, and intellectual property law.[68] Funding for universities and the kind of programs needed to foster economic development has been, at best, erratic and sometimes diverted to other priorities. And while public sentiment has recognized the importance of higher education, there is widespread sentiment that the system is relatively corrupt, and not entirely fair or meritocratic.

## Higher Education Evolution

In the 1940s and 1950s, Soviet higher education was officially infused with an ideological content that was an integral part of a system of political socialization. Official Soviet pedagogy emphasized rote learning over critical thinking, favored abstract theory over practical knowledge, and limited student choice in curriculum design. This was most evident in the social sciences and humanities, though in this period ideological priorities even shaped the biology and cybernetics curricula. Yet in a number of areas, especially the natural sciences, the official rhetoric had only a modest impact on the quality of education. Mathematics, physics, and chemistry were never really affected by ideology despite what the party line may have pretended. Universities and institutes in what is now Russia produced graduates with serious academic backgrounds, a comprehensive knowledge of particular disciplines, and a capability for producing original research.

The evolution of HEIs actually began before the dissolution of the Soviet Union. During the perestroika period, the consolidation of bureaucracies responsible for higher education began under Mikhail Gorbachev, and curricular reforms were initiated.[69] Some Russian academics (VNIK-shkola) advocated what was called "education of cooperation," which called for fundamental changes in the style of instruction to focus on the individual student, to encourage creativity, and to adopt more flexible programs of study.[70] In keeping with the policy of the Soviet Union, the Russian government continued to guarantee open and free access to public higher education on a competitive basis, as it continues to do today.[71]

Reforms implemented starting in 1991 led to many fundamental changes in higher education, including diversification, decentralization (and, thus, greater university autonomy), and the creation of a nonpublic (private) sector of higher education.[72] During this period, more than three hundred private universities were opened. Also, the number of students increased considerably, and university entrance became more competitive.[73] Russia was able to reorganize institutes and polytechnics to universities and academies, launch new areas of specialty studies, and garner increased international support.[74]

Russian universities became less isolated and more globalized as the crucial role that study-abroad experiences can play in a student's future career was more widely recognized.[75] According to officials in the Russian Ministry of Education, the number of students studying in the United States began to grow by the end of the 1990s.[76] And American schools, as well as schools from other countries, began to open branches and otherwise have more of a presence in Russia, such as through the establishment of joint degree programs. Observers from outside Russia were often struck by the magnitude of the changes that were occurring inside higher education. A 2000 report published by the Carnegie Corporation of New York noted that the days of the Soviet era when instructors were told what they must teach had ended.[77] For instance, previously condemned by Soviet officials as a "bourgeois pseudo-science," political science became one of the most popular new subjects at universities across Russia by the end of the twentieth century.[78] Business schools became popular, and students were required to learn English and navigate the Internet.

According to the 2000 Carnegie report, "Recognizing and adapting to these new market forces, along with the many other practical considerations imposed by living in a country with a new, global outlook, may finally be transforming the face of something that heretofore seemed immutable: the Russian intelligentsia."[79] After ten years of reform, the more abstract reflections of the intelligentsia started being replaced by the practical applications of knowledge by Russia's new breed of intellectuals, who started going into politics, business, and other settings where they could use their knowledge. Russian higher educators started realizing that they needed to teach students how to market themselves.

Yet the direction of Russian higher education was by no means one-dimensional. Public budgetary support during the 1990s declined precipitously.[80] From 1991 to 2001, state financing was cut by almost a half in real terms.[81] As of 2000, Russia was spending less, as a percentage of GDP, on education than any major industrialized country.[82] Graduates found it increasingly difficult to find a job corresponding to their university specialization.[83] Also, the return on investment in education was found low compared with other countries and very low compared with market interest rates, as reported in a number of studies.[84]

The proliferation of private colleges and universities in response to declining state support can be viewed as a positive means of stepping into a void created by shifting state policies. At the same time, these institutions have struggled with their own challenges as well. Many of the institutions are under-resourced and do not even have the basic access to library resources considered essential to higher education. The need to support the maintenance of their activities and staff has made it difficult to develop an orientation focused on the future requirements of the Russian economy and society. And the institutions have been the subject of various charges of corruption, ranging from unqualified staff to the sale of diplomas. The main point of reference has been the existing condition—not the future needs—of the labor market, and such efforts by HEIs have not always been aimed at the objectives of society and the state.[85]

During the last decade, Russian authorities have continued to speak about organizing the system of higher education to meet the needs of a knowledge economy. The Russian Ministry of Education developed an official doctrine that set forth a philosophy that education should be individualized and that it should be lifelong and responsive to the rapidly changing conditions of the contemporary technological world.[86] A number of practical steps were taken to implement the official commitment. In 2003, Russia joined the Bologna process (the European higher education reform effort).[87] In 2005, Russia launched an academic mobility program to facilitate pathways between its own and other systems of higher education throughout the world.

Russia's effort to once again become a major global actor has reinforced some of these tendencies. The nation's G8 chairmanship in 2006 included a global focus on innovation societies in the twenty-first century.[88] Agreements on education and innovation that were reached at the G8 summit centered on education and prosperity, human capital, knowledge-based economies, and critical thinking. Another example of globalization's influence on twenty-first-century Russian higher education reform efforts emerged from Russia's quest to be admitted to the World Trade Organization. Russian interest in becoming a WTO member has prompted both reform of business practices and instruction about commerce and business in HEIs.[89]

In addition to curricular and administrative reform, fiscal reform has occurred in Russian higher education through a combination of government efforts and foreign aid. In recent years, the Russian government has begun to reverse the decline in funding of higher education that took place in the 1990s after the collapse of the Soviet Union, so that support is now roughly the same as it was before perestroika.[90] There is a general sense, however, that elite universities in Moscow and St. Petersburg have been the principal beneficiaries of the new funding policies and prospered far more than others. External funders have bolstered efforts by the Russian government. Grants from foundations such as the Carnegie Corporation, Ford, MacArthur, and the Open Society Institute have sponsored Internet communication, funded research projects, and made it possible for students and teachers to travel abroad and return to Russia to apply their knowledge. A $50 million World Bank loan was earmarked in 2000 for improving social science education at several Russian universities.[91]

Russia also has recently created within its HEIs an array of initiatives— business innovation centers, business incubators, research and technology parks, engineering firms, and consulting firms—designed to enhance the society's capacity to participate in the knowledge economy. As of 2002, more than seventy technoparks had been established under the auspices of Russia's leading higher educational institutions, with these parks serving as a base for establishing innovation technology centers and complexes. In addition, by 2002 more than ten regional innovation centers had been created, along with sixteen regional centers for training specialists in innovation entrepreneurship, twelve regional information-analytical centers, and twelve regional centers for promoting the development of scientific-technical entrepreneurship. Also, more than 1,300 small innovative enterprises producing and marketing science-intensive products were operating within the Russian Ministry of Education system as of 2002.[92]

The intent of these efforts is not very different from what we have seen in the United States and elsewhere: incentivize academics to think about the practical applications of their work. Bring academics into closer contact with individuals and groups that have interests in commercializing scientific work. Encourage students to become involved in the activities and careers related to commercialization. But perhaps most importantly, position academic institutions as regional centers for developing innovation activity in the scientific-technical and educational spheres.[93]

At the moment, Russian higher education appears to be moving in two separate directions simultaneously. In some respects, the loosening of state control has led to a serious decline in quality. Many observers believe that a number of the new institutes of learning are essentially fraudulent and are not providing students with a level of education that is comparable to what was previously offered. There is concern that, even in traditional universities, the curriculum has become less purposeful and more chaotic and less capable of developing serious scholars. At the same time, Russian higher education is more innovative than ever before, more capable of linking research to practical applications that benefit society, and more interested in utilizing knowledge to address the wide range of challenges in contemporary society.

## Moscow State University

Moscow State University (MSU) is one of the best examples of the manner in which Russia is striving to organize its academic effort more effectively for a knowledge society. MSU enrolls more than forty thousand undergraduate students, seven thousand graduate students, and more than five thousand specialist students.[94] Each year, MSU enrolls about two thousand international students from all over the world.

MSU is committed to promoting innovation activity through its departments, research centers, and institutes, as well as to enterprises dedicated to innovation. Providing leadership for MSU's innovation structure is the university's Innovation Policy and Innovation Project Management Department, which includes a unit dedicated to innovation and technologies transfer and a unit dedicated to international and regional cooperation in science and innovation. Reporting up to the Innovation Policy and Innovation Project Management Department is an Office of Technologies Transfer, to which MSU's Innovation BIOincubator and Science Park report.[95]

The world-class research conducted by the university, along with the advanced promotion capacity of the university's Science Park (SP), creates a solid foundation for their productive cooperation. The SP of Moscow State University, established in 1992 by MSU and named after M. V. Lomonosov, contains the Risk Investment Company, with sponsorship by the Russian Federation Ministry of Science and the Foundation for Assistance to Small Innovation Enterprises.[96] It is one of the oldest science parks in Russia and, in 2000, was Russia's first organization to receive the certificate of State and Public Accreditation.[97]

The mission of the SP is to stimulate innovation activities at MSU and in the region. The SP fulfills its mission by creating favorable conditions for scientists, students, and graduates to start high-tech businesses; helping with the development of start-ups and small to medium-size businesses through consulting services; and building a comfortable environment for businesses interested in cooperation with the university.[98] The SP seeks to provide turnkey assistance to aspiring entrepreneurs, as well as to small and medium-size businesses in the high-tech sector, whether they are mature companies or in the early stages of operation.[99]

The SP includes more than 125,000 square feet of rental space, forty-five small innovation businesses, and 2,500 employees, most of whom are graduates, students, or professors of MSU.[100] The average age of SP employees is thirty-five years.[101] Firms located at the SP operate in a variety of areas, such as software production, information technologies, telecommunications, laser medicine, ecology, biotechnology, and electronics, as well as in the selection and financing of research projects.[102] IT and software production constitute about 60 percent of the activity at the SP.[103]

About 40 percent of the firms at the SP are up to three years old, with the remaining 60 percent over three years old.[104] Major firms located at the SP include Garant, REDLAB, Neural Net Technology Center—Intellectual Security Systems, Complekt-Ecology, Vitta, Neurock, Rambler Internet Holding, Agama, and DEC.[105]

Another key player in MSU's innovation enterprise is the National Training Foundation IT Incubator. The IT incubator has twenty seed-stage projects each year.[106] It provides mass Internet services, as well as offices, business analytics, and programmer support. In addition to several closed deals, the IT incubator has several projects in process. Project areas include social networking for offline meetings; promotion and targeted ads; online tools to develop expert systems; photo hosting for mobile phones; online music jams; and a hybrid of eBay and Craigslist.

The Innovation Technology Center (ITC) represents another vehicle for promoting innovation activity at MSU and in the region. The ITC, which was set up within the SP in 1999 in a brand-new facility, offers three levels of services.[107] First, it offers technical services, such as office space rental, telecommunications services, and security. Second, ITC provides consulting services, including advice on business planning, protection of intellectual property rights (IPR), and technology transfer; assistance in attracting preferential financing (including government allocations), as well as venture capital; accounting and auditing; and identifying and recruiting strategic partners. The third service area of the ITC is the synergetic interaction with SP companies it provides, which helps unite separate efforts to generate new initiatives that would be individually unaffordable.

Future MSU innovation development will be focused on the creation of a technology cluster at MSU through technology cluster development institutions. The creation of technology clusters at MSU will center on information technologies, new chemical materials and technologies, natural resources, and modern biotechnologies and medicine. Technology cluster development institutions will include the MSU Medical Center, MSU Institute of New Carbonic Materials and Technologies, MSU Center of Natural Resources, and the BIOincubator.[108] And the Central Russian government and the Moscow City government have committed millions of rubles for the development of new facilities at MSU to further the University's role in economic development.

The dramatic changes that have occurred at MSU are especially evident when compared with MSU in the spring of 1981. MSU was then a rigid Soviet institution where innovation was not welcome.[109] Today, it is vibrant, entrepreneurial and innovative, and making major contributions to economic development. The problem for Russians is that such support needs to become more widespread and not just limited to the highest level institutions such as MSU and St. Petersburg State University.

## INDIA

### Economic Backdrop

In the mid-eighteenth century, before the zenith of the Industrial Revolution, India had the second-largest economy in the world, with exports contributing more than 20 percent of its total economic output.[110] But for the next century, India's role in the world economy was significantly diminished. Protectionist tariffs, reliance on low-productivity subsistence agriculture, and a manufacturing strategy that did not prioritize global competitiveness prevented India from being a serious player in the world economy.[111]

The last twenty years have seen a powerful revival of India's economic fortunes and its reintegration into the global economy. Reforms have brought about liberalized foreign investment and exchange regimes, significant reductions in tariffs and other trade barriers, modernization of the financial sector, adjustments in government monetary and fiscal policies, improvements to highways and ports, and improved safeguarding of IPR.[112] Since 1991, foreigners have invested in more than one thousand Indian companies via the stock market.[113] India has welcomed many American corporations, such as Coca-Cola, General Motors, and Citibank, and 125 of the world's Fortune 500 companies now have R&D bases in India.[114] As of 2007, India had the world's twelfth-largest economy and the third largest in Asia behind Japan and China.[115] According to Goldman Sachs, "If things go right . . . India's economy . . . could be larger than Japan's by 2032."[116] In 2006, Pawan Agarwal, a Fulbright New Century Scholar and former employee of India's primary higher education regulatory agency (the University Grants Commission), authored a report for the Indian Council for Research on International Economic Relations (ICRIER).[117] According to that ICRIER report, despite India's subpar performance in R&D, there is general optimism about India's potential in the global knowledge-based economy, given several characteristics of the new India: continued growth of the business services sector, demographic trends, indigenous entrepreneurship, large institutional and social capital, the ability of Indians to manage diversity, and a huge pool of underutilized brainpower.[118]

This potential has already been manifested in several important ways. India's rapidly growing software sector is boosting service exports and modernizing its economy.[119] Combined, software and business-process outsourcing exports grew practically from nothing to $20 billion in 2006.[120] In addition, the recent worldwide integration of job markets has led to an emerging global occupational structure that has provided strategic opportunities for India. Revolutionary advances in telecommunications have lowered the costs of sending vast amounts of information rapidly

and have improved coordination in real time across continents, leading
to the emergence of large-scale off-shoring industries over the last few
years.[121] India is now an international services hub, having started with
IT-enabled services, both voice and data, and expanded to all knowledge
sectors, including pharmaceuticals and biotechnology. In the manufacturing sector, India is already on its way to becoming an important base for
off-shoring engineering services; and through entrepreneurship and skill
upgrading, the Indian manufacturing sector could become competitive in
other areas as well.

As with China, the power of large numbers is critical to the assessment of India's potential impact and influence. With 1.1 billion people,
India constitutes 15 percent of the world's population. The increase in
the size of the middle class has translated into 1 percent of India's poor
crossing the poverty line each year. In the last few decades, the size of
India's middle class has quadrupled.[122] Currently estimated at 325 million to 350 million people (already exceeding the entire U.S. population),
India's middle class could increase by nearly fourteen times over the next
decade.[123] India's median age is twenty-five, with some 40 percent of its
population younger than eighteen, making it one of the youngest among
large economies.[124] Although 700 million Indians still live on $2 per day or
less, the large and growing middle class not only is increasing the nation's
supply of disposable income for consumer goods, but also provides a
tremendous competitive advantage for the overall economy. Responding
to questions about the rapid increase in multinationals outsourcing jobs
to India, one of India's best-known journalists, Vir Sanghvi, pointed to
his country's competitive advantage: "One of our natural resources (educated Indians) is much cheaper than anything in the West."[125]

## India's Education Anxiety

Political figures in the West regularly point to India's enormous population and the number of scientists and engineers it is producing compared, for instance, with the United States as means of instructing the
citizenry about the competitive challenges emerging from India and the
BRIC nations. Yet close observers of the Indian system are equally likely
to remark upon the challenges that are facing India's educational system
at all levels, including higher education.

Goldman Sachs' 2007 report on the BRIC economies included India's
system of education as one of the potential obstacles to its growth, noting, "To embark upon its growth story, India will have to educate its
children and its young people (especially its women), and it must do so in
a hurry."[126] Inequalities in the distribution of India's recent economic success threaten the country's future growth. Millions of people are unem-

ployed, and only a small fraction of Indians are employed in the modern, unionized sector.[127] Unfortunately, the vehicle with the most potential for turning such statistics around—public education—is the government's most damaging failure.

Examinations of higher education raise similar concerns. In a 2004 report for the Center for International Development at Harvard University titled "Indian Higher Education Reform—from Half-Baked Socialism to Half-Baked Capitalism," Devesh Kapur (at Harvard at the time, and now at the University of Pennsylvania) and Pratap Bhanu Mehta (of the Center for Policy Research in New Delhi) stated, "The veneer of the few institutions of excellence masks the reality that the median HEIs in India have become incapable of producing students who have skills and knowledge."[128] They warned that India is facing a deep crisis in higher education, which is being masked by the success of narrow professional schools.

Philip Altbach opened his 2005 opinion piece in *The Hindu* by stating, "India is rushing headlong toward economic success and modernisation, counting on high-tech industries such as IT and biotechnology to propel the nation to prosperity."[129] But Altbach followed with, "Unfortunately, its weak higher education sector constitutes the Achilles' heel of this strategy. Its systematic disinvestment in higher education in recent years has yielded neither world-class research nor very many highly trained scholars, scientists, or managers to sustain high-tech development."[130]

Likewise, in his 2006 assessment of Goldman Sachs' BRIC predictions, Carnoy took a close look at issues with India's higher education system, specifically related to its role in one key element in the economic growth process—producing human capital, especially higher-end human capital. Carnoy concluded, "Although many analysts believe that India has sufficient absolute numbers of engineers and scientists and has advantages over China in moving towards an information-based advanced service economy, Tilak (2005) and others have pointed out that, proportionately, India . . . has very few highly educated technical and service personnel."[131]

A number of educational output indicators appear to confirm these concerns. Expenditure on R&D as a percentage of GDP from 1996 to 2003 in India was merely 0.81 percent, compared with 2.6 percent in the United States, 3.15 percent in Japan, and 2.5 percent in Germany; the figures for the other BRIC economies were 1.31 percent in China, 1.28 percent in Russia, and 0.98 percent in Brazil. From 1996 to 2004, India had only 119 researchers and technicians engaged in R&D activities per million of population, versus Japan's 5,287 and the United States' 4,484 researchers per million of population.[132] Looking at the other BRIC nations, Russia had 3,319, China had 663, and Brazil had 344 per million of population, making India the lowest of the four emerging economies.

Publication data for refereed scientific and technical journals show that India's output was on the decline or remained nearly flat from 1993 to 2003, whereas countries such as Brazil, China, and South Korea have improved their performance significantly and outpaced India.[133] According to data on patents filed under the Patent Cooperation Treaty (PCT) under the aegis of the World Intellectual Property Organization, not only are a very small number of PCT applications being filed from India, but their numbers declined during 2005. Even smaller countries like Switzerland and the Netherlands filed a much larger number of PCT applications in 2005. In terms of high-technology exports and royalties and license fees from technology licensing, India's performance is dismal, ranked as the lowest among the top-ten economies and other selected countries.

## Capacity Building in Higher Education

As of 2005, India's higher education system had a total of 17,973 institutions (348 universities and 17,625 colleges), which is four times the number of institutions in both the United States and all of Europe, and makes India's system the largest in the world in terms of number of institutions.[134] And the total enrollment reached 10.48 million in 2005, giving India the third-largest higher education system in the world in terms of number of students (after China and the United States). Yet few believe that the status quo is sustainable. In 2006, the chair of the National Knowledge Commission stressed to the prime minister that the overhaul of India's higher education system is essential "because the transformation of economy and society in the twenty-first century would depend, in significant part, on the spread and the quality of education among our people, particularly in the sphere of higher education."[135] While the details of reform plans for Indian higher education vary, there are a number of points where consensus appears to have developed.

## Funding

There is a general belief that Indian universities must be better capitalized if the institutions are to become global leaders. In addition, the National Knowledge Commission recommended that universities could tap into a larger reservoir of resources if they were able to use land as a source of financing.[136] Besides the general issue of university capitalization, the specific challenge of funding scientific research initiatives is drawing substantial attention. This is essentially the question of how a nation can set national research priorities, develop an infrastructure that can coordinate and incentivize scientists to compete and collaborate, enlist the private sector in the effort, and develop fruitful partnerships with major research universities and institutes around the globe.[137]

## Expansion

The National Knowledge Commission made several recommendations related to increasing India's production of human capital. One of its key recommendations was to increase the number of universities nationwide to around 1,500 (up from around 350 now), which would enable India to attain a gross enrollment rate of at least 15 percent by 2015.[138] Another key element of the commission's set of recommendations on the expansion of higher education was the creation of fifty national universities capable of providing education of the highest standard at both the undergraduate and graduate levels. Toward the longer-term objective of fifty such universities, the commission recommended beginning with at least ten new national universities within the next few years.

At the same time, balancing growth and excellence has become a significant challenge. The unregulated expansion of private universities has resulted in a growing concern about academic quality and comparability of degrees. Emerging for-profit universities have been the targets of special attention. These institutions have been widely criticized for hiring unqualified staff, for squeezing salaries to unacceptably low levels and for the lack of rigor in the curriculum. Calls for enhanced regulation of private institutions in the name of quality control have become routine in discussion of Indian higher education.

## Inclusion

Studies of higher education in India regularly note that its long-term success will require its capacity to be more inclusive in its reach, ultimately being far more accessible for the majority of the population. The power of large numbers can be effectively realized only if more individuals have access to high-quality postsecondary education. Reports have noted that the expansion of higher education in India during the past few decades has not proceeded equitably in terms of access. There is a significant urban-rural divide. Moreover, a 2008 report noted that the participation rate of Indian Muslims in higher education lags far behind that of Christians and Hindus. Officials at the highest level now acknowledge that social equity in higher education is one of the system's most significant challenges.

## Governance

Analysts have also proposed mechanisms for comparability and harmonization of academic standards across universities, in order to enable the mobility of students, as well as to ensure that degrees from different universities send similar signals to the job market.[139] Ideas that support excellence on an institutional level have also been advanced. Agarwal suggested that, in order to extend the modernization efforts that have been launched by certain Indian HEIs in the areas of governance and administration, more widespread initiatives are needed in staff development, procedural simplifications, and computerization efforts. Likewise, Altbach called for managerial reforms and the introduction of effective administration practices.[140] Altbach also proposed that merit-based hiring and promotion policies be instituted for the academic profession, and that merit-based practices be instituted for the recruitment, selection, and instruction of students. In addition, the National Knowledge Commission has advocated reforming the structures of governance of universities to promote autonomy and accountability.[141]

## Market Relevance

There is substantial impetus in India to develop a national strategic vision and policy that would encourage higher education to be more innovative and responsive to market demands.[142] Most recommendations that have been offered focus on establishing better and ongoing relationships with the Indian and multinational business community through internships, curricular reform, joint membership-based organizations, and formal involvement of industry representatives in higher education through increased board membership. But there is also an obvious need for a more formalized program of continuing education that provides lifelong learning in an environment where skill development is an ongoing process.

The manner in which universities can foster entrepreneurship and promote economic vitality has become especially important. An article on the role of the Indian Institute of Technology Bombay in promoting entrepreneurship in India stated, "In the developed west, governments had realized and passed bills to increase the role of universities in new business development to help strengthen local economies. When colleges and universities use business incubation as a strategy to achieve academic, research and community service missions, academia, entrepreneurs and society all benefit."[143] The article goes on to say, "Universities like Harvard, MIT, Stanford, etc. in U.S.A[.] understood that it is their civic duty to be an ally in this effort to promote enterprises based on technologies developed by them, to make U.S.A. a world leader. In India, the only parallels to such universities of west are IITs (Indian Institutes of Technology)."[144]

## Indian Institute of Technology Kharagpur

At VCU, we were able to develop a partnership with the Indian Institute of Technology Kharagpur (IITK), an institution that has directly addressed a number of the challenges facing Indian higher education. In 1946, a committee was set up to explore the establishment of technical institutes of higher education for the postwar industrial development of India. Eventually, seven IITs were established; they now offer undergraduate and graduate degrees in more than twenty-five engineering, technology, and business and management disciplines, as well as conduct world-class research. The first IIT was founded in 1950 in Kharagpur.[145]

IITK now has more than twenty departments, running the gamut from the humanities and social sciences, biotechnology, agricultural and food engineering, to medical science and technology; four centers of excellence on educational technology, reliability engineering, rubber technology, and rural development; and three schools—the G. S. Sanyal School of Telecommunications, the Rajiv Gandhi School of Intellectual Property Law, and the Vinod School of Management.[146] The institute has about eight thousand students.

One way in which the network of IITs has been contributing significantly to India's economic development is through quality improvement of instructors in technical arenas and the continuing education of the professional workforce, which is assuming tremendous importance in shaping the human capital of the nation. As the largest and most diversified technical institute in the country, IITK has been upholding this responsibility almost from its inception. IITK's Continuing Education Center recognizes that, in the face of the rapid technological advancement taking place around the globe, it is important for engineers and scientists to continue to learn new technologies and update and upgrade their knowledge base, long after completing their formal education. IITK's Quality Improvement Program and Curriculum Development Cell help meet the need for lifelong learning of some of the most important segments of India's twenty-first-century workforce.[147]

IITK has an expansive R&D enterprise, with more than eighty-five technologies that have been developed and are ready for commercialization, ranging from agricultural breakthroughs to advances in materials engineering. Whether conducting pioneering R&D in novel techniques for manufacturing instant tea or on the recovery of lead metal using green technology, IITK is positioning itself to transfer its technology to the market and to apply it to solutions to pressing problems in India.[148]

A special R&D unit at IITK, Sponsored Research & Industrial Consultancy (SRIC), was set up in 1982 as an interface between funding agencies and the institute. SRIC has handled more than 1,200 projects to date and currently has more than 450 sponsored projects from national and international clients. IITK's IPR policy supports the protection and commercial exploitation of individual IPR. So far, more than 125 patents have been filed on various innovations and development of technologies; about twenty-five of those patents have been granted. In addition, several technology transfer agreements have been executed. SRIC operates consultancy projects in almost thirty departments, centers, and schools of IITK, and works with approximately 330 clients around the world. Its sponsorship also comes from around the world and from various sectors within India, including the government.[149]

In December 2007, General Motors Corporation (GM) and IITK announced their intention to carry out joint research in the areas of electronics, controls, and software, as well as jointly develop a new educational curriculum leading to a graduate degree in those fields. The Collaborative Research Lab (CRL) will be comanaged by GM's India Science Lab in Bangalore and IITK's SRIC unit, and GM will commit more than $1 million for research to be done over five years within the new CRL.[150] And, in August 2009, IITK announced that it will partner with the University of California–San Diego to create a new full scale medical school at IITK "to bridge the gap between two distant disciplines of medicine and engineering."[151]

## HIGHER EDUCATION AND
## THE FUTURE OF THE BRIC NATIONS

There are many factors that will ultimately make or break the future for the BRIC nations. National security policies, decisions about economic priorities and directions, the capacity to align the political and economic system with the interests and aspirations of their public, and the overall quality of leadership will all be key contributors in determining whether the social and economic potential of the countries is maximized. But it is also evident that higher education policies are a crucial linchpin in their aspirations to become part of the world economy's first echelon.

When we look at the challenges faced by these nations' higher education systems, we see that size and numbers alone cannot guarantee ultimate success. Each of the BRIC nations that we have examined has to address some similar problems, albeit within their own distinctive cultures. How do you fund and organize a system of higher education that provides access and quality instruction to far greater numbers of people? How does a nation establish, fund, and grow a scientific infrastructure that encourages innovation, that links students and faculty to market needs, and that perpetuates itself over time? And what does fostering the spirit of experimentation and innovation in education mean for cultures that have not always been fully supportive and hospitable to unplanned change and individual self-expression?

In each of the countries discussed in this chapter, we see an expanded understanding of the relationship between higher education and national success in a global knowledge-based economy. We also can observe a number of practical steps that have been taken to implement this understanding. Yet the ultimate outcome is not preordained in any of these nations, perhaps because of the nature of the political choices that are inextricably related to the direction that higher education policies actually assume. In fact, the evolution of higher education policy in each of the BRIC nations will be a very clear signal of the real direction in which the government and society are moving.

## NOTES

1. Jim O'Neill, "Introduction," in *BRICs and Beyond*, Goldman Sachs (The Goldman Sachs Economics Group, 2008), http://www2.goldmansachs.com/ideas/brics/book/BRIC-Full.pdf (accessed April 8, 2009), 5; Goldman Sachs, "About Us," *Goldman Sachs* (Goldman Sachs, 2008), http://www2.goldman sachs.com/our-firm/about-us/index.html (accessed April 25, 2008), 1; Dominic Wilson and Roopa Purushothaman, "Dreaming with BRICs: The Path to 2050," *Global Economics, Paper No. 99* (New York: Goldman Sachs, October 1, 2003), 1.

2. O'Neill, "Introduction," 5.

3. Martin Carnoy, *Higher Education and Economic Development: India, China, and the 21st Century—Working Paper No. 297* (Stanford, CA: Stanford University, Stanford Center for International Development, 2006), http://scid.stanford.edu/pdf/SCID297.pdf (accessed October 2, 2006), 3.

4. Goldman Sachs, *BRICs and Beyond* (New York: The Goldman Sachs Economics Group, 2007), http://www2.goldmansachs.com/ideas/brics/book/BRIC-Full.pdf (accessed April 8, 2009), 131.

5. William Saint, "Tertiary Education and Economic Growth in Sub-Sahara Africa: The World Bank Report," *International Higher Education*, no. 54 (2009), Center for International Higher Education, The Boston College, http://www.bc.edu/bc_org/avp/soe/cihe/newsletter/Number54/p14_Saint.htm (accessed April 14, 2009), 1, 2.

6. Saint, "Tertiary Education and Economic Growth," 1.

7. Saint, "Tertiary Education and Economic Growth," 5, 8.

8. Ma Wan-hua, "Economic Reform and Higher Education in China," *Center for International & Development Education (CIDE) Occasional Papers Series: Higher Education, CIDE Contributions No. 2 (July 2003)* (Los Angeles: CIDE and UCLA Graduate School of Education & Information Studies), 20; Rondo Cameron, *A Concise Economic History of the World: From Paleolithic Times to the Present*, 3rd ed. (New York: Oxford University Press, 1997), 83.

9. Toshiya Tsugami, "Ascension Years," *Research Institute of Economy, Trade and Industry—Fellows in the Press* (2002), http://www.rieti.go.jp/en/papers/contributions/tsugami/ (accessed July 5, 2007), 1.

10. Dominic Wilson, Roopa Purushothaman, and Themistoklis Fiotakis, *Global Economics Paper No: 18—the BRICs and Global Markets: Crude, Cars and Capital* (New York: Goldman Sachs, October 14, 2004), 4–6, 22.

11. Wan-hua, "Economic Reform," 1.

12. Wei Xiao, "The New Economy and Venture Capital in China," *Perspectives* 3, no. 6 (September 30, 2002), Overseas Young Chinese Forum, http://www.oycf .org/oycfold/httpdocs/perspectives2/18_093002/Economy_Venture_China.htm (accessed August 23, 2007), 8.

13. Xiao, "The New Economy," 8.

14. Xiao, "The New Economy," 8.

15. Wan-hua, "Economic Reform," 3, 4.

16. Wan-hua, "Economic Reform," 21.

17. WES, "International Rankings and Chinese Higher Education Reform," *World Education News and Reviews* 19, no. 5 (2006): 2.

18. WES, "International Rankings," 15, 16; Ruth Hayhoe and Julia Pan, "China's Universities on the Global Stage: Perspectives of University Leaders," *International Higher Education* (Spring 2005), Center for International Higher Education, Boston College, http://www.bc.edu/bc_org/avp/soe/cihe/newsletter/News39/ text012.htm (accessed July 6, 2007), 1.

19. Michael M. Crow, "U.S. Universities and Global Competition," *The Globalist*, September 5, 2006, http://www.theglobalist.com/StoryId=5552 (accessed October 9, 2006), 12.

20. WES, "International Rankings," 22, 23.

21. Paul Mooney, "The Long Road Ahead for China's Universities," *Chronicle of Higher Education* 52, no. 37 (2006): A42.

22. Mooney, "The Long Road Ahead," A42; Wan-hua, "Economic Reform," 5, 20.

23. Wan-hua, "Economic Reform," 11.

24. "China Expands Higher Education to Back Economic Development," *People's Daily Online*, August 11, 2004, http://english.peopledaily.com.cn/200408/11/ eng20040811_152497.html (accessed June 28, 2007), 1–2.

25. Wan-hua, "Economic Reform," 20.

26. Wan-hua, "Economic Reform," 20.

27. Wan-hua, "Economic Reform," 5, 15; Mooney, "The Long Road Ahead," A42.

28. Mooney, "The Long Road Ahead," A42; Paul Mooney, "New Program Planned in U.S.-China Trade," *Chronicle of Higher Education* 53, no. 29 (2007): A38.

29. Wan-hua, "Economic Reform," 14.

30. Wan-hua, "Economic Reform," 19.

31. "China Expands Higher Education," 3, 4.

32. Wan-hua, "Economic Reform," 18.

33. Wan-hua, "Economic Reform," 18.

34. Mooney, "The Long Road Ahead," A42.

35. Paul Mooney, "The Wild, Wild East," *Chronicle of Higher Education* 52, no. 24 (2006): A46.

36. Mooney, "The Wild, Wild East," A46.

37. Mooney, "The Wild, Wild East," A46.

38. Arizona State University, "Institute for University Design," Arizona State University, http://www.asu.edu/china/education.html (accessed April 18, 2007), 3.

39. WES, "International Rankings," 24.

40. The Alliance for Global Education, *Contemporary Chinese Society and Language in Shanghai or Intensive Chinese Language Hosted by Fudan University* (The Alliance for Global Education, 2006), http://www.allianceglobaled.org/program/fudan_contemporary_society_and_language/ (accessed September 5, 2007), 1; China Today, "Fudan Leads the Way in Higher Education Reforms," All-China Women's Federation, http://www.womenofchina.cn/focus/education/4217.jsp (accessed September 5, 2007), 1.

41. Shenghong Wang, "President's Message," Fudan University, http://www.fudan.edu.cn/englishnew/about/premessage.html (accessed September 5, 2007), 1; Foreign Students Office, Fudan University, "Introduction to Fudan University," Fudan University, http://www.fso.fudan.edu.cn/en/fd_info.htm (accessed September 5, 2007), 1; Fudan University, "History of Fudan," Fudan University, http://www.fudan.edu.cn/englishnew/about/history.html (accessed September 5, 2007), 2.

42. WES, "International Rankings," 23.

43. Fudan University, "History of Fudan," 8.

44. Fudan University, "Shanghai Medical College, Fudan University," Fudan University, http://www.fudan.edu.cn/englishnew/medical/medicine.html (accessed September 5, 2007), 1.

45. Fudan University, "Shanghai Medical College, Fudan University," 1, 2; Fudan University, "Affiliated Hospitals," Fudan University, http://www.fudan.edu.cn/englishnew/medical/hospitals.html (accessed September 5, 2007), 1–8.

46. Quacquarelli Symonds Limited, "Fudan University," Quacquarelli Symonds Limited, http://www.topuniversities.com/university/217/fudan-university (accessed September 5, 2007), 2.

47. Quacquarelli Symonds Limited, "Fudan University," 8.

48. China Today, "Fudan Leads the Way," 2.

49. China Today, "Fudan Leads the Way," 4.

50. Mooney, "The Long Road Ahead," A42.

51. Mooney, "The Long Road Ahead," A42; China Today, "Fudan Leads the Way," 8.

52. John Herman, VCU professor of Chinese history, e-mail message to Kelly Myles, July 7, 2007.

53. China Today, "Fudan Leads the Way," 9.

54. China Today, "Fudan Leads the Way," 8.

55. Fudan University, "Research," Fudan University, http://www.fudan.edu.cn/englishnew/research/research.html (accessed September 5, 2007), 1, 2.

56. Fudan University, "Brief Introduction," Fudan University, http://www.fudan.edu.cn/englishnew/about/intro.html (accessed September 5, 2007), 7.

57. China Center for Venture Capital Investment, "China Center for Venture Capital Investment," Fudan University, http://www.econ.fudan.edu.cn/english/c5.htm (accessed September 5, 2007), 1.

58. Fudan University, "Joint Project," Fudan University, http://www.fudan .edu.cn/englishnew/research/project.html (accessed September 5, 2007), 1.

59. China Today, "Fudan Leads the Way," 11; Foreign Students Office, Fudan University, "Introduction to Fudan University," 6.

60. Fudan University, "Brief Introduction," 4; Quacquarelli Symonds Limited, "Fudan University," 7.

61. Sergei Bobylev et al., eds., *Human Development Report, Russian Federation 2004—towards a Knowledge-based Society* (Moscow: United Nations Development Programme, 2004), http://hdr.undp.org/en/reports/nationalreports/europethecis/russia/russia_federation_2004_en.pdf (accessed March 26, 2008), 11.

62. Carnoy, *Higher Education and Economic Development*, 2; Bobylev et al., *Human Development Report*, 11, 12.

63. Bobylev et al., *Human Development Report*, 11; Sergei A. Mitrofanov, A. A. Kharin, and I. L. Kolensky, eds., "Innovation Activity in Russian Higher Education," *Successes and Difficulties of Small Innovative Firms in Russian Nuclear Cities: Proceedings of a Russian-American Workshop* (The National Academy of Science, Higher Education Technopark and Elion Experimental Development Plant, Russian Federation Ministry for Higher Education, 2002), http://books.nap.edu/openbook.php?record_id=10392&page=24 (accessed March 13, 2008), 30.

64. Bobylev et al., *Human Development Report*, 2, 4.

65. Bobylev et al., *Human Development Report*, 19.

66. Mitrofanov et al., "Innovation Activity in Russian Higher Education," 24.

67. Sergei Bobylev et al., *Human Development Report*, 11; Sophia Kishkovsky, "A Bright Future: Russian Higher Education," *Carnegie Reporter* 1, no. 1 (Summer 2000), Carnegie Corporation of New York, http://www.carnegie.org/reporter/01/russia/index.html (accessed March 13, 2008), 12.

68. Mitrofanov et al., "Innovation Activity in Russian Higher Education," 31.

69. Deaver, "Democratizing Russian Higher Education," 47; Margaret Dobrow-King, "New Structure of Higher Education in Russia," *World Education Services* 12, no. 3 (1999), WES, http://www.wes.org/ewenr/99may/practical.htm (March 13, 2008), 5.

70. Deaver, "Democratizing Russian Higher Education," 47.

71. Shirobokov, "Civil Society: Reforming Higher Education in Russia," Omsk State Pedagogical University, http://www.prof.msu.ru/publ/omsk1/3_08.htm (accessed March 13, 2008), 6.

72. Shirobokov, "Civil Society: Reforming Higher Education in Russia," 5.

73. Mikhail Drougov, *Higher Education Expansion in Russia: What Stands Behind? (Working Paper #BSP/01/048)* (Moscow: New Economic School, 2001), http://www.nes.ru/english/research/pdf/2001/Drougov.pdf (accessed March 13, 2008), 3.

74. Irina Arzhanova, *Recent Developments in Russia—Challenges for Higher Education Institutions and Academic Cooperation* (Moscow: NTF, May 2006), http://www .lut.fi/kevatpaivat/Recent%20developments%20in%20Russia%20%96%20Challenges%20for.ppt#1 (accessed March 11, 2008), 3.

75. Shirobokov, "Civil Society," 13, 15.

76. Kishkovsky, "A Bright Future," 35.

77. Kishkovsky, "A Bright Future," 6.

78. Kishkovsky, "A Bright Future," 9.

79. Kishkovsky, "A Bright Future," 56.

80. Carnoy, *Higher Education and Economic Development*, 16.

81. Drougov, *Higher Education Expansion in Russia*, 3.

82. Jodi Koehn, "The Demise of a Great Power: Education and Russian National Security in the 21st Century," *Russian Education and National Security* (January 10, 2000), Woodrow Wilson International Center for Scholars, Kennan Institute, http://www.wilsoncenter.org/index.cfm?fuseaction=events .print&event_id=3846&stoplayout=true (accessed March 11, 2008), 8.

83. Drougov, *Higher Education Expansion in Russia*, 3.

84. Drougov, *Higher Education Expansion in Russia*, 3.

85. Mitrofanov et al., "Innovation Activity," 31.

86. Shirobokov, "Civil Society," 16, 17.

87. Arzhanova, *Recent Developments in Russia*, 13.

88. G8/2006 Russia, "Education for Innovative Societies in the 21st Century," *G8 Summit 2006, Saint Petersburg*, G8 Presidency of the Russian Federation in 2006, http://en.g8russia.ru/docs/12-print.html (accessed March 11, 2008).

89. Arzhanova, *Recent Developments in Russia*, 17.

90. Anna Nemtsova, "In Russia, Corruption Plagues the Higher-Education System," *Chronicle of Higher Education* 54, no. 24 (2008): A18.

91. Kishkovsky, "A Bright Future," 10.

92. Mitrofanov et al., "Innovation Activity," 27.

93. Mitrofanov et al., "Innovation Activity," 30.

94. Moscow State University (MSU), "Home," MSU, http://www.msu.ru/en/ (accessed March 28, 2008), 2.

95. Oleg Movsesyan, *Moscow State University Science Park* (PowerPoint presentation given to author in Moscow) (Moscow: MSU Science Park, September 2007), 4.

96. MSU Science Park, *ITC "MSU Science Park"* (Moscow: MSU Science Park, n.d.).

97. Movsesyan, *Moscow State University Science Park*, 7; MSU Science Park, *ITC "MSU Science Park."*

98. Movsesyan, *Moscow State University Science Park*, 6.

99. MSU Science Park, *ITC "MSU Science Park"*; Movsesyan, *Moscow State University Science Park*, 13–15.

100. MSU Science Park, *ITC "MSU Science Park."*

101. Movsesyan, *Moscow State University Science Park*, 12.

102. MSU Science Park, *ITC "MSU Science Park"*; MSU Science Park, "Companies, Situated in the SP," *About Science Park*, Science Park, http://www.science park.ru/eng/firms.htm (accessed March 28, 2008).

103. MSU Science Park, "History," *About Science Park*, Science Park, http://www.sciencepark.ru/eng/history.htm (accessed March 28, 2008).

104. MSU Science Park, "History."

105. MSU Science Park, *ITC "MSU Science Park."*

106. Movsesyan, *Moscow State University Science Park*, 17.

107. MSU Science Park, *ITC "MSU Science Park."*

108. Movsesyan, *Moscow State University Science Park*, 5.

109. Eugene Trani served as Senior Fulbright Professor at Moscow State University for four months in the spring of 1981, teaching in the American Studies Program at MSU.

110. Tushar Podder and Eva Yi, "India's Rising Growth Potential," in *BRICS and Beyond*, ed. Goldman Sachs Global Economics Group (New York: Goldman Sachs, 2007), http://www2.goldmansachs.com/ideas/brics/book/BRIC-Chapter1 .pdf (accessed April 24, 2008), 11.

111. Carnoy, *Higher Education and Economic Development*, 2.

112. U.S. Department of State, "Profile (October 2007)," *Background Note: India*, Bureau of South and Central Asian Affairs, http://www.state.gov/r/pa/ei/ bgn/3454.htm (accessed April 10, 2008), 44.

113. Gurcharan Das, "The India Model," *Foreign Affairs* 85, no. 4 (2006): 6.

114. Shailaja Neelakantan, "In India: No Foreign Colleges Need Apply," *Chronicle of Higher Education* 54, no. 22 (2008): A23; Das, "The India Model," 6.

115. U.S. Department of State, "Profile (October 2007)," 43.

116. Wilson and Purushothaman, "Dreaming with BRICs: The Path to 2050," 3.

117. Pawan Agarwal, *Higher Education in India: The Need for Change—Working Paper No. 180 (June 2006)*, Indian Council for Research on International Economic Relations, http://www.icrier.org/publication/working_papers_180.html (accessed April 11, 2008), ii, 183.

118. Agarwal, *Higher Education in India*, 66.

119. U.S. Department of State, "Profile (October 2007)," 48.

120. Das, "The India Model," 9.

121. Agarwal, *Higher Education in India*, 43.

122. Das, "The India Model," 2.

123. U.S. Department of State, "Profile (October 2007)," 2, 43.

124. U.S. Department of State, "Profile (October 2007)," 5; Somini Sengupta, "India Attracts Universities from the U.S.," *New York Times*, March 26, 2007, http://www.nytimes.com/2007/03/26/world/asia/26india.html (accessed March 28, 2007), 3.

125. Vir Sanghvi, "The Indians Are Coming," *Hindustan Times* (October 8, 2006), 10; *Vir Sanghvi: The Suave Charmer* (HT Media Ltd., 2006), http://www. hinustantimes.com/news/181_29349,0023.htm (accessed October 16, 2006), 1.

126. Podder and Yi, "India's Rising Growth Potential," 22.

127. Das, "The India Model," 14.

128. Devesh Kapur and Pratap Bhanu Mehta, *Indian Higher Education Reform: From Half-Baked Socialism to Half-Baked Capitalism—CID Working Paper No. 108 (September 2004)*, Center for International Development at Harvard University, http://www.cid.harvard.edu/cidwp/pdf/108.pdf (accessed April 11, 2008), 27.

129. Philip G. Altbach, "Higher Education in India," *The Hindu—Opinion*, April 12, 2005, http://www.hindu.com/2005/04/12/stories/2005041204141000.htm (accessed April 17, 2008), 1, 20.

130. Altbach, "Higher Education in India," 1, 20.

131. Carnoy, *Higher Education and Economic Development*, 1.

132. Agarwal, *Higher Education in India*, 60–61, 165.

133. Agarwal, *Higher Education in India*, 61.

134. Agarwal, *Higher Education in India*, 5, 7.

135. Sam Pitroda, chairman, National Knowledge Commission, *Letter to Prime Minister on Higher Education (November 29, 2006)*, National Knowledge Commission, http://knowledgecommission.gov.in/downloads/recommendations/HigherEducationLetterPM.pdf (accessed April 22, 2008), 1.

136. Pitroda, *Letter to Prime Minister*, 2.

137. Agarwal, *Higher Education in India*, 69–76.

138. Pitroda, *Letter to Prime Minister*, 1; Shailaja Neelakantan, "Commission Calls for Overhaul of Higher Education in India," *Chronicle of Higher Education* 53, no. 21 (2007): A44.

139. Agarwal, *Higher Education in India*, 97.

140. Altbach, "Higher Education in India," 17.

141. Pitroda, *Letter to Prime Minister*, 4, 5.

142. Agarwal, *Higher Education in India*, 18.

143. Indian Institute of Technology Bombay (IITB), "Role of IIT Bombay in Entrepreneurship in India," *Society for Innovation and Entrepreneurship*, http://www.sineiitb.org/india_incubation_and_iitb.html (accessed April 17, 2008), 4.

144. IITB, "Role of IIT Bombay," 4.

145. Indian Institute of Technology (IIT) Alumni, "IIT—History," IIT Alumni—IIT—About, http://iit.org/about-iit/iit-history (accessed April 17, 2008), 2, 3; IIT Alumni, "IIT—Overview," IIT Alumni—IIT—About, http://iit.org/about-itt (accessed April 17, 2008), 1; Indian Institute of Technology Kharagpur (IITK), "Institute History," Indian Institute of Technology Kharagpur, http://www.iitkgp.ac.in/institute/history.php (accessed April 17, 2008), 14.

146. IITK, "Departments, Centres and Schools," IITK—Academics, http://www.iitkgp.ac.in/departments/ (accessed April 17, 2008).

147. IITK, "Continuing Education Centre," Indian Institute of Technology Kharagpur, http://www.iitkgp.ac.in/cep/ (accessed April 17, 2008), 1.

148. IITK, "Technologies Developed and Ready for Commercialization," IITK—Research & Development, http://www.iitkgp.ac.in/rnd/technologies.php (accessed April 17, 2008).

149. IITK, "Sponsored Research and Industrial Consultancy (SRIC)," IITK—Research & Development, http://www.iitkgp.ac.in/sric/ (accessed April 17, 2008).

150. General Motors Corporation, "General Motors and Indian Institute of Technology Kharagpur Expand R&D and Educational Collaboration," *News*, December 7, 2007, General Motors Corporation, http://www.gm.com/explore/technology/news/2007/indian_institute_120707.jsp (accessed April 17, 2008), 1, 2, 4.

151. Pradipta Mukherjee, "IIT-Kgp Ties Up with US Varsity [sic] for Hospital," Business Standard, http://www.business-standard.com/india/storypage.php?autono=367048 (accessed August 18, 2009).

## Chapter 9

# Conclusions: Colleges and Universities Indispensable to Economic and Community Development

The relevance of colleges and universities to regional economic development can be seen both across the spectrum of higher education and over the range of local environments where these institutions are located. A community college, for example, may be as indispensable to its region as the University of North Carolina–Chapel Hill, Duke University, and North Carolina State have been to the formation and growth of the Research Triangle Park in the Raleigh-Durham area.

Rural areas in the United States that have been adversely impacted by the economic dislocations that have accompanied the globalization of manufacturing have often made community colleges the linchpins of regional efforts to maintain the industry they have and attract new companies to their area. The workforce development and training efforts of community colleges are key selling points for a region striving to maintain a reasonable quality of life in a global, competitive environment that has put local economies under tremendous pressure.

At the same time, community colleges serve as powerful engines for the economic and cultural aspirations of the new Americans who have come to the country seeking a better chance for themselves and their children. Again, it is the access to higher education and the workforce training that community colleges provide that enable large metropolitan areas to utilize the ambitions and skills of their newest residents most productively. When we recognize just how much of this population is served by community colleges and not traditional four-year institutions, we begin to understand the extent of the impact these institutions have.

In some crucial ways, even though the form that is taken can be very different, elite institutions at the pinnacle of American higher education

have increasingly become more involved in regional development strategies. Yale University is a key player in the revitalization of New Haven, as
is the University of Pennsylvania in West Philadelphia. The University of
Southern California has utilized its location in a global entertainment and
communications capital to develop a set of world-class programs that can
contribute to the further development of the related industries. The scientific experts that gather in and around these institutions and the spin-off
businesses that emerge from the collected brainpower can begin to shape
the economic DNA of the surrounding region. Studies of Silicon Valley, for
instance, often point to the importance of Stanford University and the intellectual capital that it created as crucial to the development of the region.

The indispensability of higher education institutions to regional economic development is increasingly seen across the globe. We have seen
it in a very personal way at Virginia Commonwealth University (VCU)
with how interested the leaders of our partner institutions in Europe,
Latin America, South Africa, the Middle East, and Asia are in thinking
about how their institutions can be relevant to regional economic development strategies. And we have discovered time and again that the
political leaders of their regions and nations are extraordinarily interested
in transforming their universities to place a greater emphasis on the economic development role that they can play for the nation at large.

The academic literature confirms our experiential impressions. Across
the globe, considerable attention is being paid to how university systems
ought to be funded, internally managed, and held accountable to encourage more extensive partnerships with external constituencies in bettering
the region and nation at large. These tendencies have sometimes come into
conflict, occasionally very bitter conflict, with the beliefs of those who have
felt that the preservation of academic values is dependent on a full separation of higher education goals from the practical, day-to-day realities of the
state and the marketplace. But given the enormous sums of dollars spent
on higher education, the pressure, for example, to develop a system of
higher education in the Euro-zone that can serve the interests of multiple
states, and the virtual impossibility of thinking about major scientific and
commercial invention without including universities, it is difficult to believe that the traditionalists can deflect these trends from escalating.

This chapter draws upon the case studies in the previous six chapters
to offer a set of final reflections on the role of colleges and universities in
the modern knowledge economy. In particular, we focus on three areas
that we believe are of special relevance. The chapter begins by describing
the role of university presidents and demonstrates why their personal assumption of a regional leadership role is crucially important to both their
institutions and the broader community. The second part of the chapter
focuses on the "business" operations of colleges and universities and con-

tends that institutions that have developed the strongest partnerships and the most influence on their communities have understood the range of impact that higher education can exercise through the day-to-day operations of purchasing, employing, and developing real estate. Finally, we suggest that colleges and universities should focus less on replicating other institutions and more on enhancing their own distinctiveness. Contemporary economic development theory suggests that regional differentiation and specialization are often the key to local prosperity. There is good reason to believe that the notion is applicable to higher education also.

## THE PRESIDENT AS REGIONAL ACTOR

College and university presidents can have a substantial impact on the role that their institutions play in promoting regional economic and community development. But this is a choice that has to be made consciously and deliberately. Much of the literature about higher education leadership points to the expansion of roles that presidents are expected to perform and,the growth in the number of constituencies that they are required to serve. The conflicting demands on the time and energy of university leaders, their own assessment of their interests and abilities, and the nature of the specific challenges that they must address in their own institutions have led universities to respond very differently to the prospect of becoming a partner in regional economic development efforts.

We have described in the previous chapters a set of colleges and universities that have fully embraced the opportunity, developing creative partnerships that can enhance the institution and the region. On the other hand, there are many universities that may continue to remain at arm's length from their own communities and regions or become involved in a perfunctory way that may contribute some level of expertise to community initiatives but fail to involve the full range of the college or university. Given the fundraising pressures on presidents and the continuing demands of negotiating the legendary bitterness of internal university politics, this response is understandable. But we think that establishing a fuller level of engagement is often important not only for the surrounding community and region, but for the ultimate success of the institution.

## THE COMMUNITY POWER NEXUS

Communities are, in many ways, built around a series of personal and institutional relationships. In any city and region, there are various "communities" that exercise influence in which the key participants are likely to know one another and interact in a regular way over time.

The business community has its clubs where its members dine, "round-tables" where its leaders discuss and develop viewpoints on the key issues of the region, and "public-private partnerships" where private-sector leaders work on joint projects with officials from the political arena and the nonprofit sector.

The political community is often more divided than the business community (especially along whatever lines constitute the competition for power in a region) but it also has its own distinctive culture and customs. It has a set of temporary and permanent leaders—those who are currently elected and those who exercise power over longer periods. It normally has a few individuals who have remarkable access to power, who have built personal relationships with the key players for decades, and who do not seem to be impacted by changes in electoral fortunes. It has its own set of social environments—some of which are closed to people who have self-identified with a party or faction. But others, such as power restaurants and grand openings, are available to all members of a regional community.

Regions almost invariably have nonprofit, arts, and activist "communities" that are primarily interested in promoting social justice, inclusion, and cultural enrichment. The leaders of the arts communities regularly interact with the key members of the business and political communities around matters such as downtown redevelopment and continuing support for the arts. Nonprofits work with the business and political elites around a wide range of matters, as they have become integral to community revitalization, workforce training, pre-kindergarten education, and health care for those without access to insurance. Activist groups tend to have a more complex relationship with local community elites, sometimes collaborative and sometimes adversarial. Yet over time, it is not uncommon for "spokespersons" for these activist groups to obtain a relatively permanent status in the community, either as a result of media prominence or through successful negotiations with the leaders of the business and political class.

Until recently, media outlets were also essential players in communities and regions, but a changing environment has put their role in flux. Television stations still have remarkable capacity to focus public attention through the visual power of the medium. Yet the day-to-day focus on traffic crashes, street crimes, storms, and sports has made these outlets less vital to the crucial decisions that are made about business and community development. Under tremendous financial strain as their business model collapses, newspapers in most markets have attempted to refocus almost exclusively on "local news." But doubts about their capacity to remain solvent as well as the ability of small-scale entrepreneurs to utilize the Internet to create sites of local interest, have made the media establishment less prominent as each day passes.

## The Role of Higher Education in the Community Power Nexus

College and university presidents have to decide how much time they are willing to devote to participating in these communities and what role they want to occupy within them. How should they respond to the myriad invitations to speak to community groups? How do they prioritize the requests for resources that will invariably be made? How much of the university's community time are they willing to allocate to tasks that are not essential for instructing students and conducting peer-reviewed research? And how much of a player should the institution and its leaders be in helping to determine the future of the broader region? It is hard to imagine that these questions would not have to be answered by any president at almost any higher education institution.

We have suggested that college and university presidents are not simply leading institutions that happen to be located in a particular environment, but are instead the chief executives of academic enterprises that are indispensable to the overall success and progress of their region and its citizens. In a knowledge economy, the existence of successful higher education institutions is becoming ever more vital to the capacity of regions to compete successfully for talent and jobs. Indeed, contemporary economic development theory tends to place a heavier emphasis on talent availability than on other factors that may have previously exercised a greater impact on regional prosperity. In addition to their role in economic development, we have also shown that colleges and universities are increasingly seen by their communities as essential to social and cultural progress. The research capacities of faculty in addressing matters that may appear intractable, the energy and enthusiasm of students, and the university's potential role in convening groups that address major social challenges are all vital assets for building social capital in contemporary society. In fact, universities often have the kind of credibility that enables them to bring disparate groups together to focus on shared interests more successfully than many other community institutions.

Acknowledging the role that colleges and universities actually occupy in contemporary society should have an impact on the manner in which their presidents define their job. It is our belief, for example, that they should become an essential part of the community leadership groups that help to define and establish regional economic strategy. In some places today, we see presidents become heads of the Chamber of Commerce, executive board members of regional development authorities, leaders of area-wide visioning exercises, chairs of research parks, key members of regional and statewide trade missions, and vital players in the recruitment of new industries to regions. While these roles may be far afield from what individual presidents studied in graduate school or even from the experiences they had on their way up the administrative hierarchy, possessing the capacity to contribute in these ways may be a crucial element in the overall success of the modern college and university presidency.

The intellectual diversity of the institutions that college and university presidents lead can provide them with a unique vantage point and the capacity to mobilize a set of resources that are typically not available to leaders of most community organizations. A major university, for example, typically offers science, technology, engineering, and mathematics programs that are of considerable interest to business and health care leaders in a community. In the modern knowledge economy, companies thinking of relocating to a region want to know about the scientific capacities of local universities. The professional programs in large universities often provide the trainees and interns for local governments and state governments and the faculty expertise utilized in major regional initiatives. At the same time, a university often makes significant contributions to arts and culture through its theater program, music department, and fine arts faculty. Think about how many university-centered regions have become meccas for retirees who want to be able to draw on the cultural resources of a world-class institution.

Universities that include medical centers occupy an even more prominent role. They provide employment opportunities across a wide range of occupations and professions. Hospitals may be the principal customers of vendors of goods and services, from janitorial supplies to flowers to sophisticated lab equipment. University-based medical centers are often the provider of choice for patients in the community suffering from debilitating, potentially life-threatening or chronic illnesses. In urban and rural areas, university medical centers often serve the vast majority of indigent patients who could not access high-end medical care in any other way.

The upshot is that modern colleges and universities possess resources—scientific, commercial, medical, and cultural—that are vital to the entire range of community and regional development activities relevant to the contemporary knowledge economy. The capacity of communities and regions to tap these resources in the most creative way can be crucial to their ability to flourish and prosper. A region that does not tap its higher education institutions as part of its competitive strategy is likely to underperform. Likewise, college or university presidents that do not understand the history of the community, do not see how their institutions fit into the broader fabric of regional identity, and do not make a determined effort to contribute to its growth and development are likely to miss out on opportunities to make their own universities more distinctive.

### Leadership Development and Higher Education's Community Role

University boards and others charged with the selection of college and university presidents ought to be mindful of the new responsibilities of higher education in a knowledge economy when making leadership decisions. This is an especially challenging task because it often requires a "leap of faith" regarding the capacities of the individual being chosen. The typical academic administrative career ladder—department chair, dean, provost, and president—provides almost no guarantee that candidates pick up this kind of knowledge and training while they are preparing to be presidents. Deans may well pick up some fundraising experience and involvement in technology transfer issues, depending on the school they are leading. But there is no organized and coordinated effort to ensure that this is the case. There is clear evidence that college and university boards have become more willing to think "outside the box" in recruiting and hiring presidencies, but this has often been more related to the fundraising requirements of the position than to an understanding of the indispensable role the university plays in economic and community development.

Here are two concrete suggestions. First, higher education leadership development programs, especially those conducted inside universities, should place more emphasis on linking academic leadership to community involvement in a sophisticated manner. Colleges and universities should create vehicles by which individuals on an administrative path assume real responsibilities on projects that are important to the institution and the community that will enable aspiring presidents to understand their potential role in economic development and develop some understanding of their strengths and weaknesses. Second, college boards should examine the range of external relations that potential candidates for president have built in their previous jobs—fundraising is a part of that evaluation, but it should be only a part. And once it is widely apparent that this is a job qualification, the very smart individuals who are seeking these positions are far more likely to develop the appropriate experience on their own.

## CAPITALIZING ON THE BUSINESS
## OPERATIONS OF COLLEGES AND UNIVERSITIES

Colleges and universities that have become successful partners in regional development efforts have understood that their own business operations—real estate development, procurement, establishing public-private partnerships to meet institutional aims, and the provision of medical care—enable the institutions to have a significant impact on the future of their areas. In recent years, a cottage industry that provides economic impact studies for colleges, universities, and their medical centers has developed. These studies describe for legislators and business leaders the fiscal effect of colleges and universities on their communities. One of the most striking pieces of information contained in just about every one of these studies is that colleges and universities and, in many instances, their medical centers are invariably one of the major employers in their region. In small and midsize localities, they are often the single largest employer. But what is even more interesting is that the situation is not very different in even the largest cities. We saw, for example, in chapter 3 that Steve Sample, the president of the University of Southern California, reminds other leaders in Los Angeles that the university is one of the largest employers in L.A.

As a major regional employer, colleges and universities have the same kind of impact that is seen with private-sector companies that have a large employee base and with major governmental operations. This effect is only magnified by the number of students, often in residence, who spend dollars on services and activities other than what the institution officially provides. The range of economic activity that takes place on and next to a modern college or university is extensive and highly varied.

A set of firms tend to locate near universities for the express purpose of supplying goods and services to the business operations of colleges, universities, or medical centers. Retailers view the students and employees as an enviable customer base to be tapped. Just think of the food service, restaurant, and catering operations that surround colleges and universities. Thirty years ago, colleges and universities provided their own food service and an entire generation went to college sharing complaints about miserable food. Not any longer. Higher education institutions compete for students, at least in part, by competing on the services offered, striking deals to bring to campus branded restaurants with high name recognition among young people. Starbucks, Chili's, Coldstone Creamery, and Five Guys all have a substantial on-campus presence now.

Architects, interior designers, real estate developers, construction trade operators, and material suppliers see the growth of colleges and universities as an opportunity to extend the reach of their services. On-campus construction, renovation of conventional buildings for scientific use, the creation of research parks, rehabilitation of older structures for retail use, the construction of privately owned, dorm-style apartments, and joint ventures with universities in which the private sector purchases land and constructs buildings where the universities guarantee rental for a specified period have provided a regular stream of business for these companies. The physical footprint of universities extends far wider today, is far more distinctive, and is far more integrated with the surrounding neighborhoods than the insulated campus environments of thirty years ago.

Until recently, business operations were rarely considered integral to the strategic directions of colleges, universities, and medical centers. These tasks had an "eat your peas" quality, something that had to be done but was not directly related to the more substantial activities of teaching and research. The process of negotiating town-gown relationships occasionally highlighted the significance of these operations, especially if campus expansion impinged on the quality of life in surrounding neighborhoods. But it was unusual for a college or university to utilize business operations in a positive manner to shape the kind of effect it would have on the broader community challenges and to partner with businesses and neighborhood and regional development strategies. Procurement, for example, was assigned to a mid-level official primarily responsible for preventing fraud and ensuring compliance with federal and state regulations. Most of the universities that we have examined have adopted a very different and more contemporary approach. The leaders almost invariably have a clear understanding of the institution's economic heft and the influence that decisions about how to exercise this can have.

### Developing Minority Partners

Colleges and universities invariably spend large sums as purchasers of goods and services. Some are purchased nationally and internationally, some equipment is available from specialized suppliers, and some public systems operate within a strictly regulated context that makes for a highly bureaucratized process. But these constraints, with the exception of government regulation, may not be very different from those experienced by any large business. Owners of commercial enterprises within a community typically view colleges, universities, and medical centers in the same way they would any large firm—as potential customers. Universities that pay minimal attention to the community consequences of their business operations can easily and inadvertently incur the animus of local small businesses if they appear aloof and uninterested in their concerns. On the other hand, college and university leaders who devote attention and interest to procurement matters can make a positive impact on small-business opportunity in their community and generate new sources of support for their initiatives and activities.

This is particularly true for colleges and universities located in areas with large minority populations. Although colleges and universities are traditionally considered politically liberal and highly supportive of minority rights and inclusion, the historic relationship between higher education and surrounding minority communities is more complex and complicated. University staff and faculty members have frequently been very supportive of community-based organizations and some have gained excellent reputations for their selflessness in advancing aims of civil rights and equal opportunity. But institution-community relationships have rarely evoked universally positive sentiments. In many instances, there are lingering tensions that result from admissions policies, the history of university expansion (most especially in urban renewal areas), and a perceived lack of genuine commitment to social goals. The establishment of effective minority supplier and vendor programs can be an important mechanism for rebuilding trust when its strands have been frayed over time. Moreover, the creation of effective minority supplier programs is seen by segments in the community as a better indicator of the institution's real commitment than the rhetoric of diversity that is voiced almost uniformly by college and university presidents today.

Procurement is an area where effective leadership can make a genuine difference. In the Commonwealth of Virginia, where we reside, minority firms receive 2.2 percent of overall state contracting dollars. At VCU, the overall performance rate is far greater, with minority firms obtaining 8.26 percent of overall purchasing. College and university presidents and key vice presidents can use their influence to emphasize the importance of the issue throughout the organization. They can be certain that the use of minority firms is measured on an annual basis. And they can hold individuals accountable in the institution for making progress toward the goals that are established. In most instances, the establishment of effective minority supplier programs also requires effective outreach by the institution to businesses in the community. The president's public appearances and speeches set an overall tone. Units responsible for university contracting can hold workshops for minority firms and provide advice on how these companies might bid for university contracts or partner with non-minority firms in joint ventures. And the college or university can highlight its major accomplishments through its public relations activities as a means of encouraging more companies to view the institution as a potential customer.

## Real Estate Development

The growth in the number of college-eligible students over the last two decades, the increase in the percentage of students seeking higher education, the internal pressure to improve facilities to compete in the marketplace for students, and the space requirements associated with conducting advanced research in the basic and applied sciences have pushed almost all colleges and universities into the real estate development business. This is an area where very few college presidents have much experience and training, but where skillful decision making can not only enhance the institution's capacity, but can also make a significant contribution to neighborhood and regional economies.

### Links to Regional Economic Development Strategies

A knowledge-based economy relies extensively on the research and applications of research that are produced inside universities for innovation and progress. University-affiliated research parks have become a visible symbol of these linkages. At times, many of the companies in the parks are spin-offs from the work of researchers who remain associated with the university. In some instances, companies that did not begin through an institutional affiliation want to locate near the university because of the potential synergies that could emerge. But in all instances the companies involved in the park view proximity to the university as a major plus factor.

Research parks have the capability of branding a regional economy with a distinctive identity. This is certainly the case of the Research Triangle Park, which originated in the 1950s when North Carolina governor Luther Hodges hired five academics from the major universities and told them to go out and recruit research laboratories. Fifty years later, it is one of the nation's most vital regions with a per capita income far above the state and national averages.

While it is extremely difficult to replicate the extraordinary success of the Research Triangle Park, the development of viable research parks can still help to focus a regional economic identity. Built and coordinated correctly, research parks have the capacity to bring together clusters of like-minded companies that can attract and retain talent in a region. University leaders can work with the local business community to create and enhance existing parks in ways that can provide a locus for high-tech employment, a recruiting tool for companies and talent, and a distinctive identity for the regional economy. Colleges and universities that do not think of how they can utilize their real estate potential in similar ways are missing an opportunity and are not taking full advantage of possible community partnerships.

### Community Revitalization

The traditional role of colleges and universities as real estate developers probably has engendered more community animosity in more places than any other activity in which higher education has engaged. In small towns, midsize cities, and major metropolitan areas, plans for university expansion have often been met with community resistance. In many places, universities have been obtuse in their approach, proceeding with expansion programs without taking into account the impact on the community or the views of the residents. In some venues, especially urban areas with significant minority populations, university behavior has taken on racial overtones as predominantly white administrators made decisions without bothering to consult the minority communities that were most affected by them.

In recent years, many colleges and universities have worked very hard at reversing this perception. To some extent, this has been a matter of process—creating community advisory boards, developing surveys and holding focus groups to assess neighborhood sentiment, and involving faculty with local schools and nonprofit organizations that serve neighborhood needs.

But perhaps what has been even more interesting has been the joint planning among higher education institutions, nonprofits, and local governments to address actual neighborhood needs within the context of college and university real estate development. At Ohio State University, the institution worked to rehabilitate housing in the adjoining neighborhoods as a way of improving the quality of life for residents and creating a better environment for students. At VCU, the placement of university dorms and athletic facilities on a main thoroughfare combined with private-sector investment in student-oriented apartments spurred a broader commercial revitalization. National restaurant chains opened locations in the area to serve students and patrons of the sports and recreational facility. But even more important, a big-box hardware chain and a national grocery chain, for the first time in decades, opened stores in downtown Richmond, providing choice and convenience to neighborhood residents who previously had to travel a considerable distance to buy groceries at a reasonable price.

We are not Pollyannaish about the potential for eliminating all tensions that are likely to emerge between higher education institutions and their communities over college and university expansion plans. These tensions can flare up whenever a new plan has been developed. Even institutions that have been very thoughtful in their overall approach in recent decades, such as the University of Pennsylvania, can see old animosities resurface, at least with a segment of the community, when a new expansion proposal is not uniformly endorsed.

But what we are saying is that higher education institutions that develop a genuine partnership with their communities have an enormous asset at their disposal—the capacity to develop real estate in a deliberate and large scale manner—that can serve the interests of the university and the residents of their neighboring communities. What was once almost always a source of controversy can become an instrument of mutual development, if the leaders of colleges and universities fully recognize and utilize the means at their disposal.

## PROMOTING DISTINCTIVENESS

The tasks of redefining presidential leadership and utilizing the business operations of colleges and universities to promote social development are often easier to accomplish than efforts to redefine the academic orientation of higher education institutions to place more emphasis on these goals. Colleges and universities with long traditions of collegial self-governance look very skeptically at efforts to advance an administrative vision about the academic focus of an institution. Countries that have decentralized systems of higher education often resist the establishment of goals and metrics that work in other systems to evaluate the success of the academic enterprise according to strict, competitive criteria. And it is very difficult for administrators to tell faculty members what they should be researching and students what they should be studying. Indeed, there is little to warrant the belief that university administrators will really get this right. Cutting-edge research is best developed by those in the labs and the field. And students may have a better understanding of the direction that the wider culture is moving than many adults.

But what college and university leaders can do is to provide the opportunities for work that allows economic and social development to flourish. They adopt tech transfer policies that protect intellectual property, but also advance genuine collaborations with cutting-edge industries. They work to establish conflict-of-interest policies that protect the university and public interest but provide incentives for commercial partnerships. They find creative ways of supporting interdisciplinary, problem-oriented centers. They develop outreach centers for community partnerships and sustainable practices that work with local groups on enhancement efforts. They develop ways of linking student interests to the community-oriented goals of the institutions. They develop creative programs in experiential learning, involve students in community partnerships, and nurture student research that studies real needs in their region. In effect, they are in the business of creating a university culture that nurtures academic innovation, supports community involvement, and places resources (which sometimes can be relatively modest) behind ideas that position the university more centrally within a region's future.

But perhaps an even greater task is to help establish a framework in which these activities occur and which gives a broader meaning to the entire set. In this regard, while we think that it is very useful for colleges and universities to think about how they can replicate what occurs elsewhere, it is also important to focus on what is distinctive about their institutions and their regions. One of the most interesting features of an era of globalization is that people and institutions that have the most impact often tend to be those who have a unique voice or perform a specialized task extremely well. This observation may be very relevant to higher education in the contemporary world.

## The Matter of Distinctiveness

The literature on economic development, especially that associated with Harvard's Michael Porter, insists that regional "distinctiveness is the new competitive" imperative.[1] In a recent paper for CEOs for Cities, Joe Cortright captures the spirit of this argument extremely well. Cortright notes that regions enhance their competitive advantage when they take what they do better than anyone else and use this to propel an economic development strategy. In the early 1990s, Porter spoke about how car racing in Italy and gardening in England were the basis of globally competitive enterprises in each country.[2] Cortright himself argued that the interest in track and field in Oregon along with the popular embrace of jogging as a pastime was a distinctive local culture that served as a seedbed for the Nike corporation's global positioning.[3] Since the time of Porter's work at the beginning of the 1990s, the issue of distinctiveness has become even more important as economic success is increasingly defined as regions finding what Cortright calls the "right niche."[4]

How do colleges and universities operate within the distinctiveness paradigm? In some ways, not always so well. Many of the standard measures of academic quality are national and international program rankings. And there are tendencies in academia for smaller, less prestigious programs and universities to aspire to be recognized as a smaller, less prestigious version of an internationally known program. When we asked one of our department chairs why the faculty were not attempting to develop a distinctive niche for their department, we were told that they do the same things that Berkeley does, but on a smaller scale; so why would they compromise and do anything else? The response was perfectly understandable because in many academic disciplines the currency of individual reward and recognition has nothing to do with being a part of a distinctive local program.

Yet there is a self-defeating respect to pursuing only the traditional rankings game. Derek Bok and others have noted that the ratings of the top fifty schools have barely changed in fifty years. It is not as if there is an enormous amount of upward and downward mobility in the reputational rankings of most universities. To put it simply, the top twenty or thirty universities already have the brand monopoly and, while there may be an occasional departure or entry into the highest tier, it does not make sense for most institutions to have this as an aspiration.

At one time, of course, colleges and universities embraced a place-oriented distinctiveness in which they looked to find their "right niche." This was obviously the premise undergirding the formation of the original land-grant institutions in the nineteenth century, the "tech" schools that many states established, and many of the urban-based institutions of the twentieth century. And it can be seen in the way that some states designed a series of higher education institutions to serve multiple purposes and constituencies.

The notion of a niche-oriented distinctiveness has never completely gone away in higher education circles. Community colleges have almost always embraced the concept. Urban-based public universities have often believed that they have had a special responsibility to the metropolitan community. European professional schools have occupied an important role in offering specialized training in a number of important commercial arenas. Proprietary, for-profit universities have been very creative in identifying markets that are not always well-served by traditional institutions, military personnel, working adults, and place-bound professionals who require online programs. Yet in the last quarter of the twentieth century, trends in higher education frequently led colleges and universities to downplay their place-specific distinctiveness in favor of how well they stacked up against national and international performance criteria. A major examination of land-grant universities, for example, described the identity crisis that occurred as these institutions began to look more and more like all other colleges and universities.

Fortunately, this trend is being reversed. In recent years, there has been a growing recognition of the contribution that universities can make to their regional economies and the accompanying benefits that this can provide the institution. No one can look at the high-tech centers in Silicon Valley, Austin, Boston, and Cambridge, England, without understanding the importance of Stanford, the University of Texas, Harvard-MIT, and Cambridge to the economic vitality that was generated. Nor can anyone look at the effort to enhance social capital in a region and ignore the activities of leading universities such as Penn, Yale, USC, and Ohio State.

But there are with colleges and universities, as with regional economies, remarkable opportunities to become distinctive by focusing on program development related to what a single institution (or a group) can do better than most similarly situated ones. Colleges and universities can carve out their distinctive niche in a manner that shapes a genuine identity. The institution may never become the largest community college or the most selective liberal arts school, or be on the top twenty list in terms of federal research dollars, but it has the possibility of becoming, depending on location, a model for industry and community college collaboration, a liberal arts school that produces graduates who can function in a global economy, or one of the leading research universities on sustainability practices.

In this respect, what Porter and Cortright identify for economies at large may increasingly be the case with universities. Moreover, the tie-in with the regional culture and economy tends to be the critical feature in building this distinctiveness. Colleges and universities that utilize the asset bases that already exist in their communities and capitalize on the unique features of their areas are more likely to become distinctive institutions themselves.

## Distinctiveness and the University Community: Faculty and Students

Putting an emphasis on place-specific distinctiveness can sometimes seem to be antagonistic to faculty cultures that value disciplinary norms and where success is at least partially defined by developing an individual research record that allows scholars to be mobile and entrepreneurial, not dependent on the favor of the administrators at their own place of employment. Moreover, there is a traditionalist criticism of "engagement" that views warily all moves in this direction, suspicious that it will undermine academic independence and disinterested pursuit of truth.

But recent experience suggests that the faculty perspective can be far more supportive. In many scientific areas, the relationships that can be developed among universities, research parks, and the private sector provide a genuine sense of intellectual stimulation along with the possibility of enhanced financial compensation. Establishing effective collaborations requires excellent conflict-of-interest policies, thoughtful intellectual property guidelines, and guarantees of transparency about the actions of the institution. But it is difficult to deny that there is a growing sense among the faculty that the potential for bridging theory of practice and contributing to a region's economic future is highly attractive.

In fact, this possibility is often embraced by some of the vocal critics of university entrepreneurial commitments. Faculty who may be very concerned about industry-based contracts and establishment of spin-off businesses by their colleagues can be extremely dedicated to the institution's initiatives in developing social and cultural capital in the neighboring communities. Public health faculty, social scientists, K–12 education specialists, religious studies faculty, urban planners, and others have often been the driving forces in creatively designing a way that colleges and universities can participate effectively in the community, not as experts coming equipped with theories and answers, but as partners who listen seriously to the concerns of community members and who work with them to develop real responses to their challenges. Moreover, the research that emerges from these partnerships is often highly publishable, fundable, and perfectly consistent with the long-term aspirations of individual faculty members.

Student response to engagement opportunities with the community is almost uniformly positive. Colleges and universities, especially in the United States, have a long tradition of involving students in the broader community while they are attending school. Internships and externships have long been valuable elements in the American higher education experience, providing students with an experience that enables them to evaluate possible career choices and to understand how the real world operates. Students work at ad agencies, at television stations, in political campaigns and in myriad other venues; that period is often one of the more memorable features of their entire education. Education in the health sciences professions has invariably incorporated practicum elements as an essential feature of professional training. Nurses, doctors, pharmacists, physical therapists, and dental hygienists have worked with patients in the community in order to learn the scientific and relational aspects of the profession to which they are aspiring.

The same has been true of the applied social sciences—education, social work, urban planning, criminal justice—where a significant part of professional education is learning what the problems and challenges are in the broader environment and how to address them.

The growing number of service learning programs that has developed in the last decade builds upon this tradition of external involvement. Students may work side by side with community groups as they focus on projects and causes designed to provide better delivery of a service such as education or health care or to enhance the overall quality of life in a community. Our urban planning program at VCU, for example, has developed team projects in which students assist neighborhood organizations, business associations, and towns in creating revitalization plans for neighborhoods, downtowns, and entire communities. Once a university creates the infrastructure that enables these programs to take off, the creativity of the faculty and students kicks in, often across a wider range of programs and interests than originally envisioned. Humanities faculty develop writing courses as part of educational rehabilitation programs in jails. Language students help recent immigrants negotiate the health care and social service systems. And education students assist kids in learning how to read.

While a number of students enroll in service learning for altruistic reasons, there are very practical reasons why students are typically so positive about university involvement in the community. Put simply, it provides them with additional opportunities. They can test possible career options before actually taking a full-time job. They can compare classroom lessons with ones from real life. And these opportunities tend to be the best means of acquiring the "soft" skills critical for today's workplace—getting along with others, speaking and writing for an audience, understanding motivation within an organizational setting, and learning how people from vastly different backgrounds see the world and what is important in it.

In recent times, public higher education has taken substantial hits in the United States as state legislatures have confronted difficult choices. Private universities have seen their endowments decline in a number of instances by 20 to 25 percent. Around the globe, many countries have strained to meet the demand for higher education that an expanding population requires and to orient existing institutions to serve the needs of students who will be living within a global economy. For many college and university leaders, coping with the immediate financial crisis and working to reverse the overall decline in governmental support are the most important priorities of the moment.

But the trends that we have outlined regarding higher education's indispensable role in economic and community development are likely to become more and not less pronounced as states, regions, and nations cope with and then emerge from their current fiscal challenges. Colleges and universities will become more vital to the economic development of their surrounding regions, not less. They will become more crucial to the development of social and cultural capital in their neighborhoods, not less. Conversely, colleges and universities will benefit from responding to these challenges. They will obtain greater public support for the visible contributions they are making. They will provide a better experience for their students. And they can build a greater commitment to the institution from faculty and staff. For the foreseeable future, effectively implementing its potentially decisive role in community and economic development will become a key driver of college and university success, both in the United States and throughout the world.

## NOTES

1. Joe Cortright, "The City-University Partnership: Applying the *City Vitals* Framework to Creating a Sustainable Region" (draft white paper submitted to

Building University-Community Partnerships for a Sustainable Regional Economy at Portland State University, Portland, OR, April 30–May 1, 2009), 10.

2. Cortright, "The City-University Partnership," 10.
3. Cortright, "The City-University Partnership," 10.
4. Cortright, "The City-University Partnership," 10.

# Bibliography

2007–2008 Annual Report. Netter Center for Community Partnerships, University of Pennsylvania, 11.

Academic Planning and Analysis, Office of the Provost and the Office of Budget, Planning, and Analysis. "Data Digest 2006–2007." UW. http://www.bpa.wisc.edu/datadigest/DataDigest2006-2007.pdf (accessed December 12, 2007).

Agarwal, Pawan. *Higher Education in India: The Need for Change—Working Paper No. 180*. Indian Council for Research on International Economic Relations, June 2006. http://www.icrier.org/pdf/ICRIER_WP180__Higher_Education_in_India_.pdf (accessed April 11, 2008).

The Alliance: A University District Partnership. "Steering Committee." University District Alliance. http://www.myu.umn.edu/public/Steering%204:09%20.pdf (accessed April 23, 2009).

The Alliance for Global Education. "Contemporary Chinese Society and Language in Shanghai or Intensive Chinese Language Hosted by Fudan University." The Alliance for Global Education. http://www.allianceglobaled.org/fudan.html (accessed September 5, 2007).

Altbach, Philip G. "Higher Education in India." *The Hindu—Opinion*, April 12, 2005. http://www.hindu.com/2005/04/12/stories/2005041204141000.htm (accessed April 17, 2008).

American Association of Community Colleges (AACC). "CC STATS Home (January 2007)." AACC. http://www2.aacc.nche.edu/research/index.htm (accessed February 18, 2008).

———. "CC STATS Home (January 2008)." AACC. http://www2.aacc.nche.edu/research/index.htm (accessed September 18, 2008).

———. "Historical Information." AACC—about Community Colleges. http://www.aacc.nche.edu/Content/NavigationMenu/AboutCommunityColleges/HistoricalInformation/Historical_Information.htm (accessed May 7, 2007).

———. "Significant Events." AACC—Historical Information. http://www.aacc.nche
.edu/AboutCC/history/Pages/significantevents.aspx (accessed March 3, 2009).

American Committee for the Weizmann Institute of Science. "Weizmann Achievements." Weizmann Institute of Science. http://www.weizmann-usa.org/site/
PageServer?pagename=abt_achievements (accessed August 9, 2007).

American Distance Education Consortium (ADEC). "Advancing the Learning Society: ADEC and the 21st Century State and Land-Grant University." *Strategic
Plan: The American Distance Education Consortium (ADEC) 2001–2005.* ADEC.
http://www.adec.edu/user/2001/stratplan.html (accessed January 9, 2008).

AMIDEAST Yemen. "American and American-Style Universities in the Middle
East." *Yemen Observer—Opinions,* May 12, 2007. http://www.yobserver.com/
opinions/10012191.html (accessed June 4, 2007).

Anderson, Ross. "Analysis of the Vice-Chancellor's Proposal." Campaign for
Cambridge Freedoms. No date. http://www.cl.cam.ac.uk/~rja14/expropriation
.html (accessed November 12, 2007).

———. "Council Elections, November 2006." Campaign for Cambridge Freedoms.
November 2006. http://www.cl.cam.ac.uk/~rja14/ccf.html (accessed November 12, 2007).

Arabnet. "Qatar: Introduction." Arabnet. http://www.arab.net/qatar/qr_early-
history.htm (accessed June 5, 2007).

———. "Qatar: Location." Arabnet. http://www.arab.net/qatar/qr_location.htm
(accessed June 4, 2007).

"Arabs Bring Colleges to Them." *Caymanian Compass,* December 4, 2006. http://
www.caycompass.com (accessed June 4, 2007).

Arizona State University. "Institute for University Design." Arizona State University. http://www.asu.edu/china/education.html (accessed April 18, 2007).

Artfacts.net. "Mousharaka Day Four Ends with Design Debate Doha." Artfacts.
net. http://www.artfacts.net/index.php/pageType/instInfo/inst/14562/con-
tentType/news/nID/4696/lang/1 (accessed April 1, 2009).

Arzhanova, Irina. *Recent Developments in Russia—Challenges for Higher Education
Institutions and Academic Cooperation.* Moscow: NTF, May 2006. http://www
.lut.fi/kevatpaivat/Recent%20developments%20in%20Russia%20%96%20Chal
lenges%20for.ppt#1 (accessed March 11, 2008).

Association of American Universities. "Association of American Universities."
AAU. http://www.aau.edu/ (accessed November 5, 2007).

Association of Public and Land-Grant Universities (APLU). "The 105 Land-Grant
Colleges and Universities." APLU—the Land-Grant Tradition. http://www
.nasulgc.org/publications/Land_Grant/Schools.htm (accessed April 30, 2007).

———. "A Chronology of Federal Legislation Affecting Public Higher Education."
APLU—the Land-Grant Tradition. http://www.nasulgc.org/publications/
Land_Grant/Chronology.htm (accessed April 30, 2007).

———. "Development of the Land-Grant System: 1862–1994." APLU—the
Land-Grant Tradition. http://www.nasulgc.org/publications/Land_Grant/
Development.htm (accessed April 30, 2007).

———. "Kellogg Commission on the Future of State and Land-Grant Universities."
APLU—University Engagement. http://www.nasulgc.org/NetCommunity/
Page.aspx?pid=305&srcid=751 (accessed January 9, 2008).

———. *Shaping the Future—the Economic Impact of Public Universities.* Washington, DC: APLU, Office of Public Affairs, August 2001.

———. "Welcome to NASULGC Online." APLU. http://www.nasulgc.org/Net Community/Page.aspx?pid=183&srcid=-2 (accessed January 10, 2008).

———. "What Is a Land-Grant College?" APLU—the Land-Grant Tradition. http://www.nasulgc.org/publications/Land_Grant/land.htm (accessed September 8, 2006).

Bank of Canada. *Rates and Statistics: Exchange Rate, 2007.* http://www.bankof canada.ca/en/rates/exchform.html (accessed October 4, 2007).

Barash, Nechama Goldman. "Facets of the Israeli Economy—Biotechnology." *Israel Ministry of Foreign Affairs* (2002). http://www.israel-mfa.gov.il (accessed July 6, 2007).

Battelle. *Ohio State Extension: A Generator of Positive Economic Impacts for Ohio.* OSU, January 2005. http://extension.osu.edu/about/executive_summary.pdf (accessed February 20, 2009).

Baty, Phil. "Cambridge Rebels Hold Up Rejig." *The Times Higher Education Supplement* (THES), December 13, 2002. http://www.thes.co.uk (accessed November 9, 2007).

BBC News. "Country Profile: Qatar." BBC News. http://newsvote.bbc.co.uk (accessed June 4, 2007).

———. "Rescue Plan for Ireland's Banks." BBC News. http://news.bbc.co.uk/2/hi/business/7884925.stm (accessed February 25, 2009).

Benson, Lee, Ira Harkavy, and John Puckett. *Dewey's Dream: Universities and Democracy in an Age of Democratic Reform.* Philadelphia: Temple University Press, 2007.

Bjerga, Alan. "Richmond's Rising Tide Lifts Minority Boats, Too." *Wichita Eagle,* September 14, 2006, p. 2.

Blumenstyk, Goldie. "A Tight Grip on Tech Transfer." *Chronicle of Higher Education* 53, no. 4 (2006): A28.

Bobylev, Sergei, et al., eds. *Human Development Report, Russian Federation 2004—towards a Knowledge-Based Society.* Moscow: United Nations Development Programme, 2004. http://hdr.undp.org/en/reports/nationalreports/europethecis/russia/russia_federation_2004_en.pdf (accessed March 26, 2008).

Bok, Derek. *Behind the Ivory Tower: Social Responsibilities of the Modern University.* Cambridge, MA: Harvard University Press, 1982.

———. *Universities and the Future of America.* Durham, NC: Duke University Press, 1990.

———. *Universities in the Marketplace: The Commercialization of Higher Education.* Princeton, NJ: Princeton University Press, 2003.

Bollag, Burton. "Financing for Higher Education Shifts to Private Sector Worldwide." *Chronicle of Higher Education* 53, no. 50 (2007): A36.

Bologna.ie. "Implementation in Ireland." Irish National Information Site on the Bologna Process. http://www.bologna.ie/implement_ireland/default.asp (accessed May 6, 2008).

———. "Progress to Date on Bologna Process." Irish National Information Site on the Bologna Process. http://www.bologna.ie/progress/default.asp (accessed May 6, 2008).

———. "Welcome to Bologna.ie." Irish National Information Site on the Bologna Process. http://www.bologna.ie/home/default.asp (accessed May 6, 2008).

Bradley, John. "The Community College Movement." John Bradley. http://www.emc.maricopa.edu/faculty/bradley/organizational_leadership/edu250/comcol.htm (accessed February 19, 2008).

Bragg, Debra D. "Emerging Tech Prep Models: Promising Approaches to Educational Reform." *Centerfocus* 5 (1994). National Center for Research in Vocational Education, University of California at Berkeley. http://vocserve.berkeley.edu/CenterFocus/CF5.html (accessed March 4, 2008).

Brockwell, Kent Jennings. "Odds and Ends: The Va. BioTech Park Wins an Award." *Richmond Times-Dispatch*, June 8, 2007. http://www.richmond.com (accessed June 11, 2007).

Burke-Kennedy, Eoin. "EC Warns Ireland over 'Optimistic' Recovery Plan." *Irish Times*, February 18, 2009. http://www.irishtimes.com/newspaper/breaking/2009/0218/breaking47_pf.html (accessed February 25, 2009).

Bush, George W. "President Bush Delivers Commencement Address at Miami Dade College." Speech given at graduation ceremonies of Miami Dade College –Kendall Campus, Miami, Florida, on April 28, 2007. Office of the Press Secretary. http://www.whitehouse.gov/news/releases/2007/04/20070428-3.html (accessed February 19, 2008).

Cameron, Rondo. *A Concise Economic History of the World: From Paleolithic Times to the Present*. 3rd ed. New York: Oxford University Press, 1997.

Carnegie Mellon Qatar Campus. *Your Future Begins Here*. Doha: Carnegie Mellon Qatar Campus, n.d.

Carnoy, Martin. *Higher Education and Economic Development: India, China, and the 21st Century—Working Paper No. 297*. Stanford, CA: Stanford University, Stanford Center for International Development, 2006. http://scid.stanford.edu/pdf/SCID297.pdf (accessed October 2, 2006).

Casciani, Dominic. "Israel's New Economic Challenge." BBC News. http://news.bbc.co.uk/1/hi/special_report/1999/05/99/isreal_elections/338159.stm (accessed July 6, 2007).

Center for Community Partnerships at the University of Pennsylvania." Center Awards." University of Pennsylvania. http://www.upenn.edu/ccp/awards.html (accessed May 21, 2007).

———. "History." University of Pennsylvania. http://www.upenn.edu/ccp/history.html (accessed May 15, 2007).

Central Intelligence Agency (CIA). "Qatar: Economy." *The World Fact Book*. Washington, DC: Office of Public Affairs, Central Intelligence Agency, 2007. https://www.cia.gov/library/publications/the-world-factbook/print/qa.html (accessed June 5, 2007).

———. "Qatar: Introduction." *The World Fact Book*. Washington, DC: Office of Public Affairs, Central Intelligence Agency, 2007. https://www.cia.gov/library/publications/the-world-factbook/print/qa.html (accessed June 5, 2007).

———. "Qatar: People." *The World Fact Book*. Washington, DC: Office of Public Affairs, Central Intelligence Agency, 2007. https://www.cia.gov/library/publications/the-world-factbook/print/qa.html (accessed June 5, 2007).

CEOs for Cities and Joseph Cortright. *City Vitals: A Detailed Set of Statistical Measures for Urban Leaders to Understand Their City's Performance in Four Key Areas, Talent, Innovation, Connections and Distinctiveness, in Comparison to the Fifty Largest Metropolitan Regions in the United States.* Chicago: CEOs for Cities, n.d.

China Center for Venture Capital Investment. "China Center for Venture Capital Investment." Fudan University. http://www.econ.fudan.edu.cn/english/c5.htm (accessed September 5, 2007).

China Today. "Fudan Leads the Way in Higher Education Reforms." All-China Women's Federation. http://www.womenofchina.cn/focus/education/4217.jsp (accessed September 5, 2007).

*The Chronicle of Higher Education.* "International: A New Approach Overseas." *Chronicle of Higher Education* 53, no. 43 (June 29, 2007): A40.

———. "International: Leaders of American Universities in the Middle East Bring Their Message to the U.S." *Chronicle of Higher Education* 53, no. 31 (2007): A38.

———. "International: Study-Abroad Numbers Rise." *Chronicle of Higher Education* 52, no. 13 (2005): A45.

Clark, Mike. *The Cambridge University Policy on Intellectual Property Rights: A Critical Appraisal by Mike Clark.* January 26, 2006. http://www.cus.cam.ac.uk/~mrc7/cuipr/ (accessed November 8, 2007).

College of Engineering, UW. "Office of Engineering R&D and Technology Transfer." UW—College of Engineering. http://www.engr.wisc.edu/services/ortt/ (accessed January 31, 2008).

College of Letters & Science, UW. "Intellectual Property/Technology Transfer." UW—College of Letters & Sciences: Office of Research Services. http://www.ls.wisc.edu/oros/IP_Tech_Transfer/IP_Home.htm (accessed January 31, 2008).

Colton, Joel F. "A Middle East Knowledge Economy." Presented at the AURP 21st Annual Conference, Chicago, on October 26, 2006. Qatar Science & Technology Park, Member of Qatar Foundation. http://open.nat.gov.tw/OpenFront/report/show_file.jsp?sysId=C09600336&fileNo=011#1 (accessed June 8, 2007).

Cooperative State Research, Education, and Extension Service. "CSREES Overview." United States Department of Agriculture—About Us. http://www.csrees.usda.gov/about/background.html (accessed January 29, 2008).

CORD. "The ABCs of Tech Prep." *The Cornerstone of Tech Prep Series.* Waco, TX: CORD, 1999.

Cornejo, Dan. *The University District Alliance 2007–2009 Progress Report.* University District Alliance. https://www.myu.umn.edu/public/ALLIANCE-NIR_lowres.pdf (accessed April 23, 2009).

Cortright, Joe. "The City-University Partnership: Applying the *City Vitals* Framework to Creating a Sustainable Region." Draft white paper submitted to Building University-Community Partnerships for a Sustainable Regional Economy at Portland State University, Portland, OR, April 30–May 1, 2009.

Council for Higher Education (Israel). "General." The Council for Higher Education. http://www.che.org.il/template/default_e.aspx?PageId=265 (accessed April 1, 2009).

Cowley, Stephen. "The Right Time for a Shake-Up." *THES,* December 13, 2002. http://www.thes.co.uk (accessed November 9, 2007).

Crean, Gabriel M. "The Role of Higher Educational Sector and its Institutes of Technology in Irish Economic Development." Presented to Congres National du RCCFC, Winnipeg, Canada, November 1–3, 2007.

Criscuolo, Chiara, and Ralf Martin. "An Emerging Knowledge-Based Economy in China? Indicators from OECD Databases." *OECD Science, Technology and Industry Working Papers 2004/4.* OECD Publishing. DOI: 10.1787/256502026705.

Crow, Michael M. "U.S. Universities and Global Competition." *The Globalist*, September 5, 2006. http://www.theglobalist.com/DBWeb/printStoryId. aspx?StoryId=5552 (accessed October 9, 2006).

Cummings, Scott, Mark Rosentraub, Mary Domahidy, and Sarah Coffin. "University Involvement in Downtown Revitalization: Managing Political and Financial Risks." In *The University as Urban Developer: Case Studies and Analysis*, edited by David C. Perry and Wim Wiewel, 147–74. Armonk, NY: M. E. Sharpe, 2005.

Currie, Janice K., and J. Janice Newsom, eds. *Universities and Globalization: Critical Perspectives.* Thousand Oaks, CA: Sage, 1998.

Curtis, Polly. "Dons Clash with Cambridge over Intellectual Rights." *Guardian Unlimited.* Guardian News and Media Limited, November 22, 2005. http://education.guardian.co.uk/businessofresearch/story/0,9860,1648324,00.html (accessed November 9, 2007).

Das, Gurcharan. "The India Model." *Foreign Affairs* 85, no. 4 (2006): 2–16.

Daun, Holger. *Educational Restructuring in the Context of Globalization and National Policy.* New York: RoutledgeFalmer, 2002.

Deaver, Michael V. "Democratizing Russian Higher Education." *Demokratizatsiya*, Summer 2001. BNET.com. http://findarticles.com/p/articles/mi_qa3996/ is_200107/ai_n8987504/ (accessed March 13, 2008).

Department of Chemistry. *Screensaver Lifesaver.* University of Oxford, 2005. http://www.chem.ox.ac.uk/cancer/wgrichards.html (accessed September 24, 2007).

DeVol, Ross, and Armen Bedroussian, with Anna Babayan, Meggy Frye, Daniela Murphy, Tomas J. Philipson, Lorna Wallace, Perry Wong, and Benjamin Yeo. *Mind to Market: A Global Analysis of University Biotechnology Transfer and Commercialization—Executive Summary.* Santa Monica, CA: Milken Institute, 2006.

Dillon, Sam, and Tamar Lewin. "Pell Grants Said to Face Shortfall of $6 Billion." *New York Times*, September 18, 2008. http://www.nytimes.com/2008/09/18/ education/18grant.html (accessed September 18, 2008).

Dixon, David, and Peter J. Roche. "Campus Partners and the Ohio State University—a Case Study in Enlightened Self-Interest." In *The University as Urban Developer: Case Studies and Analysis*, edited by David C. Perry and Wim Wiewel, 268–84. Armonk, NY: M. E. Sharpe, 2005.

Dobelle, Evan. *Saviors of Our Cities—Twenty-five Urban Colleges Noted for Positive Economic and Social Benefit to their Communities.* Boston: New England Board of Higher Education, 2006.

Dobrow-King, Margaret. "New Structure of Higher Education in Russia." *World Education Services* 12, no. 3 (1999). WES. http://www.wes.org/ewenr/99may/ practical.htm (accessed March 13, 2008).

Dooley, Emily C. "Area to Feel Qimonda Demise." *Richmond Times-Dispatch*, February 4, 2009. http://www2.timesdispatch.com/rtd/business/local/article/B-QIMO04_20090203-%20222213/197474 (accessed March 25, 2009).

———. "Staff Reports: VCU Engineering School Loses Ally in Qimonda." *Richmond Times-Dispatch*, March 1, 2009. http://www.timesdispatch.com/rtd/business/local/article/QIMO01S_20090228-222430/218693 (accessed March 25, 2009).

Drougov, Mikhail. *Higher Education Expansion in Russia: What Stands Behind? (Working Paper #BSP/01/048)*. Moscow: New Economic School, 2001. http://www.nes.ru/english/research/pdf/2001/Drougov.pdf (accessed March 13, 2008).

Dvir, Dov, and Asher Tishler. *The Changing Role of the Defense Industry in Israel's Industrial and Technological Development—Synopsis*. Tel Aviv: The Henry Crown Institute of Business Research in Israel, Tel Aviv University, 1999. http://recanati.tau.ac.il/Eng/Index.asp?ArticleID=695&CategoryID=440&Page=4 (accessed August 7, 2007).

Eaglin, Nina. "Qatar: Embracing Democracy." CBS News. http://www.cbsnews.com (accessed June 19, 2007).

Economics Research Associates (ERA). *Economic Impact Analysis of the University of Southern California—Annual Operations, Fiscal Year 2005–2006: Prepared for University of Southern California (ERA Project No. 16668)*. Los Angeles: ERA, September 2006.

The Economist Intelligence Unit, Ltd. "Qatar Economy: Investing Big for a New Society." Economist Intelligence Unit—ViewsWire. http://viewswire.com (accessed June 5, 2007).

"Education City Unveils Expansion Plans." *Gulf Times*, March 27, 2007. http://www.gulf-times.com (accessed March 28, 2007).

Education Ireland. "Tanaiste Announces Establishment of Five New Science Foundation Ireland 'Strategic Research Clusters.'" *About Us: Latest News*. National University of Ireland, Galway, February 25, 2009. http://www.educationireland.ie/index.php?option=com_content&view=article&id=412%3Atanaiste-announces-establishment-of-five-new-science-foundation-ireland-strategic-research-clusters&catid=1%3Aeducation-ireland-news&Itemid=1 (accessed February 25, 2009).

Embassy of Israel. "Higher Education: A Strong Foundation." *Israel Update*, Spring 1997. http://www.israelemb.org/highered/index.html (accessed July 13, 2007).

Engel, Allison. "Owning Your Home, Sweet Home." *USC News*, July 27, 2006. http://www.usc.edu/uscnews/stories/12611.html (accessed from November 27, 2007).

Enver, Ayesha, Mark D. Partridge, and Jill Clark. *Growth and Change: Closing Ohio's Knowledge Worker Gap to Build a 21st Century Economy*. The Ohio State University, Department of Agricultural, Environmental, and Developmental Economics, Extension, September 2008. http://exurban.osu.edu/growthandchange08/educ.pdf (accessed February 20, 2009).

ESN. "Towards the European Higher Education Area." *The Bologna Process*, October 3, 2008. http://www.esnrimini.org/?q=bologna-process (accessed March 10, 2009).

Europa. "Europe in 12 Lessons." *The EU at a Glance*. N.d. http://europa.eu/abc/12lessons/lesson_1/index_en.htm (accessed March 10, 2009).

European Commission. *The Bologna Process: Towards the European Higher Education Area*. European Commission, 2007. http://ec.europa.ue/education/policies/educ/bologna/bologna_en.html (accessed October 2, 2007).

———. "Education and Training 2010—Diverse Systems, Shared Goals." *Higher Education in the Lisbon Strategy*, October 4, 2008. http://ec.europa.eu/education/policies/2010/lisbon_en.html (accessed March 10, 2009).

———. "Erasmus." Lifelong Learning Programme, January 10, 2009. http://ec.europa.eu/education/lifelong-learning-programme/doc80_en.htm (accessed March 10, 2009).

———. "FAQs." *Growth & Jobs.* N.d. http://ec.europa.eu/growthandjobs/faqs/background/index_en.htm (accessed March 10, 2009).

Excelsior Information Systems Limited. "Cambridge Tourist Information." About-Britain.com, 2007. http://www.aboutbritain.com/towns/cambridge.com (accessed September 4, 2007).

Fergany, Nader. *Arab Higher Education and Development, an Overview.* Cairo: Almishkat Centre for Research, February 2000. http://www.worldbank.org/mdf/mdf3/papers/education/Fergany.pdf (accessed January 16, 2008).

Fischer, Karin. "Reimagining the 21st-Century Land-Grant University." *Chronicle of Higher Education* 55, no. 42. (2009): A14–15.

Florida, Richard. *The Rise of the Creative Class: And How It's Transforming Work, Leisure, Community & Everyday Life.* New York: Basic Books, 2002.

Flynn, Sean. "Third-Level Capital Programmes Targeted in 56m Cutback Plan." *Irish Times*, February 4, 2009. http://www.irishtimes.com/newspaper/ireland/2009/0204/1233713216822.html (accessed February 25, 2009).

———. "University Heads Warn of Severe Impact of Cutbacks." *Irish Times*, July 28, 2008. http://www.irishtimes.com/newspaper/frontpage/2008/0728/1217013341171.html (accessed February 25, 2009).

———. "University Presidents Angry at Latest Cuts." *Irish Times*, October 3, 2008. http://www.irishtimes.com/newspaper/ireland/2008/1003/122295930 4916.html (accessed February 25, 2009).

———. "University Presidents Brace for More Cuts." *Irish Times*, September 25, 2008. http://www.irishtimes.com/newspaper/ireland/2008/0925/1222207743950. html (accessed February 25, 2009).

Foreign Students Office, Fudan University. "Introduction to Fudan University." Fudan University. http://www.fso.fudan.edu.cn/en/fd_info.htm (accessed September 5, 2007).

Forfas. *Building Ireland's Knowledge Economy: The Irish Action Plan for Promoting Investment in R&D to 2010—Report to the Inter Departmental Committee on Science, Technology and Innovation.* July 2004. http://www.entemp.ie/publications/enterprise/2004/knowledgeeconomy.pdf (accessed May 6, 2008).

Frerking, Beth. "For Achievers, a New Destination." *New York Times*, April 22, 2007. http://www.nytimes.com/2007/04/22/education/edlife/bestccs.html (accessed September 22, 2008).

Frey, William H. "Diversity Spreads Out: Metropolitan Shifts in Hispanic, Asian, and Black Populations since 2000." The Brookings Institution. http://www.brookings.edu/reports/2006/03demographics_frey.aspx (accessed September 17, 2008).

Friedman, Steven Morgan. "A Brief History of the University of Pennsylvania." UPenn. http://www.archives.upenn.edu/histy/genlhistory/brief.html (accessed May 15, 2007).

Fudan University. "Affiliated Hospitals." Fudan University. http://www.fudan
.edu.cn/englishnew/medical/hospitals.html (accessed September 5, 2007).

———. "Brief Introduction." Fudan University. http://www.fudan.edu.cn/
englishnew/about/intro.html (accessed September 5, 2007).

———. "History of Fudan." Fudan University. http://www.fudan.edu.cn/
englishnew/about/history.html (accessed September 5, 2007).

———. "Joint Project." Fudan University. http://www.fudan.edu.cn/english-
new/research/project.html (accessed September 5, 2007).

———. "Research." Fudan University. http://www.fudan.edu.cn/englishnew/
research/research.html (accessed September 5, 2007).

———. "Shanghai Medical College, Fudan University." Fudan University. http://
www.fudan.edu.cn/englishnew/medical/medicine.html (accessed September
5, 2007).

Furst, David. "Ohio—Israel Medical IT Mission: Israel—Pioneer in the Life Sciences Industry." The Israel Export & International Cooperation Institute. www
.export.gov.il/LS (accessed July 16, 2007).

G8/2006 Russia. "Education for Innovative Societies in the 21st Century." *G8
Summit 2006, Saint Petersburg*, July 16, 2006. G8 Presidency of the Russian Federation in 2006. http://en.g8russia.ru/docs/12-print.html (accessed March 11,
2008).

Galbraith, Kate. "British Universities Increasingly Look Abroad for Leadership."
*New York Times*, December 3, 2003. http://query.nytimes.com/gst/fullpage
.html?res=9401E4DF1F3AF930A35751C1A9659C8B63&sec=&spon=&pagewan
ted=print (accessed November 12, 2007).

GateWay Community College. "Early College High School." MCC. http://high-
school.gatewaycc.edu/Information/TechPrep/ (accessed March 4, 2008).

Gayle, Dennis John, Bhoendradatt Tewarie, and A. Quinton White Jr. "Governance in the Twenty-First-Century University." *ASHE-ERIC Higher Education
Report* 30, no. 1 (2003).

Geller, Harold A. "A Brief History of Community Colleges and a Personal View of
Some Issues Open Admissions, Occupational Training and Leadership." George
Mason University. http://www.eric.ed.gov/ERICDocs/data/ericdocs2sql/
content_storage_01/0000019b/80/19/95/c3.pdf (accessed March 3, 2009).

General Motors Corporation. "General Motors and Indian Institute of Technology Kharagpur Expand R&D and Educational Collaboration." *News*, December 7, 2007. http://www.gm.com/explore/technology/news/2007/indian
_institute_120707.jsp (accessed April 17, 2008).

Ghafour, Hamida, and Andrew Hibberd. "Cambridge Picks Female Vice-
Chancellor." *Telegraph*, November 27, 2002. http://www.telegraph.co.uk/ (accessed November 12, 2007).

Gibbons, Michael, Camille Limoges, Helga Nowotny, Simon Schwartzman, Peter
Scott, and Martin Trow. *The New Production of Knowledge*. Thousand Oaks, CA:
Sage, 1994.

Glazer, Emily. "Schools Abroad Try to 'Mirror' U.S. Campuses." *The Daily Northwestern*, May 11, 2007. http://dailynorthwestern.com (accessed June 4, 2007).

Golden, Lara Lynn. "Entrepreneurship Can Be Learned, Says QSTP: Great Business Innovators Are Made, Not Born, and Qatar Is Setting Up Programs That

Will Do Just That." AME Info—the Ultimate Middle East Business Resource. http://www.ameinfo.com/117972.html (accessed June 8, 2007).

Goldman Sachs. "About Us." Goldman Sachs. http://www2.goldmansachs.com/ our-firm/about-us/index.html (accessed April 25, 2008).

———. "BRICs and Beyond." New York: The Goldman Sachs Economics Group, 2007. http://www2.goldmansachs.com/ideas/brics/book/BRIC-Full.pdf (accessed April 8, 2009).

Government of Ireland. *Building Ireland's Smart Economy: A Framework for Sustainable Economic Renewal*. Dublin: Stationery Office, Government Publications, 2008.

———. *Ireland, National Development Plan 2007–2013: Transforming Ireland—a Better Quality of Life for All, Executive Summary*. Dublin: Stationery Office, Government Publications. January 2007.

Graduate School of the University of Wisconsin-Madison. "2008–2009 IEDR Proposal Instructions." *Innovation & Economic Development Research Program (IEDR)—Fiscal Year 2008–2009*. Graduate School Technology Transfer Grant Programs. http://info.gradsch.wisc.edu/research/researchfunding/IEDR/ iedrinfo.html (accessed December 14, 2007).

Gravois, John. "Number of Doctorates Edges Up Slightly." *Chronicle of Higher Education* 51, no. 18 (2005): A24.

Grogan, Paul S. "Anchor Institutions in a Shifting Economy." *Metropolitan Universities: An International Forum* 20, no. 1 (2009): 11–17.

Guttman, Monika. "USC Breaks Ground on Harlyne J. Norris Cancer Research Center." *HSC Weekly* 9, no. 20 (2003). USC Health Services, Public Relations. http://www.usc.edu/hsc/info/pr/1volpdf/pdf03/920.pdf (accessed October 30, 2007).

Halevi, Nadav. "A Brief Economic History of Modern Israel." In *EH.Net Encyclopedia*, edited by Robert Whaples. Miami University, EH.Net, and Wake Forest University, March 16, 2005. http://eh.net/encyclopedia/article/halevi.israel (accessed July 16, 2007).

Hamman, Stacey. "Biotech Center Raises Funds for Foreign Investment." RichmondBizSense.com. http://www.richmondbizsense.com/2009/03/31/bio tech-center-raises-funds-for-foreign-investment/ (accessed April 1, 2009).

Harman, Danna. "American Education Thriving . . . in Qatar." ABC News. http://abcnews.go.com/International (accessed February 22, 2007).

Hayhoe, Ruth, and Julia Pan. "China's Universities on the Global Stage: Perspectives of University Leaders." *International Higher Education*, Spring 2005. Center for International Higher Education, Boston College. http://www.bc.edu/bc_ org/avp/soe/cihe/newsletter/News39/text012.htm (accessed July 6, 2007).

Hazelkorn, Ellen. "Has Higher Education Become a Victim of Its Own Propaganda?" *Surviving the Construction of Global Knowledge/Spaces for the "Knowledge Economy."* GlobalHigherEd, February 14, 2008. http://globalhighered.wordpress.com/2008/02/14/has-higher-education-become-a-victim-of-its-own -propaganda/ (accessed May 6, 2008).

Higher Education Authority (HEA). *Higher Education Key Facts and Figures: 05/06*. April 2007. http://drupal.hea.ie/files/files/file/archive/statistics/2006/Hi gher%20Education%20Key%20Facts%20&%20Figures%2005-06.pdf (accessed May 6, 2008).

Hill, Laurence D. and James L. Madara. "Role of the Urban Academic Medical Center in U.S. Health Care." *Journal of the American Medical Association* 294, no. 17 (2005): 2219–20.

Hilker, Carl. *Where Pearls Are Found.* Washington, DC: Trade & Environment Database, American University, 1996. http://www.american.edu/ted/pearl.htm (accessed June 4, 2007).

Hood, John. "Oration by the Vice-Chancellor." *Oxford University Gazette* Suppl. 3, no. 4818 (2007).

Hopkin, D. *The Role of Universities in the Modern Economy.* Cardiff, Wales: Welsh Academic Press. (2002).

Hornblower, Margot. "The Gown Goes to Town." *Time Magazine* (2000): 70–78.

Hughes, Samuel. "The West Philadelphia story." *The Pennsylvania Gazette* 96, no. 2 (1997). Penn. http://www.upenn.edu/gazette/1197/philly.html (accessed May 15, 2007).

IFP Qatar, Ltd. "Qatar Science & Technology Park Announces $130 Million Venture Capital Funds." Industry News. http://www.ifpqatar.com/News_show_news.asp?id=2637 (accessed June 8, 2007).

IIT Alumni. "IIT—History." IIT Alumni—IIT—About. http://iit.org/about-iit/iit-history (accessed April 17, 2008).

———. "IIT—Overview." IIT Alumni—IIT—About. http://iit.org/about-iit (accessed April 17, 2008).

IIT Bombay. "Role of IIT Bombay in Entrepreneurship in India." IITB—Society for Innovation and Entrepreneurship. http://www.sineiitb.org/india_incubation_and_iitb.html (accessed April 17, 2008).

IIT Kharagpur. "Continuing Education Centre." IITK. http://www.iitkgp.ac.in/cep/ (accessed April 17, 2008).

———. "Departments, Centres and Schools." IITK—Academics. http://www.iitkgp.ac.in/departments/ (accessed April 17, 2008).

———. "Institute History." IITK. http://www.iitkgp.ac.in/institute/history.php (accessed April 17, 2008).

———. "Sponsored Research and Industrial Consultancy (SRIC)." ITTK—Research & Development. http://www.iitkgp.ac.in/sric/ (accessed April 17, 2008).

———. "Technologies Developed and Ready for Commercialization." ITTK—Research & Development. http://www.iitkgp.ac.in/rnd/technologies.php (accessed April 17, 2008).

Inc.com. "Middle East Entrepreneurship Program Launched." *New York Times,* May 30, 2007. http://www.nytimes.com (accessed June 8, 2007).

Initiative for a Competitive Inner City (ICIC) and CEOs for Cities. *Leveraging Colleges and Universities for Urban Economic Revitalization: An Action Agenda.* Boston: ICIC and CEOs for Cities, 2002.

Israel Life Science Industry (ILSI). "The Israeli Life Science Industry." ILSI. http://www.ilsi.org.il/industry_profile.asp (accessed July 6, 2007).

Israel Ministry of Foreign Affairs. "EDUCATION: Higher Education." Israel Ministry of Foreign Affairs. http://www.mfa.gov.il/MFA/Facts+About+Israel/Education/EDUCATION-+Higher+Education.htm (accessed July 23, 2007).

———. "Natural Gas Find Could Transform Israel's Economy." Israel Ministry of Foreign Affairs—Israel 21c. http://www.mfa.gov.il/MFA/

Israel+beyond+politics/Natural_gas_find_26-Jan-2009.htm (accessed April 1, 2009).

———. "Spotlight on Israel: Higher Education." Israel Ministry of Foreign Affairs. http://www.mfa.gov.il/MFA/Facts%20About%20Israel/Education/Higher%20Education (accessed July 13, 2007).

Isseroff, Ami. "Israel's Quiet Economic Miracle." ZioNation. http://www.zioism-israel.com/log/archives/00000300.html (accessed July 6, 2007).

Ivy Success. "Harvard Admits 7.1 Percent." IvySuccess.com: Admission Stats 2013. 2009. http://ivysuccess.com/harvard_2013.html (accessed April 20, 2009).

Jaschik, Scott. "Lost Opportunity in Russia." *Inside Higher Ed*, January 31, 2007. http://www.insidehighered.com/layout/set/print/news/2007/01/31/russia (accessed March 13, 2008).

———. "New Era in International Higher Education." *Inside Higher Education*, May 18, 2005. http://www.insidehighered.com (accessed June 1, 2007).

Johnson, Janet, and Jeff Baker. "Getting a Jump on College: Winning Secondary-Post Secondary Partnership Programs." Montgomery College Montgomery County Public Schools Partnership. http://www.montgomeryschoolsmd.org/departments/cte/conf/strand_c/Rigor%20through%20Relevancy%20Conference.Getting%20a%20Jump%20on%20College.ppt#1 (accessed September 22, 2008).

Kapur, Devesh, and Pratap Bhanu Mehta. *Indian Higher Education Reform: From Half-Baked Socialism to Half-Baked Capitalism—CID Working Paper No. 108 (September 2004)*. Center for International Development at Harvard University. http://www.cid.harvard.edu/cidwp/pdf/108.pdf (accessed April 11, 2008).

Kelley, Jeffrey. "Richmond's Technology Stars Honored." *Richmond Times-Dispatch*, May 10, 2007. http://www.inrich.com (accessed May 10, 2007).

———. "Va. Opens Door to Israeli Firms." *Richmond Times-Dispatch*, November 4, 2007. http://inrich.com/cva/ric/news/business (accessed November 5, 2007).

Kelley, Lawrence R., and Carl V. Patton. "The University as an Engine for Downtown Renewal in Atlanta." In *The University as Urban Developer: Case Studies and Analysis*, edited by David C. Perry and Wim Wiewel, 131–46. Armonk, NY: M. E. Sharpe, 2005.

Kellogg Commission on the Future of State and Land-Grant Universities. *Returning to Our Roots: Executive Summaries of the Reports of the Kellogg Commission on the Future of State and Land-Grant Universities*. Washington, DC: APLU, 2001.

Kelly, Jim. "Spin Out Doctors: Is the 'Cambridge Phenomenon' about to Be Revived? And If So, Can the Pitfalls of the Last Boom Be Avoided?" *The Guardian—Education Guardian Weekly*, March 2, 2004. http://education.guardian.co.uk/egweekly/story/0,5500,1159471,00.html (accessed September 11, 2007).

Kennan Institute. "Western Foundations and Post-Communist Higher Education: A Report Card." Event Summary—Kennan Institute U.S. Alumni Series. Kennan Institute. http://www.cdi.org/russia/johnson/2007-32-34.cfm (accessed March 13, 2008).

Ketels, Christian H. M., and Olga Memedovic. "From Clusters to Cluster-Based Economic Development." *International Journal of Technological Learning, Innovation and Development* 1, no. 3 (2008): 375–92.

Khalaf, Roula. "Middle East Still Hungry to Learn the American Way: Arab Enthusiasm for US-Style Education Remains Undimmed Despite Antagonism on the Streets." *FT: Financial Times—World Business Newspaper*, February 11, 2004. www.FT.com (accessed June 20, 2007).

Kimball, Roger. *Tenured Radicals: How Politics Has Corrupted Our Higher Education.* Chicago: Ivan R. Dee, 1998.

Kishkovsky, Sophia. "A Bright Future: Russian Higher Education." *Carnegie Reporter* 1, no. 1 (Summer 2000). Carnegie Corporation of New York. http://www .carnegie.org/reporter/01/russia/index.html (accessed March 13, 2008).

Kitching, Ian. "The Cambridge Phenomenon." *Cambridge—Past, Present and Future*, April 5, 1999. http://www.iankitching.me.uk/history/cam/phenomenon .html (accessed September 10, 2007).

Klein, Naomi. "Laboratory for a Fortressed World." *The Nation.* http://www .thenation.com/doc/20070702/klein (accessed August 6, 2007).

Koehn, Jodi. "The Demise of a Great Power: Education and Russian National Security in the 21st Century." *Russian Education and National Security*, January 10, 2000. Woodrow Wilson International Center for Scholars, Kennan Institute. http://www.wilsoncenter.org/index.cfm?fuseaction=events.print&event_ id=3846&stoplayout=true (accessed March 11, 2008).

Krane, Jim. "Rather Than Study Abroad, Arabs Bring Foreign Colleges to Them." *Richmond Times-Dispatch*, December 1, 2006.

Krieger, Zvika. "Dubai, Aiming to Be an Academic Hub, Strikes a Deal with Michigan State." *Chronicle of Higher Education* 54, no 8 (2007): A33.

———. "Saudi Arabia Puts Its Billions Behind Western-Style Higher Education." *Chronicle of Higher Education* 54, no. 3 (2007): A1.

LaFayette, Bill. *Impact of OSU Medical Center's Growth on the Columbus Region.* Columbus Chamber. http://b700441e9603e56472e76fceed3901483f5d7759.grip elements.com/pdf/econ_dev/OSU_Medical_Center_Impact.pdf (accessed May 18, 2009).

Lambert, Richard. *Lambert Review of Business-University Collaboration: Final Report.* London: HM Treasury, December 2003.

Lauder, Hugh, Phillip Brown, Jo-Anne Dillabough, and A. H. Halsey, eds. *Education, Globalization, and Social Change.* Oxford: Oxford University Press, 2006.

Lawton Smith, Helen, John Glasson, James Simmie, Andrew Chadwick, and Gordon Clark. "Enterprising Oxford: The Growth of Oxfordshire High-Tech Economy." *Oxfordshire Economic Observatory.* N.d. http://oeo.geog.ox.ac.uk/ research/eo.pdf (accessed September 14, 2007).

Leon, Patricia. "Bologna Meets Russia: A Case of 'Identity Crisis' over Europe?" *Surveying the Construction of Global Knowledge/Spaces for the "Knowledge Economy."* GlobalHigherEd. http://globalhighered.wordpress.com/2008/01/27/ bologna-meets-russia-is-it-a-case-of-an-identity-crisis-over-europe/ (accessed March 13, 2008).

Leonard, Andrew. "The Great Depression: The Sequel." Salon.com: http:// www.salon.com/opinion/feature/2008/04/02/depression/ (accessed April 14, 2009).

Lester, Richard K. *Universities, Innovation, and the Competitiveness of Local Economies: Summary Report from the Local Innovation Project—Phase I (2005).* Industrial

Performance Center, Massachusetts Institute of Technology, IPC Working Paper Series. http://web.mit.edu/ipc/people/director/05-010.pdf (accessed April 20, 2009).

Levinson, Evelyn. "Higher Education in Israel—What's Happening Out Here." *The European Newsletter*, May 1997. United States-Israel Educational Foundation. http://www.bibl.u-szeged.hu/oseas/newsletter/edfairil.html (accessed July 13, 2007).

Library of Congress. "Morrill Act." *Primary Documents in American History*. The Library of Congress. http://www.loc.gov/rr/program/bib/ourdocs/Morrill .html (accessed December 12, 2007).

MacArthur Foundation. "Report on Activities in Russia—Higher Education and Research." *Higher Education & Research Grants, 2007*. MacArthur Foundation. http://www.macfound.org/site/c.lkLXJ8MQKrH/b.3597939/apps/nl/content2.asp?content_id={538C24D0-E2A5-4C9C-82CA-28C447954061}&notoc=1 (accessed March 11, 2008).

MacWilliams, Bryon. "Russian Parliament Approves Standardized University Admissions Test." *Chronicle of Higher Education* 53, no. 24 (2007): A51.

Mahjoub, Taieb, and Faisal Baatout. "Qatar Seeks to Reverse Arab Brain Drain." *The Middle East Times*, March 20, 2006. http://www.metimes.com (accessed June 4, 2007).

Mangan, Katherine S. "Qatar Courts American Colleges." *Chronicle of Higher Education* 49, no. 2 (2002): A55.

Marcus, Jon "The Celtic Tiger." *National Crosstalk* 15, no. 1 (2007): 14–16.

Marcuse, Peter, and Cuz Potter. "Columbia University's Heights: An Ivory Tower and Its Communities." In *The University as Urban Developer: Case Studies and Analysis*, edited by David C. Perry and Wim Wiewel, 45–64. Armonk, NY: M. E. Sharpe, 2005.

Maricopa Community Colleges (MCC). "Demographics." About Us: Maricopa Community Colleges. http://www.maricopa.edu/about/index.php (accessed February 19, 2008).

———. "Discoveryourself." About Us: Maricopa Community Colleges. http://www.maricopa.edu/about/index.php (accessed February 19, 2008).

———. "Home." Maricopa Community Colleges. http://www.maricopa.edu/ (accessed February 19, 2008).

———. "Small Business Development." About Us: Maricopa Community Colleges. http://www.maricopa.edu/about/index.php (accessed February 19, 2008).

———. "Workforce Development." About Us: Maricopa Community Colleges. http://www.maricopa.edu/about/index.php (accessed February 19, 2008).

Mayo Foundation for Medical Education and Research and Regents of U of M. "Economic Impact Study (2009)." *Minnesota Partnership for Biotechnology and Medical Genomics*. Mayo Foundation for Medical Education and Research and Regents of U of M. http://www.minnesotapartnership.info/economic_impact/eqs.cfm (accessed February 19, 2009).

Medical School, UW. "Sponsored Projects Administration." *Medical School: Research & Graduate Studies*. UW. http://research.med.wisc.edu/research/whos_who.html (accessed January 31, 2008).

Metz, Helem Chapin. "Qatar Population." *Persian Gulf States: A Country Study*. Washington, DC: GPO for the Library of Congress, 1993. http://country studies.us/persian-gulf-states/70.htm (accessed June 5, 2007).

Miami Dade College (MDC). "About Miami Dade College." MDC. http://www .mdc.edu/main/about/default.asp (accessed February 19, 2008).

——. "Developing a Tutor Training Program for Six Campuses." Paper presented at the 40th Annual CRLA Conference, Portland, OR, Oct. 31–Nov. 3, 2007. College Reading & Learning Association Conference 2007 Presentations. http://www.pvc.maricopa.edu/~sheets/CRLA2007/presentations/1hr_CC_ 88_Lemons_Dixie.html (accessed February 29, 2008).

——. "ESL & Foreign Languages." MDC: http://mdc.edu/wolfson/academic/ ArtsLetters/esl/ (accessed February 29, 2008).

——. "Facts in Brief." MDC—About MDC. http://www.mdc.edu/main/about/ facts_in_brief.asp (accessed February 19, 2008).

——. "History." MDC. http://www.mdc.edu/main/about/history.asp (accessed February 19, 2008).

Michigan State University Board of Trustees. "About MSU Dubai." Michigan State University Dubai. http://dubai.msu.edu/quick-links/about-msu-dubai (accessed March 31, 2009).

Microsoft Corporation. *Microsoft Research Cambridge*. 2007. http://research.micro soft.com/cambridge/ (accessed September 10, 2007).

Microsoft Research. *Roger Needham*. Microsoft Corporation. 2007. http://research .microsoft.com/users/needham/default.aspx (accessed September 18, 2007).

Micucci, Dana. "Classes Span Cultural Divide." *International Herald Tribune Americas*, October 31, 2005. http://www.ith.com/articles/2005/10/17/news/Redcit .php (accessed June 7, 2007).

Mitrofanov, Sergei A., A. A. Kharin, and I. L. Kolensky, eds. "Higher Education Technopark and Elion Experimental Development Plant, Russian Federation Ministry for Higher Education. 2002. Innovation Activity in Russian Higher Education." *Successes and Difficulties of Small Innovative Firms in Russian Nuclear Cities: Proceedings of a Russian-American Workshop*. The National Academy of Science. http://books.nap.edu/openbook.php?record_id=10392&page=24 (accessed March 13, 2008).

Mohamed, Amel Ahmed Hassan. "Distance Higher Education in the Arab Region: The Need for Quality Assurance Frameworks." *Online Journal of Distance Learning Administration* 3, no. 1 (2005). State University of West Georgia, Distance Education Center. http://www.westga.edu/~distance/ojdla/spring81/ mohamed81.htm (accessed January 16, 2008).

Montgomery College (MC). "Academic Initiatives and the MC/MCPS Partnership at Montgomery College." MC. http://www.montgomerycollege.edu/ Departments/mcmcps/ (accessed September 22, 2008).

——. "Academic Support." MC. http://www.montgomerycollege.edu/ Departments/studev/support.html (accessed September 22, 2008).

——. "Assessment & Placement." MC. http://www.montgomerycollege.edu/ departments/AssessCtr/assessment-placement.html (accessed September 22, 2008).

———. "Boys to Men (BTM) Mentoring Program." MC. http://www.montgomery college.edu/Departments/studevrv/mentoring.html (accessed September 22, 2008).

———. "Courses and Programs." MC. http://www.montgomerycollege.edu/ leveltwo/academics.htm (accessed September 22, 2008).

———. "FAQ." *Gateway to College Program at Montgomery College: An MC/MCPS Partnership Initiative.* MC. http://www.montgomerycollege.edu/Departments/ mcmcps/gateway/faq.htm (accessed September 22, 2008).

———. "History of Montgomery College." MC. http://www.montgomerycollege .edu/exploremc/history.html (accessed September 22, 2008).

———. "Learning Centers." MC. http://www.montgomerycollege.edu/ exploremc/learningcenters.html (accessed September 22, 2008).

———. "Medical Learning Center Overview." MC. http://www.montgomery college.edu/Departments/medlearntp/index.html (accessed September 22, 2008).

———. "Montgomery College Student Success Stories." MC. http://www .montgomerycollege.edu/news/studentsuccess/rosettanesbitt.html (accessed September 22, 2008).

———. "Online Student Success Center." MC. http://www.montgomerycollege .edu/Departments/studevgt/onlinsts/ (accessed September 22, 2008).

———. "Project SUCCESS." MC. http://www.montgomerycollege.edu/ Departments/studevrv/Project-Success.html (accessed September 22, 2008).

———. "Student Enrollment Profile." *Office of Institutional Research and Analysis.* MC. http://www.montgomerycollege.edu/Departments/inplrsh/Fall%202006/ Complete_Fall_2006_Student_Enrollment_Profile.pdf (accessed September 22, 2008).

———. "Student Success Center—Tutoring." MC. http://www.montgomery college.edu/Departments/studevgt/ssergt/tutoring.html (accessed September 22, 2008).

Mooney, Paul. "The Long Road Ahead for China's Universities." *Chronicle of Higher Education* 52, no. 37 (2006): A42.

———. "New Program Planned in U.S.-China Trade." *Chronicle of Higher Education* 53, no. 29 (2007): A38.

———. "The Wild, Wild East." *Chronicle of Higher Education* 52, no. 24 (2006): A46.

Moore, Barry. "Silicon Fen—the Cambridge Phenomenon as a Case-History of Present-Day Industrial Clustering." The Diebold Institute for Public Policy Studies. http://www.dieboldinstitute.org/paper24.pdf (accessed September 10, 2007).

Mora, José-Ginés, and Maria-José Vieira. "Governance, Organizational Change, and Entrepreneurialism: Is There a Connection?" In *Entrepreneurialism in Universities and the Knowledge Economy: Diversification and Organizational Change in European Higher Education*, edited by Michael Shattock. Berkshire, England: Open University Press, 2009.

Moscow State University (MSU). "Home." MSU. http://www.msu.ru/en/ (accessed March 28, 2008).

Moscow State University Science Park. "Companies, Situated in the SP." Science Park. http://www.sciencepark.ru/eng/firms.htm (accessed March 28, 2008).

————. "History." Science Park. http://www.sciencepark.ru/eng/history.htm (accessed March 28, 2008).

————. *ITC "MSU Science Park."* Moscow: MSU Science Park, n.d.

Movsesyan, Oleg. *Moscow State University Science Park.* PowerPoint presentation given in September 2007. MSU Science Park.

Mukherjee, Pradipta. "IIT-Kgp Ties Up with U.S. Varsity for Hospital." *Business Standard.* http://www.business-standard.com/india/storypage .php?autono=367048 (accessed August 18, 2009).

Murray, Niall. "University Staff Vow to Resist Pay Cuts as Chiefs Outline Financial Difficulties." *Irish Examiner*, January 29, 2009. http://www.examiner .ie/story/ireland/idmhausnkf/rss2/ (accessed February 25, 2009).

Myre, Greg. "Israel Economy Hums Despite Annual Tumult." *International Herald Tribune*, December 31, 2006. http://www.iht.com/ (accessed July 6, 2007).

Naik, Gautam. "Cambridge Tries U.S. Model to Make Profits on Patents." *The Wall Street Journal*, August 16, 2002. http://www.cl.cam.ac.uk/~rja14/Papers/ wsjcam.html (accessed November 8, 2007).

Nanotechwire.com. "Israeli Nano Centers Receive New Funding Worth $230 Million." Nanotechwire.com. http://nanotechwire.com/news.asp?nid=3791 (accessed August 8, 2007).

National Center on Education and the Economy (NCEE). *Tough Choices or Tough Times: The Report on the New Commission on the Skills of the American Workforce.* San Francisco: Jossey-Bass, 2007.

National Development Plan (NDP)—Ireland. "Home." *Ireland's National Development Plan (NDP), 2007–2013.* N.d. http://www.ndp.ie/docs/NDP_Home page/1131.htm (accessed May 7, 2008).

National Governors Association (NGA) and Pew Center on the States. *Innovation America: Investing in Innovation.* Washington, DC: NGA Center for Best Practices, 2007.

National Knowledge Commission (NKC), Government of India. "National Knowledge Commission, Government of India." NKC. http://knowledge commission.gov.in/default.asp (accessed April 22, 2008).

Neelakantan, Shailaja. "Commission Calls for Overhaul of Higher Education in India." *Chronicle of Higher Education* 53, no. 21 (2007): A44.

————. "In India: No Foreign Colleges Need Apply." *Chronicle of Higher Education* 54, no. 22 (2008): A23.

Nemtsova, Anna. "In Russia, Corruption Plagues the Higher-Education System." *Chronicle of Higher Education* 54, no. 24 (2008): A18.

New York University (NYU). "NYU Abu Dhabi." NYU. http://nyuad.nyu.edu/ (accessed March 31, 2009).

————. "NYUAD—the Vision." NYU. http://nyuad.nyu.edu/about/ (accessed March 31, 2009).

NorthStar Economics, Inc. "The New Economy and the University of Wisconsin –Madison," April 16, 2003. NorthStar Economics, Inc. http://www.news.wisc .edu/misc/EIS/eis.pdf (accessed December 14, 2007).

Nunley, Charlene R., Mary Kay Shartle-Galotto, and Mary Helen Smith. "Working with Schools to Prepare Students for College: A Case Study." *New Directions for Community Colleges* 111 (Fall 2000): 59–71.

Office of Corporate Relations. "The Office of Corporate Relations." UW. http://www.ocr.wisc.edu/ (accessed December 13, 2007).

——. *The Office of Corporate Relations: Annual Report for 2006–2007*. UW. http://www.ocr.wisc.edu/images/OCRar0607.pdf (accessed December 13, 2007).

——. *Take 5: The Annual Report on the Progress, Activities and Ongoing Plans of the Office of Corporate Relations at the University of Wisconsin–Madison (2007–2008)*. UW. http://www.ocr.wisc.edu/uploads/Annual%20Report%20PDF.pdf (accessed February 23, 2009).

Office of Norm Coleman, United States Senator, Minnesota. "Coleman Says Passage of Rural Renaissance a Major Victory for Greater Minnesota." *News*, November 18, 2005. Norm Coleman, United States Senator, Minnesota. http://coleman.senate.gov/index.cfm?FuseAction=PressReleases.Detail&PressRelease_id=813&Month=11&Year=2005 (accessed January 9, 2008).

——. "Coleman Touts Rural Renaissance Plan to National Association of State Universities and Land Grant Colleges." *News*, November 15, 2005. Norm Coleman, United States Senator, Minnesota. http://coleman.senate.gov/index.cfm?FuseAction=PressReleases.Detail&PressRelease_id=802&Month=11&Year=2005 (accessed October 9, 2006).

Office of University Outreach & Engagement, OSU. *Building the Future: The Impact of Engaged Partnerships (2008)*. Office of University Outreach & Engagement. http://outreach.osu.edu/pdf/OEimpact2008-web.pdf (accessed February 20, 2009).

Ohio State University (OSU). "Ohio State History and Traditions." OSU. http://www.osu.edu/news/history.php (accessed February 20, 2009).

——. "Ohio State's Outreach Efforts Gain National Recognition." OSU. http://www.osu.edu/news/newsitem2315 (accessed February 20, 2009).

——. "Statistical Summary." OSU. http://www.osu.edu/osutoday/stuinfo.php (accessed February 20, 2009).

——. *Time and Change: A Decade of Progress at The Ohio State University—Re-accreditation Self-Study Report for the Higher Learning Commission of the North Central Association of Colleges and Schools*. OSU, Spring 2007. http://oaa.osu.edu/reaccreditation/documents/OhioStateSelfStudyReport.pdf (accessed February 20, 2009).

Ohio State University Medical Center (OSUMC). *Changing the Face of Medicine . . . One Person at a Time: Community Impact Report 2007*. OCUMC. http://medicalcenter.osu.edu/pdfs/about_osumc/Community_Benefit_Report.pdf (accessed April 27, 2009).

——. "Serving Our Community." OSUMC. http://medicalcenter.osu.edu/aboutus/community_benefits/Pages/index.aspx (accessed April 27, 2009).

The Old Schools. *Cambridge Enterprise*. University of Cambridge, n.d. http://www.enterprise.cam.ac.uk/about/about.html (accessed September 18, 2007).

O'Neill, Jim. "Introduction." In *BRICs and Beyond*, edited by Goldman Sachs, 2008. New York: The Goldman Sachs Economics Group, November 23, 2007. http://www2.goldmansachs.com/ideas/brics/book/BRIC-Full.pdf (accessed April 8, 2009).

Organisation for Economic Co-operation and Development (OECD). "Education—Expenditure on Education—Expenditure on Tertiary Education: Changes in Real Expenditure on Educational Institutions in Tertiary Education." *OECD Factbook 2007: Economic, Environmental and Social Statistics*, 2007. http://ocde

.p4.siteinternet.com/publications/doifiles/302007011P1G103.xls (accessed October 2, 2007).

——. "Education—Outcomes—Tertiary Attainment: Tertiary Attainment for Age Group 25–64." *OECD Factbook 2007: Economic, Environmental and Social Statistics*, 2007. http://ocde.p4.siteinternet.com/publications/doifiles/302007011P1G100.xls (accessed October 2, 2007).

——. "Science and Technology—Research and Development (R&D)—Expenditure on R&D: Gross Domestic Expenditure on R&D." *OECD Factbook 2007: Economic, Environmental and Social Statistics*, 2007. http://ocde.p4.siteinternet.com/publications/doifiles/302007011P1G080.xls (accessed October 2, 2007).

——. "Science and Technology—Research and Development (R&D)—Size of the Researchers: Researchers." *OECD Factbook 2007: Economic, Environmental and Social Statistics*, 2007. http://ocde.p4.siteinternet.com/publications/doifiles/302007011P1G081.xls (accessed October 2, 2007).

Organization for the Promotion of Trade Israel—Netherlands (OPTIN). "Life Sciences: Universities and Institutes." OPTIN. http://www.optin.nl/ls_uninst.php (accessed July 6, 2007).

Orr, Margaret Terry. "Community College and Secondary School Collaboration on Workforce Development and Education Reform." *The Catalyst*, Spring 2004. National Council for Continuing Education & Training. www.BNET.com (accessed March 4, 2008).

Oxford City Council. *Oxford Science Park*. 2007. http://www.oxford.gov.uk/business/oxford-science-park.cfm (accessed September 14, 2007).

Oxford Economic Observatory (OEO). "A New Eye of the High-Tech Economy: The Oxford Economic Observatory." *Annual Review 2002–2003*. University of Oxford, 2004. http://www.ox.ac.uk/publicaffairs/pubs/annualreview/ar03/05.html (accessed September 14, 2007).

Park, Al. "ECONOMICS 455: Economic Development in China, Course Description (Fall 2004)." University of Michigan. http://www-personal.umich.edu/~alpark/syllab455.pdf (accessed July 6, 2007).

Partridge, Mark D., and Jill Clark. "Our Joint Future: Rural-Urban Interdependence in 21st Century Ohio." Brookings Institution. http://www.brookings.edu/events/2008/~/media/Files/events/2008/0910_restoring_prosperity/Partridge.pdf (accessed February 20, 2009).

Percy, Stephen L., Nancy L. Zimpher, and Mary Jane Brukardt, eds. *Creating a New Kind of University: Institutionalizing Community-University Engagement*. Boston: Anker Publishing Company, 2006.

Perry, David C., and Wim Wiewel, eds. *The Urban University as Urban Developer: Case Studies and Analysis*. Armonk, NY: M. E. Sharpe, Inc., 2005.

Pippins, Shirley Robinson. "Education Essential as Ever in 'Flattening' World." *Newsday*, May 23, 2006, A37. http://www.newsday.com (accessed June 4, 2007).

Pitroda, Sam, Chairman, National Knowledge Commission. "Letter to Prime Minister on Higher Education (November 29, 2006)." National Knowledge Commission. http://knowledgecommission.gov.in/downloads/recommendations/HigherEducationLetterPM.pdf (accessed 4/22/08).

Pluviose, David. "More High-Achieving Students Are Choosing Community Colleges First." *Community College News*, February 21, 2008. Diverse Online.

http://www.diverseeducation.com/artman/publish/article_10714.shtml (accessed February 21, 2008).

Podder, Tushar, and Eva Yi. "Chapter One: India's Rising Growth Potential." In *BRICS and Beyond*, edited by Goldman Sachs Global Economics Group, 11–25. New York: Goldman Sachs & Co., January 22, 2007. http://www2.goldmansachs.com/ideas/brics/book/BRIC-Chapter1.pdf (accessed April 24, 2008).

Pohl, Otto. "Getting a Foreign Education." *International Herald Tribune*, March 25, 2005. http://www. iht.com/articles/2005/03/24/news/schools.php (accessed June 4, 2007).

Porter, Michael E. "Location, Clusters, and Company Strategy." In *Oxford Handbook of Economic Geography*, edited by Gordon L. Clark, Meric S. Gertler, and Maryann P. Feldman. Oxford: Oxford University Press, 2000.

———. "Location, Competition, and Economic Development: Local Clusters in a Global Economy." *Economic Development Quarterly* 14, no. 1 (2000): 15–34.

Porter, Mike. "VCU Hosts International Medical Science Students and Faculty." *VCU News Center*. University News Services, VCU, July 31, 2006. http://www.news.vcu.edu/vcu_view/pages.aspx?nid=1450 (accessed October 18, 2007).

———. "VCU Receives National Recognition for Community Initiatives." *VCU News Center*, December 20, 2006. http://www.news.vcu.edu/vcu_view/pages.aspx?nid=1897 (accessed December 21, 2006).

Putnam, Robert D. *Bowling Alone: The Collapse and Revival of American Community*. New York: Simon & Schuster, 2000.

Pyle, Jean Larson, and Robert Forrant, eds. *Globalization, Universities and Issues of Sustainable Human Development*. Cheltenham, England: Edward Elgar Publishing Limited, 2002.

Qatar Foundation. "Northwestern University in Qatar." Qatar Foundation. http://www.qf.org/qa/output/page283.asp (accessed March 27, 2009).

———. "Qatar Faculty of Islamic Studies." Qatar Foundation. http://www.qf.org.qa/output/page284.asp (accessed March 27, 2009).

———. "Qatar Foundation: Education City." Qatar Foundation. http://www.qf.edu.qa/output/page301.asp (accessed May 31, 2007).

———. "Qatar Foundation: Education City—the Vision." Qatar Foundation. http://www.qf.edu.qa/output/page302.asp (accessed May 31, 2007).

———. "Qatar Foundation: Education City—Today." Qatar Foundation. http://www.qf.edu.qa/output/page303.asp (accessed May 31, 2007).

———. *Qatar Foundation for Education, Science and Community Development*. Doha, Qatar: Qatar Foundation, n.d.

———. "Qatar Foundation: Governance—the Board of Directors." Qatar Foundation. http://www.qf.edu.qa/output/page298.asp (accessed May 31, 2007).

———. "Qatar Foundation: History." Qatar Foundation. http://www.qf.edu.qa/output/page294.asp (accessed May 31, 2007).

———. "Qatar Foundation: Our Vision and Mission." Qatar Foundation. http://www.qf.edu.qa/output/page293.asp (accessed May 31, 2007).

———. "Qatar National Research Fund Takes Next Step in the Creation of Qatar's Research Culture." *Qatar Foundation News*, May 15, 2007. Qatar Foundation. http://www.qf.edu.qa/output/page1669.asp (accessed May 31, 2007).

Qatar National Convention Center. "The Centre of Distinction." Qatar National Convention Center. http://www.qatarconvention.com/ (accessed March 27, 2009).

Qatar Science and Technology Park. "Current Members." Qatar Foundation. http://www.qstp.org.qa/output/page54.asp (accessed March 27, 2009).

———. "New Phase in Qatar's R&D Program." Qatar Foundation—Qatar Science & Technology Park. http://www.qstp.org.qa/output/page2222.asp (accessed March 27, 2009).

———. "What We Offer." Qatar Foundation. http://www.qstp.org.qa/output/page559.asp (accessed March 27, 2009).

Quacquarelli Symonds Limited. "Fudan University." Quacquarelli Symonds Limited. http://www.topuniversities.com/schools/data/school_profile/default/fudanuniversity (accessed September 5, 2007).

Rashid, Rick. "Roger Needham." Microsoft Corporation. http://research.microsoft.com/users/needham/needham.aspx (accessed September 18, 2007).

Redburn, Tom. "Emerging Powers Seen Taking Lead in Recovery." *New York Times*, November 19, 2008. http://www.nytimes.com/2008/11/19/business/worldbusiness/19yuan.html?_r=1 (accessed April 14, 2009).

Regents of U of M. "100 Years Old and Counting." Extension Centennial 1909–2009. http://blog.lib.umn.edu/extmedia/centennial/ (accessed February 19, 2009).

———. "About ACRC." Academic and Corporate Relations. http://www.business.umn.edu/aboutacrc.cfm (accessed February 19, 2009).

———. "About CUHCC." Community-University Health Care Center. http://www.ahc.umn.edu/cuhcc/aboutcuhcc.html (accessed April 23, 2009).

———. "About UROC." Urban Research and Outreach/Engagement Center. http://www.uroc.umn.edu/about/index.html (accessed February 19, 2009).

———. "About Us." Office for Business & Community Economic Development. http://www.ced.umn.edu/About_Us.html (accessed February 19, 2009).

———. "Academic and Corporate Relations Center—Home." ACRC Academic and Corporate Relations. http:// www.business/umn.edu (accessed February 19, 2009).

———. "AHC Overview." Academic Health Center. http://www.ahc.umn.edu/about/overview/home.html (accessed April 23, 2009).

———. "Community." University of Minnesota Extension. http://www.extension.umn.edu/Community/ (accessed February 19, 2009).

———. "Community Engagement." U of M. http://www1.umn.edu/twincities/community.php (accessed February 19, 2009).

———. "Healthcare Services." Community-University Health Care Center. http://www.ahc.umn.edu/cuhcc/healthcareservices.html (accessed April 24, 2009).

———. "History and Milestones." Community-University Health Care Center. http://www.ahc.umn.edu/cuhcc/aboutcuhcc/history.html (accessed April 24, 2009).

———. "History and Mission." About the U. http://www1.umn.edu/twincities/hist.php (accessed February 19, 2009).

———. "Programs." Community-University Health Care Center. http://www.ahc.umn.edu/cuhcc/aboutcuhcc/programs.html (accessed April 23, 2009).

———. "Programs & Initiatives." The Office for Public Engagement. http://www.engagement.umn.edu/programs/index.html (accessed February 19, 2009).

———. "Outreach." Academic Health Center. http://www.ahc.umn.edu/outreach/home.html (accessed April 23, 2009).

———. "U of M–Mayo Partnership." Academic Health Center. http://www.ahc
.umn.edu/research/u-mayo/home.html (accessed February 19, 2009).

———. "Utilizing Our Resources." Academic and Corporate Relations. http://
www.business.umn.edu/resources.cfm (accessed February 19, 2009).

———. "Welcome to the U of M." About the U. http://www1.umn.edu/twin
cities/about.php (accessed February 19, 2009).

Reuters. "Qataris Get U.S. Education without Leaving Home." *Washington Post*,
April 28, 2004. http://www.washingtonpost.com/wp-dyn/articles/A62294
-2004May3_2.html (accessed June 20, 2007).

*Richmond Times-Dispatch.* "A Conversation with the *Times-Dispatch:* The Presidents of Virginia Commonwealth University and J. Sargeant Reynolds Community College Sat Down for a Discussion with Members of the *Times-Dispatch's*
Editorial Staff and Newsroom." *Richmond Times-Dispatch* (January 20, 2008).
http://www2.richmond.com/cva/ric/search.apx.-content-articles-RTD-2008
-01-20-0114.html (accessed January 22, 2008).

———. "Top 50 Richmond Area Employers (2008)." *Richmond Times-Dispatch.*
www.inrich.com (accessed May 30, 2008).

Rifkin, Glenn. "A Classroom Path to Entrepreneurship." *New York Times*, May 1,
2008. http://www.nytimes.com/2008/05/01/business/smallbusiness/01sbiz
\.html (accessed May 1, 2008).

Rio Salado College Online. "General Educational Development (GED)." Maricopa
Community Colleges. http://www.riosalado.edu/abe/ged/main.shtml (accessed March 4, 2008).

Robertson, Gary. "The Art of Expansion." *Richmond Times-Dispatch*, March 16,
2005. http://timesdispatch.com (accessed June 4, 2007).

———. "Community College First Choice for Many." *Richmond Times-Dispatch*,
June 25, 2007. http://www.inrich.com (accessed June 25, 2007).

———. "Trani Plans Steady Course to Close Tenure." *Richmond Times-Dispatch*,
April 14, 2007. http://www.timesdispatch.com (accessed April 16, 2007).

Rodin, Judith. *The University and Urban Renewal: Out of the Ivory Tower and Into the
Streets.* Philadelphia: University of Pennsylvania Press, 2007.

Rohde, Laura. "Cambridge May Sue Oracle, KPMG for Failed System." *Mossavar-
Rahmani Center for Business & Government, John F. Kennedy School of Government:
In the News.* IDG News Service, an InfoWorld affiliate, November 9, 2001.
http://www.ksg.harvard.edu/m-rcbg/ethiopia/Publications/Cambridge%2
0may%20sue%20Oracle,%20KPMG%20for%20failed%20system.pdf (accessed
November 9, 2007).

Romero, Simon. "Qatar Finds a Currency of Its Own: Natural Gas." *New York
Times*, 2005, p. 1. http://query.nytimes.com/gst/fullpage.html?res=9F07E2D9
1430F931A15751C1A9639C8B63

Rosan, Gillad, and Eran Razin. "The College Chase: Higher Education and Urban
Entrepreneurialism in Israel." *Tijdschrift voor Economische en Sociale Geografie* 98,
no. 1 (2007): 86–101.

RTE News. "€500m to Be Invested in New Venture Fund." (December 18, 2008).
http://www.rte.ie/news/2008/1218/economy.html (accessed February 25, 2009).

Sadeh, Sharon. "Israel's Beleaguered Defense Industry." *MERIA—Middle East
Review of International Affairs* 5, no. 1 (2001): 64–77.

Saïd Business School. "Entrepreneurship at Oxford." University of Oxford, 2005. http://www.sbs.ox.ac.uk/about/Entrepreneurship+at+Oxford.htm (accessed September 14, 2007).

———. "Who We Are." University of Oxford, 2005. http://www.sbs.ox.ac.uk/about/ (accessed September 14, 2007).

Saint, William. "Tertiary Education and Economic Growth in Sub-Sahara Africa: The World Bank Report." *International Higher Education* no. 54 (Winter 2009). Center for International Higher Education, Boston College. http://www.bc.edu/bc_org/avp/soe/cihe/newsletter/Number54/p14_Saint.htm (accessed April 14, 2009).

Sample, Steven B. "Southern California's Hidden Economic Engine." Reprinted from the *Los Angeles Times*, May 22, 1994. USC. http://www.usc.edu/president/speeches/1994/economic_engine.html (accessed November 6, 2007).

Samuel, Anoop. "Israel: National ICT Policies." ICT in Israel. http://american.edu/initeb/as5415a/Israel_ICT/ictPolicy.html (accessed August 7, 2007).

Samuelson, Robert J. "How We Dummies Succeed." *Washington Post*, September 6, 2006, A15.

Sanghvi, Vir. "The Indians Are Coming." *Hindustan Times*, October 8, 2006, p. 10.

The Science Center. *Sc21—the Science Center: Powering Commercialization*. Philadelphia: The Science Center, 2006.

Scott, Peter. "Action without Reflection." *The Guardian*, December 10, 2002. http://education.guardian.co.uk/specialreports/tuitionfees/story/0,,856886,00.html (accessed November 9, 2007).

Selingo, Jeffrey. "A Chronicle Survey: What Presidents Think—Leaders' Views about Higher Education, Their Jobs, and Their Lives." *Chronicle of Higher Education* 52, no. 11 (2005): A26.

Sengupta, Somini. "India Attracts Universities from the U.S." *New York Times*, March 26, 2007. http://www.nytimes.com/2007/03/26/world/asia/26india.html (accessed March 28, 2007).

Sevlian, Silva. "No 'Grief' for Marshall Entrepreneurs." *Daily Trojan*, October 23, 2007. USC. http://media.www.dailytrojan.com/media/storage/paper679/news/2007/10/23/News/Mag-No.greif.For.Marshall.Entrepreneurs-3049874.shtml (accessed October 26, 2007).

Sharaby, Linda. "Israel's Economic Growth: Success without Security." *MERIA—Middle East Review of International Affairs* 6, no. 3 (2002): 25–41.

Shattock, Michael. "Entrepreneurialism and the Knowledge Economy in Europe." In *Entrepreneurialism in Universities and the Knowledge Economy: Diversification and Organizational Change in European Higher Education*, edited by Michael Shattock. Berkshire, England: Open University Press, 2009.

———. "Entrepreneurialism and Organizational Change in Higher Education." In *Entrepreneurialism in Universities and the Knowledge Economy: Diversification and Organizational Change in European Higher Education*, edited by Michael Shattock. Berkshire, England: Open University Press, 2009.

———, ed. *Entrepreneurialism in Universities and the Knowledge Economy: Diversification and Organizational Change in European Higher Education*. Berkshire, England: Open University Press, 2009.

——. "Research, Technology, and Knowledge Transfer." In *Entrepreneurialism in Universities and the Knowledge Economy: Diversification and Organizational Change in European Higher Education*, edited by Michael Shattock. Berkshire, England: Open University Press, 2009.

Sherwood, James E. "The Role of the Land-Grant Institution in the 21st Century." *Research & Occasional Paper Series: CSHE.6.04*, August 2004. Center for Studies in Higher Education, University of California, Berkeley. http://repositories.cdlib.org/cgi/viewcontent.cgi?article=1034&context=cshe (accessed January 9, 2008).

Shirobokov, Sergei. "Civil Society: Reforming Higher Education in Russia." Omsk State Pedagogical University. http://www.prof.msu.ru/publ/omsk1/3_08.htm (accessed March 13, 2008).

Sidra. "About Sidra." Sidra. http://www.sidra.org/output/page1720.asp (accessed March 27, 2009).

SiliconFen.com. "The Silicon Fen Story." SiliconFen.com. http://www.siliconfen.com/sfstory.php (accessed September 10, 2007).

Small Business Development Center. "Solutions for Small Businesses." UW— Small Business Development Center. http://exed.wisc.edu/sbdc/aboutus/default.asp (accessed December 13, 2007).

Smydo, Joe. "Remedial Courses Used by Many to Adjust to College." *Pittsburgh Post-Gazette*, September 1, 2008. http://www.post-gazette.com/pg/08245/908603-298.stm (accessed September 19, 2008).

Sofer, Ronny. "Peres: Nano-Technology Will Beat Rockets—Vice Premier Concludes Germany Visit, Where He Was Awarded Prestigious Peace Prize, Offers to Promote Negotiations with Palestinians through Financial Endeavors." Ynet news.com. http://www.ynetnews.com (accessed August 14, 2007).

——. "Yushchenko Offers Technological Aid to Peres—Israeli Vice Premier, Ukrainian President Meet in Berlin, Discuss Collaboration on Nano-Technology in Fight against Terror." Ynetnews.com. http://www.ynetnews.com/articles/0,7340,L-3310751,00.html (accessed August 14, 2007).

Southern Wisconsin Association for Continuing Higher Education (SWACHE). "SWACHE." SWACHE. http://www.swache.org/about.php (accessed December 13, 2007).

Spiegel, Sarah. *Profile for VCU International Partnership with The Hebrew University of Jerusalem (Hadassah University Medical Center)*. Richmond, VA: VCU Office of International Education, November 15, 2008.

Spring, Joel. *Education and the Rise of the Global Economy*. Mahwah, NJ: Lawrence Erlbaum Associates, 1998.

Steinberg, Jacques and Tamar Lewin. "For Top Colleges, Economy Has Not Reduced Interest (Or Made Getting in Easier). The Choice: Demystifying College Admissions and Aid." *New York Times*, March 29, 2009. http://thechoice.blogs.nytimes.com/2009/03/29/for-top-colleges-economy-has-not-reduced-interest-or-made-getting-in-easier/?hpw (accessed April 20, 2009).

St. John's Innovation Centre. "St. John's Innovation Center: Cambridge, UK." N.d. http://www.stjohns.co.uk/ (accessed September 12, 2007).

——. "St. John's Innovation Center: Services." N.d. http://www.stjohns.co.uk/services/index.html (accessed September 13, 2007).

Strobel, Warren P. "American Education Moves to the Middle East: Mini-Universities Educate Students in Muslim Countries." BG News: Campus. http://media.www.bgnews.com/media/storage/paper883/news/2005/04/19/Campus/American.Education.Moves.To.Middle.East-1295284.shtml (accessed June 4, 2007).

Strom, Elizabeth. "The Political Strategies Behind University-Based Development: Two Philadelphia Cases." In *The University as Urban Developer: Case Studies and Analysis*, edited by David C. Perry and Wim Wiewel, 116–30. Armonk, NY: M. E. Sharpe, 2005.

Surowski, David B. "History of the Educational System of China." *Projects for International Education Research*. Kansas State University, Department of Mathematics. http://www.math.ksu.edu/~dbski/publication/history.html (accessed April 12, 2007).

Szenasy, Susan S. "Desert Learning." Metropolis. http://www.metropolismag.com (accessed June 4, 2007).

Talcott, William "Modern Universities, Absent Citizenship? Historical Perspectives." *CIRCLE Working Paper 39*. College Park, MD: University of Maryland, 2005.

Temple, Paul. "Teaching and Learning: An Entrepreneurial Perspective." In *Entrepreneurialism in Universities and the Knowledge Economy: Diversification and Organizational Change in European Higher Education*, edited by Michael Shattock. Berkshire, England: Open University Press. 2009.

Tepper School of Business, Carnegie Mellon University. "Tepper School of Business to Begin Entrepreneurship Program in Qatar." *PR Newswire—United Business Media*, May 24, 2007. FindLaw—Legal News and Commentary. http://findlaw.com (accessed June 8, 2007).

Texas A&M University at Qatar. *Chemical—Electrical—Mechanical—Petroleum Engineering Programs*. Doha, Qatar: Office of Admissions, Texas A&M University at Qatar, 2007.

Thomas, Landon, Jr. "As Iceland Goes, So Goes Ireland?" *New York Times*, February 28, 2009, B5.

———. "The Irish Economy's Rise Was Steep, and the Fall Was Fast." *New York Times*, January 4, 2009. http://www.nytimes.com/2009/01/04/business/worldbusiness/04ireland.html (accessed February 19, 2009).

Thomson Reuters. "Israel Economy May Be in Recession—Finance Minister." Thomson Reuters. http://www.fxstreet.com/news/forex-news/article.aspx?StoryId=ada88b0b-95b6-46a4-a7b8-ef795a9ef934 (accessed April 1, 2009).

Trani, Eugene P. "The Capital Corridor: A New Vision for the Region." PowerPoint presentation given throughout 2008. Richmond, VA: Virginia Commonwealth University.

———. "Do Not Isolate Israel, Embrace It." *Richmond Times-Dispatch*, September 23, 2007, E6.

———. *Dublin Diaries: A Study of High Technology Development in Ireland*. Richmond, VA: Virginia Commonwealth University; and Dublin: Keough-Notre Dame Center, November 2002.

———. "Even in Hard Times, Colleges Should Help Their Communities." *Chronicle of Higher Education* 54, no. 36 (2008): A36.

——. *Richmond at the Crossroads: The Greater Richmond Metropolitan Area and the Knowledge Based High Technology Economy of the 21st Century.* Richmond, VA: Virginia Commonwealth University, 1998.

——. *The Role of Universities in Economic Development.* Richmond, VA: Virginia Commonwealth University, 2003.

——. "Virginia Commonwealth University: A Partner in Richmond's Revitalization." *Economic Development America* (Winter 2004): 9–11.

Tsugami, Toshiya. "Ascension Years." Research Institute of Economy, Trade and Industry—FellowsinthePress.http://www.rieti.go.jp/en/papers/contributions/tsugami/ (accessed July 5, 2007).

University of Cambridge. "Business Services Guide: Working with the University." University of Cambridge. http://www.cam.ac.uk/cambuniv/business/working.html (accessed September 10, 2007).

——. "Cambridge in the Community: Public Engagement." University of Cambridge. http://www.cam.ac.uk/cambforall/public.html (accessed September 10, 2007).

——. "Cambridge in the Community: University Students and Staff." University of Cambridge. http://www.cam.ac.uk/cambforall/univ.html (accessed September 10, 2007).

——. "Cambridge Governance Reforms." *News and Events,* June 26, 2002. University of Cambridge. http://www.admin.cam.ac.uk/news/dp/2002062602 (accessed November 9, 2007).

——. "How the University Works—the Council." *The University & Its Departments,* 2007. University of Cambridge. http://www.cam.ac.uk/cambuniv/pubs/works/council.html (accessed November 9, 2007).

——. "How the University Works—the Regent House." *The University & Its Departments,* 2007. University of Cambridge. http://www.cam.ac.uk/cambuniv/pubs/works/regenthouse.html (accessed November 9, 2007).

——. "University Governance: Notice." *Reporter* 232, no. 18. Cambridge: University of Cambridge, February 6, 2002.

——. "Volunteering: University Funding for Volunteering," University of Cambridge. http://www.cam.ac.uk/cambuniv/volunteering/activecommfund.html (accessed September 10, 2007).

University of Minnesota Physicians. "University of Minnesota Physicians." U of M. http://www.umphysicians.umn.edu/ (accessed April 24, 2009).

University of Oxford. "Business." University of Oxford. http://www.ox.ac.uk/business (accessed September 14, 2007).

——. "Business and Community Liaison." University of Oxford. http://www.ox.ac.uk/aboutoxford/community.shtml (accessed September 14, 2007).

——. "Facts and Figures." University of Oxford: http://www.ox.ac.uk/about oxford/facts/ (accessed September 14, 2007).

——. "Launch of Oxford's Genetics Knowledge Park." *News,* April 6, 2004. University of Oxford.http://www.admin.ox.ac.uk/po/news/2003-04/apr/06.shtml (accessed September 21, 2007).

——. "Oxford Appoints First Director of International Strategy." *Media,* March 7, 2007. University of Oxford.http://www.ox.ac.uk/media/news_stories/2007/070307.html (accessed January 23, 2008).

University of Pennsylvania. "Converting the Former G.E. Building." *Almanac* 45, no. 20 (1999), 1.

——. "Introduction to Penn." University of Pennsylvania. http://www.upenn.edu/about/welcome.php (accessed May 11, 2007).

——. "Penn—'05–'06 Annual Report: Tercentennial Anniversary of the Birth of Penn's Founder." University of Pennsylvania. http://www.finance.upenn.edu/comptroller/accounting/AnnualRpt/Financial_Report_06.pdf (accessed May 17, 2007).

——. "The Penn Compact—Engaging Locally." University of Pennsylvania. http://www.upenn.edu/compact/locally.html (accessed May 11, 2007).

——. "Penn and Philadelphia." Penn. http://www.upenn.edu/campus/penn_philadelphia.php (accessed May 21, 2007).

——. "Penn's Heritage." University of Pennsylvania. http://www.upenn.edu/about/heritage.php (accessed May 16, 2007).

——. "Penn's West Philadelphia Initiatives—Clean and Safe Streets." University of Pennsylvania. http://www.upenn.edu/campus/westphilly/streets.html (accessed May 17, 2007).

——. "Penn's West Philadelphia Initiatives—Creating New Jobs and Economic Growth." University of Pennsylvania. http://www.upenn.edu/campus/westphilly/economic.html (accessed May 17, 2007).

——. "Penn's West Philadelphia Initiatives—Improving Housing and Home Ownership." University of Pennsylvania. http://www.upenn.edu/campus/westphilly/housing.html (accessed May 17, 2007).

University of Southern California (USC). "About." USC—University Park Master Plan. http://www.usc.edu/community/upcmasterplan/about/ (accessed November 1, 2007).

——. "About Us." USC—Research. http://www.usc.edu/research/about/ (accessed November 28, 2007).

——. "A Brief History." USC Catalogue 2006–2007. USC. http://www.usc.edu/dept/publications/cat2006/about_usc/history.html (accessed January 27, 2009).

——. "Business and Economic Development." USC—Community Building. http://www.usc.edu/neighborhoods/community/programs/business.html (accessed November 28, 2007).

——. "Galen Center—Fact Sheet: The Galen Center at USC." USC. http://www.usc.edu/neighborhoods/galencenter/ (accessed October 31, 2007).

——. "History." USC—About USC. http://www.usc.edu/about/history/ (accessed November 1, 2007).

——. "MAP 17: Los Angeles City Council Districts and USC Neighborhood Outreach Boundaries (2005)." USC. http://www.usc.edu/ext-relations/ccr/private/atlas/vol_2/MAP17.pdf. (accessed October 30, 2007).

——. "Mission." USC–USC Stevens. http://stevens.usc.edu/about_mission.php (accessed October 26, 2007).

——. "Neighborhood Academic Initiative Program: Education—Opportunity—Community." Los Angeles: USC, n.d.

——. "Our Approach." USC–USC Stevens. http://stevens.usc.edu/about_approach.php (accessed October 26, 2007).

———. "Our History." USC–USC Stevens. http://stevens.usc.edu/about_history
.php (accessed October 26, 2007).

———. "USC and Its Neighborhood." USC—Galen Center. http://www.usc.edu/
community/galencenter/neighbors.html (accessed October 30, 2007).

———. "USC at a Glance." USC—About USC. http://www.usc.edu/about/
ataglance/ (accessed November 1, 2007).

———. "USC's Plan for Increasing Academic Excellence: Building Strategic
Capabilities for the University of the 21st Century." October 6, 2004. USC.
http://www.usc.edu/private/factbook/StrategicPln_12_10_04.pdf (accessed
November 1, 2007).

University of Wisconsin (UW). "About Us." Campus Community Partnerships.
http://www.ccp.wisc.edu/aboutus.html (accessed December 12, 2007).

———. "About Us." Morgridge Center for Public Service. http://www.morgridge
.wisc.edu/about.html (accessed December 13, 2007).

———. "About Us." Wisconsin Institutes for Discovery. http://www.discovery
.wisc.edu/about/ (accessed January 8, 2008).

———. "Almanac." University Communications. http://www.uc.wisc.edu/
docs/2006_almanac.pdf (accessed December 12, 2007).

———. "Amplify the Wisconsin Idea." Connecting Ideas 2001–09: Strategies for the
University of Wisconsin–Madison. http://www.chancellor.wisc.edu/strategic
plan/areasOfFocus/amplify.html (accessed December 12, 2007).

———. "Areas of Focus 2007–09." Connecting Ideas 2001–09: Strategies for the
University of Wisconsin–Madison. http://www.chancellor.wisc.edu/strategic
plan/areasOfFocus/ (accessed December 12, 2007).

———. "Building Wisconsin's Economy." The Wisconsin Idea. http://www.
wisconsinidea.wisc.edu/buildingEconomy.html (accessed January 31, 2008).

———. "Classes and Programs." UW–Madison Continuing Studies. http://www
.dcs.wisc.edu/classes/index.html (accessed December 13, 2007).

———. "Community, Students, and Degrees." UW Facts. http://www.wisc.edu/
about/facts/community.php (accessed December 14, 2007).

———. "Connecting Ideas: Strategies for the University of Wisconsin–Madison
(2001–2009)." UW. http://www.chancellor.wisc.edu/strategicplan/Exec_Sum
.pdf (accessed December 12, 2007).

———. "Employer Resources." Adult & Student Services. http://www.dcs.wisc
.edu/info/employers.htm (accessed December 13, 2007).

———. "Evening and Distance Learning for Credit." Adult & Student Services.
http://www.dcs.wisc.edu/info/distance.htm (accessed January 9, 2008).

———. "Groundbreaking Held for Wisconsin Institutes for Discovery." News.
http://www.news.wisc.edu/15174 (accessed February 23, 2009).

———. "Outreach." UW. http://www.wisc.edu/outreach/ (accessed December
12, 2007).

———. "Research." UW. http://www.wisc.edu/research/ (accessed December
14, 2007).

———. "Speakers Bureau." UW. http://www.speakers.wisc.edu/ (accessed December 13, 2007).

———. "Strategic Plan: Goals and Initiatives (Revised—August 2005)." UW.
http://www.chancellor.wisc.edu/strategicplan/2005-2006.pdf (accessed January 31, 2008).

———. "Study: UW–Madison's Essential to State's Economic Growth." *News*, April 23, 2003. Board of Regents of the University of Wisconsin System: http://www.news.wisc.edu/8573 (accessed December 14, 2007).

———. "The Wisconsin Idea Today." The Wisconsin Idea. http://www.wisconsinidea.wisc.edu/ (accessed January 31, 2008).

University Research Park. "About the Park." UW—University Research Park. http://universityresearchpark.org/about/ (accessed December 11, 2007).

The Urban Institute. "Sprawl, Smart Growth and Economic Opportunity." The Urban Institute. http://www.urban.org/UploadedPDF/410536_Sprawland Equity.pdf (accessed February 28, 2008).

U.S. Census Bureau. "New York." *State & County QuickFacts*. U.S. Census Bureau, May 7, 2007. http://quickfacts.census.gov/qfd/states/36000.html (accessed August 7, 2007).

U.S. Congress. *Congressional Record*, vol. 141, August 1, 1995, p. S11124.

U.S. Department of Education. "Secretary Spellings and Russian Education and Science Minister Fursenko Sign New Higher Education Memorandum of Understanding." ED.gov. http://www.ed.gov/news/press releases/2006/05/05312006.html (accessed March 11, 2008).

———. *A Test of Leadership: Charting the Future of U.S. Higher Education*. Washington, DC: U.S. Department of Education, 2006.

U.S. Department of State. "Backgrounder on the Morrill Act." USINFO.STATE .GOV. http://usinfo.state.gov/usa/infousa/facts/democrac/27.htm (accessed April 30, 2007).

———. "Profile (July 2008)." *Background Notes: Ireland*. Bureau of European and Eurasian Affairs. http://www.state.gov/r/pa/ei/bgn/3180.htm (accessed February 26, 2009).

———. "Profile (October 2007)." *Background Note: India*. Bureau of South and Central Asian Affairs. http://www.state.gov/r/pa/ei/bgn/3454.htm (accessed April 10, 2008).

———. "Profile (October 2007)." *Background Notes: Ireland*. Bureau of European and Eurasian Affairs. http://www.state.gov/r/pa/ei/bgn/3180.htm (accessed May 6, 2008).

UW–Extension. "Agricultural Innovation Center." UW Extension Impact Report: Emerging Markets Team. http://www.uwex.edu/ces/ag/impactreports/documents/ag%20innov.pdf (accessed April 23, 2009).

———. "AgTech Fund Continues AgVest Legacy." UW Extension News. http://www.uwex.edu/ces/news/cenews.cfm?ID=3294 (accessed April 23, 2009).

———. "Emerging Agricultural Markets Team." UW Cooperative Extension. http://www.uwex.edu/ces/agmarkets/ (accessed April 23, 2009).

UW School of Medicine and Public Health. "About the UW School of Medicine and Public Health." UW School of Medicine and Public Health. http://www.med.wisc.edu/about/main/35 (accessed April 23, 2009).

———. "About Urban Medicine." Urban Medicine. http://www.med.wisc.edu/education/md/urban/about.php (accessed April 23, 2009).

———. "Urban Medicine Curriculum." Urban Medicine. http://www.med.wisc.edu/education/md/urban/curriculum.php (accessed April 23, 2009).

VCUQ. "About VCUQ." VCUQ. http://www.qatar.vcu.edu/output/page139 .asp (accessed June 7, 2007).

Virginia Commonwealth University (VCU). "Biography." *Dr. Eugene P. Trani.* May 23, 2008. VCU. http://www.vcu.edu/president/biography/index.html (accessed May 30, 2008).

———. *Innovation Is Our Tradition.* Richmond, VA: Virginia Commonwealth University, 2006.

———. "Scope." VCU—VCU Life Sciences. http://www.vcu.edu/lifesci/scope/scope.html (accessed May 29, 2008).

———. "Vice Provost's Message." VCU—VCU Life Sciences. http://www.vcu.edu/lifesci/scope/sco_mes.html (accessed May 29, 2008).

———. " Virginia BioTechnology Research Park." VCU. http://www.vcu.edu/biotech/ (accessed May 29, 2008).

Virginia Israel Advisory Board. "Virginia Israel Bioscience Commercialization Center Opens in Richmond Virginia." *The Virginia-Israel Alliance* 1, no. 22 (April 6, 2007). http://www.enewsbuilder.net/viab/e_article000789645.cfm?x=b11,0,w (accessed April 2, 2009).

"Vir Sanghvi: The Suave Charmer." HT Media Ltd. http://www.hindustantimes.com/news/181_29349,0023.htm (accessed October 16, 2006).

Walters, Helen, and Kerry Miller. "USC's New Institute for Innovation." *BusinessWeek*, March 29, 2007. http://www.businessweek.com/innovate/content/mar2007/id20070329_553215.htm (accessed October 26, 2007).

Wang, Shenghong. "President's Message." Fudan University. http://www.fudan.edu.cn/englishnew/about/premessage.html (accessed September 5, 2007).

Wan-hua, Ma. "Economic Reform and Higher Education in China." *Center for International & Development Education (CIDE) Occasional Papers Series: Higher Education, CIDE Contributions No. 2.* Los Angeles: CIDE and UCLA Graduate School of Education & Information Studies, July 2003.

Watzman, Haim. "Israel's Regional Colleges, Ambitious but Frustrated, Seek New Role." *Chronicle of Higher Education* 51, no. 34 (2005): A37.

The Weatherall Institute of Molecular Medicine. *Welcome to the Weatherall Institute of Molecular Medicine.* University of Oxford, 2004. http://www.imm.ox.ac.uk/ (accessed September 24, 2007).

Weill Cornell Medical College in Qatar. *Admissions Brochure.* Doha, Qatar: Office of Admissions, Weill Cornell Medical College in Qatar, 2006.

Weiss, Kenneth R. "No Longer the University of Second Choice." *Los Angeles Times Magazine*, September 17, 2000.

WES. "International Rankings and Chinese Higher Education Reform." *World Education News and Reviews* 19, no. 5 (2006). WES: New York.

The Wharton School, University of Pennsylvania. "Executive Education—Certificate of Professional Development." University of Pennsylvania. http://executiveeducation.wharton.upenn.edu/cpd/index.cfm (accessed May 22, 2007).

Wiefel, Elisa and Sally Stewart. "The USC Stevens Institute for Innovation Opens Shop on USC Health Sciences Campus." *PR Newswire*, October 8, 2007. http://www.prnewswire.com/ (accessed October 26, 2007).

Wiley, John D. "From Crossroads to Crisis," *Madison Magazine*, September 2008. http://www.madisonmagazine.com/article.php?story_id=235966 (accessed May 27, 2009), 1.

———. "Report of the Chancellor's Task Force on University-Business Relations (April 21, 2003)." UW. http://www.chancellor.wisc.edu/businessrelations .html (accessed January 31, 2008).

Williams, Gareth. "Finance and Entrepreneurial Activity in Higher Education in a Knowledge Society." In *Entrepreneurialism in Universities and the Knowledge Economy: Diversification and Organizational Change in European Higher Education*, edited by Michael Shattock. Berkshire, England: Open University Press, 2009.

Williams, Wendi A. "History & 1890 Land-Grant Institutions." *Metro News: Making Extension Connections* 1, no. 5 (2002). Alabama Cooperative Extension System. http://www.aces.edu/urban/metronews/vol1no5/history.html (accessed January 22, 2008).

Williams June, Audrey. "$175-Million Gift Goes to Film School." *Chronicle of Higher Education* 53, no. 6 (2006): A37.

Wilson, David McKay. "Yale and New Haven Find Common Ground." *New York Times*, December 16, 2007. http://www.nytimes.com/2007/12/16/nyregion/ nyregionspecial2/16yalect.html?_r=3&oref=slogin&oref=slogin&oref=slogin (accessed June 5, 2008).

Wilson, Dominic, and Roopa Purushothaman. "Dreaming with BRICs: The Path to 2050." *Global Economics, Paper No. 99*. New York: Goldman Sachs, October 1, 2003.

Wilson, Dominic, Roopa Purushothaman, and Themistoklis Fiotakis. *Global Economics Paper No: 18—the BRICs and Global Markets: Crude, Cars and Capital*. New York: Goldman Sachs, October 14, 2004.

Wisconsin Alumni Research Foundation (WARF). "Quick Facts." WARF. http:// www.warf.org/about/index.jsp?cid=27&scid=36 (accessed January 7, 2008).

Woolf, Steven H., and Robert E. Johnson. "The Health Impact of Resolving Racial Disparities: An Analysis of U.S. Mortality Data." *American Journal of Public Health* 98, suppl. 1 (2008): S26–S28.

Worthington, Tom. "The Cambridge Phenomenon: Summary of the Report." Net Traveller. http://www.tomw.net.au/nt/cp.html (accessed September 10, 2007).

Xiao, Wei. "The New Economy and Venture Capital in China." *Perspectives* 3, no. 6 (September 30, 2002). Overseas Young Chinese Forum. http://www.oycf .org/perspectives/18_093002/Economy_Venture_China.htm (accessed August 23, 2007).

Xinhua News Agency. "China Expands Higher Education to Back Economic Development." *People's Daily Online*, August 11, 2004. http://english.people.com .cn/200408/11/ (accessed June 28, 2007).

Zawya. "ConocoPhillips Says Qatar Science & Technology Park Will Attract World's Best." Zawya. http://www.zawya.com/Story.cfm/sidZAWYA20090304115132/ ConocoPhillips%20says%20Qatar%20Science%20&%20Technology%20Park%20 will%20attract%20world's%20best (accessed March 27, 2009).

Ziegler and Partner. "Learning Russian in Moscow at the Famous Lomonosov-University." Ziegler and Partner. http://www.studyrussian.com/MGU/ russian-education-system.html (accessed March 13, 2008).

Zoepf, Katherine. "In Qatar's 'Education City,' U.S. Colleges Build Atop a Gusher." *Chronicle of Higher Education* 51, no. 33 (2005): A42.

# Index

# About the Authors

As the fourth president of Virginia Commonwealth University (VCU) and the president and chair of the board of directors of the VCU Health System, **Eugene P. Trani** positioned the university as a key driver in regional and statewide economic development. Currently president emeritus and university distinguished professor at VCU, Trani has authored, coauthored, annotated, and edited eight books and published more than one hundred articles and op-eds, including two major books on foreign policy.

**Robert D. Holsworth** was the founding director of both the Center for Public Policy and the Wilder School of Government and Public Affairs at Virginia Commonwealth University. He has authored or coauthored five books and numerous articles on American politics and public policy. His observations on national and Virginia politics have appeared in the *Wall Street Journal*, the *Washington Post*, the *New York Times*, and numerous other media. He runs the nonpartisan political website VirginiaTomorrow.com and is a principal in two research and planning groups.